BRITISH HUMANITARIANISM AND THE
CONGO REFORM MOVEMENT, 1896–1913

To my wife, in gratitude

British Humanitarianism and the Congo Reform Movement, 1896–1913

DEAN PAVLAKIS
Carroll College, USA

ASHGATE

© Dean Pavlakis 2015

All rights reserved. No part of this publication may be reproduced, stored in a retrieval system or transmitted in any form or by any means, electronic, mechanical, photocopying, recording or otherwise without the prior permission of the publisher.

Dean Pavlakis has asserted his right under the Copyright, Designs and Patents Act, 1988, to be identified as the author of this work.

Published by
Ashgate Publishing Limited
Wey Court East
Union Road
Farnham
Surrey, GU9 7PT
England

Ashgate Publishing Company
110 Cherry Street
Suite 3-1
Burlington, VT 05401-3818
USA

www.ashgate.com

British Library Cataloguing in Publication Data
A catalogue record for this book is available from the British Library

The Library of Congress has cataloged the printed edition as follows:
Pavlakis, Dean.
  British humanitarianism and the Congo reform movement, 1896–1913 / by Dean Pavlakis.
    pages cm
  Includes bibliographical references and index.
   ISBN 978-1-4724-3647-4 (hardcover)—ISBN 978-1-4724-3648-1 (ebook)—ISBN 978-1-4724-3649-8 (epub) 1. Congo Reform Association (Great Britain) 2. Humanitarianism—Political aspects—Great Britain—History—19th century. 3. Humanitarianism—Political aspects—Great Britain—History—20th century. 4. Congo (Democratic Republic)—Politics and government—1885–1908. 5. Belgium—Colonies—Administration. I. Title.
   DT655.P38 2015
   361.7'309675109041—dc23
                                                                                    2015004401

ISBN: 9781472436474 (hbk)
ISBN: 9781472436481 (ebk – PDF)
ISBN: 9781472436498 (ebk – ePUB)

Printed in the United Kingdom by Henry Ling Limited,
at the Dorset Press, Dorchester, DT1 1HD

Contents

List of Figures and Tables	vii
List of Abbreviations	ix
Preface	xi

1	Context and Questions	1
2	Origins	29
3	Organizing Congo Reform	67
4	Adherents	103
5	Alliances	131
6	The Internationalist Congo Reform Movement	157
7	Contested Representation	175
8	Politicians and Bureaucrats: The Art of the Possible	201
9	Effectiveness	233
Conclusion		261
Appendix I—About the Donor Database		269
Appendix II—Congo Reform Association Auxiliaries		273

Select Bibliography	275
Index	295

List of Figures and Tables

Figures

1.1	Average annual crude rubber price per pound (US), for each year ending June 1892–1915	11
1.2	Congo rubber prices at Liverpool, 1905–14	11
2.1	Henry Richard Fox Bourne, Secretary, Aborigines' Protection Society	35
2.2	Old Congo hands who critiqued the Congo Free State: Edward Glave, William Parminter, Herbert Ward, and Roger Casement	38
2.3	E.D. Morel in 1908	40
2.4	Sir Charles Dilke	47
2.5	W.T. Stead	48
2.6	Dr Harry Grattan Guinness, Acting Director, Regions Beyond Missionary Union	52
3.1	The first issue of the *Official Organ of the Congo Reform Association*	68
3.2	The First Executive Committee of the CRA	70
3.3	William Cadbury, the CRA's largest single donor and Morel's chief patron	92
3.4	John Harris	97
4.1	Alice Seeley Harris	120
5.1	Rev. John Clifford, served as President of the Baptist Union, National Free Church Council, and World Baptist Alliance	142
5.2	Rev. Frederick Brotherton Meyer served as President of the Baptist Union, Free Church Council, and PSA Brotherhood, as well as on the Committee of the Regions Beyond Missionary Union	146
6.1	Félicien Cattier	170
6.2	Emile Vandervelde, Belgian reformer and Socialist leader	172

| 7.1 | *West African Mail* masthead with Morel's motto | 195 |

Tables

1.1	Congo rubber production in tonnes, 1891–1913	9
3.1	Sources of CRA funds, 1904–13	86
4.1	CRA Executive Committee members, 1904–13	107
4.2	The 25 largest donors to the Congo Reform Association	110
4.3	CRA donations by women	114
4.4	Religious affiliation: comparing the 1911 population to the CRA's religiously identifiable donors	124
4.5	Occupational breakdown of donations	126
5.1	Recorded Congo meetings by religious affiliation	143
7.1	Congo reform meetings, and resolutions 1904–10	190

List of Abbreviations

Sources, references beginning with

380 COMI	Chamber of Commerce collection, Liverpool City Library Archives
380 HOLI	John Holt collection, Liverpool City Library Archives
Add.	British Library Manuscript Department's Additional Manuscripts (Add. MSS.)
Afr.	MSS Africa at the Bodleian Library of Commonwealth and African Studies at Rhodes House, Oxford
B/JH(A)	National Museums Liverpool, Archives Department, Maritime Archives & Library
Brit. Emp.	Anti-Slavery papers, at the Bodleian Library of Commonwealth and African Studies, Oxford
DAV	Randall Davidson papers, Lambeth Palace, London
F	Morel papers, London School of Economics and Political Science Archives
MS Emmott	Emmott papers at Nuffield College Library, Oxford University
Osborne	handwritten notes by John Bremner Osborne, Jr of archival material
Reel	RBMU archival footage at Harvard University

Other abbreviations

AIC	*Association Internationale du Congo*
AM	*African Mail*
Anti-Slavery	Until June 1909, the British and Foreign Anti-Slavery Society; after June 1909, the amalgamated British and Foreign Anti-Slavery and Aborigines' Protection Society
APS	Aborigines' Protection Society
ASR&AF	*Anti-Slavery Reporter and Aborigines' Friend*, the organ of the amalgamated Society beginning in October 1909
BMS	Baptist Missionary Society
CBM	The Congo Balolo Mission of the RBMU
CRA	Congo Reform Association

IU	W.T. Stead's International Union
Organ	*Official Organ of the Congo Reform Association*, from LSE Library
RBMU	Regions Beyond Missionary Union, network of missions and training schools
Reporter	*The Anti-Slavery Reporter*
WAM	*West African Mail*

Throughout, Hardinge refers to Arthur Hardinge, Buxton to Travers Buxton, and Harris to John Harris.

The proper name for Leopold's Congo, *L'État Indépendant du Congo*, strictly translates as the Independent State of the Congo or Congo Independent State: I have used the more familiar Congo Free State throughout. This book follows the practice of the early twentieth century in referring to it as "the Congo."

Preface

The study of the Congo reform movement has, at its core, the question dogging all humanitarian efforts: how can distant strangers ameliorate suffering despite the forces arrayed against their efforts? The question contains a plethora of issues: metaphysical concerns of morality and justice, practical elements of strategy and tactics, mundane problems concerning money and interpersonal conflict, and how to overcome obstacles of all kinds. The present work takes as its subject the reform movement in its many forms, bringing new information to light in some areas while using a fresh look at the sources to evaluate and synthesize earlier interpretations. The movement's expanse prevents an all-encompassing account of its every action, but this study's object has been to pull its many factors together. Britain receives the most attention as the movement's locus of origin and its primary source of momentum, but the study is not limited to that country. The perspective is, by its nature, European; African suffering, accommodation, and resistance deserve book-length attention, but this examination cannot do them justice while focusing on the reform agitation—replicating its subject's Western and indeed hegemonic nature. The reform movement's motives, methods, and effectiveness dominate this story, giving us insight into a campaign to make a better world that has implications for our understanding of that world and our own.

I owe much to the assistance of the archives mentioned in the Bibliography, especially Lucy McCann at the Bodleian Library of Commonwealth and African Studies at Rhodes House and Sue Donnelly and the staff at the British Library of Political and Economic Science. Thanks particularly to Patrick McDevitt of the University of Buffalo for his advice and correctives, as well as to readers William Roger Louis, Sasha David Pack, and Claire Schen. Paula Tavrow at UCLA ignited my interest in the reform movement. It was a great pleasure to receive help and encouragement from the scholars I met along the way, such as Robert Burroughs, Martin Ewans, Aidan Forth, Cherry Gertzel, Kevin Grant, Adam Hochschild, Óli Jacobsen, and Sharon Sliwinski. John Bremner Osborne generously shared his Foreign Office notes, introduced me to US archival information, and proved a good host. Richard Harris, Rebecca Seeley Harris, and Judy Pollard Smith joined me in my research into Alice Harris. Finally, I am grateful for the gracious friendship and insightful conversations of Morel biographer Donald Mitchell and his wife Susanna. Donald sharpened my thinking on the effectiveness question and saved me from errors; any remaining are my responsibility alone.

The support of my children, parents, sisters, and friends has made the process better than bearable. Most of all, many thanks to my wife, Patricia Christian, for her patience, encouragement, and affection through my self-absorption and travels.

Dean Pavlakis

Portions of Chapter 1 appeared in the *Journal of Colonialism and Colonial History* 11, no. 1 (spring 2010). © 2010 Johns Hopkins University.

Chapter 1
Context and Questions

Victory or Delusion?

On 16 June 1913, the final meeting of the Congo Reform Association (CRA) convened at London's Westminster Palace Hotel. Delegates from all over the United Kingdom gathered to celebrate the organization's triumph over a terrible colonial evil. The Association's *Official Organ* listed 67 attendees by name; many others attended as well. Observing the Anglican, Baptist, Methodist, and Congregational luminaries on the platform, including the Archbishop of Canterbury, one might have thought this was a religious convocation. Aristocrats, MPs, former colonial governors, newspaper editors, and philanthropists rounded out the gathering. Sir Gilbert Parker, the Canadian-born novelist and Conservative Member of Parliament, opened the meeting by praising his fellow MPs as a victorious army—one that had fought for human dignity and against criminal behavior. This army, he observed, had united different parties, political beliefs, and religions, in unspoken contrast with the divisive Boer War. Their arguments over Britain's behavior in that war had been subsumed in a cause they could agree on: the battle for justice in the Congo. Parker reminded attendees that both Houses of Parliament had taken up the question for ten years without regard for party allegiances.

Edward Talbot, Bishop of Winchester, read the motion to dissolve the Association because "its main purposes have now been secured." He then introduced E.D. Morel, praising him as the man that God had raised up to lead the movement to success. Morel touched on the movement's long history and the current state of affairs in the Congo, now administered along normal lines. In the world outside, Bulgaria attacked Serbia and Greece that very day, starting the second Balkan war in an ominous prelude to the coming world war. But in the meeting room, the world was becoming a better place, thanks to the persistence of good men and women determined to end one of the great evils of the world.[1]

The dissolution of the Congo Reform Association invites skepticism. Some accounts have compared the reformers' boasts to the world situation and concluded that the organization had failed. With the Great War beginning

---

[1] E.D. Morel, "Final Meeting of the Association," *Organ* 2, no. 12 (July 1913): 1008–20.

just over a year later, one scholar posited that European security needs had trumped the reform movement, forcing it to dissolve in despair. Although this theory has been disproved, it still surfaces because of the endurance of academic writing in scholarly journals.[2] More recently, some historians have attributed the dissolution to its failure to sustain public interest, especially after several missionary societies abandoned the cause in 1910.[3] Another version of the failure thesis concludes that the Association had little to boast of because the Belgian regime that replaced the Congo Free State was itself far from being a paragon of colonial virtue.

In contrast to these gloomy pictures, some have agreed with the speeches at the last meeting and held up the Congo Reform Association as a model organization, succeeding at its objectives and deserving of the accolades at the Westminster Palace Hotel. This study concludes that the Congo reform movement could boast of a triumph, albeit an incomplete one. As Morel told the organization's Executive Committee the month before, the Congo Reform Association could not be responsible for healing the Congo; its job had been to stop the bleeding by overturning an iniquitous system of rule, and it could claim success in that. The specific conditions that it had fought had largely ended, leading to a material change in the lives of the Congolese people. (Though the inhabitants of the Congo Free State did not think of themselves as "Congolese" at the time, Europeans used this term, and this book will follow their lead.)

However, the reformed Congo suffered from three weaknesses. Most immediately, the reforms were incomplete: some rights, such as access to land, were not codified in law, and those that were legally promulgated were vulnerable to reversal. A dramatic reduction in forced labor for private purposes had not eliminated the practice. More broadly, the reform movement left an institutional vacuum in its wake. The Association advocated principles that could apply to all tropical colonies, but there was no international mechanism to monitor and enforce them in French Congo, Portuguese Angola, German Kamerun, and the Belgian Congo itself. The final flaw, obvious decades later, was that the movement did not contemplate self-government. But it is a mistake to evaluate the movement's degree of success or failure against a standard based on the ideologies and values professed half a century later. The movement is

---

[2] The theory presented in Mary Elizabeth Thomas, "Anglo-Belgian Military Relations and the Congo Question, 1911–1913," *Journal of Modern History* 25, no. 2 (June 1953): 157–65, was demolished by Myron Echenberg in "The British Attitude toward the Congo Question, with particular reference to the work of E.D. Morel and the CRA, 1903–1913" (MA thesis, McGill University, 1964), 202–3, and, with even more evidence, by Silvanus J.S. Cookey, *Britain and the Congo Question, 1885–1913* (London: Longmans, Green and Co., 1968), 312–13.

[3] Kevin Grant, *A Civilised Savagery* (New York: Routledge, 2005), 77.

best judged by considering its own goals in the context of the ideas, actions, possibilities, and material conditions of the times.

This particular movement was not a mass force that then found leaders. It had to be coaxed into existence, given institutional form, and sustained by a few individuals whose importance is still a matter of debate, none more so than E.D. Morel. His centrality comes not just from his role as Honorary Secretary, so called because the CRA did not pay him a salary. His papers provide much of the surviving documentary evidence. His correspondence shows him to be sensitive to criticism and in constant need of reassurance; consequently, the archives brim with praise for the man and his work. In addition, his sometimes cantankerous interpersonal relationships loom large in the archival record—so large that they can overshadow the main story. Morel's role in the movement, his conflicts, and his affections need to be put in their place, neither glorified nor dismissed, to understand the movement and how the initiative for reform shifted over time.

Morel and others claimed that the movement was comparable only to the battle against the slave trade a century before. This is a distraction. Though the movement had unusual aspects, it had far more in common with other reforming and humanitarian campaigns than the participants admitted in their pursuit of support and impact. However, invoking the heroic past did have a purpose beyond inspiring its adherents with the borrowed finery of abolitionism. The Congo reformers used the imagined golden age of British humanitarian intervention as a standard to measure the government's handling of the Congo question. The government often failed this test, provoking mounting criticism from the reformers until the entire structure of British foreign policy-making was at issue.

This idealized humanitarianism also spoke to British anxieties that reached far beyond the Congo question. The movement flourished at a time when an increasing sense of uneasiness and vulnerability hit British society and government. Many of the old certainties about the stability and reasonableness of the British imperial nation-state had come under attack by social stresses and international threats that loomed larger than in previous decades, leading to what Roy Hattersley calls the "strange mixture of confidence and uncertainty" in Edwardian society.[4]

The reformers assured the public and government that, by embracing Congo reform, they were restoring British moral leadership in the world. At a time when national *degeneration* and *regeneration* were commonly used terms, the reformers

---

[4] Roy Hattersley, *The Edwardians* (New York: St Martin's Press, 2005), 16, 334, 338; Peter Broks, "Science, Press, and Empire," in *Imperialism and the Natural World*, ed. John Mackenzie (New York: St Martin's Press, 1990), 141–63; David Brooks, *The Age of Upheaval: Edwardian Politics, 1899–1914* (New York: St Martin's Press, 1995), 1, 5.

offered a way to regenerate Britain's national pride and confidence. This trope appears in letters, articles, CRA publications, and in speeches made throughout the campaign. In a time of uncertainty, the Congo Reform Association offered Britons a way to reconnect with a positive image of their country, in much the same way that the anti-slave trade movement helped British society rebuild its moral capital over a century earlier.[5]

This book takes the reform movement itself as its primary object of study. It examines the ideologies of the movement's pioneers; its goals, evolving structure, membership, strategy, and tactics; its international connections; and its impact on the Congo. As an episode in the long tradition of British overseas humanitarianism, the movement relied heavily on well-established motivations and practices. It was simultaneously a humanitarian lobbying effort to influence British foreign policy, a research organization, and a mass movement that rallied large numbers of people to express their support for change. Understanding the depth of popular support for the movement complicates some recent accounts of how that support translated into pressure for change.

The oft-praised agency of the Congo Reform Association did not bring about change by itself. The British Foreign Office, initially reluctant to speak against Leopold's system, became an increasingly important reforming force in its own right, and the initiative shifted from the Association to the Foreign Office. Morel's personal influence with the Foreign Office waxed through 1908, illuminating policy choices and principles for its staff, then precipitously waned, beginning with his public attack on the foreign policy establishment in June 1909. After this, the Association became more a gadfly than a mover of events or even ideas, though it kept the informed British public from forgetting the Congo by pricking its conscience in a world of distracting events that struck much nearer home.

With affiliates in other countries and personal contacts with key individuals in Belgium, the British reformers were at the hub of a transnational movement that generated its own dynamic. The reformers and organizations in other countries, most importantly in Belgium, are reintegrated into the story of Congo reform in the later discussion of transnationalism.

This analysis also questions Morel's emphasis on his own centrality to every event while giving due credit for his perseverance, energy, and his vision of the movement as an organization. Like his contemporary, Lenin, he believed in the importance of a centralized movement that was well disciplined in its message and tactics. His ability to enforce this discipline made the Congo Reform Association far more effective than previous efforts. On the other hand, the loss of influence in the Foreign Office in 1909 was primarily Morel's responsibility.

---

[5] Christopher Leslie Brown, *Moral Capital: Foundations of British Abolitionism* (Durham: University of North Carolina Press, 2006); J.R. Oldfield, *Popular Politics and British Anti-Slavery* (New York: Manchester University Press, 1995).

This new interpretation of the movement neither adulates nor trivializes Morel but makes an effort to incorporate the human and structural factors that created the movement's flawed success.

The Westminster Palace Hotel was the site of different kinds of activism. The Museum of London displays a shard of glass from the window of the hotel's main dining room, where the CRA officially disbanded in 1913. Suffragists fanning out from Parliament had broken windows there on 21 November 1911. Police arrested over 200 activists, including Emmeline and Frederick Pethick Lawrence, who had donated £5 to the Congo Reform Association.[6] Sent to prison, their jailers force-fed them when they went on hunger strike. The fight for the Congo entailed no such risks for its British participants, secure in their great distance from the scene of the crime. Their battle against what they perceived as the natural indifference of the British public and the hesitation of the Foreign Office did not require violence. Though this fits into a half-century of law-abiding Britons demanding reform, the early 1900s had undermined this pacific tradition, with increasing strife over women's suffrage, labor relations, and the Irish question. The Congo reform movement illuminates a different aspect of that world: an arena where reformers could invoke British virtue to spur their compatriots and government to be once again a force for good in the world, as they imagined it had been in years past.

The Rise and Fall of Leopold's Congo Empire: A Brief Overview

The fascinating story of the founding and functioning of the Congo Free State is beyond the scope of the present work. Readable accounts include Barbara Emerson's *Leopold II of the Belgians*, Adam Hochschild's *King Leopold's Ghost*, Jean Stengers and Jan Vansina's "King Leopold's Congo, 1886–1908" in *The Cambridge History of Africa*, Neil Ascherson's *The King Incorporated*, and similar titles in the bibliography. A brief introduction will suffice.

In the 1880s, King Leopold II of the Belgians had staked a claim to an area of the Congo basin as large as Western Europe in the name of the International Association of the Congo, an organization that was his personal vehicle. After voyages of exploration and treaty-signing by Henry Stanley and others, Leopold secured the recognition of the Association's sovereignty (and thus his own personal sovereignty) in bilateral treaties before and during the Berlin West Africa Conference of 1884–85. Furthermore, Leopold's International

---

[6] "Women Smash London Windows," *New York Times*, 22 November 1911; "Suffragette Outrages," *Poverty Bay Herald*, 11 January 1912, 2 (dateline 1 December 1911), http://paperspast.natlib.govt.nz/cgi-bin/paperspast?a=d&d=PBH19120111.2.3&l=mi &e=-10-1-0-.

Association of the Congo acceded as a sovereign power to the Act of the Berlin Conference, which committed him to free trade and to improving the moral and material lot of the people living there. In this way, Leopold carried out his colonial ambitions through a territory that was not technically a colony of any country, but instead a free-standing government headquartered anomalously in Brussels that functioned primarily as a vehicle for a commercial enterprise.

Within months he had declared himself the king-sovereign of the Congo Free State, which he ruled as an autocrat from 1885–1908, extracting huge sums of money from the sale of Congo ivory and rubber through a system of government that comingled administration and commercial exploitation. All lands not actively cultivated or inhabited by Africans became the property of the state and thus of Leopold. He granted large tracts to concession companies in exchange for fees and a large ownership stake. Government officials and company agents alike had instructions to increase rubber production, reinforced with the carrot of financial incentives and the stick of possible dismissal or reassignment. In remote districts away from prying eyes, these Europeans terrorized villages to deliver rubber, ivory, provisions, men, and women, relying on the use of armed men—the Free State's official European-led, African-staffed military, the Force Publique, or the euphemistically named sentries of the concession companies. The massive disruption of local society, the system's tendency to encourage violent behavior in the pursuit of profits, and the consequent death toll made the Free State a dramatic epitome of exploitation and oppression, a colony in intent if not strictly in name. However, the marriage of commerce and administration, the absence of any checks on state power, and the prioritizing of profit above all other considerations meant that a vast area suffered a level of violence with few colonial parallels.

After a few false starts, the sporadic calls to reform the administration of the Congo became a sustained campaign when the venerable London-based Aborigines' Protection Society took up the cause under the leadership of its Secretary, Henry Richard Fox Bourne. Despite the Society's efforts, the British government would not act. Conservative British foreign secretaries Lord Salisbury and Lord Lansdowne were reluctant to interfere in another country's business and felt that no colonial power's hands—even Britain's—were altogether clean. The movement for reform accelerated in 1900 when E.D. Morel, a shipping company department head, compared the falsified official reports of the Free State with shipping records and sales statistics from the Antwerp rubber market. Far from being a money-losing enterprise, as Leopold complained, the Free State had changed years before into a highly profitable venture, on the scale of £500,000 in two years (1899–1900), or over £40,000,000 in today's money.[7]

---

[7] E.D. Morel, "History of the Congo Reform Movement," in *E.D. Morel's History of the Congo Reform Movement*, eds William Roger Louis and Jean Stengers (Oxford: Clarendon Press, 1968), 39–40; currency deflator at www.measuringworth.com.

Finding that the Free State's imports consisted primarily of munitions, Morel concluded that the Congo Free State reaped these large sums from the coerced labor of unwilling subjects. Morel published his findings, arousing public concern. Information from the Aborigines' Protection Society and Morel, supported by some chambers of commerce, the Regions Beyond Missionary Union, and journalist W.T. Stead, convinced Parliament in 1903 to pass a resolution protesting mistreatment of the Congo people and Leopold's trading monopoly. As a result, the Foreign Office dispatched Consul Roger Casement to investigate conditions in the interior. Casement's report provoked a public outcry. To sustain the outcry and exert pressure on the British government, Casement convinced missionary leader Dr Harry Grattan Guinness, cotton manufacturer and MP Alfred Emmott, and African trader John Holt to join Morel in founding the Congo Reform Association in 1904.

A Commission of Inquiry appointed by Leopold to exonerate the Free State surprised the world by corroborating Casement's findings. The agitation quickly became international. The CRA supported reformers in Belgium and inspired the formation of an American Congo Reform Association and similar organizations in France, Switzerland, and Germany. By early 1906, the new Liberal Foreign Secretary, Sir Edward Grey, had committed British foreign policy to reform. Yielding to international pressure from Britain and the United States as well as to alarmed Belgian politicians who fretted that the King's difficulties could become Belgium's problem, King Leopold agreed in late 1906 to negotiate the transfer of the Congo to Belgium. After difficult debates and bargaining in Belgium, this occurred in 1908 in exchange for a large financial settlement. A year later, the Belgian government announced substantial reforms to Leopold's system that became effective in phases from 1910–12. By 1913, British consuls in the Congo and other observers provided evidence that the reforms had largely ended Leopold's colonial system. Grey presented their reports to Parliament and the Association dissolved as Britain officially recognized Belgium's annexation of the Congo.

Material Foundations of the Congo Red Rubber Regime

Until the mid-1890s, the brutality evident in the conquest of the Congo had limited impact on European or American public opinion. All colonial powers used violence. Britain's record had notorious examples, such as the massacres of Australian and Tasmanian aborigines and the treatment of the Xhosa in South Africa. The occupation and early administration of the Congo foreshadowed what was to come; within a few years, material factors transformed the Congo Free State into an ongoing regime of astonishing harshness. Its output became known among reformers as red rubber for its high cost in human suffering.

By 1891, Congo expenditures had swallowed up much of Leopold's fortune.[8] When selling Congo bonds met with difficulties, he pursued three new ways to raise money: revising the Berlin treaty to allow him to collect import duties, obtaining loans from the Belgian government, and recasting the colonial state as a vast moneymaking enterprise based on ivory, copal (a resin), and most of all, rubber. He succeeded in all three of these initiatives, leading to an immense cash flow as well as the Congo humanitarian outcry that was to prove his nemesis.

Leopold's secret decree of 29 September 1891 and public decree of 5 December 1892 reserving to the state all trade in ivory, copal, and rubber in most of the country could not have been better timed. World demand for rubber was rising rapidly. In the decades since vulcanization was patented in the 1840s, rubber consumption had grown as its uses expanded to consumer goods such as apparel and industrial purposes such as machinery and insulation for electric wiring. After the 1888 invention of the pneumatic rubber tire, bicycle production exploded in the 1890s to nearly 2,000,000 a year. Automobile tires began to have a material impact on rubber demand after 1900.[9] Worldwide rubber consumption doubled in the decade after 1890 to over 53,000 tons. Leopold rode this wave of demand and the associated price bubble. Under his direction, state agents and concessionary companies made it their top priority to get the local people to collect rubber by persuasion or force; fair payment was not an option, though token payments occurred in most places. The rubber thus collected traveled on the steamers of Liverpool-based Elder Dempster to Antwerp, where it was auctioned. Merchants re-exported much of it via Liverpool to points around the world.[10]

Few reformers advocated a boycott of Congo rubber. Unlike sugar and cocoa, consumer discretionary goods that were the subject of principled boycotts, rubber had become an integral part of all manner of industrial and consumer production. A boycott would have harmed not only the Liverpool shipping and warehousing companies that purchased and resold much of the Congo's rubber, but also the British manufacturers that used rubber both as an input and in the industrial machinery that kept their plants running.

Spurred by the hunger for rubber, Congo exploitation expanded dramatically after the secret decrees of 1891. As Table 1.1 shows, Congo wild rubber production rose more than fourteenfold from 1891 to 1896 and more than fourfold in the next five years to 1901, when the Congo Free State supplied 12 percent of the world market for rubber, less than Brazil but still a force to be

---

[8] Guy Vanthemsche, *Belgium and the Congo, 1885–1960*, trans. Alice Cameron and Stephen Windross (Cambridge: Cambridge University Press, 2012), 53, fn. 47.

[9] Erik Eckermann, *World History of the Automobile* (Warrendale, PA: Society of Automotive Engineers, 2001), 48.

[10] *India Rubber World*, February 1912, 254.

reckoned with. The extraordinary growth in Congo production, averaging 54 percent per year for ten years, was possible only because of coercion. But 1901 was its best year. After this, rubber production slowly declined, shrinking on average 6 percent a year for the next 12 years. Nonetheless, the reformed Belgian Congo of 1913 produced more rubber than the Congo Free State had in 1898, when the red rubber regime was in full swing.

Table 1.1   Congo rubber production in tonnes, 1891–1913

Year	World	Congo wild rubber	% Congo	Plantation	% Plantation
1891	N/A	82			
1892	N/A	156			
1893	N/A	241			
1894	N/A	348			
1895	34,277	576	2%		
1896	37,725	1,317	3%		
1897	39,890	1,662	4%		
1898	45,260	2,113	5%	1	0%
1899	49,790	3,747	8%	4	0%
1900	53,931	5,317	10%	4	0%
1901	51,852	6,023	12%	5	0%
1902	52,346	5,350	10%	8	0%
1903	55,948	5,918	11%	21	0%
1904	62,123	4,831	8%	43	0%
1905	69,507	4,862	7%	179	0%
1906	67,918	4,849	7%	646	1%
1907	68,646	4,529	7%	1,175	2%
1908	67,031	4,263	6%	2,120	3%
1909	69,372	3,492	5%	3,700	5%
1910	est. 75,000	3,106	4%	N/A	
1911	88,000	3,176	4%	14,200	16%
1912	99,000	3,230	3%	28,590	29%
1913	105,670	2,886	3%	47,200	45%
1914	120,977	N/A		71,977	60%

Note: N/A = information not available.

Source: World Production from L&W Van de Velde's India-Rubber Statistics, in *India Rubber World*, March 1910, 227; March 1912, 290; March 1913, 290; February 1914, 238. Congo data 1891–1909 from Gann and Duignan, 123 (correlated with Mackie to Grey, 14 June 1910, FO 881/9854:12 and *Economist*, 3 June 1911, 1180–81); Congo 1910–13 from Antwerp rubber arrivals, *India Rubber World*, February 1911–14. Pre-1909 Antwerp statistics are slightly lower than Gann & Duignan.

The expansion of rubber plantations in Asia after 1901 transformed the market by 1913. Though plantation rubber was initially of lesser quality than wild rubber, economies of scale made it cheaper to produce, and by 1912 its sheer volume was pulling down prices and eroding profit margins for all producers. Entrepreneurs and speculators frenetically promoted plantation rubber. The *India-Rubber Journal* reported the formation of 31 new rubber plantation companies in London in 1905, 58 in 1906, and 103 in 1907, the year of the greatest frenzy.[11] Some companies sought to create new plantations, but most bought up existing plantations to combine, expand, or convert from other products to rubber. The new companies operated mostly in Ceylon, Indochina, and the Indonesian archipelago, with a small number in Africa and Latin America. New rubber trees became reliable producers in just a few years. In 1912, a study of 43 Asian companies showed they had planted 13,377,928 trees, of which 12,006,713 were expected to produce rubber by 1915.[12] Not so the Congo rubber vines. With the danger to self, family, or village if they did not meet the rubber quota, the rubber-gatherers had every incentive to kill the vine to get as much rubber as quickly as possible. *India Rubber World* bemoaned this as early as 1903: "The rubber consumer may or may not be concerned about the cruelty of this system ... he cannot be indifferent long, however, to the exhaustion of rubber which the Congo system is bringing about."[13] Leopold required new plantings and soon boasted that millions of vines had been planted. Because regulations provided no incentive to care for the new plants, few lived to maturity.[14] For all intents and purposes, there were no functioning rubber plantations in the Congo Free State.

The boom was marked by a rise in prices (Figure 1.1). The peak prices reached in 1900, 1906–07, and 1910–11 may have created incentives for plantations but they also led to greater pressure on the people of the Congo. Daniel Lagergren has showed that the worst abuses existed when the crown or concession companies extended the rubber tax to a new area. Once the locals had been terrorized into submission, with resisters driven away or killed, a comparatively stable situation emerged and abuses declined (though they did not disappear) until there were no rubber vines within many days' walk. At this point, vicious treatment and atrocities proliferated again as the authorities used brutality in a vain attempt to stave off rapidly declining production.[15] Because the rubber frontier continued to move, the areas reporting the worst abuses shifted also until the end of the

---

[11] *IRJ*, various issues, 1905–08.

[12] *IRW*, November 1911, 64.

[13] *IRW*, July 1903, 328.

[14] John Harris, "Present Conditions in the Congo," 1911, section II, 1–10.

[15] David Lagergren, *Mission and State in the Congo: A Study of the Relations between Protestant Missions and the Congo Independent State Authorities with Special Reference to the Equator District, 1885–1903* (Uppsala: Almqvist and Wikshells, 1970), 234, 264, 275–89, 293.

rubber tax, notably to areas farther from missionary stations, such as the Ubangi and Kwango regions.[16]

One reason for the Belgians' elongated three-year timetable to introduce reforms in the Congo from 1910–12 was their desire to get as much value as possible from the most productive remaining areas before reforming them. As the graph of prices in Figure 1.1 shows, these were important years, with rubber prices at 20-year highs.

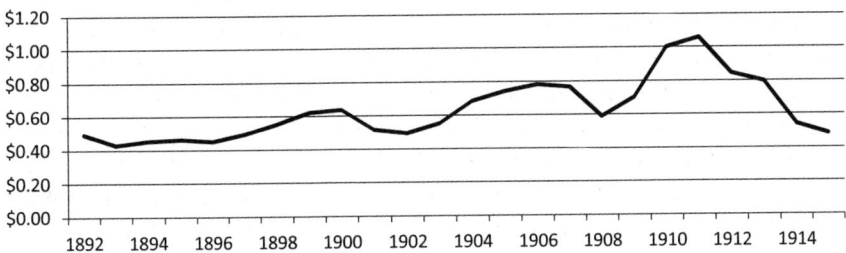

Figure 1.1   Average annual crude rubber price per pound (US), for each year ending June 1892–1915

Source: India Rubber World.

Brief falls in 1902 and 1908 did not last, and during the speculative peak of 1910–11, prices briefly reached $2 per pound in New York on 31 March 1910, treble the price of just two years earlier. Because it uses full-year averages, Figure 1.1 understates the speculative peaks that are more visible in Figure 1.2. The Congo concession companies were extremely profitable in their heyday.

Subsequently, prices fell, as shown in stark relief in Figures 1.1 and 1.2. Congo rubber prices had fallen by 1914 to levels not seen since the 1890s due to the long-anticipated explosion in plantation rubber production shown in Table 1.1.

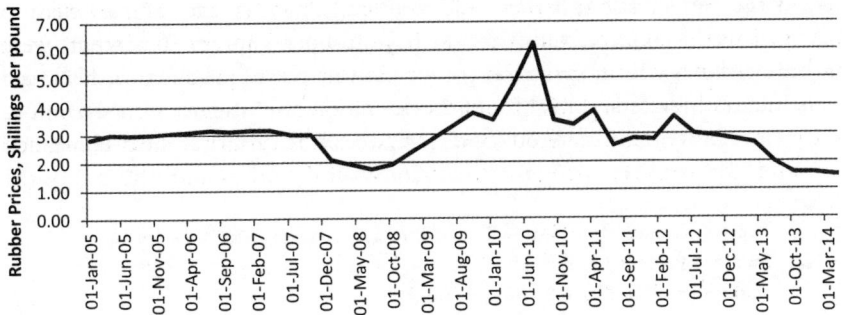

Figure 1.2   Congo rubber prices at Liverpool, 1905–14

Source: West African Mail, African Mail, and *India Rubber World.*

---

[16]   Jack Proby Armstrong, memorandum, 25 January 1910, FO881/9730:30–39.

High prices led Leopold to emphasize rubber production over all other considerations through 1908 and motivated the Belgian government to introduce reforms by region thereafter. This opens the possibility that the patterns of rubber exploitation may have created the material conditions conducive for reform through exhaustion of supply. Historian Robert Harms, after studying some of the most notorious concession companies, found that ruthless exploitation had largely exterminated the wild rubber vine in the Abir, Anversoise, and Lulonga concessions by 1906, the very year Leopold agreed to surrender the Congo.[17] From 1903–05, rubber production in the three concessions fell by 70 percent. Eradication of rubber vines rendered the rubber tax and the concession itself profitless and obsolete, and thus easy to end. This appears to be a regional story. As production in some concessions fell, it expanded in others. For example, the Kasai Company's rubber output, which had been similar to the Abir's in 1903, had risen by 48 percent by 1905.[18] The statistics in Table 1.1 show that rubber production in the Congo as a whole fell 18 percent from 1903 to 1905. This indicates that the decline in coerced rubber production was relatively small because dramatic shrinkage in some areas was largely offset by expansion in others. The fate of the Abir, Anversoise, and Lulonga concessions was years away from affecting the country as a whole.

This pattern continued. From 1905 to Belgian annexation in 1908, Congo rubber production declined slowly, at just 4 percent a year. The new Belgian administration made changes with an immediate impact; in its first year, stories of atrocities largely ended and rubber output fell 18 percent. As other reforms phased in from 1910–12, production held steady at just over 3,000 metric tonnes annually.[19] The first phase, in 1910, applied to depleted areas and areas not suitable for rubber. Reforms went into effect last in areas most recently opened to rubber collection. In 1910–12, British consuls reported coerced rubber labor and associated abuses ending region by region as the Belgian government ended the rubber tax and the trade monopoly.[20] Once the reforms were in place across the country, rubber production dropped another 10 percent, again indicating the less brutal practices meant a lower level of production. Although humanitarian ideals and tradition, representation, and the use of power drove the reform movement, material conditions were at the heart of the problem and

---

[17] Robert Harms, "The End of Red Rubber: A Reassessment," *The Journal of African History* 16, no. 1 (1975): 88.

[18] *India Rubber World*, September 1906, 399.

[19] L.H. Gann and Peter Duignan, *The Rulers of Belgian Africa 1884–1914* (Princeton: Princeton University Press, 1979), 123. 1910–12 from Daniel Vangroenweghe, *Du Sang sur les Lianes* (Bruxelles: Didier Hatier, 1986), 302.

[20] John Bremner Osborne, Jr, "Sir Edward Grey, the British Consular Staff, and the Congo Reform Campaign," (PhD thesis, Rutgers University, 1971), 277–80.

changes in these conditions affected the reform movement's ability to influence events, particularly after 1910.

Imperialism

The last quarter of the nineteenth century was the heyday of the so-called New Imperialism, when European powers, the United States, and Japan used their technological and military superiority to expand their colonial empires. Leopold's Congo Free State was born of the age of the New Imperialism and in many ways exemplified it. The heart of imperial ideology was the belief that it was appropriate to control the people of physically and/or culturally separate territories without regard to their opinions in the matter. The acceptability of colonial rule was widespread, not least in Britain where the symbols, products, and profits of empire pervaded society. Imperial ideas ranged from the aggressive expansionism associated with Rhodes and Milner to reluctant annexationists such as Gladstone who believed that conquest was a tool to use sparingly in dealing with threats to British interests and to others who felt that Britain should be satisfied with the empire it had. Very few argued *against* empire. The activists of the Congo reform movement were by and large critics of empire but not anti-empire.

Proponents of imperial expansion often justified the New Imperialism in contemporary rhetoric involving race and Social Darwinism. In the mid-Victorian years, British attitudes towards racial questions had hardened, at the same time that thinking in evolutionary terms had become pervasive, creating a general sense of the unity of the human race that did not include racial equality.[21] The new language of Social Darwinism labeled cultures dynamically: successful societies progressed and expanded, and others degenerated. In this context, conquest of so-called degenerate or primitive peoples appeared to be a law of nature. Even a passionate critic of empire like Roger Casement reflected this line of thinking when he wrote that colonies were necessary outlets for the population and power of leading European countries.[22] This rhetoric merged with commercial self-interest, which increasingly seemed to require territorial domination because Britain's commercial rivals protected their colonial markets to secure outlets for manufactured goods and sources for raw materials and tropical produce. Social Darwinism could apply to competition among great powers as well as between civilized and primitive peoples, as implied in a 1905 essay by Lady Lugard, who before marrying colonial administrator Sir Frederick

---

[21] Douglas A. Lorimer, *Colour, Class, and the Victorians* (New York: Leicester University Press, 1978), 202–6.

[22] Casement to Morel, 14 September 1909, F8/23:431–3.

Lugard had achieved fame in her own right as Flora Shaw, the African expert at *The Times*:

> The first fact which we have to face in regard to the tropical Colonies—the fact indeed which has generally determined our acquisition of them—is that if they were not British they would almost of necessity belong to some other Western Power. There is no such thing as the possibility of leaving them neutral and independent. They must by their nature be either for us or against us.[23]

Religion too played a role in imperialism. Many religious people saw the rise of European empires as the work of divine Providence.[24] The missionary movement, though sometimes critical of imperial practice, was at heart an imperialist cultural venture dedicated to converting people's beliefs and ways of life. Although missionary universalism assumed fundamental racial equality, missionaries reinforced racial stereotypes by publicizing cultural chauvinism. They justified their work with reports of those African practices most likely to shock metropolitan readers. The frequent and selective misrepresentation of African culture by missionaries had the unplanned consequence of stimulating racial and cultural arrogance.[25] Andrew Porter describes this complex interaction of missionary idealism, empire, and race as characterized by expediency and ambiguity, with different responses to specific situations that also reflected the background and outlook of the participants.[26]

Imperialism also coordinated well with national ideology. It was a commonplace belief that Britain's comparatively free society and its voluntary rejection of slavery and the slave trade made the country particularly well-suited to rule. Both enthusiastic imperialists and critics of empire believed that British moral superiority entitled and obligated it to set an example for others.[27]

These racial, commercial, religious, and moral bases for a colonial empire permeated the discourse of the day. For instance, a British program of tropical development would, of course, use the African "reserve of labour" just as Japan

---

[23] Flora Lugard, "The Tropics of the Empire," in *The Empire and the Century: A Series of Essays on Imperial Problems and Possibilities*, ed. Charles Sydney Goldman (London: J. Murray, 1905), 817, http://books.google.com/books?id=-hELAAAAYAAJ.

[24] D.W. Bebbington, "Atonement, Sin, and Empire, 1880–1914," in *The Imperial Horizons of British Protestant Missions, 1880–1914*, ed. Andrew Porter (Grand Rapids, MI: W.B. Eerdmans, 2003), 18.

[25] Philip Curtin, *The Image of Africa* (Madison: University of Wisconsin Press, 1964), 326.

[26] Andrew Porter, *Religion Versus Empire? British Protestant Missionaries and Overseas Expansion* (New York: Manchester University Press, 2004), 281, 314.

[27] Antoinette Burton, *Burdens of History* (Chapel Hill: University of North Carolina Press, 1994), 39.

was taking advantage of Chinese labor.[28] This was a racial argument, based on notions of European superiority as much as on African resistance to tropical diseases. Some, like Morel, felt that development would depend on African labor because tropical Africa would never be white man's country. Others in Britain and elsewhere, taking Social Darwinism to a logical extreme, believed that Africans would disappear altogether in the face of superior Europeans, seeing this as "a law of nature" and "a blessing."[29]

Whether Africans were surviving or disappearing, there was great interest in using their labor and great concern about their reluctance to work for Europeans under the conditions and for the pay offered to them. A persistent trope was that African men needed to be trained to work. Morel and others believed that Africans needed only free access to markets as free labor to be converted to European notions of work. But others disagreed. Frederick Lugard opined that the work of women in garden plots, the abundance of forest produce, and the absence of population pressure led to abundant leisure for the men, which was "apt to be devoted to indolence, quarrelling, drink, or sensuality."[30] As two practical men reflected in an article about growing rubber on plantations through a combination of paternalistic philanthropy and forced labor for "only" one eight-hour day per week: "it is against the nature of the negro to work without compulsion; he is lazy and happy-go-lucky."[31] This current set the tone for Leopold's Congo: for the foreseeable future, Congolese labor would be procured only by coercion.

The reasons given by Europeans for the necessity of forced labor ranged from the grimly practical to the socially progressive. For example, Africans' forced labor would pay for the services of European governments, such as suppression of intra-African wars and slave-raids, road-building, and port improvements. Many Europeans also felt that African culture needed to adapt to a world without warfare by adopting a new gender division of labor: forced labor for African men would reduce the slave-like burdens of African women by imposing a European domestic model, where men would be wage-earners and providers, supporting women whose first responsibility would be to raise children and make a home while supplementing male wages by gardening or selling goods

---

[28] Flora Lugard, "The Tropics of the Empire," 817, 826.

[29] "Captain Baccardi's Report," *Congo Supplement to the WAM*, September 1904, 388; Dr Paul Rohrbach quoted in Kingsley Kenneth Dike Nworah, "Humanitarian Pressure-Groups and British Attitudes to West Africa, 1895–1915" (PhD thesis, University of London, 1966), 8; Charles Dilke, *Greater Britain* (London, 1868), 130, quoted in Duncan Bell, *The Idea of Greater Britain* (Princeton: Princeton University Press, 2007), 115.

[30] Frederick Lugard, "West African Possessions and Administrations," in *The Empire and the Century*, ed. C.S. Goldman (London: J. Murray, 1905), 835–60.

[31] Wildeman and Gentil, *IRJ*, 21 November 1904, 521.

at markets. If the current inhabitants could not see this, then compulsory labor would teach them.

Like African labor, African resources were the objects of much European interest. Imperialists often claimed that they were acting as trustees for their subjects, with a legal or even sacred charge to rule them for their own good, in the same way that a bank acts as trustee for those without the ability, knowledge, or inclination to take care of their own assets. In Britain, this argument had a component of atonement for past misdeeds associated with slavery.[32] The tension between ensuring the most profitable use of the assets and ensuring the best outcome for the beneficiaries made trusteeship a flexible concept; most Europeans believed they could use the resources of Africa better than the inhabitants. Whether taking control of resources or altering cultural practices, for European purposes or for the supposed benefit of local people, the result was imperial control.

Only a few people contested the idea that conquest and rule were the natural order of things. Recent studies show that the number of anti-imperialists remained small through the late Victorian and Edwardian eras.[33] Many were socialists whose overall program marginalized their views on colonialism, but some anti-imperialists were in prominent positions and could make themselves heard. Their ideas had roots in the application of theory and in reaction to the realities of imperial rule. The philosopher and social scientist Herbert Spencer focused on the harmful effects on home societies as a necessary byproduct of imperial control. The British Positivists, whose secular religion of humanity combined formal rituals with trust in science to answer questions about both nature and society, rejected colonial rule as a violation of the principles of human equality. For Frederic Harrison, President of the English Positivist Committee, "all are our brothers and fellow-citizens of the world."[34] The Irish historian Alice Stopford Green came at the question from a more practical perspective: her reflexive anti-imperialism sprang from her sympathy for the plight of her native Ireland.[35]

---

[32] William Bain, *Between Anarchy and Society: Trusteeship and the Obligations of Power* (Oxford: Oxford University Press, 2003), 55.

[33] Gregory Claeys, *Imperial Sceptics: British Critics of Empire, 1850–1920* (Cambridge: Cambridge University Press, 2010); Mira Matikkala, *Empire and Imperial Ambition: Liberty, Englishness and Anti-Imperialism in Late-Victorian Britain* (New York: I.B. Tauris, 2011).

[34] Frederic Harrison, "Empire and Humanity," in *National and Social Problems* (New York: Macmillan, 1908), 247.

[35] Herbert Spencer, "Imperialism and Slavery," in *Facts and Comments* (New York: D. Appleton and Company, 1902), 157–71; Robert Wuliger, "The idea of economic imperialism with special reference to the life and work of E.D. Morel" (PhD thesis, University of London, 1953), 25; Brenda Clarke, "Alice Sophia Amelia Green," in *A Historical Dictionary of British Women* (London: Europa Publications Ltd., 2003), 192.

It is no accident that Spencer, Harrison, and Green all supported the attack on the Congo regime.

The more numerous critics of empire steered a middle path to seek a better sort of imperial rule.[36] J.A. Hobson tied imperialism to flaws in the operation of the capitalist system: unequal distribution of wealth in European societies brought about underconsumption and thus surplus capital, which led financial interests to seek investment opportunities in less advanced countries. For Hobson, the founding and functioning of the Congo Free State sprang from this very problem and served as an object lesson about the need for government control of colonies. Leopold's Congo Free State existed for the benefit of private economic interests: the concession companies and Leopold's government itself, which functioned as a commercial enterprise. This illustrated Hobson's contention that the absence of a proper colonial power such as Britain in a less advanced region would open the floodgates for the unregulated agents of surplus capital to exploit the local people without limitation.[37]

Most critics—including all the early Congo reformers—accepted the basic fact of imperial rule, arguing for improving its practice based on religious, humanitarian, and commercial ideas that resonated with their society. Morel's own idealization of empire appeared when he wished that Belgian socialists

> could be induced to modify their sweeping condemnation of all colonial enterprise without exception … It is a thousand pities that the Belgian Socialist leaders do not make it their business to really study the work of Great Britain in Western Central Africa and of France in her West African dependencies proper. They would then realise not only that it is possible for the management of overseas dependencies to be conducted on lines materially advantageous to both Europeans and natives, but they would realize how inextricably interwoven are the economic and humanitarian sides of all such enterprise.[38]

J. Compton Rickett, MP, captured this spirit when he wrote of "the Imperial idea sanely expressed" in a 1902 letter to Liberal leader Sir Henry Campbell-Bannerman asking him to meet with Nonconformist religious leaders, most of whom became active in the Congo reform campaign.[39]

The question of a sane imperialism had divided British public opinion and especially the Liberal party during the Boer War of 1899–1902. The war's

---

[36] Bernard Porter, *Critics of Empire: British Radical Attitudes towards Colonialism in Africa*, 2nd ed. (New York: I.B. Tauris, 2008).

[37] J.A. Hobson, "Free Trade and Foreign Policy," *Contemporary Review*, no. 74 (August 1898): 167–80; Hobson, *Imperialism: A Study* (London: J. Nisbet & Co., 1902) 209, 243–5.

[38] *Organ*, July 1907, 15.

[39] J. Compton Rickett to Campbell-Bannerman, 3 March 1902, Campbell-Bannerman papers, Add. 41237:18–22.

supporters called its opponents pro-Boers and, occasionally, traitors.[40] In the immediate aftermath of the war, the Congo regime provided a target that could unite a broader array of the British public, transcending political, confessional, and other boundaries. Critiquing British imperialism in the age of the New Imperialism meant attacking government officials and powerful interests in British society. Concerns about Russia, a great power, and the Ottoman Empire in Bulgaria, Armenia, and Macedonia, a focus of great-power rivalry, similarly could lead to conflict because of the complications of international diplomacy. Leopold's personal imperialism had few prominent defenders in Britain and much less risk of great-power complications. The Congo campaign restored a sense of unity that the Boer War had jeopardized without aggravating the unhealed wounds of the debates over the war.

The British Humanitarian Context

The British Congo reform movement began late in Victoria's reign, flourished under a sympathetic Edward VII, and concluded under George V. This "long Edwardian" period is a useful timeframe for analyzing both Britain and Europe. Philipp Blom has referred to this period as the "vertigo years," emphasizing the uncertainty that permeated European culture.[41]

The movement for reform began in Britain long before it had a foothold anywhere else, and the British movement was the centerpiece even after the movement became transnational. Other countries developed reform movements because of the inspiration and prodding of the CRA, and those movements, except in America, never developed a large popular following, and no country's reformers, except in America and Belgium, had any influence on government policies. Britain's centrality sprang in part from a combination of cultural factors that had no parallel elsewhere, with the exception of the sense of uncertainty referred to by Blom. In Britain, a long relative economic decline during a period of economic growth triggered this anxiety while naval competition spawned fears of war and invasion. The Congo reformers responded to the uncertainty with the hope that the old British confidence could be renewed if they could resurrect the will, vigor, and moral compass required. To do so, they expressed, used, and wrestled with Edwardian assumptions about Britain's role in the world, imperialism, national honor, and economics.

---

[40] John W. Auld, "The Liberal Pro-Boers," *Journal of British Studies* 14, no. 2 (May 1975): 78–101; W.T. Stead, "Restoration of the Transvaal to the Boers," *American Monthly Review of Reviews* 35, no. 4 (April 1907), 429.

[41] Philipp Blom, *The Vertigo Years: Europe 1900–1914* (New York: Basic Books, 2008).

Another special factor was evangelical religious feeling, a potent political force for the last time in British history.[42] For over a century, moderate British evangelicals relied on free will and individual initiative to save others, body and soul, because they believed that God would not otherwise intervene in human affairs and that their faith would be demonstrated by their efforts to redeem wrongs in the world.[43] Among other demands it made on its adherents, evangelicalism called for atonement for sin through positive action and for conversion of the heathen. Because helping the Congo promised both, the reform movement attracted churchgoing Nonconformists and evangelical Anglicans. This spirit energized even the Quakers in the mid-nineteenth century and, with an infusion of liberal thought, set the stage for an unparalleled Quaker engagement with the problems of Britain and the world during the vertigo years, in what Thomas Kennedy has called the "Quaker Renaissance."[44]

This emphasis on atonement, saving, and action in the world had spread beyond the evangelicals. Less devout persons like Morel and secularists like Fox Bourne used language that echoed evangelical themes, including the will of God, without overtly doctrinal content. All evidenced a strong responsibility toward the unprivileged, which some analysts have seen as connected with the value the evangelicals placed on the human soul and thus, the individual.[45] Indeed, a commitment to humanity bridged many divides in British society in what historians Georgios Varouxakis and Eugene Biagini have called "enlightened patriotism," which could unite evangelicals, positivists, and secularists in campaigns against cruel practices, just as it did in the Congo reform movement.[46] John Halstead traces the roots of this sensibility to the blending of Enlightenment philosophies with evangelicalism in the late eighteenth century that, a century later, had thoroughly permeated nearly every institution of

---

[42] John F. Glaser, "English Nonconformity and the Decline of Liberalism," *The American Historical Review* 63, no. 2 (January 1958): 352–63.

[43] Amanda Bowie Moniz, "'Labours in the Cause of Humanity in Every Part of the Globe': Transatlantic Philanthropic Collaboration and the Cosmopolitan Ideal, 1760–1815" (PhD diss., University of Michigan, 2008), 340.

[44] Thomas C. Kennedy, *British Quakerism, 1860-1920: The Transformation of a Religious Community* (Oxford: Oxford University Press, 2001), 6–7, 193.

[45] David Lambert and Alan Lester, "Geographies of Colonial Philanthropy," *Progress in Human Geography* 28, no. 3 (2004): 323, citing Ernst Howse, *Saints in Politics: The "Clapham Sect" and the Growth of Freedom* (London: George Allen and Unwin. 1953), 7.

[46] Eugenio F. Biagini, *British Democracy and Irish Nationalism 1876-1906* (New York: Cambridge University Press, 2007), 3–4; Georgios Varouxakis, "'Patriotism,' 'Cosmopolitanism,' and 'Humanity' in Victorian Political Thought," *European Journal of Political Theory* 5, no. 1 (January 2006): 100–118.

British society with some level of concern for the underdog.[47] Likewise, religious atonement and secular notions of honor came together in the Congo reform movement, building on the argument that Britain had enabled the formation of the misgoverned Congo Free State. This sense of national honor reflected widely held beliefs that Britain's role in the world was fundamentally a force for good: a beacon of freedom, the guarantor of the *Pax Britannica*, the suppressor of the slave trade, and the home of enlightened colonial administration. In this view, countervailing examples of British greed, perfidy, cruelty, or immorality were exceptions, or better yet, exceptions that proved the rule, because Britain was more self-critical than its rivals.

Most of the British public and political elite accepted the inherent virtues of competition and free trade; Campbell-Bannerman observed that questioning free trade was like arguing about the law of gravity.[48] The electorate rejected Joseph Chamberlain's advocacy for protection in the 1906 election, giving the Liberals a tremendous victory; free trade was the chief plank in the party's platform.[49] The Congo Free State's trading monopolies violated not only the 1885 Berlin treaty but also free-trade principles that were more pervasive in Britain than in her major rivals.

Britain's humanitarian tradition had more depth than any other country's. Since the late seventeenth century, Britain had been the leading country in philanthropy conducted by formally organized voluntary associations, a part of the expansion of its public sphere. The United States was the only country in the same league. An 1803 survey counted almost 10,000 British societies, while by mid-century France had 2,000, Italy 443, and Russia only six.[50] The associations did not rely on state, church, or aristocratic authority to set goals, obtain funding, or operate, shifting control to members of the middle class who were the associations' officers, committee members, and donors.[51] Nonconforming Protestants, who had limited political rights until the nineteenth century, found outlets for their energies and political dissatisfaction in these associations.[52] Just as the joint-stock company led to larger and better-capitalized commercial

---

[47] John P. Halstead, *The Second British Empire: Trade, Philanthropy and Good Government* (Westport, CT: Greenwood Press, 1983), 18.

[48] Colin Cross, *The Liberals in Power* (London: Barrie and Rockliff, 1963), 3.

[49] Biagini, *British Democracy*, 351; Herbert Gladstone papers, 1906 election, Add. 46063.

[50] Joanna Innes, "State, Church, and Voluntarism in European Welfare, 1690–1850," in *Charity, Philanthropy, and Reform*, eds Innes and Hugh Cunningham (New York: St Martin's Press, 1998), 41. Italy's total includes savings banks.

[51] David Edward Owen, *English Philanthropy, 1660–1960* (Cambridge, MA: Belknap Press, 1964), 13.

[52] G.M. Ditchfield, "Rational Dissent and Philanthropy, c. 1760–1810," in *Charity, Philanthropy, and Reform*, 196.

ventures, the parallel development of similarly organized associations improved access to funding, quality of governance, and ability to grow and even incorporate.[53] Subscriptions from a large number of people meant independence from individual donors and enabled larger budgets while encouraging wider involvement and better oversight.[54] In a parallel development, philanthropists broadened their purview from local to regional and national causes, and some began casting their eyes overseas.[55] Multiple causes used British philanthropic modes of organization to pursue a cause of redemption by using the force of public opinion to influence Parliament and thus government policy.

Beatrice Webb called late Victorian humanitarianism a secular religion, but religious motivations remained important for many.[56] Traditional Anglican and Catholic charity was a religious duty to comfort a suffering recipient while benefiting the giver in the hereafter. However, since the late seventeenth century, duty increasingly called dissenting Protestants and evangelical Anglicans to identify moral wrongs and to try to redeem society. British Positivists blended secular morality and religious fervor to create their vision of an improved world. Gregory Claeys has shown that their ideas influenced ways of thinking far beyond the few formal adherents of their "religion of humanity" where there were "no distinctions of skin or race, of sect or creed" according to Positivist leader Frederic Harrison.[57]

Humanitarianism reflected other cultural values. Enlightenment ideas about fighting injustice and solving problems through reason lived on in philanthropic institutions of all kinds.[58] For some, involvement provided an opportunity for social climbing, perhaps simply to make contacts in higher classes or else to stake a claim to a higher-class status.[59] Humanitarian relief sometimes served

---

[53] For groups such as libraries with limited subscribers, membership could be sold like shares of stock. R.J. Morris, "Clubs, Societies and Associations," in *Cambridge Social History of Britain 1750–1950, Vol. 3: Social Agencies and Institutions*, ed. F.M.L. Thompson (Cambridge: Cambridge University Press, 1990), 406–7.

[54] Benjamin Kirkman Gray, *A History of English Philanthropy: From the Dissolution of the Monasteries to the Taking of the First Census* (London: B.J. King and Son, 1906), 80–82; Owen, *English Philanthropy*, 11–12; M.J.D. Roberts, *Making English Morals: Voluntary Association and Moral Reform in England, 1787–1886* (New York: Cambridge University Press, 2004), 67; Donna T. Andrew, *Philanthropy and Police: London Charity in the Eighteenth Century* (Princeton: Princeton University Press, 1989), 42, 48, 49.

[55] Gray, *History*, 156–7, 171ff.

[56] Gertrude Himmelfarb, "The Age of Philanthropy," *Wilson Quarterly* 21, no. 2 (Spring 1997): 51.

[57] Claeys, *Imperial Sceptics*, 55–6; Harrison, 'Empire and Humanity,' 247.

[58] Susan Thorne, *Congregational Missions and the Making of an Imperial Culture in Nineteenth Century England* (Stanford: Stanford University Press, 1999), 34–5.

[59] Owen, *English Philanthropy*, 165.

economic interests, as when British slaveholders wished to see others similarly deprived of slave imports after 1807.

Pride in British morality reinforced the arrogance of British power. The British sense of superiority as the world's leader in liberty accorded with their view of themselves as uniquely benevolent among nations.[60] This self-regarding aura became strongest after 1815 when the coincidence of power (the defeat of Napoleon) and virtue (the ending of the slave trade) suggested a connection that no evidence of British colonial oppression could challenge thereafter. At best, these incidents became betrayals of the mythic British national character. For 60 years, the British used their power to bring other European states into conformity with their own recent revulsion against the slave trade, acculturating the people and government to a new practice in statecraft, in which Britain wheedled and bullied other countries to achieve humanitarian objectives.

While other overseas humanitarian organizations came and went during the Victorian era to address famines, oppression, and injustices around the world, the British and Foreign Anti-Slavery Society (Anti-Slavery) and the Aborigines' Protection Society (APS) carried the legacy of abolition through the nineteenth century. They saw downtrodden aboriginal peoples and slaves as having little agency in an imperial world save violent rebellion and therefore needing British government intervention to help them. With overlapping membership and similar tactics, they often worked together. The Anti-Slavery Society endured despite dwindling public interest and a stubbornly persistent slave trade.[61] Its income in 1899–1908 fluctuated greatly from a high of £3467 in 1901 to a low of £625 in 1907, with the number of donors falling steadily from 469 in 1901 to 240 in 1908. The Aborigines' Protection Society argued for native rights with less success. It had fewer than 200 donors, subscribers, and life members in 1841.[62] In 1897, as it began its Congo agitation, donations hit a low point of £242 from 166 people though they did rebound to £677 from 201 donors by 1903.

The two societies' inability to grow led to pessimistic assessments. One historian notes an ebbing of evangelical fervor and the subsidence of British self-confidence, factors not conducive to sympathy for the troubles of distant strangers.[63] Fox Bourne, the last APS Secretary, believed that Britain's

---

[60] Andrew, *Philanthropy and Police*, 20–22.

[61] Susan Willmington, "The Activities of the Aborigines Protection Society as a Pressure Group on the Formulation of Colonial Policy 1868–1880" (PhD thesis, University of Wales, 1973), 9–10.

[62] *The Fourth Annual Report of the Aborigines' Protection Society* (London: P. White and Son, 1841).

[63] Willmington, "Activities," 9–10, 34–5.

humanitarian spirit had decayed.[64] This sentiment should not be taken at face value. For example, when Fox Bourne was writing, the National Society for the Prevention of Cruelty to Children was able to mobilize 6,000 female collectors to explain the work of this society and raise money.[65] Similarly, British interest in overseas humanitarianism rebounded in the 1890s. In the decade before 1904, a new band of humanitarian organizations had arisen, including, among others, the Society for the Recognition for the Brotherhood of Man against lynching and segregation in the US, the Armenian Relief Fund, the Friends of Russian Freedom, the Native Races Aid Association and Society of Universal Brotherhood, the Macedonian Relief Fund, and the Balkan Committee. Expanded concern for faraway peoples coincided with the spread of imperialist sentiment in the 1890s, though interest in their souls was more widespread than concern about oppression, rights, and ill-treatment. Each major missionary society had an annual cash flow more than 100 times greater than the APS or Anti-Slavery.[66]

Although overseas humanitarianism found new energy, a relatively small group of humanitarians kept these flames burning, including members of families with strong philanthropic traditions, such as Buxtons and Wilberforces, and some manufacturing, retailing, and merchant magnates, such as William A. Albright, whose company made the igniting chemicals for matches. Notable Quakers such as the lawyer Joseph G. Alexander, Anglican clergymen such as Canon Scott Holland, and crusading editors such as John St Loe Strachey had links to these causes as well. The CRA's London Committee boasted Richard Cobden's daughter, Jane Cobden Unwin, who was a leader of the Friends of Russian Freedom, a notable suffragist, and the first woman to serve on the Committee of the Aborigines' Protection Society. The CRA brought some new blood into overseas humanitarianism, but it largely relied on the same networks of leaders and donors as the societies that preceded it.

Methods of organization, information-gathering, publicity, fundraising, and influencing government were much the same for all overseas humanitarian societies, with variations for groups actually sending people overseas as missionaries or famine relief workers. Each had a president or chairman, a treasurer, and a secretary. At the Anti-Slavery Society before 1910, the president led the organization, while the Secretary filled this role at the APS, backed by a largely ceremonial president. Occasionally a vice-president or vice-chairman had

---

[64] Kenneth D. Nworah, "The Aborigines' Protection Society, 1889–1909: A Pressure-Group in Colonial Policy," *Canadian Journal of African Studies* 5, no. 1 (1971): 87–8.

[65] Frank Prochaska, "Philanthropy," in *The Cambridge Social History of Britain 1750–1950, Vol. 3*, ed. F.M.L. Thompson (Cambridge: Cambridge University Press, 1990), 384.

[66] E. Boothroyd, *Low's Handbook to the Charities of London, 1903–1904* (London: Sampson Low, Marston & Co., 1904), 11, 40, 42, 117–19, 164, 231.

executive duties, but in most cases these were non-executive positions handed out to influential or generous sympathizers as an honor to flatter the individual and boost the organization's prestige. A Committee or Executive Committee represented the membership, provided oversight, and in many cases determined policy and strategy. Many organizations used local auxiliaries or branches to get the word out, raise funds, and organize lectures. The Peace Society was particularly vigorous in this regard.[67] The APS was not organized this way in the late 1800s, despite founding a short-lived Liverpool branch and a similarly ephemeral "Native Races" group in Manchester in 1898.[68]

Overseas humanitarian organizations sought international connections where possible to lend weight to their entreaties at home, abroad, and at international conferences. The Aborigines' Protection Society had honorary foreign members and correspondents, and the Anti-Slavery Society collaborated with similar groups in Belfast, America, France, Germany, Italy, and even Malta.[69] In addition, both groups received information from overseas missionaries. The Congo Reform Association adapted these practices for its own purposes.

Humanitarian organizations used public meetings, the press, pamphlets, and books to publicize their causes. Public meetings entertained, informed, and advocated in this era before broadcast radio and television. Often public meetings culminated in passing resolutions to influence politicians or government officials. Missionary and humanitarian societies frequently used illuminated images from magic lanterns to attract people to meetings and reinforce their emotional attachment to the cause.[70] Sometimes the entire audience paid to attend, while at other times admission was free for the gallery, with a fee for reserved seating, with most funds coming from a collection taken after the speakers had inspired the audience. Any money remaining after paying for room rental, travel expenses, and refreshments would go to the sponsoring organization. However, humanitarian organizations raised much more money through annual mailings, special appeals, and, for larger donors, personal contact. They tried to lure people as subscribers who would receive publications, attend annual members' meetings, and donate year after year.

Newsletters, often called official organs, let organizations communicate relevant news, official positions, and financial needs to subscribers and influential non-subscribers in the press, in political life, or at other societies. Most overseas

---

[67] For examples, see *The Herald of Peace and International Arbitration*, 1 June 1894, 70–73, http://books.google.com/books?id=tF0PAAAAIAAJ&pg=PA427.

[68] *Aborigines' Friend*, February 1899, 392–4 and November 1899, 455–6.

[69] Lewis Tappan, "Correspondence of Lewis Tappan and Others with the British and Foreign Anti-Slavery Society (Parts 1, 6, and 13)," *The Journal of Negro History* 12, no. 2 (April 1927): 202–3, 309, 542; Douglas H. Maynard, "The World's Anti–Slavery Convention of 1840," *The Mississippi Valley Historical Review* 47, no. 3 (December 1960): 452–71.

[70] See Chapter 6.

humanitarian societies aimed to influence the British government to take action in the colonies or exert pressure on foreign countries. In addition to public meetings and resolutions, they worked with friendly MPs to raise questions in Parliament or sponsor legislation, met privately or in formal delegations with government ministers, wrote letters and memoranda to officials, and used influential people to advocate with government ministers. The Congo Reform Association drew on all these methods.

When the Aborigines' Protection Society took up the cause of Congo reform in 1896, the society had over 50 years' experience arguing for the humane treatment of colonized peoples.[71] Its actively Christian motivation and close ties to missionaries had become more secular over time.[72] In its middle years, the society espoused an imperial humanitarianism: the best solution for an abridgement of aboriginal rights was British annexation. Annexationist sentiment ebbed in the APS when the New Imperialism was in its heyday, but an imperial mindset continued to color the society's attitude towards human rights and prevented it from working with educated Africans interested in self-government.[73] The society continued to believe that European powers had a right and even an obligation to rule societies that were weaker, non-Christian, and less civilized. Advocating imperial trusteeship rather than independence, the APS for the most part saw Africans not as partners but as objects of their attention.[74]

Lack of popular support meant that the APS addressed injustices by lobbying. Using information from correspondents, its Secretary asked the Colonial Office, Foreign Office, and/or Parliament for remediation. The Colonial Office was sometimes grateful to the society for acting as its eyes and ears, but during Fox Bourne's tenure as Secretary (1889–1909), the Colonial Office became more skeptical about the quality of the society's information, suspecting that he was too gullible to detect his correspondents' errors, mendacity, or self-interest. This skepticism was to impede the APS's Congo advocacy in the late 1890s.[75]

---

[71] Nworah, "Aborigines' Protection Society," 79–91; Charles Swaisland, "The Aborigines' Protection Society, 1837–1909," in *After Slavery: Emancipation and Its Discontents*, ed. Howard Temperley (London: Frank Cass, 2000), 265–80; Willmington, "Activities."

[72] Ruth Slade, *King Leopold's Congo* (New York: Oxford University Press, 1962), 277–8.

[73] Swaisland, "Aborigines' Protection Society," 277; Nworah, "Aborigines' Protection Society," 85–6.

[74] Andrew Porter, "Trusteeship, Anti-Slavery and Humanitarianism" and "Religion, Missionary Enthusiasm and Empire," *The Oxford History of the British Empire*, vol. 3, *The Nineteenth Century* (Oxford: Oxford University Press, 1999), 198–221.

[75] Swaisland, "Aborigines' Protection Society," 266–7; Willmington, "Activities," 31–2; and Nworah, "Aborigines' Protection Society," 83, 87.

Scholars have disputed some of the society's successes; sometimes others, such as missionaries, could take credit.[76] This raises the question of how to measure relative influence in a campaign where each element may have been necessary but not sufficient, a question relevant for the Congo Reform Association. Because the APS seemed to be inadequate to the Congo question, many reform advocates sought another organizational vehicle by 1903, ending with the 1904 formation of the CRA.

The CRA's leadership emphasized the uniqueness of the Congo problem and the CRA, a theme that helped them influence the public, the press, and the Foreign Office. However, the CRA used technologies of humanitarianism common to other organizations. Similarly, colonial misrule on the Congo was not as unusual as Morel claimed. Imperial powers mistreated and slaughtered people on a large scale in Africa, Asia, and even Europe. Some Congo reformers publicized and condemned other imperial excesses. Mark Twain campaigned against the brutal American war in the Philippines, W.T. Stead and others had been active Pro-Boers, groups condemned lynching in the United States, and Fox Bourne publicized Portuguese cocoa slavery in São Tomé and Príncipe as well as the Angolan slave trade that fed it. Roger Casement, in alliance with John Harris, later tried to remedy rubber atrocities in the Peruvian Putumayo. Although (or perhaps because) his close allies played a leading role in these exposés, Morel took care to emphasize that the scale of the Congo problems exceeded these situations. Even when he publicly called for action on Portuguese cocoa slavery in 1906, he told his readers that it was "mild in comparison with the horrors of the rubber slavery of the Congo State."[77] Regarding the Putomayo, Morel stressed its limited extent:

> For devilish ingenuity in torture, the [Congo] comparison may stand. In the numbers affected, the area concerned, and the cumulative effects comparison is absurd. Where the Putumayo Indians have perished in thousands, the Congolese have perished in *millions* ... Modern history has no parallel to this.[78]

This rhetoric of uniqueness had many uses. It reassured Morel and the Harrises that the cause to which they had devoted years of their lives was worth their sacrifices. It spurred donors to continue their financial support year after year. And finally, it helped draw attention from MPs and Foreign Office personnel with a multitude of other calls on their time. Nonetheless, the Congo reform

---

[76] John H. Darch, "Missionaries as Humanitarians? Opposition to the Recruitment of Indentured Labour for Queensland in the 1860s and 70s" (Paper, Henry Martyn Seminar, Westminster College, Cambridge, 2 March 2006), https://www.academia.edu/793405.

[77] *WAM* (8 June 1906): 242; "The Angolan-San Thomé question," *AM* 3, no. 144 (8 July 1910).

[78] *Economist*, 27 July 1912, 177. Also, *AM* 5, no. 251 (26 July 1912): 422.

movement, despite its claims of uniqueness, was firmly embedded in the humanitarian tradition.

Questioning Motives, Methods, and Effectiveness

Many of the questions about the Congo reform movement become those that pertain to any humanitarian campaign. The present study addresses these topics thematically in a roughly chronological fashion, starting with those that primarily concern the movement's beginning.

Chapter 2 addresses the movement's motivations and origins, culminating in the creation of the CRA. Chapter 3 examines the CRA's structures and practices, which could determine success or failure, as well as the impact of the evolving relationship of Morel and John Harris. Because so much of the documentary record comes from his correspondence, it is important not to blindly follow Morel's lead, particularly in his understanding of his own actions, his choice of heroes and villains, and his conclusions about the motives or actions of others.

The CRA was also the sum of its adherents. Chapter 4 analyzes the demographics of the CRA's leadership and donor base to draw conclusions about how this makeup enabled and constrained the movement. This chapter also examines the ways this highly masculine movement depended on women and how their roles fell into the shadows in historical accounts.

Chapter 5 reviews how the group's essential alliances linked it to other humanitarian societies, missionary organizations, religious bodies, and chambers of commerce. The CRA's web of alliances was also transnational, with independent forces for reform in several countries working in cooperation the CRA, as covered in Chapter 6.

Because Leopold had portrayed his enterprise as a paragon, the primary battleground was the representation of the Congo Free State itself. Chapter 7 shows how the reformers contested Leopold's rosy picture in the press, other printed matter, public meetings, and courtrooms.

The point of the battle of representation was to convince government leaders to acknowledge the Congo's problems and to take responsibility for resolving them. The government's evolving relationship to the reform question appears in Chapter 8, culminating in government control of the reform effort.

The crux of the matter is the question posed at the onset: was the victory of the Congo reform movement real or a delusion? Chapter 9 undertakes an examination of the determinants of success or failure and the role of causality in the outcome, synthesizing the work of Africanists with the mechanics of the reform movement. To the extent that the Congo reform campaign succeeded, what was effective in creating the possibility and reality of change?

To address these questions, this work combines archival research and analysis with the insights of a historiography from multiple disciplines from scholars on three continents.[79] The particulars of the political, cultural, and material context were responsible for the Congo situation and the possibilities for confronting it, and the movement's responses to those specific situations have resonance for the study of other humanitarian movements.

---

[79] For historiography, see Dean Pavlakis, "The Congo Reform Movement in Britain, 1896–1913" (Unpublished PhD dissertation, 2011), 9–34 or Pavlakis, "Historiography of Congo Reform," http://congofreestate.com/2014/05/22/historiography-of-congo-reform/, updated 22 May 2014.

Chapter 2
Origins

> We must unite in organized association having one clear sole aim—namely to enlighten, systematically and continuously, public opinion in this country, and abroad, upon the actual condition of the Congo people.[1]—Roger Casement, 1904

Men and women stirred by concern for others may take action, but to make that action constructive they require a common vision. The Britons arguing for Congo reform before the foundation of the Congo Reform Association came from eclectic backgrounds and were not always in agreement about priorities. Traders, philanthropists, businessmen, journalists, diplomats, politicians, and missionaries tried to get government and international attention, sometimes as allies, other times as rivals. An attempt by W.T. Stead to unite the reformers led to acrimony and divergence in late 1903. With the Roger Casement's intervention, the reformers reunited in a disciplined movement which synthesized their ideas into a coherent program.

Early Critiques

Before 1885, Leopold had astutely cultivated humanitarians, missionaries, free-traders, Belgian commercial interests, and foreign statesmen. The reality of the Congo Free State slowly undermined this support, due to the violence of the administrative culture, pursuit of profits by the state and state-granted monopolies, royal favoritism, and exploitation of the people. Increasingly disaffected commercial, humanitarian, and religious constituencies might oppose the regime, if they could be organized and motivated. Support dwindled, but Leopold no longer needed broad public support so long as he did not face outright hostility from Belgium or the more powerful governments that could affect Belgium's fate or the Congo's.

Complaints began early from British traders on the lower Congo. In a lantern lecture at the Manchester Geographical Society on 27 October 1886, the trader and anthropologist Richard E. Dennett described conditions in the Congo Free State very much at odds with its philanthropic and scientific claims, emphasizing

---

[1] Casement to Morel, 25 January 1904, F8/16:25.

its "mismanagement and bullying propensities."[2] The next year he complained of its "arbitrary and despotic" treatment of traders and observed that the Congo government, unlike other colonial governments, "cannot resist the temptation of trading."[3] In 1889, the Manchester Geographical Society reviewed traders' evidence to the effect that, "the Belgians' methods of trade were to employ 100 armed soldiers round each station to terrorise the natives into bringing them produce," all, as one added bitterly, "in the name of philanthropy."[4] Traders had begun worrying about their potential customers, the people of the Congo.

George Washington Williams achieved far more publicity than any trader. An African-American pastor, journalist, and historian, he believed that the Congo could be a land of the future for American blacks. Before heading there, he met with Francis W. Fox, a Quaker who served on the Committee of the Aborigines' Protection Society.[5] This conversation may have led to his first doubts; on his journey to Congo, Williams discussed the injustices of European colonialism with people he met on board ship and at each port.[6] On arrival, he encountered Dennett, who filled his ears with stories of misrule.[7] His journey 1,300 miles up the Congo River convinced him of the government's "deceit, obtrusiveness, ignorance, and cruelty."[8]

Although coerced rubber production had not begun in earnest, the Free State's brutal culture horrified Williams. After reaching Stanley Falls in July 1890, he compiled a comprehensive indictment in *An Open Letter to His Serene Majesty Leopold II*, and two other reports in the same vein, denouncing state-sponsored slavery, the abuse of military power, trade monopolies, and cruelty.[9] He accused the Congo authorities of lying to the world and criticized the mayhem of Stanley's last expedition (1886–89). Williams held Leopold responsible, in contrast to other early critics who assumed that problems occurred despite, not because of, the King's intentions. Williams appealed to the signatories of the Berlin Act, the Belgian people, humanitarians, Christians, and statesmen to act together against Leopold and his Congo regime.

This call reached a wide audience, beginning while Williams was in transit: Stanley read the *Open Letter* in October 1890, and, in November, it featured

---

[2] "Reports of Meetings," *Journal of the Manchester Geographical Society* (*JMGS*) 2 (July to December 1886): 283–306, 369.

[3] Dennett letter, 6 February 1887, *JMGS* 3 (March 1887): 117.

[4] E.D. Morel, *King Leopold's Rule in Africa* (London: William Heinemann, 1904), 103.

[5] Fox to Morel, 15 November 1906, F9/6:42.

[6] John Hope Franklin, *George Washington Williams* (Chicago: University of Chicago Press, 1985), 189.

[7] Dennett to Morel, 23 December 1914, F8/38:9–18.

[8] Williams to Huntington, 16 July 1890, quoted in Franklin, *Williams*, 195.

[9] The reports are reproduced in Franklin, *Williams*, 244–79.

in a London meeting of European traders regarding Leopold's petition at the Brussels Anti-Slavery Conference to exempt the Congo from the Berlin Act's ban on import taxes.[10] Richard Cobden Phillips, a merchant with Congo experience, used the *Open Letter* to demonstrate that the evils there went far beyond Leopold's proposed tax.[11] His critique anticipated the reformers' key arguments: "the aim of the Congo State was a commercial monopoly of the products of the country which they occupied by forged treaties in Africa, false declarations at home, and afterwards maintained by endless violence and extortion."[12] However, the meeting remained narrowly focused on import taxes. The next month, at an APS public meeting on Stanley's last expedition, Phillips again brought up the prevalence of atrocities, but the meeting's tepid resolution did not address this issue.[13]

As newspapers in the United States, Belgium, Britain, and France informed their readers about the *Open Letter*, Leopold's allies went into action. Stanley accused Williams of blackmail.[14] Speeches in the Belgian Parliament attacked Williams and praised Leopold. For now, the counterattack succeeded. Williams, gravely ill, returned to Britain and died two months later, on 2 August 1891. He had accomplished this much: the controversy had torn Leopold's cloak of philanthropy, leaving a general sense that all was not well in the Congo.

This did not translate into action. Leopold had little to fear from Belgium, where most of the press and Parliament were on his side. Decrees in 1891 monopolizing trade elicited complaints from Belgian, Dutch, and British commercial interests, but Leopold mollified them with the opportunity to secure concessions.[15] The APS largely ignored the Congo from 1891–96 and missionaries almost always expressed their concerns in private. Dr Harry Guinness, head of the Congo Balolo Mission (CBM), went silent after publicizing problems in 1890–91.[16] The Foreign Office filed the accounts of cruelty it received without public comment. Williams's assertion of Leopold's personal culpability gave way to the view that "Crimes against humanity have been committed," but were not the King's fault, because "he is in the hands of his officials."[17]

---

[10] Franklin, *Williams*, 197–9, 207–9.
[11] "Report of the Proceedings of the Conference of African Merchants on the Congo Free State and Import Duties" (Manchester: Manchester Press, 1890), 33–4.
[12] *JMGS* 8 (1892): 201–2.
[13] "The Congo Atrocities," *AF*, April 1891, 155–64; Cookey, *Britain*, 35.
[14] Franklin, *Williams*, 211–14; *New York Times*, 15 April 1891, 5.
[15] Cookey, *Britain*, 14, 24.
[16] Ruth Slade, *English-Speaking Missions in the Congo Independent State* (Brussels: Academie Royale des Sciences Coloniales, 1959), 239–42.
[17] John Scott Keltie, *The Partition of Africa*, 2nd ed. (London: Stanford, 1895), 219–25, 515.

The Foreign Office was more interested in British subjects recruited by the Congo authorities as workers and soldiers. These men found themselves used as beasts of burden, imprisoned or killed for complaining, pressed into military service, and kept after their contracts ended. To address these issues, in 1892 the Foreign Office appointed Edward Bannister, a British trader, as Vice-Consul in the Congo under Consul William Clayton Pickersgill in Loanda (now Luanda) in Portuguese Angola. Until his dismissal at the Congo government's request two years later, Bannister energetically pursued these cases, the first of many British consular officials in the story of Congo reform.[18]

The fate of one British subject particularly aroused the ire of the British public and the Foreign Office, run at this time by Prime Minister Salisbury: Charles Henry Stokes. In August 1895, the British government learned from Germany that the Force Publique had arrested and executed this Irish trader seven months earlier for allegedly selling weapons. The issue became a public and diplomatic sensation. The journalist Lionel Decle argued that his research into the Stokes execution showed that Leopold's regime was not fit to govern.[19] Again, nothing of substance resulted, but the treatment of British subjects contributed to an understanding of the Congo government as flawed, mendacious, and brutal.[20]

Protestant missionaries had to this point complained to local officials or their home offices, without result.[21] In 1895, two missionaries defied their superiors to come forward in the press: John H. Weeks of the Baptist Missionary Society (BMS) in October and John B. Murphy of the American Baptist Missionary Union (ABMU) in November.[22] The publicity machine went into action; Stanley excused murders as isolated crimes and accused missionaries of mistreating local people and buying slaves to free them as the government did.[23] The furor faded when the missionaries did not reply. Once again, publicity had tarnished the Congo Free State's armor but not breached it.

The pace of disclosure increased. In April 1896, an English officer formerly in the Force Publique, Captain Philip Salusbury, wrote of Congo "murder, rapine, plunder, and cruelty in the most awful degree ever reached."[24] Salusbury had less

[18] Cookey, *Britain*, 26–30.
[19] William Roger Louis, "The Stokes Affair and the Origins of the Anti-Congo Campaign, 1895–1896," *Revue Belge de Philologie & d'Histoire* 43, no. 2 (January 1965): 572–84.
[20] Cookey, *Britain*, 31–4; Adam Hochschild, *King Leopold's Ghost* (New York: Houghton Mifflin, 1998), 174.
[21] Lagergren, *Mission and State*, 138–46.
[22] *The Times*, 14 October 1895, 6; *The Times*, 18 November 1895, 6; Charles Harvey to Morel, 12 November 1906, F9/8:133; Lagergren, *Mission and State*, 148–52.
[23] Lagergren, *Mission and State*, 152–4.
[24] Phillip Salusbury, "The Congo State: A Revelation" *United Service Magazine*, June 1896, 314–30; "Defenders of the Congo State," *United Service Magazine*, July 1896, 420–48.

press than Williams, but was more influential because of the Congo Free State's worsening reputation. Sir Charles Dilke, Radical MP, former cabinet minister, and parliamentary spokesman for the APS, used the dire conditions revealed in Congo official documents to argue that its government violated the Berlin Act and the rights of the Congolese.[25] Guinness returned to the fray, calling for an end to the slaughter resulting from the rubber tax. In July, the APS urged European public opinion and governments to apply pressure to Leopold.[26] In September, Alfred Parminter, who had worked in the Congo for nine years, reported his firsthand knowledge of atrocities and revealed the existence of the bonuses that government employees earned on the rubber they coerced from the local people.[27] The counterattack began immediately, painting Salusbury as an unreliable witness interested in extracting money from Leopold.[28] In *The Times*, Stanley suggested that Salusbury and Parminter had believed false rumors.[29]

Stanley warned Leopold not to appear to disregard English public opinion: "it only requires a few more incidents from the Congo to confirm her in the opinion that everything must be radically wrong."[30] The answer came from another diehard British advocate for the Congo, Sir Hugh Gilzean Reid, a former MP, newspaper editor and publisher (President of the Society of Newspaper Proprietors and Managers in 1898–99), and Liberal activist. At his suggestion, Leopold instituted a Commission for the Protection of the Natives in September 1896, comprised of six long-time Congo missionaries.[31] In addition to three Belgian Catholics, Leopold appointed three British Protestants: George Grenfell and William Holman Bentley of the BMS, both distinguished authors who had praised the Congo Free State, and Dr Aaron Sims, a Scotsman in the ABMU. Grenfell correctly predicted that the Commission was likely to become "a mere farce."[32]

Grenfell's change of heart occurred in March 1896, while captaining the new BMS mission steamer *Goodwill*. His passenger, Rev. Edvard Viktor Sjöblom, a Swedish minister at the American Baptist mission, was headed to Europe on

---

[25] Charles Dilke, "Civilisation in Africa," *Cosmopolis*, 3 (July 1896), 18–35.
[26] "The Congo Free State," *AF*, July 1896, 55.
[27] *The Times*, 8 September 1896, 3 and 18 September 1896, 3; Lagergren, *Mission and State*, 188.
[28] FO 881/6813; Henry Stanley, "Captain Salusbury's Congo 'Revelations,'" *United Service Magazine*, September 1896, 645–52.
[29] *The Times*, 18 September 1896, 3.
[30] Stanley to Leopold, 16 September 1896, quoted in Barbara Emerson, *Leopold II of the Belgians: King of Colonialism* (New York: St Martin's Press, 1979), 437.
[31] *The Times*, 21 September 1896, 3; Plunkett to Salisbury, 20 September 1896, FO 881/6893:131; Lagergren, *Mission and State*, 195–6.
[32] Lagergren, *Mission and State*, 200.

furlough. Sjöblom's eyewitness descriptions of the cruelties in rubber areas convinced Grenfell, the first of his many converts to the cause of reform.[33]

The month before, Sjöblom, frustrated by the indifference of Congo officials, sent an article for publication to his ABMU superiors, to Guinness, and to the Swedish Baptists. The ABMU forwarded it to the Congo government through the US State Department, but not to the American press. It did not reach the English press either, because the Congo Balolo Mission's Council (hereafter, the Congo Council) directed Guinness to communicate it only to the Congo government in Brussels.[34] The matter might have died, but the Swedish Baptists published Sjöblom's letter in their journal, the *Wecko-Posten* (*Weekly Post*) on 23 July 1896. His accusations rippled through the Swedish press and became internationalized in September thanks to the Swedish correspondent of a Swiss paper. Soon it had appeared in Georges Clemenceau's paper *La Justice* in France and Georges Lorand's *La Reforme* in Belgium. The story spread across Europe, though not to the UK or USA, the two places Sjöblom most wanted to reach.[35] Sjöblom would find an audience in Britain the next year.

From Complaint to Campaign

In late 1896, the Aborigines' Protection Society (APS) took up the Congo. Its humanitarian ethos had its roots in evangelicalism, anthropology, and the 1837 Parliamentary report endorsing compassionate policies toward colonized peoples. Its governing Committee had a strong Quaker element, including Edward W. Brooks, Francis W. Fox, and Thomas Hodgkin by 1896.[36] Over time, the Society had added the language of native rights to the language of compassion. In the words of its Secretary, Fox Bourne, the APS worked for "the protection of ... rights" for "uncivilised races," meaning "the fundamental rights of humanity" to justice, property, and fair treatment, not political participation or full equality. The APS supported the "legitimate" extension of British authority over peoples whose condition could be improved in this way. Indeed, every civilized nation had a right to conquer less favored communities as long as they did not rule oppressively.[37]

---

[33] Lagergren, *Mission and State*, 167, 180–81.
[34] Congo Council, 24 June 1896, reel 11, 2.
[35] Lagergren, *Mission and State*, 185–92.
[36] *Report of the Parliamentary Select Committee on Aboriginal Tribes (British Settlements), Reprinted, with Comments, by the Aborigines' Protection Society* (London: William Ball and Hatchard & Son, 1837).
[37] Fox Bourne, *The Aborigines' Protection Society: Its Aims and Methods* (London: P.S. King, 1900), 3, 6–8.

Figure 2.1 H.R. Fox Bourne
Source: WAM Special Monthly Congo Supplement, July 1904, from LSE Library's collections, MOREL F1/11/5.

The APS had hesitated for years. Based on Williams's work, F.W. Fox raised Congo atrocities at its Committee meeting of 11 June 1891, but Fox Bourne concluded that the evidence was insufficient after consulting with Alfred Baynes, the BMS Secretary, and Grenfell, home on leave.[38] In late 1892, William Parminter (Alfred's uncle), who, as governor of Vivi province, had been the Congo administration's most highly placed Englishman, submitted a statement to Fox Bourne documenting the government's attacks on the rights of the local people and European merchants, but the APS did not act on his testimony, in part because Parminter shortly thereafter reconciled with Leopold.[39]

After a few more years of gradually accumulating information, the APS decided to support calls for change. This began as a discreet approach to the Congo government's chief functionary in Brussels, Edmond Van Eetvelde, but, when this led nowhere, Fox Bourne published a comprehensive statement of the evidence in December 1896, ending, "Our Committee, therefore, earnestly appeals to the Government of the Congo State to institute such changes in the administration as may be necessary to attain the humane objects contemplated and undertaken by it when the State was established."[40] In March 1897, he followed up with an article titled "The Congo Failure."[41]

Dilke brought the Congo before the House of Commons on 2 April 1897, calling for the Berlin Conference to reconvene, but his motion failed. Speaking for the Foreign Office, George Curzon stated the government's position: "it is no part of ... the duty of Her Majesty's Government to act as guardians of the public trust imposed on the Congo State by the Acts of Brussels and Berlin."[42] The following week, the APS held a public meeting on the treatment of colonized peoples, with Congo speeches by noted Liberals John Morley and Leonard Courtney covered by at least 19 newspapers.[43]

At this point Sjöblom arrived in Britain, where he convinced Guinness to introduce him to Fox Bourne, who quickly organized a public meeting in St Martin's Town Hall to review evidence from Sjöblom, Guinness, and Salusbury. Although reporters attended with the stipulation that the witnesses would remain anonymous, Fox Bourne gave Sjöblom's name in the *Aborigines' Friend*

---

[38] *AF*, February 1892, 215.

[39] Fox Bourne, *Civilisation in Congoland: A Story of International Wrong-doing* (London: P.S. King, 1903), 132–9.

[40] *AF*, December 1896, 61–81; *The Times*, 3 June 1897, 12.

[41] Fox Bourne, "The Congo Failure," *New Review* 16, no. 94 (March 1897): 342–52.

[42] 48 Parl. Deb. (4th ser.) (1897) 425–55.

[43] *The Times*, 8 April 1897, 11; Fox Bourne, *Civilisation in Congoland*, viii–ix; *AF*, April 1897, 160.

and the Swedish reporter ignored the stipulation altogether.[44] Sjöblom's account finally appeared in the British press, too late for the parliamentary debate, but used effectively thereafter.

Publicity accelerated due to some factual errors in Dilke's parliamentary speeches. A response from the Congo Consul General in Britain, Jules Houdret, triggered a volley of at least ten letters in *The Times* from April to June 1897, with Dilke and Fox Bourne countering Houdret, Gilzean Reid, and Adolphe de Cuvelier, the Congo Secretary-General for Foreign Affairs.

The campaign seemed to be developing momentum. The brutality and stupidity of Congo officials, driven half-mad with illness, isolation, and the demands of their concession company, featured in an 1897 short story by Joseph Conrad published simultaneously in London, Paris, and Berlin.[45] An indictment in the *Speaker* appeared from poet and African linguist Alice Werner.[46] *Century* increased the pressure by reproducing the journals of the late British adventurer Edward J. Glave in installments, culminating in "Cruelty in the Congo Free State." Glave had found the new Congo of the rubber zones to be a dismaying result of his pioneering 1880s work with Stanley.[47] A book by a Belgian traveler, Edmond Picard, was equally critical.[48] Congo defenders (known as Congophiles or apologists) counterattacked, but the uncoordinated campaign was working. By 1897, the notion that "everything must be radically wrong" with the Congo Free State was spreading.

Several forces worked in Leopold's favor. The British government's hands-off attitude persisted into 1903. The Foreign Office did not publicize corroborating information from its consular officials, such as the report from Bannister's successor, Leonard Arthur, that a captain in the Force Publique demanded a severed hand for each expended cartridge.[49] Consul Pickersgill met with missionaries, including Sjöblom, in 1896–97, and documented their damning stories and the intimidating response of the Governor-General of the Congo, Théophile Wahis. Pickersgill summed up, "To my mind the amazing thing about the Congo atrocities is not that they occurred but that they have been so impudently denied."[50] Worried about public reaction, the Foreign Office issued a bowdlerized report under Pickersgill's name (1898) that did not mention

---

[44] *The Times*, 13 May 1897, 7; *AF*, May 1897, 131–7; *Stockholm Dagblad*, 21 May 1897 cited in Lagergren, *Mission and State*, 207–8.

[45] Joseph Conrad, "An Outpost of Progress," *Cosmopolis*, June 1897, 609–20, and July 1897, 1–15.

[46] Alice Werner, "The Civilised World and the Congo State," *Speaker*, 5 June 1897, 625.

[47] Edward Glave, "Cruelty in the Congo Free State," *Century Magazine*, September 1897, 699–714.

[48] "The Congo State," *Athenaeum*, no. 3647 (18 September 1897): 378–9.

[49] Cookey, *Britain*, 38–9.

[50] FO 881/7109:45–9.

Figure 2.2   Glave, Parminter, Ward, and Casement

Source: E.J. Glave, W.G. Parminter, Herbert Ward, and Roger Casement (b/w photo), English Photographer (nineteenth century)/Private Collection/Bridgeman Images.

atrocities, alluded vaguely to the methods of procuring food and rubber as "open to abuse," and praised the administration.[51]

In 1899, a report from the new Congo Vice-Consul reiterated that "the methods employed in the collection of rubber are cruel in the extreme," but this followed Pickersgill's report into the files.[52] This was the year of the Fashoda crisis, when a French military force reached the Nile via the Congo Free State, almost leading to war. Salisbury's Foreign Office feared that pressure could provoke Leopold into closer relations with France.

The APS's lack of focus did not help the campaign. In 1897 alone, the APS addressed no fewer than 24 causes around the world.[53] Financial pressures also

---

[51] "Report on the Congo Independent State," 1898, c.8649–30, no. 459 Misc., FO 10/731; Jules Marchal, *E.D. Morel contre Léopold II: L'Histoire du Congo 1900–1910* (Paris: L'Harmattan, 1996), Vol. 1, 182; Lagergren, *Mission and State*, 219–20.

[52] Pulteney to Foreign Office, 15 September 1899, FO 10/731, no. 5.

[53] *AF*, 1897.

took a toll. In 1897, its income fell precipitously, leading to a major fundraising effort in 1898 that provided a higher and more stable cash flow for the next decade, but suspended the Congo agitation.[54] Furthermore, the 1896–97 campaign was exclusively British. Fox Bourne had not yet made connections to the Belgian opposition to Leopold, which included the Radical legislator Georges Lorand, some of the King's former allies, and the anti-imperial socialists from the *Parti Ouvrier Belge* (Belgian Labour Party), particularly the party's future leader, Emile Vandervelde.

In Britain, criticism continued. The journalist Harold Spender, reviewing a book by the adventurer A.B. Lloyd, noted, "Unhappily it is clear from this narrative that throughout the region of the Congo Free State Europe stands for little else but cruelty and extortion."[55] He might have aptly made the opposite point; in Europe, the Congo Free State was coming to stand for little else than cruelty and extortion. Fox Bourne and the APS renewed the campaign in June 1899, the same year that Conrad's *Heart of Darkness* appeared. This time, with new allies in Belgium and Britain, the campaign created the possibility that complaint could lead to action.

E.D. Morel's Conversion

Morel was the next campaigner to take up the Congo. Although he had been born Georges Edmond Pierre Achille Morel de Ville in France in 1873 to a French father who died when he was three and an English mother, he had come to Britain in his youth and now went by the simpler George Morel de Ville. He joined Liverpool's Elder Dempster shipping company as a clerk in 1891, and became the head of the new Congo department in 1895 when Elder Dempster started service between Antwerp and the Congo, a service that became a lucrative monopoly in 1901.[56] Elder Dempster's senior partner, Alfred Jones, became the Consul in Liverpool for the Congo Free State and one of its staunchest defenders.

De Ville had moonlighted as a journalist since 1893, often using the pen name E.D. Morel. Most of his articles in the 1890s covered West African issues, usually taking positions that supported the Liverpool merchants generally and Elder Dempster in particular.[57] The merchants had not hired Morel for this purpose,

---

[54] *The Times*, 26 May 1899, 6; *AF*, June 1899; *AF*, April 1900, 503–5.

[55] Harold Spender, "Review: *In Dwarf Land and Cannibal Country*," *Speaker*, 25 November 1899, 201–2.

[56] J. Plas and Victor Pourbaix, *Les sociétés commerciales belges et le régime économique et fiscal de l'Etat Indépendant du Congo* (Brussels: Van Assche, 1899), 111; Marchal, *Morel contre Léopold*, Vol. 1, 24 and Vol. 2, 304.

[57] Catherine Cline, *E.D. Morel 1873–1924* (Belfast: Blackstaff Press, 1980), 10.

Figure 2.3   E.D. Morel
Source: From LSE Library's collections, MOREL F1/8/5/9.

but by putting himself forward in this way, he made connections among them and made himself more valuable to Alfred Jones, a leading spokesman for the colonial commercial lobby as President of the Liverpool Chamber of Commerce and the Chairman of its African Trade section.[58] He must have been pleased about Morel's articles in the influential *Pall Mall Gazette* defending Leopold's regime: one responding to press criticism in 1894 and another refuting the APS and Dilke in 1897.[59]

Historians Catherine Cline, Jules Marchal, and Donald Mitchell have traced the young man's conversion from rising commercial star to humanitarian activist, but it remains a challenge to explain why he was the one who could turn knowledge of the Congo Free State's misdeeds into leadership of a movement—a movement that had already begun but needed to become more coherent, disciplined, and persistent to be effective.[60] It appears to be the result of his position, his character, and his imperial ideologies. At Elder Dempster, he had an insider's access while remaining an outsider who had not compromised himself in Leopold's service. Shipping and financial information showed him the violence and its origins in Leopold's system of rule. As an Elder Dempster rising star, Jones kept him on and tried to win him over after they had begun to disagree about the Congo, allowing him the space to make a principled resignation. As a journalist, Morel could write quickly and knew editors who could print his Congo articles. Like Williams, he was constitutionally inclined to denounce wrongdoing with little concern for personal risk. Most importantly, his ideas were changing, mostly because of Mary Kingsley, the woman who had burst from obscurity in the mid-1890s with books, articles, and lectures based on African voyages that included exploration, scientific discovery, ethnography, and a new conception of how imperial powers should rule their African subjects.

Mary Kingsley was a different kind of imperialist, contrasting with Flora Shaw (later Lady Lugard). Kingsley observed disparagingly that Shaw was "imbued with this modern form of jubilee imperialism, it is her religion." Unlike Shaw, Kingsley saw misguided practices everywhere.[61] She tirelessly advocated for a new African colonial policy, based largely on her own observations.

When Morel began corresponding with Kingsley in 1899, he had already begun to incorporate consideration for Africans into his commercially oriented free-trade ideas. This intellectual stew led Kingsley to first contact the kindred spirit she saw in "E.D.M.," intrigued by an article supporting her position on

---

[58] Morel, "History of the Congo Reform Movement," 30.

[59] "The Belgians in Africa," *Pall Mall Gazette*, 22 February 1894; "A Word for the Congo State," *Pall Mall Gazette*, 19 July 1897; Cline, *Morel*, 24.

[60] Cline, *Morel*, 15–20; Marchal, *Morel contre Léopold*, Vol. 1, 16–18; Donald Mitchell, *The Politics of Dissent: A Biography of E.D. Morel* (Bristol: Silverwood Books, 2014), ch. 1.

[61] Kingsley to Holt, 20 February 1899, B/JH(A) 1/1/6:125.

colonial expenditure.[62] In his brief correspondence with "Dear Miss Kingsley" (February 1899 to March 1900), Morel honed his ideas and absorbed many of hers. They were of one mind about the flaws of imperial administration. They believed free trade made for a mutually beneficial relationship between Europeans and Africans, economically, culturally, and administratively. This reflected their robust respect for Africans and African culture, including practices such as polygamy that were distasteful to most Europeans. They supported traditional African authority structures in a framework of indirect rule, abhorred most punitive military expeditions, condemned coercion and forced labor, and supported African legal practices. Kingsley's ideas sprang in part from a backward-looking desire to return to the administrative practices of informal empire, but her respect for African culture marked her also as a progressive.[63] Morel expressed profound gratitude for years to come, writing, "any good ideas that I may have on these subjects, are almost entirely attributable to her influence. I ... propose to the best of my ability to carry on her teachings and the lessons she inculcated."[64]

The transformation of Elder Dempster's George de Ville into the activist journalist Edmund Dene Morel paralleled the maturing of his thought. Mary Kingsley always addressed him as Mr Morel, and within two years he was asking his most elevated contacts, Alfred Jones and John Holt, to do the same.[65]

Kingsley wanted her ideas to become the cornerstone of a "Liverpool Sect" or "Liverpool School" uniting business leaders in sustained and coherent lobbying on colonial administration that would grow into true collaboration with the authorities.[66] Although she found a ready welcome, and even friends, among leading men in the Liverpool, Manchester, and London Chambers of Commerce, they disappointed her; they seldom spoke with a single voice and had no staying power on issues that mattered to her.[67] Kingsley's dream of the Liverpool Sect as a broad alliance of the three great Chambers of Commerce never materialized.[68] To Morel, she identified only one man as a true believer: John Holt, the head of the John Holt Ltd African trading company. Holt used her, as the others did, to advance his commercial interests, but he was in broader

---

[62] Kingsley to Morel, 10 February 1899, F8/97A:115.

[63] John E. Flint, "Mary Kingsley—A Reassessment," *Journal of African History* 4, no. 1 (1963): 95–104.

[64] Morel to Stephen Gwynne, 13 March 1903, F10/3:402.

[65] Jones to Morel, 31 January 1902, F8/95:53; Holt to Morel, 22 May 1902, F8/83:209.

[66] Kingsley, *West African Studies*, 274; Kingsley to Holt, 13 March 1898, B/JH(A) 1/1/6.

[67] Bernard Porter, *Critics of Empire*, 279; Holt to De Ville, 5 July 1901, F8/83:112; Holt to Morel, 5 November 1902, F8/84:263.

[68] Dea Birkett, *Mary Kingsley: Imperial Adventuress* (London: Macmillan, 1992), 103, 121; Kingsley to Holt, 11 July 1899, B/JH/(A) 1/1/6:152.

harmony with her ideas and willing to say so even when it was inexpedient.[69] Like Kingsley, Holt had harsh words for his fellow African merchants when Morel tried to enlist them in Congo reform activism: "They take too shallow an idea of their lives and duties. They do not think of the basic laws affecting their trade and existence. They do not think below the surface of things."[70] The Liverpool Sect consisted of what Nworah calls the "family compact" of just three people: Kingsley, Holt, and Morel, with a few sympathizers, such as Dennett, who lectured with Kingsley, the adventurer Ralph Durand, the journalist Stephen Gwynn, and Kingsley's close friend Alice Stopford Green, but no trade magnate besides Holt, who came to his concern for Africans through long residence among them and a keen appreciation for their value as customers.[71]

After Kingsley's untimely death in 1900 at the age of 37, the Sect survived because of the growing rapport between Holt and Morel. Kingsley had engineered this connection. After Morel wrote articles against the monopoly held by Sir George Goldie's Royal Niger Company, Kingsley had commended Morel to Holt's protection: "E.D.M. is a struggling young man with a family and Goldie is always nagging at Jones to get rid of him and I should be sorry for the family if Jones did."[72] Holt began working with Morel to seek redress for the confiscation of his goods in French Congo, where authorities had imitated Leopold's monopoly concession system. From this inauspicious beginning of pity and self-interest, Holt became Morel's new mentor and more. Their relationship was both the echo and the culmination of their relationships with Kingsley. Holt found someone who could fight for his ideals as well as his interests, while Morel had an enthusiastic patron. In comparison to his strained relationship with Fox Bourne and his disappointing disagreement with Alfred Jones, it must have been a pleasure for the fatherless young man to have Holt's effusive praise and nearly unconditional support, sometimes interrupted by paternal scolding.

Holt transmitted and reinforced Kingsley's principles, leavened with his fundamental sympathy for the colonized.[73] This appears in an 1895 letter to Fox Bourne regarding a briefly shared concern in West Africa:

> I am a trader and as such am guilty in your eyes of many things ... but when it comes to protecting the native of the Niger basin I am willing to put selfish

---

[69] Kingsley to Morel, 5 March 1899, F8/97A:119; Kingsley to Holt, 26 October and 22 November 1898, B/JH(A) 1/1/6.

[70] Holt to De Ville, 5 July 1901, F8/83:112.

[71] Holt to Morel, 28 September 1905, F8/85 394; Kingsley to Holt, 8 September 1899, B/JH(A) 1/1/6:173; K. Dike Nworah, "The Liverpool 'Sect' and British West African Policy 1895–1915," *African Affairs* 70, no. 281 (1971): 349, 358; Nworah, *Humanitarian Pressure-Groups*, 110; Birkett, *Kingsley*, 170.

[72] Kingsley to Holt, 25 July 1899, B/JH(A) 1/1/6:154.

[73] John Grace, *Domestic Slavery in West Africa* (New York: Harper and Row, 1975), 52.

considerations and differences aside and to work all I can with you in what may help to advance a human being (to whom I owe so much) in the scale of civilisation and protecting him from unfair treatment and cruelty. My heart revolts at the idea of sacrificing human lives to spread trade or to further our humane ideas—I am with you in enforcing gentle and persuasive treatment when dealing with native races. Even on economical grounds I have ever considered it supreme folly to kill our customers as we sometimes do.[74]

When a colonial abuse would seem to benefit an African trader, as in the use of forced labor for highway construction, its effects worried Holt:

If road-making is to be accomplished by injustice or oppression, for heaven's sake let us have no roads for ever ... It is imperative that we should get rid of this military idea of doing everything by force ... It is a pity that these helpless people who are under our rule are not to be subjects of our care, and should be victims of such an inhuman and unjust system.[75]

Morel's approach to the Congo question reflected the same sympathy.

In February 1901, Morel left Elder Dempster on good terms and became assistant editor of the journal *West Africa*, which gave him more time to devote to his writing and freedom to pursue Congo reform. When the Congo apologists accused him of being a merchant lobbyist in 1902, Morel indignantly responded, "That is utterly erroneous. I am subsidized by no one and in no particular interest."[76] No longer a merchant spokesman, Morel's vision of what was right for Africa dominated his writing for the next decade.

Morel's attack on the Congo Free State stressed the rights of the Africans living under colonial rule. Historians have disagreed about the source of this focus. Jules Marchal posits that it came from Mary Kingsley, but she did not use this language in her letters to him or in her books, which talked of preferred methods of administration: what was better, not what was due.[77] Kevin Grant sees a connection with Fox Bourne's ideas about rights; under his leadership the APS actively promoted aboriginal rights.[78] However, Fox Bourne's letters to Morel never bring up African rights, and his 1897–1902 writings about the Congo almost never spoke of rights, concentrating on the response required by

---

[74] Holt to Fox Bourne, 16 February 1895, Brit. Emp. s.18 C151:145.
[75] Holt to Fox Bourne, 13 July 1906, Brit. Emp. s.18 C.151:155.
[76] Cline, *Morel*, 12; Wuliger, "Economic Imperialism," 33; Morel to Sir William Macgregor, 19 December 1902, F10/2:19; Nworah, *Humanitarian Pressure-Groups*, 94–6.
[77] Marchal, *Morel contre Léopold*, Vol. 1, 16–18.
[78] Grant, *Civilised Savagery*, 32; Fox Bourne, "The Duty of Civilised States to Weaker Races," *Transactions of the APS*, April 1891: 169–76; Fox Bourne to J. Chamberlain, 31 December 1901, F8/65:40.

justice, mercy, and treaty obligations.[79] Goldie observed that Morel's approach was "a perfectly good one but it was not the point that was usually taken by the Aborigines' Protection Society."[80]

Morel's intellectual guide was John Holt, who urged him to advocate for "more regard for the rights and interests of the people God has called us to rule over" and "protection of their rights and liberties."[81] Although Kingsley did not talk about rights, Holt attributed to her "a just recognition of human rights among those we govern, no matter what their colour, intelligence, or degree of natural mental evolution."[82] Rights, God's will, compassion, and humanitarianism mingled with the benefits of free trade in Holt's ideology as expressed to Morel. When Morel first publicly criticized Leopold's regime in 1900, with nine anonymous articles and letters in *The Speaker*, he referred to treaty obligations but not to rights.[83] Although rhetoric of native rights had been available to Morel from the APS and the Positivists, it is telling that he did not adopt it until after he engaged with Holt.

By this point, the APS's Congo agitation had revived. Fox Bourne connected with Belgian critics of the Congo, leading to better information flow. The cause benefited from new missionary testimony, most notably that of Rev. William Sheppard of the American Presbyterian Congo Mission (APCM) in the Kasai region, delivered by his superior, Rev. William Morrison. Morel's vigorous attack on the Congo in *The Speaker* and other publications contributed to this revival and brought him into contact with Fox Bourne and Dilke. Morel maintained a somewhat tense collaboration with Fox Bourne in 1900–03, punctuated with apologies on both sides for real and imagined slights.[84] Fox Bourne took information from Morel and used him to disseminate testimony that the APS had gathered. In return, he introduced Morel to men such as Lorand and Vandervelde.[85] Morel grumbled that Fox Bourne, "lives ... on my efforts, but, after all the main thing is to get the thing publicly ventilated."[86] Fox Bourne

---

[79] *AF*, November 1897, 276–8; Fox Bourne to Leopold, 21 October 1899, *AF*, April 1900, 503–5; Fox Bourne, "The Congo Free State," *Imperial and Asiatic Quarterly Review*, July 1901, 86–100.

[80] Stead to Morel, 8 December 1902, F8/133:6.

[81] Holt to De Ville, 8 November 1901, F8/83:149–51; Holt to Morel, 19 March 1903, F3/4.

[82] Holt to De Ville, 20 June 1900, F8/82:22.

[83] Of Morel's seven articles and two letters in *The Speaker* in 1900, historians often cite the last six articles, which formed a series. See "E.D. Morel, anonymously," in the Bibliography.

[84] Fox Bourne to Morel, 2 June 1903, F8/66:118.

[85] Fox Bourne to Lorand, 24 July 1901, F8/65:19; Fox Bourne to Morel, 29 April and 13 June 1903, F8/66:102, 123.

[86] Fox Bourne to Morel, 27 June 1901, F8/65:16.

intended that the APS and Morel should "press away on parallel lines," which meant keeping Morel at a distance.[87] All the same, they moved the cause along.

Morel's emphasis on the perverse nature of Leopold's system of government and its economic underpinning revolutionized the hitherto ineffective movement. As Louis first observed, this conceptualization gave the campaign energy and staying power.[88] Fox Bourne's previous tropes of poorly supervised officials and badly enforced rules did not attract much interest. After all, every colonial power had miscreant officials. But if the Congo government's policies and underlying principles were at fault, then change would come only through the use of power to force Leopold to transform or surrender the Congo. Dilke highlighted this as Morel's chief intellectual contribution: "You showed us that all depended upon the right of the original black inhabitants of the soil to own their property and carry on trade."[89]

British commercial interests should have been natural allies for this approach, but Fox Bourne had not reached out to them.[90] Morel's campaign against French Congo monopolies led his contacts at the Chambers of Commerce, such as London's Francis Swanzy (of the West African trading firm F. & A. Swanzy Co.), to take note of the Congo Free State's concession system.[91] In 1902 several chambers came out in support of Congo reform.[92]

Both Morel and Fox Bourne were writing books condemning Leopold's Congo using the language of native rights. In November, Morel's *Affairs of West Africa* devoted three scathing chapters to the Congo, followed in January 1903 by Fox Bourne's more extensive *Civilisation in Congoland*, detailing Free State history, atrocity reports, and failed attempts to work through Leopold. Both books received wide publicity and contributed to the parliamentary resolution of 20 May 1903 that asked the British government to consult with other powers regarding the Congo Free State's adherence to the Berlin Act.

Stead Enters the Fray

W.T. Stead, who brought a deep religious fervor to his crusading journalism, was already a force to be reckoned with, though his campaigns were not always successful. Stead's activism sprang directly from a deeply felt Christianity, which

---

[87] Fox Bourne to Morel, 15 April 1902, F8/65:50.
[88] Louis, "The Stokes Affair," 577.
[89] Dilke to Morel, 6 February 1908, Add. 43897:210; Wuliger, "Economic Imperialism," 20.
[90] Wuliger, "Economic Imperialism," 73.
[91] Green to Morel, 19 November 1901, F8/71:32.
[92] Fox Bourne, *Civilisation*, 279.

Figure 2.4   Sir Charles Dilke
Source: Look and Learn/Elgar Collection.

Figure 2.5   W.T. Stead

Source: William Thomas Stead (1849–1912) (litho), English Photographer (twentieth century)/Private Collection/Ken Welsh/Bridgeman Images.

led him to promote women's equality, morality, peace, and ending misrule.[93] An enthusiastic imperialist, he envisioned Britain as a new Rome, uniting English-speaking countries to keep the peace and spread liberty, civilization, and Christianity.[94] Combining his imperial and moral ideas, Stead believed in humanitarian military intervention; he cheered for the US victory over Spain and hoped the US would capture Istanbul to end Ottoman misrule.[95]

In late 1901, Morel wanted someone to organize and lead the Congo reform movement. He asked Holt, who found the idea "enough to make me tremble at the thought of the responsibility ... Have I the power by sacrifice to secure the freedom of the millions of the Congo region from the scourge of European brutality? ... So far as I am able to discern my destiny arranged by Providence is to be a distributor of merchandise."[96] Holt suggested Stead, whom Morel had met through the *Manchester Guardian*'s editor.[97] Stead hesitated; the information about the Congo had worried him, "but it is no use pecking at the subject. If any good is to be done, it has to be handled with both hands, and with all one's strength. For that at present I have not the time."[98]

Stead had been debating the issue with his old friend Sir Hugh Gilzean Reid, a vigorous apologist. Gilzean Reid praised Leopold and assured Stead he would expose the paid slanderers (meaning Morel, Fox Bourne, and the missionaries). Between May and October 1902, Morel convinced Stead that Gilzean Reid was wrong.[99] Gilzean Reid's reaction was to threaten Stead in January 1903.[100] Despite, or perhaps because of, Gilzean Reid's hostility, the Congo had hooked Stead.[101] He met with the reformers in February and, in March, formalized the campaign under the auspices of the International Union, an organization he had founded to promote peace.[102]

---

[93] Grace Eckley, *Maiden Tribute: A Life of W.T. Stead* (Philadelphia: Xlibris, 2007).

[94] W.T. Stead, *The United States of Europe* (New York, Doubleday & McClure, 1899), 60, quoted in Richard Gamble, "The Americanization of the World: William T. Stead's Vision of Empire," presented at the "War and Empire" conference at Grand Valley State University, Grand Rapids, Michigan, 6–7 October 2005.

[95] Stead, *United States of Europe*, 424–7, quoted in Gamble, "Americanization."

[96] Holt to Morel, 31 December 1901, F8/83:168.

[97] C.P. Scott to Morel, 14 and 18 May 1901, F8/127:4, 6.

[98] Holt to De Ville, 28 December 1901, F8/82:165; Stead to Morel, 29 May 1902, F8/133:2.

[99] Marchal, *Morel contre Léopold*, Vol. 1, 20; Whyte, *Stead*, 215–16.

[100] Stead to Morel, 21 October 1902, 24 October 1902 and 24 January 1903, F8/133:4, 5, 8.

[101] Morel to Holt, 26 January 1903, F10/2:226.

[102] BFASS papers, Brit. Emp. s.18, C89/26.

Stead had vision, contacts, and experience campaigning far beyond Fox Bourne's.[103] In 1903, Stead brought together Congo reformers of all stripes on 27 February, 13 March, 6 May, and 17 December, at least.[104] Many of those who attended later became CRA members: Holt, Swanzy, Liverpool merchant Hahnemann Stuart, MPs Herbert Samuel and Alfred Emmott, colonial administrator Harry H. Johnston, Travers Buxton, Guinness, Rev. John Clifford of the Baptist Union, and Canon Scott Holland of the Church of England.

Stead also invited Stanley and Gilzean Reid, but both refused to attend; things might have gone very differently if Stead had changed their minds.[105] He also invited Stanley's close friend and admirer, May French Sheldon, a journalist and African adventurer. She attended and became the Congo Committee's most significant investment when she accepted £500 from Stead to conduct a voyage of inquiry to the Congo. At the same time, she became the beneficiary, with Lord Mountmorres and Marcus Dorman, of £3,000 that Alfred Jones told Guinness he spent on the three travelers to conduct investigations into the Congo.[106] After 14 months in the Congo spent mostly with Free State officials, she returned to Britain as an apologist; not surprisingly, she had chosen her friend Stanley and highest bidder Jones over Stead.[107]

Stead wanted the new group to become the center of agitation, led by a core Committee of Stead, Fox Bourne, Morel, and Emmott.[108] Despite Stead's later claim that the Congo Reform Association had held its earliest meetings in his offices, the IU Congo Committee failed and was the CRA's predecessor, not its embryo.[109] Stead's own limitations weakened it: his naiveté, his many commitments, his difficulty in bringing together different viewpoints, and his personal antipathy to Dilke, the reformers' strongest ally in Parliament.[110] Morel could not convince Stead to include Dilke. Fifteen years before, Dilke had sued

---

[103] Stead to Morel, 11 March 1903, F8/133:16.

[104] Travers Buxton to Stead, 20 March 1903, Brit. Emp. s.19 D1/2:120.

[105] Stead to Morel, 23 February, 26 February, 7 May, 18 May, and 12 June 1903, F8/133:14–39.

[106] Guinness to Holt, 3 November 1905, Afr. s.1525 13/4:35; Guinness to Morel, 4 November 1905, F8/74:114.

[107] Robert Burroughs, "The Travelling Apologist: May French-Sheldon in the Congo Free State (1903–4)," *Studies in Travel Writing* 14, no. 2 (June 2010): 135–57; Tracey Jean Boisseau, *White Queen: May French-Sheldon and the Imperial Origins of American Feminist Identity* (Bloomington: Indiana University Press, 2004), 108–23; Stead to Morel, 13 May 1904, F8/133.

[108] "Action by International Union," *WAM*, 20 May 1903, 225.

[109] Stead, "After Twenty-one Years," *Review of Reviews*, January 1911, 6.

[110] Roy Jenkins, "Dilke, Sir Charles Wentworth, second baronet," *Oxford Dictionary of National Biography* (Oxford: Oxford University Press, September 2004; online ed., May 2008).

a young woman who had accused him of seducing her into adultery, which had poisoned his reputation among religious people and particularly Stead, who wrote, "He lied to me so atrociously and endeavoured to make me his tool by a combination of hypocrisy and treachery that it is quite impossible for me ever to meet him or to hold any communication with him."[111] Characteristically, Morel persisted, but Stead responded, "Your idea that Dilke and I should fall upon one another's necks at the Albert Hall before the world is quite out of the question."[112] As Morel feared, Stead's inability to work with Dilke hobbled the IU's reform agitation.

Guinness and the Regions Beyond Missionary Union

In 1903, a fourth force entered the lists: Dr Harry Grattan Guinness of the Regions Beyond Missionary Union (RBMU), the umbrella organization that included the Congo Balolo Mission. Many accounts of the reform movement understate the role of the religious elements, and Guinness was a particular casualty from the 1970s until Kevin Grant rescued him from obscurity in 2004.[113] Harry Guinness was the son of the famed divine Rev. Henry Grattan Guinness, DD, a preacher with close ties to several Protestant denominations.[114] He and his wife, Fanny, married in a Friends' meeting house and baptised their children with the Plymouth Brethren. Harry himself married in a Baptist tabernacle.[115] For years, the senior Guinness had overseen a web of training schools in England and missions mostly outside the British Empire as a family enterprise thanks to Fanny's able administrative work. The RBMU missions' doctrinal requirements were a basic Protestantism, and the missions were nondenominational.[116]

Harry Guinness studied at the London Hospital from 1880–85 to become a medical missionary, but discovered a vocation for preaching that diverted him

---

[111] Stead to Morel, 12 March 1903, F8/133:17.

[112] Stead to Morel, 23 March, 29 March, 18 May, 20 September, and 22 December 1903, F8/133:21, 24, 32, 47, 68.

[113] Grant, *Civilised Savagery*, 60–65.

[114] It is easy to confuse Guinness father and son; even the senior Guinness's death notice did so, *Annual Register*, June 1910, 128. This occurred in Pavlakis, "British Overseas Humanitarianism," but is remedied here.

[115] Klaus Fiedler, *The Story of Faith Missions* (Oxford: Regnum Books International, 1994), 36, 196.

[116] Fiedler, *Faith Missions*, 36; Hardinge to Grey, 28 May 1909, FO 881/9530:201; Joseph Conley, *Drumbeats that Changed the World: A History of the Regions Beyond Missionary Union and the West Indies Mission, 1873–1999* (Pasadena, CA: William Carey Library, 2000), 30, 39, 67; Lagergren, *Mission and State*, 36; Slade, *English-Speaking Missions*, 99.

Figure 2.6   Dr Harry Grattan Guinness
Source: Catherine Mackintosh, *The Life of Dr. Harry Grattan Guinness.*

from his medical training. As his parents aged, he took increasing responsibility for running the family mission enterprise, starting with its East London missionary training school, Harley House. He developed the Congo Balolo Mission and, after finishing his MD in Brussels in 1891, traveled to the Congo to set up its first mission stations. When Fanny died in 1898, 37-year-old Harry became Acting Director of the family missionary enterprise, now renamed the Regions Beyond Missionary Union.

Guinness was heir to a missionary tradition undergoing major changes.[117] The new faith missions movement, which included the Guinnesses, undertook its work with urgency based on the impending end of days. Doctrinal particulars and formal conversion were less important than preaching the Gospel to prompt repentance and acceptance of Christ to prepare for the imminent apocalypse.

Guinness's first Congo criticisms had appeared in the house journal, *Regions Beyond*, in May 1891, then stopped when the Congo Council (which Guinness chaired) set a policy to avoid any chance of a public exposé.[118] Five years later, the CBM suppressed Sjöblom's report, though he had trained at Harley House and served at a CBM station before joining the ABMU. This policy led to the controversy about reporters at the 1897 APS Congo meeting. Guinness arrived at what he thought was a private meeting to find Dilke, whom he loathed, chairing, reporters taking notes, and Houdret, the Congo's Consul General, watching the proceedings for Leopold. Guinness spoke after being promised anonymity and carefully praised the King for listening to his concerns.

Guinness's top priority was saving souls, and Congo Free State misgovernment impeded that objective. In 1895, Murphy and Sjöblom convinced him that the problems were pervasive, but he still hesitated to speak out for fear of repercussions, preferring to discuss his concerns in private with Leopold, who sometimes transferred abusive agents away from CBM missions.[119] As Fox Bourne wrote to Morel, "He told me a good deal about atrocities of which he knew but always on the understanding that I was to publish nothing, as he thought it would hinder his missionary work."[120] Events proved him right; the more public his statements, the more constraints his missions faced; his near-perfect public silence from 1898 to 1902 earned the CBM a new station.[121]

---

[117] Andrew Porter, *Religion Versus Empire? British Protestant Missionaries and Overseas Expansion* (New York: Manchester University Press, 2004), 192–6, 198, 200, 256, 261, 269–72.

[118] *Regions Beyond*, May 1896, 253–4; Ruth Slade, *English-Speaking Missions*, 241, 243.

[119] Catherine W. Mackintosh, *The Life Story of Henry Grattan Guinness, M.D., F.R.G.S.* (London: RBMU, 1916), 69–71.

[120] Fox Bourne to Morel, 24 November 1903, F8/66:180.

[121] Lagergren, *Mission and State*, 244–5, 255, 260–67; Roger T. Anstey, *King Leopold's Legacy* (New York: Oxford University Press, 1966), 57; Guinness to Morel, 16 December 1902, F8/74:5.

When Morel sought information from the RBMU in late 1902, Guinness would not release it without the Congo Council's permission. "The problem is to do good without doing harm," Guinness explained, "We do not want to incur the restriction of the benevolent operation of our mission except for the promulgation of facts more serious than what we have to complain of now."[122] Morel badgered Guinness for months, even when Guinness did not answer his letters.[123] Morel's appeals coincided with a RBMU Congo Council investigation begun in November 1902 into accusations against several missionaries: Rev. Daniel J. Danielson, who ran the mission steamer, whipped his crew with a hippopotamus-hide whip, or chicotte, and put local people in the stocks for not bringing enough wood; Rev. Somerville Gilchrist and others knew that another missionary had used the chicotte several times; yet another had used it on a woman and two little girls; Rev. John Harris asked an Abir agent to whip an African mission worker; and Rev. William Armstrong took cookware and fowl from villagers when they would not listen to him preach or satisfy his demand for food.[124]

To their credit, Guinness and the Congo Council took the bull by the horns, meeting a week later with all the Congo missionaries home on furlough. They confirmed many of the accusations and identified other incidents; the missionary who had first accused the others had beaten his personal servant with a stick. Their conclusion, documented by James Irvine, a devout Liverpool merchant on the Congo Council, was that only Danielson had seriously abused his power. The Council believed that it was "necessary and wise" to disciple Africans parentally, a concept they distinguished from the practices of the concession companies and the Congo government. The Council also confirmed the missions' existing ban on corporal punishment, especially the chicotte.[125]

This investigation was a major issue; if the allegations were true, the RBMU would be vulnerable when it revealed its evidence of Congo State abuses. All Protestant missionary societies were wary because the Congo Free State's apologists routinely attacked critics by accusing them of similar behavior.[126] Gilzean Reid gloated in a letter to Van Eetvelde, "One by one from Salusbury to Murphy to that Danish 'missionary' so-called, I have destroyed them and even stopped the hostile criticism in our Parliament. The need never ceases for action."[127] Leopold's publicists could have used the missionaries' use of floggings,

---

[122] Guinness to Morel, 8 November and 16 December 1902, F8/74:1, 5.
[123] Morel to Guinness, 24 November 1902, F10/1:281–90 and 7 February 1903, F10/2:321–3.
[124] Congo Council, 27 November 1902, Reel 11, Vol. 3, 72–3.
[125] Congo Council, 4 December 1902, Reel 11, Vol. 3, 77.
[126] Grant, *Civilised Savagery*, 49.
[127] Gilzean Reid to Van Eetvelde, 6 December 1897, quoted in Slade, *English-Speaking Missions*, 250.

imprisonment, and the stocks to damage the cause and undermine the mission's ability to raise money.

After the investigation, the Congo Council began moving toward more publicity in February 1903.[128] They asked Guinness to confer with Fox Bourne and with Baynes, the BMS Secretary, to determine if Morel could be trusted. Guinness proceeded slowly, writing to Fox Bourne almost a month later.[129] Meanwhile, Guinness notified the Field Committee in the Congo that he would publish their reports only if publicity would aid the missions.[130] Morel told him that his delays were tantamount to a defense of the Congo Free State:

> I can only say that so long as the Missionary Societies will not join us openly in our efforts to better the state of things, our efforts are bound to be paralyzed all along the line. I do earnestly beg of you to consider this matter once again, and see if you cannot do anything. I had a talk with Mr Irvine, who belongs to your Mission, yesterday, and he fully shares my view.[131]

On 26 March, the Congo Council, with Irvine in attendance, permitted Guinness to write a Congo article for *Regions Beyond*. There is no discussion of Morel's request in the minutes, and, a few days later, having not heard anything, Morel's annoyance was palpable: "We will never get anything out of these missionaries."[132]

But the Congo Council appears to have given Guinness permission to cooperate. Morel's annoyance notwithstanding, Guinness publicly condemned the Congo Free State. Morel had left *West Africa* after acrimonious disputes with its proprietor and started his own weekly journal in April 1903, the *West African Mail*. Guinness launched his Congo reform campaign that month, with simultaneous and identical articles in *Regions Beyond*, Fox Bourne's *Aborigines' Friend*, and the third issue of the *West African Mail*, just in time to influence the May 1903 Congo debate in Parliament. The *Regions Beyond* of June 1903 further discussed the atrocities, including their commercial aspect, announced a forthcoming pamphlet, and praised the MPs willing to take up the charge, even the old reprobate, Dilke.[133] The same issue reproduced the correspondence of BMS missionary John Weeks with the Congo government, showcasing the State's unwillingness to deal with abuses.

---

[128] Congo Council, 5 February 1903, Reel 11, Vol. 3, 88ff.

[129] Ruth Slade, "English Missionaries and the Beginning of the Anti-Congolese Campaign in England," *Revue Belge de Philologie d'Histoire* 33, no. 1 (1955): 55.

[130] Guinness to Field Committee, 12 February 1903, Archives Africain, Brussels M584 (96), quoted by Lagergren, *Mission and State*, 307.

[131] Morel to Guinness, 12 and 17 March 1903, F10/4:234, 478.

[132] Morel to Stead, 31 March 1903, F10/4:317.

[133] *Regions Beyond*, June 1903, 173ff.

However, Guinness was an unreliable ally, alternating between caution and boldness. Alfred Jones, as Leopold's Consul in England, sought to manipulate Guinness by interceding with Leopold and obtaining an offer of subsidies for the mission.[134] The implied *quid pro quo* for this payment from rubber profits was silence. The Congo Council discussed and rejected the offer; after more prodding from Morel and Stead, Guinness's campaign against the Congo Free State came to life again in October 1903.[135] He gushed to Morel, "I rejoice that you are able to be of such splendid service in enlightening the British public in regard to what seems to me the most dastardly outrage that civilized Europeans could possibly perpetrate on defenceless Africans."[136]

A CBM missionary briefly became a key figure in late 1903: Rev. Daniel Jacob Danielson, by background a sailor from the Faroe Islands.[137] The Congo Council dismissed him in March 1903 after their investigation into missionary cruelty, but withdrew the dismissal shortly thereafter, because Guinness told the Council that the charges had turned out to be false or gross exaggerations. In July, while the reprieved Danielson was travelling downriver to go to Britain on furlough, he encountered Roger Casement at the BMS Bolobo mission as the Consul was about to transfer to the ABMU steamer *Henry Reed*. On 17 July Danielson agreed to skipper the *Henry Reed* as replacement for Arthur Billington. Danielson accompanied Casement for the rest of his journey of investigation, through 15 September.[138] Historian Óli Jacobsen has shown that Danielson used his journey with Casement to take some of the earliest atrocity photos and develop his own campaign against the Congo Free State.

In October, Danielson arrived in Britain, eager to share his photographs and to speak out against the atrocities. After Foreign Office personnel encouraged the Congo Council to publicize the information Danielson had learned while traveling with Casement, the Council allowed him to go on a speaking tour in Scotland and decided to publish his evidence.[139] His talks were well-attended, with audiences reaching the thousands, but there was little press coverage, no recorded resolutions to government offices, and thus little lasting impact apart

---

[134] Congo Council, 24 September 1903, Reel 11, Vol. 3, 108–9.

[135] Morel to Guinness, 13 October 1903, F10/8:265; Morel to Stead, 20 October 1903, F10/8:330.

[136] Guinness to Morel, 16 October 1903, F8/74:14.

[137] For more detail on Danielson's contributions to Congo reform and his dealings with the Congo Council, see Óli Jacobsen, *Daniel J. Danielsen and the Congo: Missionary Campaigns and Atrocity Photographs* (Brethren Archivists and Historians Network, 2014), www.olijacobsen.com.

[138] Congo Council, 26 March and 24 September 1903, Reel 11, Vol. 3, 101, 108–9, 112; Lagergren, *Mission and State*, 260.

[139] Guinness to Morel, 16 October 1903, F8/74 14; Congo Council, 24 October 1903, Reel 11, Vol. 3, 115; RBMU Directors, 6 and 26 November 1903, Reel 1, Vol. 1.

from his photographs, which continued to appear in Congo reform literature without correct attribution for the duration of the movement. Despite his obvious star-power, in January 1904 the Congo Council once again talked of dismissing Danielson, noting that he was hard to work with and that his agitation had made him unwelcome in the Congo. After further consideration, they paid his passage back to the Faroes in June 1904.[140]

Inspired by Danielson's lectures and a similar meeting Guinness had held on 24 November in Colston Hall, Bristol, the RBMU directors agreed on 26 November 1903 that Guinness should hold large meetings on the Congo. But Guinness hesitated; de Cuvelier, the Congo State's Foreign Secretary, accused him of inciting natives to rebel.[141] Guinness's silence for the next week may indicate second thoughts, but if so, he quickly recovered his gumption.

Roger Casement, the Crisis of January 1904, and the CRA's Founding

Previous histories have not addressed the crisis that jeopardized the movement in January 1904. Each reformer had been proceeding along his customary lines with similar but not identical aims. For instance, Fox Bourne did not want to advocate a specific solution, such as annexation by Belgium, but Morel did.[142] Danielson consulted separately with Fox Bourne and Morel and organized his own meetings through December 1903.[143] There had been talk of a Guinness-sponsored meeting in Liverpool, and Guinness had mentioned to Morel that a lecture tour would boost the cause.

On 11 December, encouraged by Casement, Guinness went to Stead to discuss the planned Scotland lecture tour and suggested Stead bring the IU Congo Committee together to develop a pamphlet he could distribute.[144] At the resulting 17 December meeting, which Morel could not attend, Guinness agreed to two conditions: the lectures would be under the auspices of the International Union and that revenues would not benefit the CBM.[145] Fox Bourne doubtfully wrote to Morel, "I hope he will keep the promise I got him to make that they

---

[140] Congo Council, 26 January, 25 February, 14 June, and 6 October 1904, Reel 11, Vol. 3; RBMU Directors, 28 January 1904, Reel 1, Vol. 1.

[141] De Cuvelier to Guinness, 2 December 1903, FO 881/8268:334.

[142] Fox Bourne to Morel, 26 June 1903, F8/67:133.

[143] Fox Bourne to Morel, 24 November 1903, F8/67:180; Danielson to Morel, 4 December 1903, F9/4.

[144] Fox Bourne to Morel, 21 November 1903, F8/66:178; Stead to Morel, 11 December 1903, F8/133:64.

[145] Stead to Morel, 17 December 1903, F8/133:66; Guinness to Morel, 18 December 1903, F4/1.

shall *not* be merely Congo Balolo missionary meetings."[146] The group voted to pay Morel £10 for a pamphlet.

The meeting resulted in disaster, with the reformers quickly at odds and apologists scrambling to counter Guinness's tour, presumably informed by someone at the meeting.[147] Morel took offence at being treated like a hack writer who would crank out pamphlets for a fee. Fox Bourne dissociated himself from the pamphlet vote while trying to soothe Morel's injured pride.[148] The Anti-Slavery Committee, suspicious of Guinness, asked Travers Buxton "not hastily to pledge this Society."[149] Their concern was well-founded: Guinness backtracked within days on his promises; he thought Stead's IU would collect any profits from his meetings while the mission would have to cover any shortfall. Without the RBMU's support, the APS or IU could have hosted meetings in London, but with much smaller audiences: dozens of attendees as opposed to hundreds or thousands.[150]

Guinness resumed his original plan of a Congo Balolo Mission tour. Fox Bourne, having warned Morel to be wary of the "slippery character," immediately backed out: "It seems to me quite clear that he is now rushing the Congo question much more in the interests of his Society than in those of the natives."[151] Morel tried to solve the impasse with a position statement endorsed by Holt, Fox Bourne and Emmott: Guinness's CBM-sponsored Congo meetings would damage the cause by misleading audiences about the reformers' goals and lead to criticisms by the apologists that the reformers were sectarian; "In this we may be right, or wrong. But we, at any rate, have been consistent."[152] This proud statement did not conciliate Guinness.

With Guinness on his own path, Fox Bourne distancing himself, and Morel feeling slighted, Stead's efforts to unite the reformers collapsed. The International Union Congo Committee vanished. The impasse seemed intractable until Roger Casement intervened.

Casement was no stranger to the Congo. He had been, variously, an employee of Elder Dempster, a member of the Sanford Exploring Expedition that prepared the exploitation of the Congo, a lay employee at a BMS mission, and Joseph

---

[146] Fox Bourne to Morel, 20 December 1903, F8/66:186.

[147] Gilzean Reid to Van Eetvelde, 28 December 1903, quoted in Slade, "English Missionaries," 70.

[148] Fox Bourne to Morel, 29 December 1903, F8/66:189; Fox Bourne to Morel, 11 January 1904, F8/67:191.

[149] BFASS Committee, 1 January 1904, Brit. Emp. s.20 E2/12:1230.

[150] Guinness to Irvine, 19 January 1904, F4/2:18–25.

[151] Fox Bourne to Morel, 21 and 24 November, 29 December 1903, F8/66:178, 180, 189.

[152] Morel to Fox Bourne and Emmott, January 1904, F4/2; Holt to Morel, 18 January 1904, F8/85:350; Morel to Holt, 19 January 1904, Afr. s.1525 18/2:1.

Conrad's roommate. After this he became a British consular official in present-day Nigeria (where he met Mary Kingsley), Mozambique, and Angola. In 1899, he became consul in Loanda with Congo jurisdiction, and in 1900 the Foreign Office sent him to the Congo as Consul, leaving a Vice-Consul in Loanda, to have a more senior official to help British subjects in the Congo. In his new role, he met with Leopold twice on 10–11 October 1900, but the monarch's charm did not win him over.[153] Casement had long been suspicious of the Free State system, possibly dating from his days with Conrad, or at least from the mid-1890s, when his uncle Edward Bannister was Vice-Consul. Casement had urged the Foreign Office to work with Germany to put an end to the "reign of terror" there.[154] When the Foreign Office selected Casement for the position, they were deliberately putting someone in the job who already believed that the Congo State misruled its people, the first sign of a shift in the Foreign Office approach.

Casement divided his time between Portuguese Cabinda and three towns on the lower Congo: Boma, Matadi, and Leopoldville, which kept him so busy with the problems of British subjects that he could not get firsthand insight into conditions in the interior. He proposed an investigative journey to the upper Congo, which the Foreign Office approved on 22 August 1902.[155] However, he headed back to Britain in October without making the trip, delaying the day of reckoning for the Congo Free State. After he returned to Boma on 1 May 1903 he repeated the proposal, but the Foreign Office instructed him to finish his report on British subjects first. The 20 May House of Commons resolution caused the Foreign Secretary, Lord Lansdowne, to reverse those instructions, telling him to set out as soon as possible.[156]

His travels from June to September were not as extensive as Williams's. He cut his trip short when he believed he had enough information to make a comprehensive indictment of misgovernment. Arriving in Britain on 1 December, he delivered the first draft of his report to the Foreign Office on 12 December, provided additions on 18 December, and completed requested revisions from 25–28 December.[157] He became involved with the reformers, starting with his 10 December visits from Guinness and, more fatefully, Morel. Morel had been brought into correspondence with Casement earlier that year by

---

[153] Cookey, *Britain*, 76.

[154] Casement to Gosselin, 30 April 1900, FO 403/304, in Cookey, *Britain*, 64; Marchal, *Morel contre Léopold*, Vol. 1, 185–7; Casement to FO, 13 February 1903, FO 403/398, in Cookey, *Britain*, 76.

[155] 21 July 1902, FO 881/8212:110.

[156] B.L. Reid, "A Good Man—Has Had Fever: Casement in the Congo," *Sewanee Review* 82, no. 3 (Summer 1974): 460–61, 469.

[157] Roger Casement's 1903 diary, Séamas Ó Síocháin and Michael O'Sullivan, *The Eyes of Another Race: Roger Casement's Congo Report and 1903 Diary* (Dublin: University College Dublin Press, 2003), 293, 295, 297–8.

a mutual friend, Herbert Ward, an artist and author who lived most of the year in Paris. Ward and Casement had met in the Congo long before, where Ward had served on several major expeditions. Ward intrigued Morel by saying Casement wanted to speak out, but could not because of his government position.[158] For months, Ward served as a go-between, all the while singing Casement's praises: "No man walks the earth who is more absolutely good and honest and noble-minded than RC."[159]

In October 1903, as Casement journeyed home, he wrote confidentially to Morel.[160] The two men met on 10 December at Ward's unoccupied London house in Chester Square. Casement's brisk diary entry shows that the discussion lasted far longer than his talk with Guinness: "E.D.M. first time I met him. The man is honest as day. Dined at Comedy together late & then to chat till 2 A.M. M. sleeping in study."[161] Morel formed an immediate, intense feeling for Casement—born of a shared interest and a shared way of thinking, as well as mutual admiration, but also of a passionate connection reflected in Morel's memory of Casement's physical presence in a darkened room, lit by the fire, and recreating with his almost magical voice the horrors in the Congo valley.[162]

Casement's comments about Morel warmed each time they met. He visited Morel at his home in Hawarden near Liverpool on 5 January. The Congo report completed, Casement had the time and energy to deal with the reformers' disarray. A whirlwind of activity ensued, with Casement writing to Morel, Fox Bourne, Stead, and Guinness and discussing the Congo with his many contacts, even David Lloyd George, whom he met on the train coming back from Hawarden.[163] Meanwhile, Morel found himself confined to bed with what was probably lumbago, a condition which was likely made worse by stress.[164] The movement's disarray troubled him. He was particularly furious with Guinness, complaining to Holt about the missionary's selfishness and recalling how he threw "cold water on Fox Bourne's persistent and courageous crusade" in 1897, conveniently omitting that he had done the same in the *Pall Mall Gazette*.[165]

Casement wanted the reformers to unite in a single disciplined organization to publicize his report and agitate for reform for the months or years that might be required. Speed was essential, because the Foreign Office would present his report to Parliament soon. He wrote as much to Guinness, engendering

---

[158] Ward to Morel, 12 March 1903, F8/143:3.
[159] Ward to Morel, 25 August 1903, F8/143:12.
[160] Casement to Morel, 23 October 1903, F8/16:13.
[161] Casement's diary, Ó Síocháin and O'Sullivan, *Eyes of Another Race*, 293.
[162] Morel, "History," 160–62.
[163] Casement's diary, 6 January 1904, in Ó Síocháin and O'Sullivan, *Eyes of Another Race*, 302.
[164] Fox Bourne to Morel, 18 January 1904, F8/67:192.
[165] Morel to Holt, 19 January 1904, Afr. s.1525 18/2:1.

his enthusiasm for a third time in less than two months. Almost immediately, Guinness wrote to Morel on 21 January 1904, agreeing to all Morel's terms, a victory Morel attributed to Casement, though it helped that Holt agreed to guarantee the finances of the large Liverpool meeting that would follow the Scottish tour.[166] Guinness's pitch to the RBMU directors for the new approach suggests he kept his word.[167] The other reformers may have deplored the religious tone of his meetings but they did not complain of sectarianism or mission fundraising. This was no guarantee for the future; Guinness's resolve on any topic could easily reverse.

Casement's letter to Guinness also made the case for a single-purpose organization headed by Morel. On 22 January 1904, Guinness hastily wrote to Morel, forwarding Casement's letter suggesting the idea and committing himself to adhere to the new group if Morel would found it.[168] Guinness wrote Morel again the next day, explaining why Stead could not run the new organization and discussing how it could operate.[169] Historians have correctly attributed the idea of the CRA to Casement, but the letters show that Guinness brought the idea to Morel. Casement had also written about it to Stead, but not Morel. Morel's oft-quoted letter to Holt on 24 January about Casement's idea was based on Casement's letter to Guinness; there is no letter from Casement to Morel suggesting the CRA. Casement may have hesitated to broach it because of the burden he wanted Morel to take on.[170]

The moment of truth came on 25 January, when Morel acceded to the advice of his wife, Mary, to undertake the leadership of a combined Congo reform movement.[171] Talk of duty and perhaps dreams of fame had overcome Morel's hesitations about his not very robust constitution and his familial and journalistic responsibilities.[172] He boarded a ship for Ulster and met with Casement at the Slieve Donard hotel, Newcastle, County Down.[173] By that night, the die was

---

[166] Guinness to Morel, 21 January 1904, Afr. s.1525 18/2:11; Morel to Emmott, 22 January 1904, F10/8:884; Morel to Emmott, 26 January 1904, F4/2:43–4; Morel to Dilke, 26 January 1904, F10/9:6.

[167] RBMU Directors, 25 February 1904, reel 1, Vol. 1, 36–7.

[168] Guinness to Morel, 22 January 1904, F4/2:28.

[169] Guinness to Morel, 23 January 1904, F4/2:32.

[170] Morel to Holt, 24 January 1904, 380 HOLI 18/2; Cookey, *Britain*, 109.

[171] Morel, "History," 163. The founding year is incorrectly stated as 1903 in Dean Pavlakis, "The Development of British Overseas Humanitarianism and the Congo Reform Campaign," *Journal of Colonialism and Colonial History* 11, no. 1 (Spring 2010), but is corrected here.

[172] Morel to Guinness, 26 January 1904, F4/2:40.

[173] Ó Síocháin and O'Sullivan, *Eyes of Another Race*, 27, date the meeting on Sunday 24 January based on a later document, but 24 January was Saturday. Morel said the meeting occurred "yesterday" on 26 January and "Sunday" for the next few days.

cast. In an encouraging letter that he wrote immediately after their meeting, Casement memorialized their discussion in a manifesto which emphasized the need for unity, organization, and systematic publicity in the UK and overseas. He went on to warn, "Sporadic meetings and occasional lectures—articles in the press from time to time are not sufficient ... only systematic effort can get the better of them."[174] He enclosed a £100 contribution that he could little afford on his straightened means—roughly equivalent to £9,400 in 2013.[175] He wanted Guinness to announce the CRA on his lecture tour, which began shortly thereafter.[176] Four paid employees of the RBMU arranged the meetings, which took place in the largest public or private halls in each location on the following February dates: 1-Glasgow, 2-Alloa, 3-Govan, 8-Aberdeen, 11-Dundee, 15-Edinburgh, 16-Dumferline, 17-Stirling, 18-Falkirk, and 19-Greenock.[177]

Morel immediately recruited Holt, Guinness, and Emmott for a preliminary governing Committee.[178] When Emmott balked at Guinness's presence, Morel assured him, "He is an eloquent speaker, and will command many adherents, and I am going to do my very best to work with him."[179] To Dilke he wrote, "He is a man that up to the present I have not regarded with any confidence, but I recognise with Casement that he can tap people that we cannot tap."[180] He was more open with Holt, writing: "I am quite sure we will have to keep our eye on him."[181] He envisioned running the print campaign while Guinness handled public meetings, Emmott managed Parliamentary relations, and Holt provided guidance. Emmott and Holt were wealthy men who could assist with funding and fundraising.[182] Guinness agreed at once and reported enthusiastically to the RBMU directors on 28 January, "It was noted with thankfulness that a new organization, to be called the 'Congo Reform Association' was likely to come into existence in a few days, and to form an extended platform in connection with which important meetings would be held throughout the country."[183] Morel

---

[174] Casement to Morel, 25 January 1904, F8/16:25.
[175] MeasuringWorth, http://www.measuringworth.com/calculators/exchange.
[176] Grant, *Civilised Savagery*, 61, reflects preliminary plans, not actual events. RBMU Directors, 28 January 1904; *Regions Beyond*, February 1904, 39–40; *Regions Beyond*, March 1904, 72–3; Guinness to Irvine, 19 January 1904, F4/2:18–25; Gifford et al., *Stirling and Central Scotland*, 74, http://books.google.com/books?id=MN2nvtWc35UC&pg=PA74.
[177] *WAM*, 26 February 1904, 1223 referenced a 10 February meeting in Stirling, but this was not on Guinness's itinerary. Either the date of the prior week's meeting was misstated or another missionary spoke.
[178] Morel to Stead, 27 January 1904, F4/2:36–8.
[179] Morel to Emmott, 26 January 1904, F4/2:43–4.
[180] Morel to Dilke, 29 January 1904, F4/3:67–9.
[181] Morel to Holt, 3 February 1904, Afr. s.1525 18/2:15.
[182] Morel to Guinness, 26 January 1904, F4/2:40.
[183] RBMU Directors, 28 January 1904, Reel 1, Vol. 1.

asked for Stead's support but did not invite him to join the Committee, primarily because of his refusal to work with Dilke, whom Morel believed essential.[184]

However, initial efforts to recruit Dilke and Fox Bourne failed. Casement had written them arguing that the APS was not capable of directing the movement, despite its noble efforts.[185] Morel also wrote a respectful letter that nonetheless contained disrespectful phrases: the APS was unpopular in certain quarters, it did not have the funds necessary, and the movement needed a centralized effort under one leader. If Casement could convince Guinness to limit his sectarianism, "it is our duty to put our personal feelings in our pockets."[186]

This did not find a sympathetic response. Fox Bourne was considering starting a Congo Committee of the Aborigines' Protection Society, with himself as Honorary Secretary and Dilke as Chairman.[187] The APS would insulate it from the charge of religious fanaticism, a constant risk with Guinness involved. He disliked that Morel had asked him to join the CRA "privately" and not as the APS's official representative. He complained of the

> reckless haste with which you are rushing a plan which you have sprung upon men who have been working at the Congo question long before you took it up, and whom you now expect, on the spur of the moment, to bow to your decision and submit to your leadership.[188]

A meeting with Morel in London on 2 February eased his anger somewhat; he agreed not to launch the APS Congo Committee but refused to join the provisional CRA Committee, using Guinness as his excuse.[189] Fox Bourne anticipated that the CRA would further divide the movement. It lacked the APS's contacts and reputation, and, even worse, would siphon off funds from the APS, which could not afford any drop in its annual income of £550–£700.[190] After he obtained the backing of the APS Committee for his position, Fox

---

[184] Morel to Stead, 27 January 1904, F4/2:36–8; Morel to Emmott, 26 May 1904, F10/11:196.

[185] Casement to Fox Bourne, 25 January 1904, quoted in Cline, *Morel*, 41; Casement to Morel, 13 February 1904, F98/16:30.

[186] Morel to Fox Bourne, 30 January 1904, F4/1.

[187] Fox Bourne to Morel, 29 January 1904, F4/3:56–7.

[188] Fox Bourne to Morel, 1 February 1904, quoted in Cline, *Morel*, 42. It is not in the Morel papers.

[189] Morel to Dilke, 3 February 1904, F10/9:42; Morel to Holt, 3 February 1904, Afr. s.1525 18/2:15.

[190] APS Annual reports, 1899–1903. Contrary to Grant, *Civilised Savagery*, 63, this income was sufficient for the APS; other lobbying groups had similar funding. BFASS Annual Report, 1903; *Low's Handbook to the Charities of London*, 1904, http://books.google.com/books?id=n7NbAAAAQAAJ.

Bourne tried to reassure Morel they could work in parallel: "If you do start it I'll loyally stand aside and do what I can in my own humble way."[191]

For his part, Dilke believed the organization was unnecessary because Parliament and the press were nearly unanimous for Congo reform. Morel argued that this support was shallow; it was necessary to awaken public opinion.[192] However, Dilke refused to join out of loyalty to Fox Bourne.

Morel would not compromise. He saw the APS as old-fashioned and outdated; it never held large public meetings, its leader could not act without its Committee's approval, and it seemed unable to stir popular support.[193] A special purpose organization was more likely to awaken public opinion, raise money, and wield influence. Casement, Holt, and Emmott believed that Morel was superior to other possible leaders: the elderly and fussy Fox Bourne, the mercurial Guinness, and the controversial Stead. The new organization could benefit from their talents, but Morel had to lead it.

For Fox Bourne, "loyally standing aside" initially meant telling people how much he regretted the CRA's existence.[194] Soon, this coldness gave way to a renewed alliance. He agreed to join Morel on the platform for the CRA's founding meeting on 23 March in Liverpool.[195] Three days later, he assured Morel of his high regard and his desire to work with him and the CRA "as heartily and loyally as we can in our uphill fight."[196]

Fox Bourne was as good as his word. The April *Aborigines' Friend* said that the founding of the Congo Reform Association would be remembered as "the death-knell of the new African slavery."[197] Cooperation accelerated, and, in June, Fox Bourne, Dilke, and Fox accepted the CRA's renewed invitation to join its expanded Executive Committee as APS representatives. The *Aborigines' Friend* welcomed the CRA with great satisfaction.[198] Fox Bourne continued to pursue his habitual methods, but Morel developed similar capabilities, and, within two years, Fox Bourne conceded the work to the CRA. For his part, Morel continued to be respectful of Fox Bourne, referring frequently to his persistence in keeping the Congo issue alive in the late 1890s.

---

[191] Fox Bourne to Morel, 29 January 1904, F4/3:58; Morel to Guinness, February 1904, F4/3:90; APS Committee, 4 February 1904, Brit. Emp. s.20 E5/10.

[192] Morel to Dilke, 29 January 1904, F4/3:67–9.

[193] Morel minute on copy, Guinness to James Irvine, 19 January 1904, F4/2:18–25; Morel to Cadbury, 31 October 1905, F8/11:98.

[194] Fox Bourne to Morel, 4 March 1904, F8/67:193.

[195] Morel to Fox Bourne, 7 March 1904, F8/67:195. He did not attend, however, due to illness.

[196] Fox Bourne to Morel, 10 March 1904, F5/1.

[197] *AF*, April 1904, 63–4.

[198] *AF*, June 1904, 157–8.

The Congo Reform Association was Casement's brainchild, but it represented the merging of ideological strains: Stead's humanitarian interventionism, Guinness's evangelical fervor, Kingsley's respect for aboriginal cultures, liberal free-trade dogma, and the promotion of native rights propounded by Holt and the Aborigines' Protection Society, leavened with the compassion of Holt, Casement, and the APS. Anointing Morel to run the CRA meant that, in the end, the organization would pursue Holt's vision of human rights as interpreted through the Berlin Treaty and the golden rule.[199] Because the Congo could not be settled by Europeans, one or more European states should control it as a normal colonial dependency, guaranteeing freedom of commerce, providing freedom of operation for missionary groups, and safeguarding rights for the Congolese people that complemented their own traditions.[200] These rights included freedom to trade, land rights over most of the country, and traditional cultural practices with a few exceptions such as slave-trading, cannibalism, and internecine warfare. Ideally, there would be no forced labor, though an exception could be made for purposes that benefited the people. Over all this would be a benevolent colonial authority, concerned with protecting these rights, promoting improved public health, and maintaining the peace so critical to the development of Africa on African lines. Organized public opinion would secure this outcome. Though this proved an unattainable dream, the reforms it prompted in administration, commerce, and land rights ended the governing system that was its chief target.

---

[199] Holt to De Ville, 22 August 1901, F8/83:120.
[200] Morel, "The Outlook," *Organ*, July 1908, F4/31.

Chapter 3
Organizing Congo Reform

> In matters like organising a national campaign, many things have to be considered and the thing has to be worked out on business lines and with <u>grim hard labour</u>. I have experience! ... I want to keep this machine rolling with <u>one steady purpose</u> in view, not distracted at all by side winds.[1]—E.D. Morel, 1909

With the creation of the Congo Reform Association, the resilience, resources, and institutional impact of a voluntary association opened avenues for protest that had been previously unavailable. Its structure and activities could enable or hinder efforts to make the most of these opportunities. Within a well-designed structure, the movement could capitalize on the reformers' energies and talents, but a poorly functioning organization would squander their work. On one hand, the hagiographic tradition sees the CRA as Morel's tool for a successful campaign, but one historian takes the opposite view, describing it as Morel's vehicle for "the failed strategies of protest," becoming successful only after it engaged Quaker financial resources and John and Alice Harris's talents to develop a mass movement.[2] The Association's organization and finances illuminate this question and provide another way to understand the movement. Its structure affected how the CRA functioned, limiting as well as enhancing possibilities.

Casement, Morel, and their allies formed the Association because they recognized that the battleground had changed. Through agitation in the press and lobbying, loosely affiliated activists had brought about the critical Parliamentary debate of May 1903. The young MP Herbert Samuel, coordinating with Morel, Fox Bourne, and Dilke, put forward a resolution calling on His Majesty's Government to confer with the Berlin Act signatories regarding the Congo Free State's treatment of natives and trading monopolies.[3] After amendment at the government's request to soften the presumption of the Congo Free State's guilt, the resolution passed without a division, meaning that its passage could be described as unanimous, although not many MPs were present.

The consequences were momentous. Foreign Secretary Lansdowne commissioned Casement's voyage of inquiry, communicated in August to the 12 European Berlin Act signatories, and published Casement's report in

---

[1] Morel to Doyle, 13 August 1909, F8/49:4.
[2] Grant, *Civilised Savagery*.
[3] 122 Parl. Deb. (4th ser.) (1903) 1289–332.

Figure 3.1 The first issue of the *Official Organ of the CRA*
Source: LSE Library's collections, MOREL F1/11/5.

February 1904. However, a turning point is not victory. The Foreign Office did not convince the other signatories to act even after receiving Casement's report.[4]

In Britain, Casement's report created a sensation but, as Casement predicted, it did not lead to the decisive action favored by the reformers. Casement argued that it would take a dedicated organization to keep the flames of indignation alive, which in turn would push the Foreign Office and the government to put pressure on Leopold. This was a conventional approach taken by special-purpose organizations such as the Society for the Suppression of the Opium Trade and the Friends of Armenia. Morel, coming from outside this culture, initially planned for not much more than a press campaign in conjunction with Guinness's public meetings.[5] Casement would provide unofficial guidance behind the scenes; as a Foreign Office official, he could not formally join. Just after the CRA's inauguration on 23 March 1904, Morel proposed a more sophisticated plan of action, which required a more robust organization, the first of a number of changes put into place as the CRA's needs evolved.[6]

Morel asserted that the CRA was altogether new: "This Association has been conducted as probably no Association of the kind has ever been conducted, or ever will be."[7] However, the group organized along lines set down by hundreds of voluntary associations in the previous century. Morel had no formal guide for good governance, but the British Charity Commission since published such a guide, listing common-sense criteria for a well-run association. The organization should be clear about its purpose and direction, have a strong board, be structured appropriately for its purpose, improve its practices, manage its finances prudently, and be financially and operationally transparent.[8] As time went on, the CRA adopted more of the practices that characterized well-run associations then and now.

Morel's first steps were to assemble an Executive Committee, develop a written program, and recruit an aristocratic president. Overall direction was to be in Morel's hands, as Casement and Guinness had insisted. Today this role is often called executive director or CEO, but in Morel's day, the Secretary usually led the organization, as was the case with Fox Bourne at the Aborigines' Protection Society and at the Society for the Suppression of the Opium Trade, where Secretary (and Congo activist) Joseph G. Alexander was the group's leading figure. However, this depended on the Secretary's character. The Anti-Slavery Society's paid Secretary, Travers Buxton, was, in his own words, not

---

[4] *New York Times*, 10 June 1904.
[5] Morel to Guinness, 26 January 1904, F4/2:40; Morel to Stead, 27 January 1904, F4/2:36–8.
[6] Morel's draft plan, 31 March 1904, F4/4:141–58.
[7] Morel letter, *New Age*, 21 December 1907, 149.
[8] "The Hallmarks of an Effective Charity," Charity Commission, July 2008. http://www.charity-commission.gov.uk/Publications/cc10.aspx.

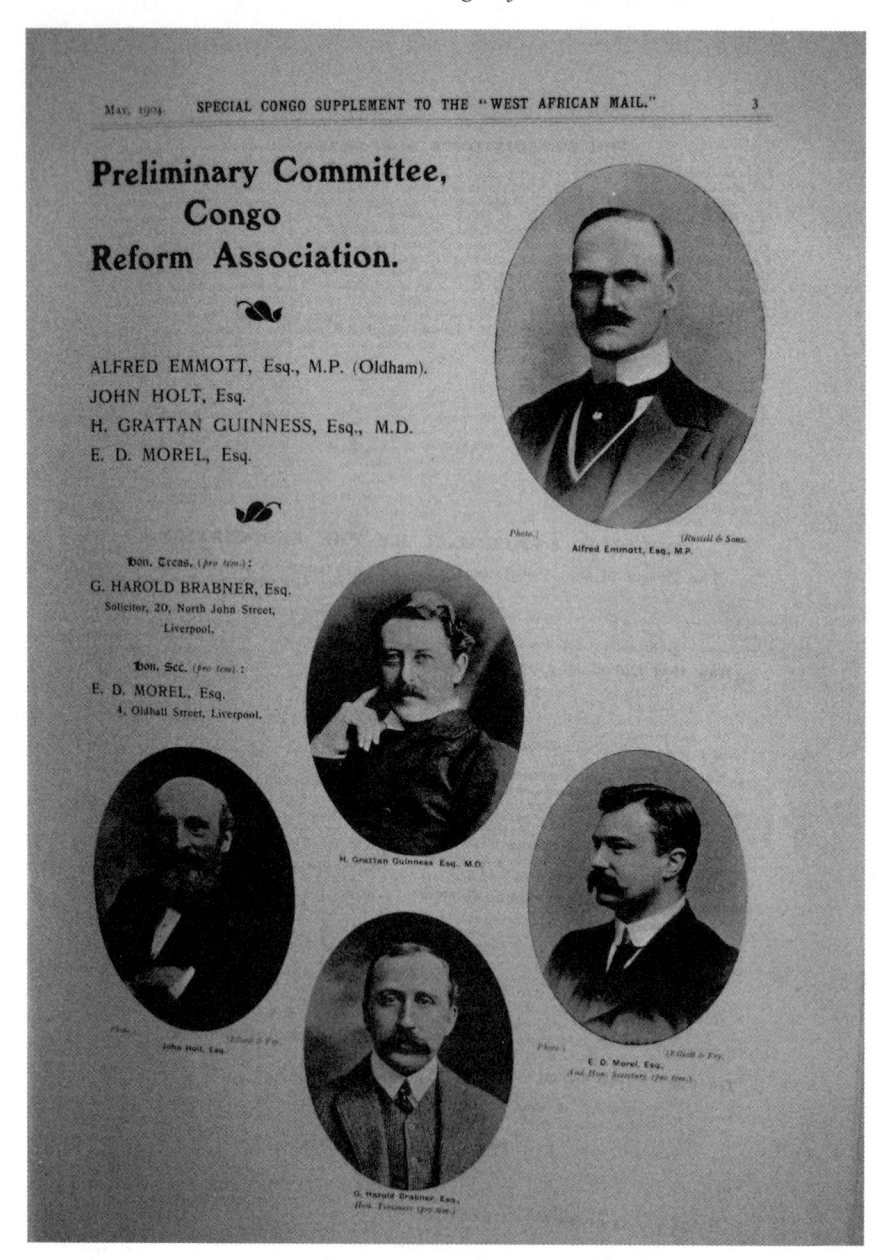

Figure 3.2 The First Executive Committee of the CRA

Source: West African Mail Special Monthly Congo Supplement, May 1904, from LSE Library's collections, MOREL F1/11/5.

"strong in initiative."[9] He handled routine business and published the Society's journal but otherwise followed the direction of the group's Committee or its President, Sir Thomas Fowell Buxton, a distant relation. After John and Alice Harris joined it as Organising Secretaries in 1910, however, John Harris became the chief figure, eclipsing the Buxtons and the Committee. Harris, in this as in many other things, had modeled his practices on Morel's.

The Executive Committee and President

The equivalent of a modern board of directors in turn-of-the-century voluntary associations was the Committee. Its members were typically people of influence, wealth, or both who would oversee the Secretary, worry about finances and major management problems, and set overall direction. At the CRA, Morel called it an Executive Committee and wanted it small, with each member working on a set of tasks, leaving himself free as Secretary to operate without oversight or regular meetings. Its members met each other for the first time at the CRA's founding on 23 March 1904, after two months of intensive organizing work.[10] However, this structure was inadequate. A month later, Emmott complained about the demands it placed on him. With Holt and Morel in Liverpool and Guinness traveling, he found himself in London, making important decisions on his own. However, he wrote, "Even if we met often, it is not practicable to carry on our present work with the heterogeneous committee of four we now have." He especially did not want to rely so much on Guinness. They must expand the Committee and clearly delegate powers to Morel for most of the work.[11] Emmott also revived the invitation to Fox Bourne to join the Executive Committee with two other APS representatives.[12] Emmott soon had his wish. By August, the Executive Committee had expanded to 24 members on its way to more than 30 three years later.

With his allies' help, Morel attracted additional committeemen of standing, including three aristocrats, six MPs of both parties, a bishop, three high-profile clergymen, another African trading company owner, one newspaper editor, and two bearers of famous humanitarian names: a Gladstone and a Wilberforce. The impressive list of names showed how far the movement had come in a short time. The Committee also included Morel's trusted Liverpool friend Harold Brabner as Treasurer and Alice Stopford Green's brother, Col. J.G.B. Stopford, who was her eyes and ears.

---

[9] Buxton to Sir T.F. Buxton, 15 January 1906, Brit. Emp. s.19 D1/3:16–20.
[10] Guinness to Holt, 2 March 1904, Afr. s.1525 13/4:1.
[11] Emmott to Morel, 27 and 28 April 1904, F8/53:56, 57.
[12] Emmott to Morel, 30 May 1904, F8/53:76.

The new body met Emmott's immediate concerns by reducing his workload and substituting Morel for Guinness on the American trip.[13] New questions of governance arose, initially from Emmott, who had experience as head of his family's cotton spinning business and as mayor of Oldham. In 1905, he urged Morel to "regularize" his practices by consulting with his Executive Committee consistently about strategy.[14] William Cadbury, another business executive, told him to expand his staff and make the Executive Committee responsible for fundraising.[15] Morel did not make many changes, and in 1906 complained about Executive Committee meetings, triggering an admonishment from Holt: "Committee meetings are not the useless things you think." Meetings would sustain the participants' personal interest and could help find the CRA a new president; the first President, Lord Beauchamp, had resigned to join the new Liberal government five months earlier. Holt also pointed out, not for the last time, that Brabner should submit regular financial reports to the Executive Committee.[16]

Morel continued to resist what he thought of as old-fashioned methods.[17] For example, he did not consistently keep minutes of the Executive Committee's meetings. In the early years, he did not fully record attendance for seven meetings, and meeting summaries in the *Organ* differed from references in correspondence or other documentation.

In October 1906, the Executive Committee created a Finance Committee of six: Monkswell, the President; Morel and Harris, the headquarters and London Secretaries; and Brabner, Buxton, and Arthur Black, the headquarters, London, and Liverpool Treasurers.[18] However, it did not function properly until March 1907.[19] The Finance Committee grew to 12 members, with three to eight men attending its monthly meetings. However, there were no records of this body's deliberations in its first two years.

Morel's carelessness about meeting minutes at the Executive and Finance Committees reflected his disregard for written documentation of debates and decisions, likely because it would limit his freedom of action. He preferred to keep Committee conversations casual and to rely on correspondence with his most trusted contacts to keep people informed and make decisions. This gave him greater control.

---

[13] *Congo Supplement to the West African Mail*, August 1904, 113.
[14] Emmott to Morel, 5 April 1905, F8/3:50.
[15] Cadbury to Morel, 9 November 1905, F8/12:8.
[16] Morel to Albright, undated 1906, F10/14:45; Holt to Morel, 26 July 1906, F8/86:444; F10/13:456.
[17] Morel to Cadbury, 31 October 1905, F8/11:98.
[18] Harris to Cadbury, 9 October 1906, F8/76:284.
[19] Morel to Monkswell, 21 April 1908, F10/16:441.

An example of Morel's control of information through informality occurred in October 1905. Leopold's ally Sir Thomas Barclay invited the CRA to recommend specific improvements the King could make to Congo administration, which Morel answered angrily as if it were insulting.[20] When Cadbury disapproved of his brusque reaction, Morel assured him that Emmott and Casement supported his position. This was patently untrue; Emmott and Casement (and three others) had also written that he had mishandled the situation.[21] Barclay's offer was made at the same time as similar offers via Alfred Jones to the RBMU and via Hugh Gilzean Reid to the APS, and thus needed discussion it did not receive at the Executive Committee. Morel's lack of transparency and self-serving prevarication successfully deflected negative feedback at the time and since.

When Harris became the Finance Committee's Secretary in 1908, his meticulous minutes put pressure on Morel to do the same for the Executive Committee; its records improved soon thereafter. Morel printed some of its discussions verbatim in the *Organ* in 1910 and in 1912 published complete meeting transcripts.

Financial statements were a particular source of concern. Morel believed that publishing financials would let their enemies know how meagre their resources were. Thomas Hodgkin, a retired banker on the Executive Committee, disagreed. He told Harris and hinted to Brabner that they needed audited financial statements.[22] Violet Simpson wrote Harris how she wished "Mr Morel's Good Angel would lead him to see the necessity" of properly audited accounts.[23] This Good Angel appeared in the form of John Holt, who could chastise Morel directly when others shied away. In mid-1907, after Morel had vented his fury at Harris for, among other things, publishing audited financial statements of the London Auxiliary, Holt reprimanded Morel:

> If Brabner was as businesslike in his accounts as Harris appears to be, it would be more satisfactory. So far as I remember I have never seen a printed account of Brabner's. All the local associations should copy the business-like method of the London Association and if the parent concern would do the same, it would be an advantage.[24]

Swallowing his undoubted annoyance at having to follow John Harris's example, Morel regularized financial reporting. On 1 October 1907, Brabner gave the

[20] *Messenger* 44, no. 5 (November 1905): 519.
[21] Emmott to Morel, 22 October 1905, F4/6:40; Casement to Morel, F8/18:120; Morel to Cadbury, 1 November 1905 F8/12:1; Morel to Samuel, 25 October 1905, F10/12:843.
[22] Hodgkin to Harris, 31 December 1906, F8/80:2.
[23] Simpson to Harris, 7 July 1907, F8/76:327.
[24] Holt to Morel, 8 July 1907, F8/86:513.

Executive Committee a cumulative revenue and expense statement from March 1904 to September 1907.[25] This enabled Morel to respond to MP Hilaire Belloc's December 1907 attack on the CRA's mysterious finances in the *New Age*.[26] Morel sent the financials confidentially to the *New Age* editors so they could assure Belloc that things were on the up-and-up. Publishing of accounts started in 1909 when, under continuing public attack by Belloc and others for the possible nefarious interests shielded by secretive financial practices, Morel printed the previous year's audited financial statements in the *Organ*. Belloc found this unconvincing, so Morel put together the first comprehensive list of donations received, which he published along with cumulative audited financials, finally silencing Belloc.[27] From then on, the CRA regularly disclosed donors and financial statements.

Morel's early failure to meet these common standards demonstrated inexperience and arrogance tantamount to incompetence. He believed he had a compelling new way of organizing that may have been attractive and even functional from moment to moment in terms of the flexibility and power they gave him, but weakened the organization and made it vulnerable to attacks and set back the movement unnecessarily due to his hasty reactions. Sometimes it took pressure from his enemies as well as demands from his supporters for Morel to conform to good practice.

In one arena Morel did not compromise: annual meetings of subscribers. Humanitarian organizations such as the APS, Anti-Slavery Society, and RBMU used annual meetings to endorse new Committee members, approve rule changes, hear stirring reports of recent victories and new challenges, and speak out on issues. Morel dispensed with this practice. Subscribing to the CRA merely provided literature. The CRA's third anniversary commemoration on 19 April 1907 brought together subscribers, but its purpose was to celebrate the CRA's existence and energize the members.

The Executive Committee came to serve as Morel's sounding-board in developing the CRA's program, ongoing strategy, and public documents. Morel also used a few other trusted people for this purpose, especially Casement, the journalist T.L. Gilmour, Alice Stopford Green, and, later, Randall Davidson, the Archbishop of Canterbury.

The Executive Committee made the major decisions regarding Morel's status as the organization's unpaid chief executive. At the Aborigines' Protection Society, Fox Bourne received £400 annually, and the British and Foreign Anti-Slavery Society paid Travers Buxton £240, but both men had other sources of income. Morel, who could not rely on his minimal investment income, tried

---

[25] Morel to Hodgkin, 2 October 1907, F10/15:937.
[26] *New Age*, 12 December 1907, 149.
[27] Morel to Brabner, 26 June 1908, F9/13:31; *Organ*, June 1909, 283–90.

to support his family with the *West African Mail* and its post-bankruptcy reincarnation as the *African Mail*, but these perpetually struggling publications could not provide what he needed, leaving him reliant on subsidies from Holt and Cadbury, who were unwilling to have their subsidies publicized. In answer to suggestions from Casement, Cadbury, and others that he give up the *WAM* and draw a salary from the CRA, Morel insisted that this would expose him to charges of self-interest in the Congo agitation.[28] This backfired; the lack of a salary for a man obviously without independent means led his detractors (correctly) to suspect that hidden benefactors were privately subsidizing him, and also (incorrectly) to say that these benefactors would profit from changes in the Congo. Because of the incorrect coda as well as his patrons' wishes, Morel always hotly denied the allegations of secret CRA funding, misrepresenting his position if not strictly lying.

The *West African Mail* became increasingly dependent on the CRA. In early 1905, Morel arranged for the CRA to pay the *WAM* to print its *Official Organ* at £150 annual profit to the paper.[29] Later that year, Morel refused the £300 salary the Executive Committee offered him, but, with their permission, he used CRA funds to hire an Assistant Editor for the *West African Mail* at a £208 salary (£240 in 1908).[30] In return, the *WAM* gave the CRA rent-free office space and its staff often worked late on CRA business. Morel estimated that the CRA was worth £640 a year to the *WAM*; Holt, Cadbury, and the CRA poured up to £1,000 annually into Morel's paper so the CRA could avoid paying him a salary. But the financial needs of Morel's family grew, while his journalism income fell. Although the CRA Executive Committee again voted to pay him a salary in 1908, Morel did not have to accept because the Liverpool Auxiliary raised £1,000 for him.[31] In 1911, Casement, Green, Emmott, Doyle, and Lord Cromer raised a further £4,000 testimonial that left Morel financially secure through the Congo agitation and beyond.[32] He never drew a CRA salary.

The Executive Committee took on new importance in late 1906, when Leopold agreed to transfer the Congo to Belgium, triggering protracted negotiations between the King, the Belgian government, and the Chamber of Deputies. Instead of simply asking the Executive Committee to endorse his plans, Morel assembled the group to fashion the CRA's official position. On 21 January

---

[28] Casement to Morel, 28 August 1905, F8/20:248; Executive Committee, 1 November 1905, F4/7:30; Beauchamp to Emmott, 2 December 1905, MS Emmott 3 f.331; Memorandum, 31 July or 1 August 1906, F10/14:66.

[29] Morel to Swanzy, 25 January 1905, F10/10:984.

[30] Morel to Holt, F4/77:80.

[31] Morel to Holt, 20 September 1908, F4/9:202–8; Testimonial, 29 January 1909, F4/10:5.

[32] "The Public Presentation to Mr. E.D. Morel," 29 May 1911, https://archive.org/stream/publicpresentati00cromiala#page/n0/mode/2up.

1908, they declared the draft annexation treaty unacceptable, calling on the British government to bully Belgium into cooperating by denying recognition of the annexation, defending with military force any Britons exercising free-trade rights, placing gunboats on the Congo, closing the Nile to Congo traffic, refusing British ports to Belgian steamers in the Congo trade, increasing consular staff, and establishing consular jurisdiction. Consular jurisdiction meant denying the local government's authority over British subjects and using military force to keep the peace in lands adjacent to British territory.[33] This muscular response marked the ascendancy of the Executive Committee's most aggressive members, such as Monkswell. Although Hodgkin had urged Morel to let Monkswell chart out his own policy, Morel had not accepted this advice, preferring to ensure a consistent message.[34] This forced Monkswell and others to bring their ideas to the Executive Committee, where, in this case, they won their point. They feared British leverage would dwindle once Belgium annexed the Congo. It would be better to be forceful now and friendly later.

On 9 October 1908, the Executive Committee weighed in again after the Belgian Chamber of Deputies and Senate ratified a treaty that removed Leopold but left his system, including the concession companies, in place. The CRA would continue asking the British government to lean on Belgium to implement meaningful reforms.[35] However, the British Cabinet adopted only one measure: it refused to recognize Belgian annexation, which occurred on St Leopold's Day, 15 November 1908.[36] As discussed in Chapter 8, the Foreign Office was not ready to risk European complications. The 11 February 1909 Executive Committee meeting expressed frustration that the government had not taken stronger measures.[37]

Between June and December 1909, several events changed Morel's relationship to the Committee. In June he publicly denounced the government's Congo policies, its dealings with France and Germany, and the way the Foreign Office developed and executed foreign policy. This alarmed many Committee members, who had been willing to criticize Britain's Congo policy but would not follow Morel in attacking the entire foreign policy edifice. Morel was no longer the Committee's moderate center; the Committee increasingly hesitated to push the government to act forcefully, especially after Belgium announced reforms in November 1909 and Monkswell's death the following month. The Executive Committee continued to advocate for British pressure on the Belgians to move faster and to warn of the dangers of officially recognizing

---

[33] *Organ*, January 1908, 7–8.
[34] Hodgkin to Morel, 5 January 1907, F4/80:4.
[35] *Organ*, November 1908, 22.
[36] Cabinet minutes, 28 October 1908, CAB 41/31/69.
[37] *Organ*, 1909, 166.

the annexation too soon, but talk of gunships and blockades died away.[38] The Executive Committee's role in setting policy had grown since 1904.

The CRA President's role expanded from 1904 to 1909. In 1904, the provisional Committee wanted an aristocratic president to give it visibility and standing. Although Morel did not intend to burden the President with much work, finding one proved difficult.[39] To avoid embarrassing the candidates or the CRA, they vetted and approached potential presidents informally. Emmott and Green provided most of the suggestions because of their connections in the aristocracy. Emmott's list included William Lygon, Lord Beauchamp. Only 31 years old, Beauchamp had entered political life early as mayor of Worcester and had most recently been Governor of New South Wales. However, Green reported that Beauchamp "carries no weight," so they moved on to others. They asked Green's friend Lord Northbourne, Lord Aberdeen (president of several humanitarian groups), Lord Percy (extensive Foreign Office experience), John Morley, and others.[40] One after another, they declined, though several lent their names as supporters, and a few gave money.

With the CRA's launch three weeks away, Beauchamp was the best remaining candidate. To everyone's relief he accepted, modestly offering to step aside if they found a more influential person.[41] Although Beauchamp donated £115, he was not particularly useful. He did not speak on the Congo question in the House of Lords or at the few public meetings he attended. He resigned upon taking a position in the new Liberal government in December 1905.

Holt quashed Morel's suggestion that a president was unnecessary.[42] William Cadbury refused the job because of the unresolved cocoa slavery question.[43] Providentially, that same week, the well-connected journalist Harold Spender joined the Executive Committee and suggested four names, including Robert Collier, Baron Monkswell. Spender called Monkswell "a very good chap" who was "spoiling for a job" because the new government had not offered him a position.[44]

Monkswell accepted and proved to be indefatigable, generous (£171 in three years), and fully committed. He never missed an Executive Committee

---

[38] Executive Committee, 14 July 1910, *Organ*, 1910, 634 and 21 February 1911, *Organ*, October 1911, 692–3.

[39] Morel to Emmott, 28 January 1904, F4/2:51; Morel to Russell, 5 February 1904, F4/3:98.

[40] Green to Morel, 8 February 1904, F4/3; Emmott to Morel, 3 and 20 February and 3 March 1904, F8/53:12, 36, 37; Holt to Morel, 23 and 24 February 1904, F8/85:354, 355.

[41] Emmott to Morel, 4 and 15 March, 1904 F8/53:38, 44; Beauchamp to Morel, 15 March 1904, F4/4 127.

[42] Holt to Morel, 26 July 1906, F8/86:444.

[43] Cadbury to Morel, 12 March 1906, F8/12:23.

[44] Spender to Morel, 20 July 1906, F8/132:4.

meeting, spoke at over 50 public meetings in three years, and took a strong line in the Lords in 1907 on behalf of the Association.[45] The BMS missionary Rev. Kenred Smith called Monkswell's first Congo speech well put together but delivered "without much fire."[46] This belied a forceful personality; Morel and others had to rein in his bellicosity and his "well-meant but injudicious words."[47] Monkswell developed such a liking for the work that he became chairman of the amalgamated Anti-Slavery and Aborigines' Protection Society in 1909. He gave his time and energy unstintingly to both organizations, even after his doctor diagnosed the fatal illness that killed him in December 1909.[48]

After Monkswell's death, Morel began a dilatory search for a successor. Monkswell's widow urged him to find a strong MP but rejected his suggestions: Dilke because of the divorce scandal, MacDonald because a Socialist would alienate supporters, and Sir George White because he was too conciliatory.[49] Dilke advised Morel to recruit a high-status president, but, he wrote, "the best plan is to have none—if that is possible."[50] This opened the door to a frank admission from Morel: "I don't particularly want a President, but I do feel that the Association loses caste somewhat by not having one."[51] This time he allowed the question to lapse. When the CRA embarked on its policy of watchfulness in mid-1910, a president seemed less necessary and the position remained vacant.

Purpose and Direction

From the first, Casement and Morel wanted the CRA's goals to be clear. The Association's initial program said it would use the press, public meetings, and personal influence to restore to the Congolese their land rights, their rights to the produce of the soil, and their personal freedom through a "just and humane administration," consistent with the principles of the 1885 Berlin Act and the 1890 Brussels Act, without regard to party, religious, and national differences.[52] The CRA adhered to these core principles for the next nine years. Other causes would be distractions, as Emmott said, "Chinese labour, West Australian irregularities, and Nigerian expeditions are the deadly foes of our Congo

---

[45] Holt to Morel 14 January 1907, F8/86:501; *Organ*, 1910, 366.
[46] Kenred Smith to Morel, 30 November 1906, F8/130:17.
[47] Monkswell to Morel, 17 December 1906 and 9 January 1907, F8/111:1, 3; Hodgkin to Morel, 11 October 1907, F8/80:7.
[48] Harold Spender to Morel, 1 March 1912, F4/25.
[49] Lady Monkswell to Morel, 15 April 1910, F8/111:26.
[50] Dilke to Morel, 28 April 1910, Add. 43897:243.
[51] Morel to Dilke, 4 May 1910, Add. 43897:244.
[52] "Program of the Congo Reform Association," March 1904.

movement."⁵³ Although Holt encouraged him to fight for better administration across Africa, Morel followed Emmott's advice. Dismissing all other concerns as secondary, he expected the same of others. Sir Arthur Conan Doyle, who in 1909 devoted himself full time to the CRA, gave the party line in a *Daily News* letter regarding the Putumayo rubber scandals: "It would be a great misfortune if our attention to Peru should in any way relax our vigilance upon the Congo," where British treaty rights and responsibilities made intervention imperative.⁵⁴ He had the same concern about the cocoa slavery issue, "because it obscures the big question and if it is the same men who are working on it, it gives a handle to those critics who call them busy bodies."⁵⁵ Morel seldom deviated from this Congo focus until after 1910.

Morel's position gave him standing to insist that those who spoke under the CRA's banner stayed true to its diagnosis, recommendations, and practices, such as notifying Morel of meetings and forwarding him copies of resolutions passed, which should use Morel-provided wording. The greatest challenge to this discipline was his CRA co-founder, Dr Harry Grattan Guinness.

This began over the question of public debates. During Guinness's February 1904 speaking tour, Dr Charles Sarolea, the Belgian Consul in Edinburgh, challenged Guinness to a debate. Sarolea, one of Leopold's more gentlemanly defenders, met Morel and Guinness before a small gathering of Edinburgh's elite at the University of Edinburgh's Rainy Hall on 18 March 1904. This debate had little impact and convinced Morel that such public contests were more trouble than they were worth. A subsequent challenge exposed Guinness's unreliability. This came from a more pugnacious apologist, George Herbert Head, a Cambridge lawyer. The Congo government had hired Head the previous year to help prosecute the libel trial of Captain Guy Burrows, the man who had discredited Salusbury in the 1890s and reversed himself by writing a book attacking the Congo Free State. On 19 April 1904, in front of over 2,000 people at an RBMU-sponsored Congo meeting at Exeter Hall, Head challenged Guinness to a debate.⁵⁶ He told Guinness over coffee a few days later that his pay from Leopold could defray the cost of the debate.⁵⁷ This became a controversy: Morel and Emmott were not happy about the debate in the first place, more unhappy that Congo profits might pay for it, and most unhappy that Guinness was making decisions without consulting them, risking the CRA's credibility.⁵⁸ Morel demanded that Guinness debate as a private person, because "it is hardly

---

53   Emmott to Morel, 12 September 1905, F8/55:185.
54   *Organ* 2, no. 10 (August 1912): 847.
55   Doyle to Morel, 19 September 1909, F8/49:22.
56   *West African Mail*, 29 April 1904, 109.
57   Guinness to Morel, 22 April 1904, F8/74:19. Head's uncle Albert Head was one of Guinness's closest friends. Mackintosh, *Guinness*, 109.
58   Morel to Guinness, 23 April 1904, F8/74:27.

dignified for the CRA to meet the representative of a Government whose methods it condemns, not on individual opinions, but on facts."[59] Emmott found Guinness's explanations about the affair unsatisfactory.[60] The 8 June debate with Head at St James Hall turned out to be good for the movement; both Guinness and Morel used it in their publicity. For the moment, Guinness had shrugged off the discipline that Morel was trying to impose.[61]

Guinness's erratic cooperation should not obscure his contributions. He was the only CRA founder with the ability to draw large audiences and was for a time an energetic proponent. It had been Guinness's idea to ensure that every meeting passed a resolution to send to the Foreign Office and the local Member of Parliament (MP). As the CRA formed, he proposed local branches and the creation of the CRA's *Official Organ*. Guinness also wanted to deliver a memorial to President Roosevelt in association with a US lecture tour.[62]

In 1904–05, Guinness used his lantern slides in at least 37 meetings, with some audiences numbering in the thousands. However, the lectures stopped when Guinness went to South America from June to November 1905. With Guinness's meetings producing almost nothing in the way of money, sustained interest, or local branches, Morel declined the RBMU's offer to schedule other lecturers in his absence.[63]

Morel and Fox Bourne had worried that Guinness would use Congo lectures for his mission and that too overt a religious tone would annoy potential supporters. Morel's initial plan was for a non-religious campaign: "It is purely a humanitarian movement, and must be kept on those lines; and religion and humanity, unfortunately, do not always go together."[64] As Morel put it to Guinness:

> I feel a delicacy in discussing the subject with you, for we cannot, in the nature of things, look at the matter quite in the same light. What I wish to avoid ... in the interests of the movement, is the suggestion that the movement is based on religious exaltation—I use the word for want of a better one—at any rate that outward religious manifestation should be a feature of it. I know this would alienate a lot of people. There is no earthly reason why we should not feel religious,

---

[59] Morel to Guinness, 28 April 1904, F10/9:953.
[60] Emmott to Morel, 29 April 1904, F8/53:58.
[61] "The Defence of the Congo State," *Regions Beyond*, July 1904, 193–6; *West African Mail*, 10 June 1904, 280–282.
[62] Guinness to Morel, 23 January 1904, F4/2:32–6; Morel to Emmott, 9 March 1904, F10/9:439; Draft plan of action, 31 March 1904, F4/4:141–58.
[63] Morel to Talbot, 21 Jun. 1904, F10/11:377.
[64] Morel to Holt, 3 February 1904, Afr. s.1525 18/2:15.

and there is every hope that, as you say, we shall get many religious people in the true sense of the word to join us.[65]

However, Guinness was on to something important. In advocating for lectures, petitions, and attention to religious leaders, he identified a rich vein of potential support: the energy and activism of what historian D.W. Bebbington has called "the Nonconformist conscience" of 1890–1910. In this period, the Free Churches of Nonconformist Britain were particularly willing to protest against wrongs and demand remedies through the political process. These campaigns depended on what Bebbington calls indignation meetings. In contrast to the often staid lectures of other pressure groups, indignation meetings were enjoyable and exciting. The speakers aimed to reach hearts more than minds, portraying the situation as so grim that it required wholehearted commitment. This was the core of Guinness's approach and would be used to greater effect by the Harrises and other missionaries later.[66]

The tension between their ideas was productive. The CRA reined in Guinness's tendency to run RBMU-based religious exaltation meetings, but the religious symbolism of his talks was effective. Strategically, Morel felt it would be disastrous if the CRA appeared to be Guinness's tool, which would alienate other religious groups as well as secular humanitarians.[67] However, Guinness helped Morel and the Executive Committee to see religious leaders as allies.[68] By August 1904, four had joined the Executive Committee: Rev. John Clifford (Baptist), Canon Scott Holland (Anglican), Rev. R.J. Campbell (Congregationalist), and Francis Chavasse, the evangelical Anglican Bishop of Liverpool. The Rev. Scott Lidgett (Methodist), Bishop Edward Talbot (Anglican), Rev. F.B. Meyer (Baptist), and others followed. However, it was primarily Morel, with help from Harris after 1905, who brought these men into the movement, not Guinness.

Guinness's greatest contribution was involving his missionaries. They provided much of the 1903–04 testimony. CBM missionaries spoke at CRA-related meetings from 1904–09, including Revs Whytock, Gilchrist, Whiteside, Padfield, Lower, and others. Most significantly for the future of overseas humanitarianism, Guinness arranged for the RBMU directors to second John and Alice Harris to Morel full time as chief lecturers and organizers of the CRA London Auxiliary from 29 March 1906 to 26 October 1908, continuing to pay their salary of £192 per year. Though this salary was inadequate to life in London and required supplementary payments delivered through the

---

[65] Morel to Guinness, (4) February 1904, F4/3:90.
[66] D.W. Bebbington, *The Nonconformist Conscience: Chapel and Politics 1870–1914* (London: Allen and Unwin, 1982), 15–17.
[67] Morel to Harris, 26 April 1906, F8/76:232.
[68] Guinness to Morel, 7 October 1905, F8/74:62.

Liverpool Auxiliary and Travers Buxton, it was nonetheless a remarkable act of commitment in contrast to 1905, when the CBM charged the CRA £70 16s 3d to cover the Harrises' salary for four and a half months of lectures.[69] It was the Harrises who opened the door to a much more vigorous and successful approach to meetings.

For all his contributions, Guinness was not a success as a CRA leader. Public interest declined in the 18 months after the CRA's founding despite his speeches. Not only was he unable to use his star power to benefit the movement in a sustained way, his erratic personality and willingness to pursue his own ends led him into difficulties with other leading reformers, particularly Morel. In early 1905, Morel griped that he had first heard about a Guinness talk in the Plymouth area from his in-laws.[70] Even Meyer was not comfortable with him; he refused to join the Executive Committee until after Guinness stopped attending.[71]

Guinness's erratic nature made him the target of efforts by Leopold and Sir Alfred Jones to peel him away from the movement. The first occasion, described in Chapter 2, occurred in 1903. In Fall 1905, when Barclay approached the CRA, the RBMU's Congo Council received an offer through Jones, whose shipping line between the Congo and Antwerp had become a monopoly, incentivizing Jones to curry favor by weakening the movement before publication of the Commission of Inquiry report. A new company was to be formed to replace the notorious ABIR concession, and Jones offered the CBM a seat on its board and new mission stations in the area.[72] Guinness found the offer intriguing, despite Morel's observation that Guinness would then be complicit in the forced labour necessary to turn a profit.[73] At Morel's request, F.B. Meyer conveyed to Guinness in the strongest possible terms that he should not accept the offer, and threatened to resign from the RBMU board if Guinness ignored his advice.[74] Meyer prevailed; the Congo Council rejected the offer on 7 November. After Jones publicly attacked the missionaries as hypocrites for this refusal, Guinness and Morel published the proposals and showed how they were unlikely to lead to any improvement.[75]

Although Grant portrays Harris as allied with Guinness, he had thrown his lot in with Morel.[76] While still an RBMU employee, Harris made his feelings

---

[69] Harris to Buxton, 15 September 1908, Brit. Emp. s.18, C82:100; *Organ*, July 1913, 1047.
[70] Morel to Emmott, [25 January 1905], F10/10:995.
[71] Harris to Morel, 31 August 1905, F8/75:187.
[72] Slade, *English-Speaking Missions*, 294–5.
[73] Guinness to Morel, 4 November 1905 F8/74:114; Morel to Guinness, 5 November 1905, F8/74:92.
[74] Meyer to Morel, 7 November 1905, F8/108:4.
[75] *WAM*, 24 November 1905, cited in Slade, *English-speaking Missions*, 296.
[76] Grant, *Civilised Savagery*, 76.

about his boss clear: "Neither my wife or I would go to him [Guinness] for help if we got into a tight place, indeed what self-respecting man or woman would?"[77] In 1906, Harris told Morel, "I rather think he [Guinness] resents me swearing by you on every occasion[;] well it would be difficult to swear by him, for one never knows where he is."[78]

In February 1907, matters worsened when the Congo Balolo Mission told its missionaries not to communicate with the CRA.[79] Whatever Guinness's role in this decision, it happened without a discussion with the CRA. When asked, James Irvine explained that the RBMU's Congo Council wanted to approve anything before publication to prevent libel suits. Guinness was away, making it easier for Morel and Harris, working through Irvine and Meyer, to secure a compromise: the missionaries could write to Morel and Harris but the CRA promised to obtain permission before publishing and the Council voted that the policy did not indicate any "coldness" to Morel.[80]

Wounded but not dead, cooperation with Guinness continued in 1907–08. He undertook another Scottish campaign for Congo reform in November 1907 and spoke at a dozen or more meetings in 1908. But Belgium's annexation of the Congo in November 1908 set the stage for an irreparable break. Morel, ever on the alert, learned that the CBM had requested more mission stations. When Morel asked for a statement of support, the RBMU directors conveyed their commitment but undermined this by declining to send money.[81] Guinness visited Belgium and received promising answers about new sites. While there, he told the British ambassador that his missionaries had found the Congo officials to have an "improved tone" since annexation.[82]

Improvement in the Congo led to antagonism between the CRA and RBMU, where Meyer was no longer a director. Taking offense when Morel publicly cautioned them against defiling themselves by working with the Belgian government, the Congo Council reinstated the policy that missionaries should write only to headquarters.[83] Guinness's praise for Congo progress in the *Regions Beyond* distressed the CRA.[84] After a fruitless exchange of letters, the Congo

---

[77] Harris to Morel, 16 and 18 September 1905, F8/75:192, 195.
[78] Harris to Morel, 7 September 1906, F8/76:268.
[79] Morel to Harris, 28 February and 11 March 1907, F10/15:216, 237. Grant, *Civilised Savagery*, 76, says this divided the Harrises and Morel, but Morel wrote to Harris as an ally and Harris jubilantly telegraphed Morel on 11 March that Meyer had taken the matter up.
[80] RBMU Directors, 21 March 1907; Congo Council, 12 March and 9 April 1907, Reel 11, Vol. 3, 246–7, 249, 250.
[81] Congo Council, 12 January 1909, Reel 11, Vol. 3, 317–18.
[82] Hardinge to Grey, 28 May 1909, FO 881/9530:201.
[83] *Organ*, April–July 1909, 273; Congo Council minutes, 13 July 1909, Reel 11, Vol. 3, 337.
[84] Morel to Wilkes, 25 August 1909, MS Emmott 4:249–55.

Council broke off from the CRA and resolved "should Mr Morel repeat the abuse of his position as Secretary of the CRA by attacking Mission policy, Dr Guinness be authorized to take such action as he may deem advisable."[85] This breach was permanent. Guinness no longer attended CRA events, and the Congo Balolo Mission reverted to its pre-1903 policy of not publishing negative reports.[86] Guinness raised money by lecturing on improvements in the Congo.[87]

For good and for ill, Guinness was a disruptive force. His enthusiasm for the cause and for Morel's leadership immediately after the crisis of January 1904 enabled the CRA to get off the ground quickly. His celebrity status made the Association's formal launch in March 1904 a well-attended news-making phenomenon. He first suggested many of the movement's big ideas and loaned the Harrises. At the same time, more than any other reformer, his refusal to hew to the official line and to coordinate was the most serious breach of discipline Morel contended with.

Catherine Mackintosh, Guinness's biographer, said he did not want recognition for his Congo reform activities. This may seem disingenuous in light of Guinness's strong ego and his evident pleasure at rousing large indignation meetings. But Mackintosh captured something important. Diplomatically avoiding the temptation to settle old scores, she wrote that Guinness "gently withdrew" once he was no longer essential, because public controversy interfered with his primary vocation, saving souls.[88] More than anything, he wanted to bring salvation to the world's heathens, and his Congo reform activism was a tool to reach that goal, rendering him less interested in submitting to the authority of Morel and the CRA Executive Committee.

Guinness was not the movement's only headstrong friend. In 1909, Arthur Conan Doyle recruited the novelist Henry De Vere Stacpoole, the popular author of *The Blue Lagoon*. Morel had to corral Stacpoole, who ended up contributing a novel, *The Pools of Silence* (1910), about brutality in the Congo.[89] Doyle himself needed a firm hand. Morel stayed deliberately silent when Doyle's 1909 *Crime of the Congo* urged France and Germany to partition the Congo because of Belgium's inadequate first-year reforms. This helped Morel appear more moderate and a friend to Belgium.[90] But his forbearance could not last. In November, Doyle was to share the podium with Morel for the first time. To be sure Doyle would advocate the Association's standard positions, Morel met with

---

[85] Congo Council minutes, 5 October 1909, Vol. 3, 339–45.
[86] Congo Council minutes, 4 October 1910, Vol. 3, 361–2.
[87] *Liverpool Journal of Commerce*, 18 December 1911, F8/100:156; Guinness, "Congo: Past and Future," in Morel to Buxton, 10 March 1912, Brit. Emp. s.19 D2/3/1.
[88] Mackintosh, *Guinness*, 74, 78.
[89] Morel to Doyle, 13 August 1909, F8/49:4.
[90] Morel to Claparède, 17 September 1909, F8/31.

him in advance to avoid "any public suggestion of a difference in view when it comes to a remedy."[91]

Other reformers needed to be brought into line. Morel successfully corralled Dilke and Monkswell; by 1907, Dilke was asking Morel if he found his arrangement of parliamentary speakers and content satisfactory and Monkswell gave assurances that he would "refrain from taking an aggressive attitude."[92] However, the person Morel admonished most often was John Harris, who tended to improvise in both word and action. As Morel warned repeatedly, "I must be most careful, and if any mistake is made the fact of my being alone responsible will make it easier to bear."[93] In a typical 1908 case, Harris had opined in print about ending Britain's guarantee of Belgian neutrality. Morel demanded fiercely that he not comment on the international situation without permission to avoid harming the cause in Germany or France.[94] More detail on their relationship appears in Chapter 7.

The *West African Mail* also prioritized the CRA's message. Initially, it criticized British colonial policy in the spirit of Mary Kingsley, but after the CRA formed it moderated its tone. John Holt, a major investor in the paper, considered this to be an abdication of responsibility. He complained to Morel, "The *West African Mail* is not critical enough now. It does not stir up anything but Congo affairs. We want rousing articles on our colonies in [West Africa] and the present is a splendid time for giving our Government a programme."[95] Holt wanted the *West African Mail* and its successor, the *African Mail* to advocate African rights, the traders' interests, and better administration throughout West Africa. Morel dedicated them to Congo reform, even to the point of ignoring the Herero genocide. Morel's papers demonstrated the discipline and consistency that he similarly expected of all CRA participants.

Finances, Auxiliaries, and Meetings

The search for money was a major preoccupation for the CRA. As Table 3.1 shows, individual donors (discussed in Chapter 4) provided over seven-eighths of its funds. This section discusses the next largest sources of funds in the context of historiographical debates regarding CRA finances.

---

[91] Morel to Doyle, October 1909, F8/49:30.
[92] Morel to Harris, 23 June 1906, F8/76:249; Hudson for Dilke to Morel, 15 May 1907, F8/41:115; Monkswell to Morel, 9 January 1907, F8/111:3.
[93] Morel to Harris, November 1906, F8/76 296.
[94] Morel to Harris, 18 August 1908, F8/77:374.
[95] Holt to Morel, 20 February 1906, F8/86:433; Holt to Morel, 13 October 1905, F8/85:400.

Table 3.1   Sources of CRA Funds, 1904–13
Incorporating the London Auxiliary for 1907–08

	Total	Percent	Number of occurrences
Named Individual donors	£11,081	83%	4,173
Plus Anonymous donations	£480	4%	157
Total individual donations	**£11,560**	**86%**	**4,330**
From Auxiliaries (netting out London's 1907–08 contributions)	£772	6%	59
Surplus meeting proceeds	£485	4%	133
Donated directly by churches & FCCs	£156	1%	113
Donations from other organizations	£97	1%	48
Collections, mostly from churches	£125	1%	86
Collected by magazines	£70	1%	23
Total income from donations	**£13,265**	**99%**	
Plus literature sales, bank interest, furniture sales	£155	1%	
Total income	**£13,420**	**100%**	

Notes: "Collections" includes odd amounts labeled "CRA Suppt." and "Sundry Subscriptions" but not "CRA Suppt." in even amounts which are presumed to be anonymous single donations. "Surplus meeting proceeds" does not include London's 1906–07 collection of £260 in *Rising Tide*, 1907, 11, making a total of £745 collected from all meetings.

Sources: Rising Tide, April 1908, 24–8; and *Organ*, April 1909, 181–8; June 1909, 283–92; January 1910, 483–8; May 1910, 605–8; October 1910, 657–9; May 1911, 701–4; October 1911, 743–4; August 1912, 856–60; April 1913, 974–6; July 1913, 1044.

Local auxiliaries provided the second largest funding source, 6 percent of total income. Branches were customary for humanitarian and missionary organizations. During its peak years, the Anti-Slavery Society claimed to have about 100 branches.[96] In 1899, the APS had short-lived Liverpool and Manchester branches.[97]

Morel embraced Guinness's idea for CRA branches in 1904.[98] However, none had appeared by July 1905, when Morel told supporters that new donations would help him found branches.[99] Cadbury and Morel discussed a Birmingham branch that never materialized, partly due to the *Birmingham Daily Post* editor's

---

[96] "History of Anti-Slavery International" (2001), 6, website no longer available.
[97] *Aborigines' Friend*, February 1899 and November 1899.
[98] Morel memorandum, 31 March 1904, F4/4:141–58; Morel to Charles Brunning, 27 February 1904, F10/9:225; Morel to C.R. Fox, 8 March 1904, F10/9:414.
[99] Morel to CRA Supporters, 11 July 1909, F10/12:379.

hostility.[100] Morel set up the Liverpool Auxiliary as a prototype in early 1906, run by some of his friends.[101] John Harris organized the London Auxiliary shortly thereafter, superseding Violet Simpson's ineffectual satellite operation.[102] Morel and Harris went to Newcastle in October 1906 to found an auxiliary to stir things up in Foreign Secretary Grey's constituency.[103] After this, John and Alice Harris became responsible for auxiliaries, which required extensive groundwork before they brought Morel in for the showcase meeting where an auxiliary took formal shape. Sometimes this required persistence; it took 11 months to start the Bristol Auxiliary.[104] There are references to about two dozen auxiliaries forming in 1906–10; most survived through 1913.[105]

The auxiliaries created demand for atrocity meetings, kept the Congo in the local press, and democratized policy-making through auxiliary representatives attending Executive Committee meetings. Nonconformist ministers were about a quarter of the 210 auxiliaries' Committee members in 1907, and as much as two-fifths in 1909, demonstrating the strength of the religious element in the movement.[106] However, most committee members were not ministers, and few ministers occupied leadership roles. Of the 37 representatives sent by regional branches to recorded Executive Committee meetings over the years, only 4 were ministers. Local politicians and commercial people were as numerous as ministers in the auxiliaries' Committees, suggesting that the branches approached Morel's ideal of an eclectic movement with strong religious, humanitarian, and commercial interests.

Kevin Grant has argued that auxiliaries and meetings were vital to the CRA's financial health after the 1906–07 fiscal year, because contributions from auxiliaries and collections at meetings made the difference between an income of £815 in the year ending September 1907 to £1,720 in the year ending September 1908—a £905 increase that he says ended CRA deficits and compared favorably with the perpetual deficits of the APS and the Anti-Slavery Society.[107] This argument needs examination in every respect.

---

[100] Morel's draft plan, 4 July 1905, F8/11:37; Cadbury to Morel, 5 July 1905, F8/11:31; Cadbury to Morel, 30 July 1908, F4/7 19–20.
[101] Meyer to Morel, 23 November 1905, F8/108 6; Meyer to Morel, 8 December 1905, F8/108:7.
[102] Morel to Cadbury, 2 August 1905, F8/11:41.
[103] Morel to Cadbury, 1 October 1906, F8/12:33.
[104] Harris to Morel, 8 August 1906, F4/7:53; Morel to Bristol Lord Mayor, 9 August 1906, F8/76:257; Harris to Morel, 7 September 1906, F8/76:268; Harris letter, 31 October 1906, F8/76:290.
[105] See Appendix V.
[106] Grant, *Civilised Savagery*, 74 for 1907; 23 August 1909, F10/18:2–10 for 1909.
[107] Grant, *Civilised Savagery*, 74–5.

The numbers quoted come from the London Auxiliary's annual reports, not the reports of the central CRA.[108] They show that the Harrises did an excellent job creating a solid financial basis for the London Auxiliary, which covered its burgeoning expenses for meetings, literature, travel, and rent and contributed £20 to the Bristol Auxiliary and £500 to the central CRA.

For the central CRA, fiscal year 1907 income was somewhere between £1,400–1,500.[109] For the 1908 fiscal year the CRA's financial statements show £1,579 3s 5d in income. This did not represent a revolution in CRA finances. The £1,579 included £136 in funds from the auxiliaries founded in 1907 and £26 collected at meetings and other special collections. This small financial contribution from the auxiliaries and meetings declined in each succeeding year. Excluding the London Auxiliary, which had a special fundraising mission, auxiliaries contributed £672 during the CRA's life, or 5 percent of total income. A few auxiliaries, such as Manchester and Bristol, needed subsidies despite the Finance Committee's policy that auxiliaries be self-funding. Only 222 of the CRA's 1,000-plus public meetings contributed more than they cost. Even £443 in ticket sales and other donations for the massive 19 November 1909 Albert Hall demonstration left that meeting with a £40 deficit.[110] Collections at meetings went primarily to defray costs, and most meetings had financial shortfalls.

The big story in these numbers is that the finances of the central CRA and the London Auxiliary began to overlap in mid-1907, triggering three events: improved financial reporting as previously discussed, an attack by Morel on Harris examined below, and Morel's move to London to merge the London Auxiliary into the central organization, covered in the next section. London was justly proud of its success in getting subscribers and in generating a £500 contribution to the central organization in fiscal year 1908. However, to Morel's annoyance, Harris was soliciting money from current CRA subscribers; people had sent donations to London thinking they were going to the central CRA.[111] At least 46 of the London group's 415 donors in fiscal year 1908 had previously been donors to the central organization. These overlap donors gave £304 to

---

[108] *The Rising Tide: Annual Report of the London Auxiliary of the Congo Reform Association* (April 1906–March 1907) Spring 1907, 3; also in *Organ*, June 1907, 39; for 1907–08, *Organ*, April 1908, 24, F4/36. Balances carried forward from the previous year should not be considered income.

[109] 1906–07 income is estimated because the CRA issued cumulative 1904–07 financials. Audited financial statements for March 1904–September 1907 give total income of £4,647 10s. Subtracting the £895 19s 7d income for the year to 6 January 1905 (Brabner to Executive Committee, 19 January 1905), leaves the remaining 33-month period with annual income of £1,393. Income improved after 1905, so £1,400–£1,500 is the range for 1906–07.

[110] Morel to Mrs. Emmott, 8 November 1905, F10/12:911.

[111] Morel to Harris, 3 July 1907; F10/15:808; Brabner to Harris, 3 July 1907, F8/76:325.

London. Put a different way, the central group might have collected £304 of the £500 that the London auxiliary contributed to the central CRA if London had not existed. Morel chastised Harris for cannibalizing the central organization's donors, though he directed his explosion of anger inappropriately to a man who had also convinced new donors to give a further £640, most of which paid the London Auxiliary's expenses, including meeting shortfalls.

The CRA was not in deficit before the Harrises.[112] When Brabner reported that the CRA had collected £895 in income through 6 January 1905, he also reported that it had spent £882 in the same period, indicating a small surplus in the CRA's first year.[113] From its founding to September 1907, the Association collected £4,647 10s and spent £4,557 2d, showing a surplus from 1905–07 as well.[114] The CRA's constant call for more funds was compatible with its ability to spend within its constrained means, a need Morel was well aware of, writing "We must cut our cost according to our cloth."[115]

Similarly, far from having perpetual deficits, the APS and Anti-Slavery Society were often in surplus. Their financial statements from 1899–1913 show income greater than expense for the Anti-Slavery Society in ten of 11 years, for the APS in five of 11 years, and for the combined organization in four of five years. Saying that they were always in deficit perpetuates the CRA's myth of uniqueness. Not-for-profits then and now often find that their ambitions outrun their funds and scale back their work to the money available. The surpluses show that all three groups were able to do this.

The drying up of CRA financing in October 1904 has led to speculation that Morel had difficulty attracting support from his wealthy merchant friends. After all, the organization received only £6 in October and had only £23 in the bank, of which it owed £10 to pay bills.[116] However, Morel would have been hard-pressed to solicit funds from anyone in October; he had left Britain in mid-September for a US tour and did not return until early November, while the CRA paid a substitute editor for the *WAM*. When Morel found that almost no donations had arrived in his absence, he sent an immediate and successful appeal to keep the organization going.[117] Fundraising in 1904 depended completely on Morel and his absence almost sank the organization. His push for funds upon his return brought the organization back from the brink. From 17 November 1904 to 6 January 1905, the CRA collected £143, a respectable sum for two months. Far from being unable to reach beyond his tightfisted merchant friends,

---

[112] Grant, *Civilised Savagery*, 74, asserts that the Harrises moved the CRA out of deficit.

[113] Morel to Mrs Thomasson, 11 April 1905, F10/12:136.

[114] *Organ*, June 1909, 283–90.

[115] Morel to Simpson, 14 November 1905, F10/12:922.

[116] Cline, *Morel*, 47; Grant, *Civilised Savagery*, 65; Brabner to Mrs Morel, 22 October 1904, F9/2:166–71.

[117] Morel to Stopford, 14 November 1904, F4/17:253.

Morel landed new and notable donors at the end of 1904, such as F.B. Meyer, the explorer F.C. Selous, the wealthy industrialist widow Mrs Rylands, *Liverpool Post* proprietor Sir Edward Russell, and Miss Marjory Lees, cotton heiress and daughter of Oldham's first female mayor.

Some have taken Morel's gloomy words "things look very black," written to Alice Stopford Green on 28 December 1904, to mean that the Congo Reform Association was at risk.[118] Morel made this observation at a time of difficulties for both the *West African Mail* and the CRA. On 20 December, Morel wrote a seven-page letter to tell the shareholders of the *West African Mail*, which included Green, that the paper was about to fold, with only £2,122 in revenues to cover expenses of £2,920 in the ten months to 30 November 1904, a massive £798 loss. This included £112 stolen by Stephen Gelder, his most highly paid employee at £156 annually.[119] He invited them to a shareholders' meeting in early January to consider if they could save the paper by restructuring or selling it. The letter mentioned that the CRA would be weakened if the *WAM* went out of business, but Morel does not say here or elsewhere that the CRA was in danger of collapse, simply that a bankruptcy at the *WAM* would force him to scale back his CRA work.[120] Herbert Samuel immediately replied, "I am very sorry to hear that the *WAM* is in a bad way."[121] Although Green's response to the 20 December letter is not on file, it is reasonable to assume that she wrote back about the *WAM* and that his two-sentence response on 28 December 1904 conveyed that things looked "very black" for the paper, not the CRA. Fortunately he arranged a recapitalization in early 1905, though its finances remained precarious.

This is not to say that Morel was unconcerned about the CRA's finances; however, when he called the CRA's funds "virtually exhausted," he was asking for donations.[122] Shortly after returning from the US in November, with money at its lowest ebb, Morel sent Congo police chief Antonio Benedetti £40 for travel expenses as well as £80 compensation for quitting his job in return for evidence.[123] Holt contributed the £40, and Morel was confident that he could raise the rest of the money.[124] To make a long story short, Benedetti had expected Morel and the rubber merchants who supposedly backed him to pay him well, and when more money did not materialize, he sold his services to the Congo

---

[118] Green to Morel, 28 December 1904, F10/10:823; Grant, *Civilised Savagery*, 65.

[119] Morel to Zochonis, 14 December 1904, F10/10:749; Morel to Holt, 20 December 1904, F10/10:793.

[120] Morel to Holt, 20 December 1904, F10/10:793-9; Morel to Holt, 22 December 1904, F10/10:800; Morel to Emmott, 29 December 1904, F10/10:830.

[121] Samuel to Morel, 20 December 1904, F8/125:14.

[122] Morel to Holt, 20 December 1904, F10/10:796.

[123] F8/4:53-74.

[124] Morel to Morrison, 12 February 1905, cited in Robert Benedetto, *Presbyterian Reformers in Central Africa* (New York: Brill, 1996), 238-9.

Free State. Instead of revealing Congo Free State secrets, he embarrassed the CRA by announcing in the press that the Congo reformers bribed witnesses. The Benedetti affair threatened to discredit the campaign, and Morel made it a policy henceforth to never pay for information. To make matters worse, at the same time, Fox Bourne had to retract allegations about conflicts of interest among members of Leopold's Commission of Inquiry, leading to further embarrassment.[125] Although Benedetti later revealed the plot when Leopold's people failed to pay him what he expected, December 1904 was indeed a low point for the CRA. Cookey specifically links Casement's observation that the reform movement was "practically dead" to the fallout from the Benedetti affair.[126] Financial worries were minor compared to these embarrassments and flagging public interest.

In April and May 1905, after a personal appeal from Morel, the financial picture brightened considerably with two £100 donations from philanthropic Quakers: one from William Cadbury and another from Katherine Thomasson, the APS's greatest donor. Then, in July, William Cadbury transformed the CRA's finances with a donation of £600.[127]

Fundraising was an ongoing worry; although its income rose, its expenses and plans also grew. Morel wrote pessimistic letters about finances to his closest allies right into 1909. He asked influential members to inspire donors and issued appeal after appeal for funds. One such appeal from February 1906 reminded readers that "the Association stands in urgent need of funds to continue and amplify its work of propaganda."[128] In keeping with the alliance with religious leaders that Guinness had recommended, the appeal bore the signatures of the Bishops of Southwark, Liverpool, and Durham, Rev. Stephen Gladstone (one of William Gladstone's sons), Congregationalist leaders Rev. Robert Horton and Rev. Silvester Horne, Rev. F.B. Meyer (Baptist), and Rev. Scott Lidgett (Methodist). The results of the appeal disappointed Meyer, and he worried that "we defeated our own object by its length."[129] Long or short, every appeal failed to bring in money at the levels hoped for, yet the organization continued to gather funds, carry out its work, and generally run in the black.

---

[125] Samuel to Morel, 20 November 1904, F4/17:270; Cookey, *Britain*, 127–31; *Aborigines' Friend*, December 1904, 236–7.

[126] Cookey, *Britain*, 131.

[127] Grant, *Civilised Savagery*, 66, following Louis, "Morel and the Congo Reform Association, 1904–13," 172, calls this a £1,000 gift, but Cadbury *offered* £1,000 on 26 June 1905, which he then revised to a £600 gift and £400 paid as a subsidy to Morel's *WAM* salary over two years; Morel to Cadbury, 26 June 1905, F8/11 25; Cadbury to Morel, 5 July 1905, F8/11 31; Morel to Cadbury, 2 August 1905, F8/11:40; *Organ*, June 1909, 283–90.

[128] February 1906, F4/7:11.

[129] Meyer to Morel, 19 March 1906, F4/7:11.

Figure 3.3 William Cadbury
Source: From LSE Library's collections.

John Harris and the CRA's Move to London

The CRA's move to London requires further understanding of the involvement of Alice and John Harris. They came home on furlough on 6 August 1905 hoping to make a lecture tour, which coincided with an idea Morel had floated several months before.[130] Contrary to suppositions that he resisted the tour, Morel proposed it to William Cadbury on 8 August: "I very much hope to have a series of meetings in the autumn at which Harris and others can speak."[131] Cadbury endorsed it to Casement on 25 August, and Casement enthusiastically brought it back to Morel, who had already been lining up venues and speakers for the past few days.[132] Casement briefly changed his mind after Harris wrote a letter to the *Morning Post* that he thought ill-advised, but soon set these doubts aside.[133] John Harris planned to use these meetings to draw popular support, marrying Guinness's emotional appeal with Morel's rigorous analysis without subjecting listeners to "a burden of detail."[134] Cadbury's recent gift made the Harris tour possible, partly by enabling the CRA to pay the RBMU for their services.

The timing was fortuitous. After a busy 1904, few public meetings had been held in the first eight months of 1905. Guinness and the CBM's Rev. Peter Whytock had done most of the 1904 lecturing, occasionally joined by Morel, Dilke, Samuel, and others. Whytock had died in November 1904, and Guinness had done only a few lectures since.[135] The Harris tour began in October, with John doing most of the speaking and Alice supporting him on occasion. As their skills and confidence improved, their lectures became increasingly successful.

In late January 1906, they went to the United States, where John and Alice started together but then undertook separate tours. John Harris made the nearly impossible claim that they gave 200 lectures in 49 cities in under 40 days; regardless of the exact number, they were clearly energetic and prolific speakers.[136] When they arrived in England on 10 March, flushed with success,

---

[130] Morel to Stopford, 4 April 1905, F10/12:105.
[131] Morel to Cadbury, 8 August 1905, F8/11:49. This contradicts Grant, *Civilised Savagery*, 67.
[132] Harris to Morel, 23 August 1905, F8/75:184; Casement to Morel, 28 August 1905, F8/20:249; Casement to Morel, 8 September 1905, F8/20:252; Morel to Harris, 22 August 1905, F10/12:481.
[133] Casement to Morel, 4 September 1905, F8/20:250.
[134] Harris to Morel, 19 August 1905, F8/75:179.
[135] Guinness to Morel, 7 October 1905, F8/74:62.
[136] Harris to Buxton via Alexander, 31 January 1906, Brit. Emp. s.18, C82/77a; American Congo Reform Association, *Congo News Letter*, April 1906, 16, http://books.google.com/books?id=tZUPAQAAMAAJ.

they proposed that the RBMU lend them to the CRA at the RBMU's expense, which the directors approved on 29 March 1906.[137]

They set up a CRA auxiliary in London to support their lectures, replacing Violet Simpson's satellite office. Morel encouraged this, giving John Harris advice on choosing a committee, finding a president, and general management, inadvertently encouraging the independence that he later found troubling with comments such as, "Act and consult [your Committee] afterwards."[138] John Harris recruited Travers Buxton, the Secretary of the Anti-Slavery Society, as the London Auxiliary's Treasurer. Buxton was hardly overtaxed; he had requested and received a reduction in his Anti-Slavery work schedule from six days to four because there was not enough work to keep him busy.[139] He organized the auxiliary's financial reporting to the Anti-Slavery Society's standards, with audited accounts and listed donors. To save money, the London Auxiliary moved into Anti-Slavery's offices. Meanwhile, Morel reacted sharply to every misstep that came to his attention over 170 miles away.

The distance was a minor impediment. British mail service reached its top performance in the decades before 1914, leading to mail volumes resembling twenty-first-century email; as Hodgkin complained, "The mass of letters, circulars, advertisements and so forth which every post brings is one of the most serious evils of our modern civilisation."[140] The CRA London Auxiliary could count on 12 mail deliveries each weekday between 7:15 am and 8:30 pm. Other London locations received six to 12 daily deliveries a day, while Manchester had eight and Liverpool seven. Smaller cities had fewer daily deliveries, most villages only one, and homes in the countryside two per week. In large cities, a businessman could send a letter to inform his wife he would be late for dinner.[141] Thanks to innovations such as sorting rooms on mail trains and an underground postal railroad in London, even intercity letters could arrive the day they were posted.[142]

Mail was the cheapest form of communication, at a cost of a penny for a four-ounce letter (£0.36 in 2013 currency). More expensive telegrams found uses for urgent, terse communications. The CRA had telephone service, though its limited coverage, high cost, and lack of confirming documentation meant that it was used sparingly. Using these methods, the CRA's Liverpool headquarters enjoyed rapid communication with Committee members, allied organizations,

---

[137] RBMU Directors, 29 March 1906.
[138] Morel to Harris, 26 April 1906 and undated note, F8/76:233, 243.
[139] Brit. Emp. s.19 D1/3.
[140] Hodgkin to Morel, 31 May 1912, F8/80:23.
[141] M.J. Daunton, *Royal Mail: The Post Office since 1840* (London, Athlone Press, 1985), 44–9.
[142] F. George Kay, *Royal Mail* (London: Rockliff, 1951), 113.

and auxiliaries. The move to London did not come about because of the slowness of the mails.

The CRA had formed in Liverpool because that is where Morel lived and where he earned his livelihood publishing the *West African Mail*, which depended on Liverpool advertisers.[143] Yet London had advantages. Most importantly, a London location gave easy access to the corridors of power. One could meet with MPs when Parliament was in session, drop in at the Foreign Office, and make last-minute appointments with government officials. It made connections with allies easier and more spontaneous. From Liverpool, such visits consumed a whole day or more; from London they could be accomplished in a matter of hours. London's clubs and social scene gave opportunities for informal contacts that could bring unexpected benefits, especially if one was in the good graces of a political hostess such as Alice Stopford Green.

For over four years, Morel managed the distance from the capital with a voluminous correspondence and frequent visits, sometimes traveling home by midnight trains to start work at 5:30 am.[144] But in October 1908, the Finance and Executive Committees endorsed Morel's suggestion that he and the organization's headquarters move to London.[145] Three events preceded this change. First, the Belgian Chamber of Deputies voted on 20 August to annex the Congo, followed by the Senate on 10 September; prodding Belgium to act would be a more delicate task than denouncing Leopold, making a London headquarters advantageous for more frequent and personal contact with the Foreign Office.

Second, this was the time when Morel and the Harrises were asking for salaries. After the £1,000 honorarium had relieved Morel's personal money worries, the CRA agreed to bring John and Alice Harris onto its own payroll at £460 per year. Guinness released the Harrises from the RBMU on 26 October 1908. The CRA had endorsed the Harrises but emphasized that they worked for Morel, mollifying Morel's concern that John Harris's indiscipline, creativity, and independence posed risk to the movement and, no less important, were personally offensive. His concerns arose from the responsibilities that John and Alice Harris had taken on in London.

In April 1907, the London Auxiliary published *The Rising Tide*, its first annual report, showcasing its financial success in collecting £815, mostly in donations and more than either the APS or the BFASS that year.[146] *The Rising Tide* started the chain of events that led to the move from Liverpool. Although

---

[143] In April 1903, 1904, and 1905, Liverpool firms bought 44 percent of advertising, London firms 21 percent.

[144] Morel to Green, 3 February 1903, F10/8:928.

[145] Finance Committee and Executive Committee, 1 October 1908, F4/9.

[146] *The Rising Tide*, Spring 1907, 3, 11, F4/41; Harris to Morel, 7 September 1906, F8/76:268.

Morel thought highly of the courage shown by the Harrises on the Congo and their energy and "magnificent" organizational ability in Britain, his focus on a disciplined movement implied a desire for control that their independence frustrated.[147] His sensitivity made him a difficult superior. Tension had appeared as early as November 1905, when Morel brusquely rebuffed Harris's request to attend an Executive Committee meeting or at least be available in case they wanted him. This was no routine discussion; Harris felt the need to seek reconciliation afterwards.[148] This pattern recurred: while in London or traveling, John Harris would overstep an often invisible boundary, Morel would react with anger, and Harris would apologize. The Harrises' odd position as employees simultaneously of the RBMU and CRA in 1906–08 made matters more difficult. John Harris tried to reassure Morel that he served only one master and began telling people that his Congo reform work had jeopardized and then ended his missionary career, leaving it vague as to whether this meant he was *persona non grata* with the Congo Free State, the RBMU, or both.[149]

The Harrises had chosen Congo reform over Congo mission work, but Morel remained sensitive to any signs that John was setting CRA policy, impinging on Morel's prerogatives, or impulsively communicating positions that had not been cleared. The opportunities for this multiplied as the London Auxiliary took on more work. The Finance Committee asked Harris to raise £2,000 per year, a high target he did not reach, but in the process he began asking existing subscribers for a multi-year commitment, cannibalizing the central CRA's donors.[150] Through his CRA work, John Harris built relationships with important men, such as the Archbishop of Canterbury and Lord Cromer, and the well-connected, such as Travers Buxton and Harold Spender. Morel did not view this development with favor. His personal feelings for John Harris deteriorated, though he continued to publicly praise the Harrises' work.

At the time that he and Morel were asking for salaries in 1908, Harris was also exploring other opportunities. Travers Buxton said Harris's brain had been "seething" with the possibility of merging the Anti-Slavery Society and the CRA (or at least its London Auxiliary).[151] Absent a merger, perhaps he and Alice could work for both groups, and Buxton could cover the CRA's London office while they traveled. John proposed a year-long return trip to the Congo for a year to gather fresh information, and he also considered becoming a colonial official there, if Belgium would have him, or perhaps applying for a consular position in tropical Africa. However, his unusual partnership with his wife

---

[147] Morel to Cadbury, 31 July 1906, F4/7:23 and 9 October 1906, F8/12:40.
[148] Harris to Morel, 27 November 1905, F8/75:216.
[149] *Organ*, November 1907, 60; Harris to Morel, 25 July 1908, Brit. Emp. s.18, C82/91.
[150] Harris to Brabner, 4 July 1907, F8/76:335–7.
[151] Buxton to Alexander, 19 and 27 December 1907, Brit. Emp. s.19 D1/3:813, 821.

Figure 3.4   John Harris
Source: Horner's Weekly, 22 December 1906.

constrained him. She had embarked on her missionary career before he did, and they had built their marriage on common work. Thus, he wrote, "Mrs Harris in not prepared for me to enter upon work which she cannot share."[152] As it turned out, the CRA offered him a salary and the Harrises became the CRA's Joint Organizing Secretaries.

Nonetheless, behind Morel's back, John Harris brought Monkswell and Buxton into discussions about merging the APS, the CRA, and the Anti-Slavery Society. "Everyone seems to view a closer union of the B+FAS and CRA with great pleasure," he wrote, with one big exception: Morel.[153] Harris feared that Morel's reaction to a proposed merger would interfere with the fight for reform.[154] The matter faded away. If Morel had gotten word of it, it would have further aggravated his feelings about Harris.

Meanwhile, Cadbury urged Morel to move to London: "I should think it might do away with a good deal of the friction if there were one general office."[155] Brabner, who detested Harris and believed Buxton was disruptive, concurred because the Harrises would clearly be Morel's employees. As a bonus, the movement' enemies would have to stop saying it was a Liverpool-driven tool of envious merchants.[156] T.L. Gilmour, who was close to Morel and friendly to Harris, backed the move, writing Morel:

> We are engaged in refashioning an instrument which *you* are to use. *You* ought to be taking the lead in the refashioning; but what's happening is that *Harris* is taking the lead + he will try to fashion it to suit his own ideas. You can scarcely blame him if he does ... are you justified in letting Harris get control of the reconstruction? Is it not your duty to make still another sacrifice to the cause and sink your own personal repugnance?[157]

It took Morel a while to see it this way. He complained to Gilmour, "A complicated organisation is being elaborated in order to give Mr Harris a career." He saw himself fighting "Harris and Co." over competing Liverpool and London financial centers—the result of his own dislike of fundraising.[158] He claimed to find this battle repugnant though he seemed always ready to go at it.

Planning for the merger generated more tension. Morel ignored Harris's complaint that "Organizing and Traveling Secretaries" were really two different jobs; one could not organize effectively while traveling. Morel accused Harris

---

[152] Harris to Morel, 25 July 1908, F8/77 366; Harris to Buxton, Brit. Emp. s.18, C82/97.
[153] Harris to Buxton, 30 August 1908, Brit. Emp. s.18, C82/96.
[154] Harris to Buxton, 22 August 1908, Brit. Emp. s.18, C82/94.
[155] Cadbury to Morel, 4 September 1908, F8/13:9.
[156] Brabner to Morel, 15 September 1908, F4/9:182.
[157] Gilmour to Morel, 17 September 1908, F4/9:184.
[158] Morel to Gilmour, undated but September 1908, F4/9.

of ignoring his critique of Harris's draft reorganization plan, then asking for it again a week later.[159] This petty sniping made reconciliation difficult, but Morel attempted to clarify things shortly before moving:

> I have a general supervising responsibility over the whole work which, so far as your special branch of it is concerned, I propose to exercise in no manner other than ascertaining day to day what is going on. I anticipate no difficulty in the practical application of the labours in which we shall be mutually engaged for a common end; and I think you may rest equally satisfied on that score. We shall, I hope, be colleagues working in full sympathy.[160]

They did work in sympathy through the winter and spring, until an unauthorized and unreported visit Harris made to Sir Edward Grey led to renewed conflict.[161]

Morel's move to London was the result of John and Alice's success in London, making them indispensable to the campaign while antagonizing Morel. Morel's move did realize strategic benefits. In addition to a closer working relationship with the Parliamentary Committee, the Foreign Office (for about seven months), and London notables, it led to a better relationship with John Harris as an ally after he left the CRA for the Anti-Slavery Society in 1910.

Parliamentary Committee

The CRA included an on-again, off-again group of sympathetic MPs called the Parliamentary Committee. The most effective pressure on the Congo Free State and on Belgium came from the British government, and Parliament was the best vehicle for getting the government's attention. As described in Chapter 8, MPs and Lords advanced the cause through questions, debates, and resolutions. By advocating a consistent position, they exerted pressure on the government and especially on the Foreign Office.

For a cause whose defining moment was the uncontested Commons vote of May 1903, preservation of multiparty unity had symbolic as well as practical importance. The CRA's initial program backed up its statement that its aims were "absolutely outside Party Politics" by listing eight Liberal MPs and eight Conservative/Unionist MPs as primary supporters.[162]

Emmott led the first Parliamentary Committee in 1904–05, but he resigned upon joining the new Liberal government 1905. Dilke refused to take

---

[159] F4/9, various.
[160] Morel to Harris, 7 October 1908, F4/9:225–6.
[161] See Chapter 8.
[162] *Programme of the CRA*, March 1904, F4/2:1.

over for Emmott, in part because of his own responsibilities under the new administration.[163] Socialist solidarity provided the next chairman shortly after the 1906 election when Vandervelde asked British Labour Party leaders to back Congo reform.[164] A few days later, Labour Party Secretary Ramsay MacDonald asked Morel who was handling the Congo question in the House of Commons.[165] Within weeks he had taken over the Parliamentary Committee, preparing questions and organizing a deputation to Sir Edward Grey.[166] But soon he told Morel that he would be "delighted" to turn the Parliamentary Committee over to someone else, due to pressure from his other political commitments.[167] Thus began several years of frustration during which MacDonald devoted little attention to the Parliamentary Committee. From 1907–09, Morel often worked directly with interested MPs, while the Committee's secretary, E.N. Bennett, gathered signatures when needed and provided minimal coordination, but the Committee met only a few times and had little influence on the movement. MPs continued to bring up the Congo in the House of Commons; indeed, 1908 saw more questions directed to the Foreign Secretary than any other, though the Committee was quiescent. Morel still hoped for a more effective Parliamentary Committee, but he could not find anyone else to run it and felt he could not give orders to MPs. An effort to recruit Parker led nowhere.[168] In May 1909, Morel made a last effort to get MacDonald's attention, reminding him, "The whole thing depends on your being able to put your individual initiative to it."[169] Morel assured him that Dilke and others would follow if he would lead.

After the 1910 election, Morel vented to Dilke and others, "I have received nothing from Ramsay MacDonald. He is really a most unsatisfactory chap over this Committee, and I wish to goodness we could get somebody else, but I cannot very well suggest it."[170] The broad hints reached MacDonald, who resigned.[171] Morel again begged Dilke to be chairman, conveying support from MacDonald (Labour), Parker (Conservative), and Sir George White (Liberal), but Dilke was as adamant as he had been in 1906.[172] Sir George White finally agreed to take the job on the condition that Morel would act as Secretary.[173]

---

[163] Colin Cross, *The Liberals in Power* (London: Barrie and Rockliff, 1963), 38, 58.
[164] Morel to Dilke, 19 February 1906, Add. 43897 f40.
[165] MacDonald to Morel, 21 February 1906, F8/106:1.
[166] MacDonald to Morel, March 1906, F8/106:2–8.
[167] MacDonald to Morel, 20 June 1906, F8/106:10.
[168] Parker to Morel, 12 February 1908, F8/121:22
[169] Morel to MacDonald, 25 and 26 May 1909, F8/106:25, 27.
[170] Morel to Dilke, 24 January 1910, F8/43:279.
[171] Morel to MacDonald, 20 January 1910 and MacDonald to Morel, 26 January 1910, Add. 43897:234.
[172] Morel to Dilke, 26 January 1910 and 7 February 1910, Add. 43897:236.
[173] Morel to White, 27 January 1910, F8/146:107.

This victory had a perverse outcome for Morel. White and Morel were able to get 162 MPs to sign a Parliamentary Memorial to Prime Minister Asquith in April 1910 regarding the slow pace of Congo reforms. Due to a misunderstanding, Asquith did not read it until July. He acknowledged the strength of opinion behind it but referred White to what he and Grey had already said.[174] Several weeks earlier, as if anticipating Asquith's dismissive response, the MPs and Morel had disagreed about the reform movement's next steps at the Parliamentary Committee meeting on 14 June 1910. British policy as determined by Grey and supported by the Cabinet was to refuse to recognize the Belgian annexation of the Congo until there was proof of satisfactory reforms. In late 1909 Belgium had announced a reform plan that would take effect in different regions in 1910, 1911, and 1912. The Executive Committee had denounced this timetable as far too leisurely and advocated increased pressure on Belgium, but the Parliamentary Committee preferred to wait and see, bringing up questions from time to time to ensure the government did not forget the subject. Morel called the meeting "more or less a fiasco," and wrote White:

> I have done my best, and I don't see that I can do anything more. If Parliament is not willing to act on the lines of the Memorial signed by 162 of its Members, then there is nothing for it but to sink back in the position of virtually acquiescing in the Government's policy of non-recognition, and trying to keep the Government to even *that* policy.[175]

This meeting determined the CRA's policy for the next three years.

The Parliamentary Committee henceforth played a diminished role. Dilke died in January 1911 and White in May 1912. For the CRA's last year, Parker, while not formally chairman, would gather a few MPs when needed to speak in the House.[176]

The Parliamentary Committee existed on paper from 1906–12, functioning best in 1906 and then again under White in 1910. Ironically, this final group endorsed a less aggressive strategy than what Morel and the Executive Committee wanted, pulling the CRA into the same posture. From August 1910 until 1913, the Association worked primarily to hold the Belgians to their promises and the Foreign Office to the course that Grey had adopted in 1910.

This analysis of the Congo Reform Association's structure shows that it was not simply a vehicle for Morel's reforming zeal. At times, the Executive Committee and Parliamentary Committee determined the organization's strategy. The Finance and Executive Committees pushed a reluctant Morel

---

[174] Asquith to White, 12 July 1910, F4/10:121.
[175] Morel to White, 16 June 1910, F8/146:152.
[176] Morel to Parker, 12 March 1912 and 6 January 1913, F8/121:118, 137.

toward better governance, improving how the movement functioned, reducing its vulnerability to outside attacks, and strengthening its cash flow. Auxiliaries gave the movement a broader footprint and democratized the Executive Committee. The London Auxiliary enabled John and Alice Harris to use their energies most effectively while learning everything they could from Morel and gave John Harris a laboratory for some of his many ideas. Its success made it a second headquarters for the CRA, aggravating tensions with Morel to the point where he felt that he must transfer the headquarters to London, a belated move that improved access to the Foreign Office and the CRA's philanthropic allies.

In 1904, the CRA existed only because of Morel, and largely worked the way he wanted it to. By 1908 its increasingly robust structures, which resembled those of other humanitarian organizations, meant that Morel's freedom of action had decreased. These changes gave the organization the means to function even if Morel had reduced or ended his involvement.

Chapter 4

Adherents

I am anxious that you may not mistake where your real supporters will lie. Believe me that they will be found amongst those who are pronounced Christian men and women.[1] —Dr Harry Grattan Guinness, 1904

Understanding the Movement's Dimensions

The people of the movement brought life to the CRA's structures. The reformers presented themselves as the representatives of a popular wave of enthusiasm among the population of England, Wales, and Scotland, which numbered 37 million in the 1901 census. Millions saw the newspapers that carried Congo articles and editorials, hundreds of thousands attended Congo meetings, pamphlets went out by the tens of thousands each year and people bought many thousands of copies of each of Morel's books.[2] More important were the people who devoted time and money to the cause: speakers at meetings, Executive Committee members, and donors.

At the movement's periphery were the people who agreed with what they learned about the Congo but did nothing: readers of newspapers and periodicals with an interest in foreign affairs and Protestant churchgoers who heard about the Congo from the pulpit. Although they formed the largest component of a broadly pro-reform public opinion, their unwillingness to join any organized activity limited their impact.

People who attended Congo meetings had a greater effect. Hundreds of resolutions passed at public meetings flooded the Foreign Office with copies to local MPs, showing that support for reform reached far beyond newspaper editors and CRA activists. This led Grey to say in Parliament, "No external question for at least thirty years has moved the country so strongly and so vehemently."[3]

Estimating the number who attended meetings requires both science and art. The database of 1,590 recorded UK Congo meetings (at this writing) gives attendance figures for 90 large meetings totaling 158,000–175,000. The 1,500

---

[1] Guinness to Morel, 2 Feb 1904, F4/3:87–8.
[2] John M. McEwen, "The National Press during the First World War," *Journal of Contemporary History* 17, no. 3 (July 1982): 466–7.
[3] 184 Parl. Deb. (4th ser.) (1908), 1871.

recorded meetings that did not report attendance were likely smaller. A sampling of seating capacity, where available, in these venues runs from a few dozen in a drawing room through churches and halls holding a few hundred to larger locations with capacities of 1,000–2,000. Baptist churches, the most common venue, on average had 60–100 parishioners.[4] Estimating average attendance at 100–300 people seems reasonable.

Estimating unrecorded meetings is more challenging and depends on how complete the records are. Morel wrote in October 1906 that the *Organ* did not include all the meeting notices he had received that month, but he caught up and announced that he would acknowledge every resolution, though he might miss one "here and there."[5] Evidence suggests that half to three-quarters of the meetings appeared in the *Organ*. For example, the Liverpool auxiliary sponsored 21 meetings in 1906 of which Morel recorded half.[6] Also, Morel claimed 400 meetings for the three months ending 31 January 1907, but listed 317 specific meetings.[7] Searches of 73 newspapers in the electronic British Newspaper Archive found only a few dozen meetings Morel missed. Unreported meetings seem to have been less numerous than the ones we know of. Assuming 100–300 average attendance and 1,000–1,500 unrecorded meetings, total meeting attendance from 1903–13 ranged from 400,000 to 1,100,000. Col. Stopford's claim that 7 million people attended a Congo meeting was unwarranted.[8]

Some meetings were huge, with thousands gathering in the largest halls in major cities, such as 1909's Albert Hall demonstration. More numerous were the 76 town's meetings, which had a semi-official character as recording the consensus view of the inhabitants. Town's meetings were a regular part of British civic life, called by the mayor to meet parliamentary requirements for topics such as capital spending or in response to a petition about social or humanitarian issues. Most numerous were smaller meetings organized by local worthies, ministers, private citizens, or organizations, occurring primarily in churches, which often charged no rent, or in small lecture halls, YMCA meeting rooms, schools, clubs, and homes.

Press accounts sometimes identified the prominent men and women who showed support by taking seats on the platform. A typical town's meeting platform would include the mayor and his wife, aldermen and councilors, local MPs, titled individuals, and local clergymen. Beyond the platform, there is little information about the makeup of the audience. Public meetings

---

[4] *Whittaker's Almanac*, 1912; *Hazell's Annual*, 1911.
[5] *Organ*, December 1906, 28.
[6] *Organ*, April 1907, 20.
[7] Morel to Channing, 31 January 1907, F10/15:76.
[8] Stopford memo, 30 July 1908, F4/9:134.

held at churches would have attracted people from the community as well as parishioners. Morel favored town's meetings and large public demonstrations because they reached a broader constituency. Mayors observed that their town's meetings drew people irrespective of religious belief or political affiliation, and one noted that his meeting brought together the middle and working classes.[9] With free admission except for the best seats, there was no barrier to working-class participation.

In some venues working-class men made up the entire audience. The *Organ* reported Congo meetings for 19 Bible Study and Adult School groups. Twenty-six recorded meetings appeared under the sponsorship of Pleasant Sunday Afternoon (PSA) brotherhoods, nonsectarian groups that met in churches after Sunday services for working men skeptical of organized religion but supportive of a generic Christian approach to current issues.[10] Conveniently, F.B. Meyer became President of the newly formed national PSA association in 1907. A few labor organizations sponsored Congo meetings and/or resolutions, among them the Trades Council of West Hartlepool, Derby Trades Council, and National Union of Women Workers.[11] Trade union support fell far short of Morel's original goals, which if successful would have let the CRA claim millions of supporters via the unions.[12]

Those who only attended meetings were not really adherents; they made no sacrifice for the cause. In this age before radio, television, and wide film distribution, public meetings were a form of diversion and recreation for many people.[13]

Organizing or speaking at local meetings, a more active form of support, engaged Committee members from the central CRA and auxiliaries, missionaries, political figures, writers, parish clergy, religious leaders, and Africa hands. Speaker names appear for 930 meetings in Britain, not counting purely local figures. John and Alice Harris, simultaneously CRA activists and former missionaries, appeared most frequently, with John named 406 times and Alice 221. Morel was the next most frequent speaker at 135 meetings. BMS missionary J.R.M. Stephens spoke 117 times, followed by Guinness at 76. Another 18 CBM and BMS missionaries spoke 84 times. The names of 38 other clergy appear as speakers at 76 meetings, but hundreds of pastors spoke at meetings in their own churches or preached on Congo Sundays.

---

[9] Baxxforth (Mayor of Huddersfield) to Morel, 15 April 1907, F4/24.
[10] *Whittaker's Almanac*, 1912; *Daily News Year Book*, 1912.
[11] *Organ*, February 1907, 29; *Organ*, June 1907, 14; *Organ*, December 1906, 22–7.
[12] Morel to Emmott, 10 March 1904, F10/10:464.
[13] Leonore Davidoff and Catherine Hall, *Family Fortunes: Men and Women of the English Middle Class, 1780–1850* (Chicago: University of Chicago Press, 1987), 428.

Executive Committee

The officers and committees of the CRA and its auxiliaries were the movement's core activists. The 45 Executive Committee members during the CRA's existence tended to be Nonconformist, Liberal, university-educated, London-based, middle-aged, and male (Table 4.1). The absence of women was unusual; the APS Committee had included women for many years, and the Anti-Slavery Society opened its Committee to women in 1906.[14]

The CRA leadership was relatively young. In 1905, Morel turned 32 and the Executive Committee's median age was 51. With an age range of 31 to 74, the group could draw on the experience of Brooks (71), Hodgkin (74), and Fox Bourne (68) and the energy of the men in their 30s such as Morel, Samuel, and John Harris. Three-fifths of the Executive Committee were in their 40s and 50s, many approaching the peaks of their careers. This age structure gave the CRA an advantage over the older leadership at its sister humanitarian organizations.[15]

Apart from Morel, Dilke, Fox Bourne, Samuel, and a few others, religious influences were strong among the Executive Committee. Of the men whose religious affiliations were available, just over half were Nonconformists and just under half Anglicans. None were Catholics. Among the 19 Nonconformists, five were Quakers active in overseas humanitarianism. Most of those with identified affiliations were deeply committed to and motivated by their religious beliefs.

Liberals dominated this ostensibly nonpartisan organization. The party was more receptive than the Conservatives to international humanitarian concerns and to the causes espoused by politically active Nonconformists. Local Liberal groups asked for Congo speakers and the party's leadership made independent representations to Grey regarding Congo reform.[16] Of the 33 Executive Committee members with clear political affiliations, 82 percent were Liberals. A handful of Conservatives, a Liberal Unionist, and the Labour Party's Ramsay MacDonald gave the group a multiparty fig leaf.

By occupation, 11 committeemen were clergy, providing a strong but not dominant religious element. Businessmen were the next largest contingent, with three retired bankers, five merchants, and three manufacturers. Five aristocrats were politically active men with government experience, though Aberdeen and Listowel did not attend meetings. Five men were professional writers or editors, including the novelist Sir Gilbert Parker. The others were lawyers, professors, secretaries of philanthropic organizations, professional politicians, and a retired military officer. Guinness, an MD, could be considered clergy though he was not ordained. The committee was largely middle class, mostly on the upper side of that class.

---

[14] BFASS Committee minutes, 6 October 1905, Brit. Emp. s.20 E2/12:1354.
[15] Nworah, *Humanitarian Pressure-Groups*, 658.
[16] Hudson to Morel, 11 October 1906, F9/13.

Table 4.1 CRA Executive Committee members, 1904–13

Name	Age in 1905	Religion	Donor?	Political party	Occupation
William A. Albright	51	Quaker	Yes	Liberal	Manufacturer
Joseph G. Alexander	57	Quaker	Yes	Liberal	Law
Edward N. Bennett	37	Anglican		Liberal	Journalist*
Dermot Bourke, Lord Mayo	54	Anglican	Yes	Cons.	Lord-Political
Henry Richard Fox Bourne	68			Liberal	Humanitarian
Harold Brabner	42				Law
Edward W. Brooks	71	Quaker	Yes	Liberal	Manufacturer
Travers Buxton	41	Presbyterian	Yes	Liberal	Humanitarian
R.J. Campbell	38	Congregationalist	Yes	L-Radical	Clergy
Francis Channing	64				Law, academics
Francis Chavasse	59	Anglican	Yes		Bishop
John Clifford	69	Baptist	Yes	Liberal	Clergy
Robert Collier, Lord Monkswell	60		Yes	Liberal	Lord-Political
Sir Charles Dilke	62			L-Radical	Politician*
C.M. Douglas	40		Yes	L-Radical	Professor*
Alfred Emmott	47	Anglican	Yes	Liberal	Manufacturer*
Francis W. Fox	64	Quaker	Yes	Liberal	Banker
T.L. Gilmour	46		Yes	Liberal	Journalist
Henry N. Gladstone	53	Anglican	Yes	Liberal	Merchant
Harry Guinness	44	Nonconformist	Yes		Missionary Leader
J. Hamilton-Gordon, Lord Aberdeen	58	Presbyterian		Liberal	Lord-Political
William Hare, Lord Listowel	72	Anglican		LU	Lord-Political
John Harris	31	Baptist		Liberal	Clergy

Name	Age in 1905	Religion	Donor?	Political party	Occupation
Thomas Hodgkin	74	Quaker	Yes	Liberal	Banker
Henry Scott Holland	58	Anglican	Yes	Liberal	Clergy
John Holt	64	Nonconformist	Yes	Liberal	Merchant
Silvester Horne	40	Congregationalist		Liberal	Clergy*
Thomas Law	51	Methodist			Clergy
Scott Lidgett	51	Methodist	Yes	L-Radical	Clergy, politician
William Lygon, Lord Beauchamp	33		Yes	Liberal	Lord-Political
Ramsay MacDonald	39	Unitarian		Labour	Labour politician*
F.B. Meyer	58	Baptist	Yes		Clergy
E.D. Morel	32	Anglican	Yes	Liberal	Humanitarian, editor
Sir Gilbert Parker	43	Anglican	Yes	Cons.	Novelist, politician*
Herbert Samuel	35	Jewish	Yes	Liberal	Banker*
John Shakespeare	48	Baptist			Clergy
Harold Spender	41			Liberal	Journalist
Col. J.G.B. Stopford	67		Yes		retired Military
John St. Loe Strachey	45	Anglican	Yes	Cons.	Editor
Francis Swanzy	51	Anglican	Yes		Merchant
Edward Talbot	61	Anglican	Yes		Bishop
Austin Taylor	47	Anglican		Cons.	Shipowner
Charles Trevelyan	35	Anglican		Liberal	Politician
Robert Whyte	49	Presbyterian	Yes		Merchant
L.R. Wilberforce	44	Anglican?			Physics Professor

Notes: * indicates an MP any time 1904–13. L-Radical=Liberals (Radical wing), LU=Liberal Unionist.

The Executive Committee's composition realized Morel's hope that the movement could fuse overseas humanitarianism, the religiously led activism of the Nonconformist conscience, and the philanthropic side of the world of commerce. The CRA claimed with some justification that its top echelon bridged political, sectarian, class, and geographic divisions, albeit in a token sense for some groups and not at all for Catholics.

Donors

The movement could not rely on the Executive Committee alone for funds. More than a third of committeemen contributed no money at all, and five subscribed for just one or two years. Only five Executive Committee members were among the top 30 donors. In total, the Executive Committee provided just over an eighth of all donations. A broader array of donors supplied most of the CRA's funds through onetime donations and subscriptions; a £10 standard membership included the *Organ* and all pamphlets, the £5 membership did not include the *Organ*, and an associate membership of £1 came with no literature.[17]

Initially, fundraising occurred when cash ran short. This fell to Morel, who complained about it constantly. At a January 1905 meeting, he tried to get the Executive Committee to share the burden, but they left it to Morel to broaden the donor pool. He did this through more religiously oriented fundraising; William Cadbury facilitated a four-page appeal to Quakers in *The Friend* that subsequently appeared in other newspapers, and Meyer sponsored another.[18]

In late 1905, Meyer urged Guinness, Morel, and John Harris to aggressively solicit new subscribers after each meeting for an annual commitment.[19] His advice had little impact until the Executive Committee assigned John Harris and the London Auxiliary to build an annual subscriber base in 1907. This brought the CRA its peak earning years in 1908–09. Annual subscriptions provided momentum, ensuring money would come in after the Harrises left the CRA on 31 March 1910, during Morel's 1910–11 trip to West Africa, and in subsequent years.

Of the CRA's total incoming cash flow of £13,320, £11,560 or 87 percent came from direct individual donations (Table 3.1).[20] Morel's claim of 5,000

---

[17] Morel to Newnham, 30 January 1907, F10/15:61.
[18] *The Friend*, 31 March 1905.
[19] Meyer to Morel, 23 November 1905, F8/108:6.
[20] From cumulative audited financial statements plus the London Auxiliary's 1907–08 income, subtracting London's contribution to the central CRA to avoid double-counting. Appendix 1 discusses methodology and caveats.

members was an exaggeration for public consumption.[21] There were 4,330 discrete donations from 2,034 identifiable donors and 155 anonymous givers. Not only were the individual donors vitally important to the ongoing health of the movement, they provide a window onto the demographics of the CRA's supporters.

Leading Donors

A scant 10 percent of the donors gave 76 percent of the money, and the top 25 donors, listed below, accounted for almost half the donations. With the notable exception of Roger Casement, these donors were wealthy people who regularly donated to philanthropic causes.

Table 4.2   The 25 largest donors to the Congo Reform Association

Name	Occupation	Religion	Number of donations	Total donated	Percent of total
William A. Cadbury	Manufacturer	Quaker	13	£1,241	10.7%
William A. Albright	Manufacturer	Quaker	13	£355	3.1%
Joseph Rowntree	Manufacturer	Quaker	6	£285	2.5%
Barrow Cadbury	Manufacturer	Quaker	7	£277	2.4%
Mrs J.P. Thomasson	Mfr.'s widow	Unitarian	5	£260	2.2%
George Cadbury	Manufacturer	Quaker	7	£255	2.2%
Sir William P. Hartley	Manufacturer/Wholesaler	Primitive Methodist	2	£246	2.1%
Thomas Hodgkin	Banker (ret.)	Quaker	5	£210	1.8%
John Holt	Merchant	Nonconf.	5	£205	1.8%
Lord Monkswell	Politician		3	£171	1.5%
Arthur Backhouse	Banker	Quaker	6	£150	1.3%
Sir Thomas Fowell Buxton	Philanthropist	Anglican	6	£140	1.2%
Earl of Lonsdale	Sportsman		3	£125	1.1%
Hebert Marnham	Stockbroker	Baptist	2	£125	1.1%
Miss Priscilla Peckover	Peace Activist	Quaker	7	£117	1.0%
Ludwig Deuss (German)	Merchant		5	£116	1.0%
George Freeland Barbour	Writer, Mfr. heir	Pres.	5	£116	1.0%
Mrs E.B. Backhouse	Banker widow	Quaker	6	£125	1.0%

---

[21] Edward Gaston, ed., *British Supplement to the New Encyclopedia of Social Reform* (London: Funk and Wagnall's, 1908), xvi, http://books.google.com/books?id=7DtAAAAAYAAJ&pg=PR16.

Earl Beauchamp	Politician		3	£115	1.0%
Edward Backhouse Mounsey	Banker	Quaker	6	£110	1.0%
Mrs C.R. Barbour	?	Pres.	6	£100	0.9%
Roger Casement (anon.)	Consul		1	£100	0.9%
J.R. Rayner	?		1	£100	0.9%
Sir Robert Laidlaw, M.P.	Retail	Methodist Episcopal	4	£95	0.8%
Lord Peckover	Banker (ret.)	Quaker	4	£90	0.8%
				£5,218	45.1%

Quakers (£3,205) and manufacturers (£2,918) predominated among the top 25. Quaker cocoa manufacturer William Cadbury's £1,241 was almost 10 percent of the CRA's total funds. His contribution looms even larger considering his personal subsidies to Morel, totaling at least £2,800 from 1905–12, worth over £250,000 in 2013 currency. The belief that Cadbury stopped giving the CRA money in favor of subsidies to Morel is incorrect; he donated at least once a year until 1913.[22] William's cousin Barrow and his uncle George joined him in the top tier, ranking fourth and sixth, respectively. Their Quaker competitor, Joseph Rowntree, was the third most generous. These CRA contributions were only a small fraction of what the Cadburys and Rowntrees spent on philanthropic causes, religious activities, the peace movement, and social activism. For example, George and Richard Cadbury were the main financial backers of the Free Church Council movement, contributing £1,200 annually.[23]

William Cadbury's generosity to Morel and the CRA has raised questions about his motives. Cadbury Brothers bought its cocoa from the Portuguese colonies of São Tomé and Príncipe for a decade after learning that the plantation workers were essentially enslaved. William Cadbury spent years gathering information and working with the Portuguese government to remedy the situation at a pace which drew criticism from Fox Bourne and others. Cadbury's desire to remain in the background of the Congo reform movement, which he explicitly tied to the cocoa controversy, and Morel's public belittling of the cocoa slavery issue raised suspicions that Cadbury used Congo reform and Morel to deflect attention from his own dubious ethical situation.[24] Morel failed

---

[22] Grant, *Civilised Savagery*, 75, 189, n. 145, based on the London Auxiliary's receipts, proving Morel was right to argue that having two financial centers confused people.

[23] Bebbington, *Nonconformist Conscience*, 61–72.

[24] Cadbury to Morel, 6 December 1905, F8/12:15; Cadbury to Beauchamp, 12 December 1905, F8/12:16; Grant, *Civilised Savagery*, 124–8.

to observe that he had a conflict of interest, writing Cadbury privately that a boycott was inevitable but defending his patron publicly, due to his Congo focus, his personal affection for Cadbury, and his financial dependence on him.[25] Lowell Satre concludes that Cadbury was well meaning but cautious, slow to act, and too willing to accept the Foreign Office's advice and Portuguese assurances. After traveling to the islands himself, he decided to organize a boycott, not much consolation to the Africans abducted while he had delayed.[26] Cadbury's support of Morel and the CRA seems to have been sincere and not a ruse to deflect attention, though the Congo agitation had that effect.

The second largest CRA donor was William A. Albright, a partner in the Birmingham chemical manufacturing firm of Albright and Wilson. A Quaker, Albright had been active on the Anti-Slavery Society's Committee since 1898. Unlike the chocolate manufacturers, who remained in the background, Albright joined the CRA Executive Committee.

At fifth place was the leading female donor, philanthropist Katherine Thomasson, niece of the nineteenth-century Quaker reformer John Bright. Her late husband, John P. Thomasson, had made his fortune spinning cotton in Bolton and served as an MP. Before his death in 1904, he was the APS's largest donor and supported women's suffrage, labour rights, and land reform. His fortune, one of Britain's largest, was valued at £1,159,000 at his death, or over £100,000,000 in 2013 money.[27] Although John and Katherine became Unitarians, their patterns of philanthropy had much in common with the Quaker manufacturing families.

Sir William Pickles Hartley, a Methodist jam manufacturer and wholesale grocer, had pledged a third of his income to philanthropy. His CRA donations were a tiny portion of the nearly £300,000 he gave away before he died in 1922. He financed Morel's most popular book, *Red Rubber*.

Thomas Hodgkin, a Quaker historian and retired banker, was an active member of both the APS and the Anti-Slavery Society. His uncle and namesake had discovered Hodgkin's lymphoma and cofounded the APS.

Two non-Quakers complete the top ten. John Holt was not noted for philanthropy despite his passionate attachment to human rights for Africans; the Congo reform movement was his major philanthropic commitment, through his donations and even larger subsidies for Morel. Holt stopped funding the CRA in 1907 while still subsidizing Morel. Neither Holt's nor Cadbury's subsidies to

---

[25] Lowell Satre, *Chocolate on Trial: Slavery, Politics, and the Ethics of Business* (Athens: Ohio University Press, 2005), 114–16; Grant, *Civilised Savagery*, 134.

[26] Satre, *Chocolate on Trial*, 132–47.

[27] William D. Rubenstein, "British Millionaires, 1809–1949," *Historical Research* 47, no. 116 (November 1974): 212.

Morel appeared anywhere in the CRA's records or publications, making Morel vulnerable to suspicions of secret funding from conniving commercial interests.

Lord Monkswell, CRA President (1906–09), was the tenth largest donor. Though not a Quaker himself, Monkswell was the scion of a long line of Quakers. His CRA work awakened his humanitarian spirit, leading him to become Chairman of the amalgamated British and Foreign Anti-Slavery and Aborigines' Protection Society in 1909.

Among the next 15 donors, three were notable exceptions to the dominant theme of wealthy English Nonconformist philanthropists. Roger Casement, an Irishman of no independent means, donated the CRA's first £100. Ludwig Deuss, a Hamburg merchant married to an African, donated £100 during one of the CRA's many hours of need, plus smaller sums later. The Earl of Lonsdale, Hugh Cecil Lowther, was the most unusual individual large donor of all. Not known for philanthropy, he was a *bon vivant* and a sportsman famous for a failed attempt to reach the North Pole. Donating £125 made only a small dent in his £80,000 annual allowance, but as an aristocrat he was notable for having donated at all.[28] A mere 15 aristocrats donated in their own names to the CRA, and only Monkswell gave more.

Women in the CRA

The CRA began with an almost exclusively male authority structure; a few women played key roles in the background. In the CRA's initial prospectus, only four women appeared among the 62 worthies who endorsed the new organization.[29] Over time women expanded their involvement in leadership while becoming a more significant presence among donors and meeting attendees.

Analyzing donors by sex demonstrates these patterns. Only three women appeared in the top 25 donors, but women made up 30 percent of all identified donors and gave 18 percent of funds. The female proportion of individual gifts and of their value rose over time, as shown in Table 4.3 below.

Women seldom appeared as donors in the CRA's first two years. Grant credits the involvement of missionaries, particularly the Harrises, for the growing number of women thereafter, because missionaries tapped into female religious conviction unreachable by Morel. The Harrises' London Auxiliary achieved a significantly higher female participation, a credit to their methods and greater openness to women. Alice Harris's lectures had special resonance for women. The CRA, despite its increasing appeal to women, was more masculine in its donor base than its sister organizations; 41 percent of the amalgamated

---

[28] Donald Sutherland, *The Yellow Earl* (New York: Coward-McCann, 1965), 107.
[29] CRA March 1904 Prospectus, F4/5, 281.

Table 4.3   CRA donations by women

	Number of gifts	Value of gifts
1904–05	14%	10%
1906–Sep. 1907	19%	15%
Central CRA Sep. 1907–Oct. 1908	22%	21%
London Aux. April 1907–Oct. 1908	34%	29%
Oct. 1908–March 1910	32%	19%
April 1910–June 1913	34%	21%
Overall	30%	18%

Notes: Excludes anonymous donors and mixed gender groups (brother/sister, husband/wife).

Anti-Slavery and Aborigines' Protection Society's donors in 1909 were women, accounting for 27 percent of donations.[30]

Its leadership was more male than its donors. At the auxiliaries, only three women appeared among 67 named officers: Morel's sister-in-law Winifred Richardson, Secretary, Plymouth Auxiliary; Gertie Emmott, President, Women's Auxiliary; and Alice Harris, Joint Secretary (with John), London Auxiliary, and Secretary, Women's Auxiliary. Outside the Women's Auxiliary, there were only 20 women among 247 committee members at ten auxiliaries for which records were available.[31] In several auxiliaries the Committees included no women. Although men dominated the public sphere, this was particularly low female representation, resulting from the CRA's strength in arenas that were almost exclusively male: Parliament, church leadership, missionary society leadership, and commerce.[32] The CRA had little connection to areas where women more often had formal leadership roles, such as school boards, poor law boards, compassionate charities, and women's suffrage.

The CRA's rhetoric of legal rights and obligations reflected and reproduced the movement's masculinity; the campaign directed emotional appeals to women, emphasizing the harm done to women and children. In his Plan of Campaign, Morel included a women's appeal along these lines, leading to a 1904 pamphlet, "The Treatment of Women and Children in the Congo State," written for Gertie Emmott to distribute to Women's Liberal Federations and later reproduced in America. However, in mixed meetings, Congo reform speakers brought in all the tropes at their disposal to reach every listener.

---

[30] *1909 Annual Report of the British and Foreign Anti-Slavery and Aborigines Protection Society*, 12–17.

[31] F10/18:2–10; Leeds, *Organ*, 1910; London, *The Rising Tide*, Spring 1907, 2.

[32] F.M.L. Thompson, *The Rise of Respectable Society: A Social History of Victorian Britain, 1830–1900* (Cambridge, MA: Harvard University Press, 1988), 252–3.

The CRA could be condescending to women. Casement suggested that women's energies could best be deployed by holding bazaars, because "Women love bazaars." Emmott discouraged a women's committee.[33] At a meeting in Bristol, when a Mrs Swann asked if the movement was for men only—a telling question in itself—Morel said, "No good work had ever been done without the assistance of women." Not only did the CRA welcome their aid, but "ladies were helping them in other cities."[34] Morel saw the Association as a male organization usefully assisted by women.

Masculine hegemony did not preclude women's influence. Because men generated, dominated, and recorded most of the CRA's story, examining the few women who played important but often overlooked roles shows how they functioned in a male-led movement and public sphere.

The spirit of the movement derived from Mary Kingsley, Morel's mentor, Holt's comrade-in-arms, Alice Stopford Green's friend, and Casement's acquaintance.[35] Morel and Holt invoked her name for years, codifying her as a most remarkable woman. Simultaneously, she seemed to transcend gender for her contemporaries, shown by colonial governor Matthew Nathan's complimenting her as having a man's fearlessness and sense of justice.[36]

Kingsley's friend Alice Stopford Green played a considerable behind-the-scenes role in the reform movement, mostly assisting and advising Morel. She introduced him to editors, politicians, colonial officials, and others. She labored on his behalf, for instance by trying to find a buyer for the *West African Mail* in the dark days of December 1904 and collecting funds for his 1911 testimonial.[37] She counseled him on his writing, movement strategy, and his relationships with other reformers and powerful people, always in terms of unwavering support. For her, Morel was the movement's keystone, writing, "I am a great believer in 'one-man' efforts. It is these that have ... succeeded."[38] Should his energy flag or his attention wander, the cause would be lost. At the height of the campaign she expressed her attitude more fully, feeding his ego to keep him fighting:

> Everyone to whom I have spoken in these years has argued that your ability had given the most conspicuous proof in our generation of what might be done by journalistic enterprise in honest and able hands. There has been nothing at all corresponding to it. *Every* hand against you and *nothing* with you but your

---

[33] Plan of Campaign, 31 March 1904, F4/4:141–58. Casement and Emmott comments, 1904, F4/5:165–205.
[34] *Organ*, May 1907, 36.
[35] Birkett, *Kingsley*, 102, plate 3.
[36] Matthew Nathan, 3 July 1907, *Journal of the Royal African Society* 7, no. 25 (October 1907): 28–31.
[37] Casement to Morel, 15 December 1904, F8/17:111.
[38] Green to Morel, 21 May 1902, F8/71:49.

energy and ability ... The fight with the Devil is not ended yet in this world ... The way is narrow and strait and the company is small ... And we think that God is there—and true friends—and loyal companionship.[39]

She rallied him when he felt discouraged and cheered his victories. Until his 1908 move to London, he stayed at her house when he came to the city. She was a friend in whom he could confide his worries and despair, knowing she would not break his trust.[40]

Despite her strong Irish connections, she was unable to rally the Irish Home Rule MPs to the Congo cause. Although their leader, John Redmond, was sympathetic when she and Casement approached him in 1904–05, some MPs were hostile because they prioritized Irish issues, saw the reformers as anti-Catholic, and, Morel suspected, accepted payments from Leopold.[41] By 1906 they had convinced the Irish Parliamentary Party to oppose Congo reform. Green deplored their refusal to advocate for both Ireland and the Congo.

In her letters to Morel, she praised people he thought well of and attacked people he complained about. When Morel turned against someone, she reinforced his move with vituperation. When Morel was working with Grey, she endorsed him: "I agree with you in trusting Sir Edward Grey. He may be cautious and correct but ... you might reckon there on scrupulous honor," and "He is really a humane man and I think truly hates injustice and cruelty."[42] But when Morel attacked Grey in June 1909, she called Grey a hypocrite and later asserted, "I do not think he is an honest man."[43] Whether Green saw the matter exactly as Morel did or was unwilling to disagree, she had the effect of reinforcing Morel against those allies, such as the Emmotts, who felt he had made a serious mistake.

She similarly joined Morel in his growing irritation toward John Harris, unlike Holt and Cadbury, who remained on good terms with Harris, Cadbury only for a while. "Little Harris," she wrote, was "ordinary," guilty of "treachery," and ruined by his religious training. Like other clergymen, he should have had to "serve in a shop where stealing was not allowed." She advised Tyrell at the Foreign Office not to "touch Harris nor any of his doings."[44] Her propensity to fan the flames of Morel's anger rather than to encourage him to seek solutions

---

[39] Green to Morel, 9 May 1907, F8/72:180.
[40] Green to Morel, 8 October 1901; F8/71:27; Green to Morel, late 1902, F8/71:65.
[41] Emmott to Morel, 11 April and 6 May 1904, F8/53:52, 61; Green to Morel, 8 August 1904, 2 and 8 February 1905, 24 May 1906, F8/72:136,142, 143, 169; MacDonald to Morel, 25 May 1906, F8/106:9.
[42] Green to Morel, 7 and 10 January 1907, F8/72:176, 177.
[43] Green to Morel, 20 June 1909 and 11 March 1910, F8/72:218, 244.
[44] Green to Morel, 5 January and 26 May 1910, F8/72:232, 251.

bore some responsibility for Morel's intransigence and the unnecessary drama in the CRA.

Green lived a number of gender contradictions. She assisted the movement using the tools of an actively political woman, but one who, like Kingsley, did not support women's suffrage. In keeping with middle-class practice, she had helped John Richard Green with his *magnum opus* on British history and completed the last volume after his death. With widowhood came the freedom to work under her own name. She achieved fame as a popular historian with her history of Ireland, a rarity in an androcentric profession.[45] She had long been involved in Liberal circles in London. Despite her public standing as a historian and her political connections, she took only modest public roles in the Congo campaign.

Like Green, Gertie Emmott was a political woman. She supported her husband's political career, and, after involvement in charity, undertook her own political life, beginning with her election to the Oldham Board of Guardians in 1898.[46] Once her husband left the CRA, she became his intermediary, but with her own style and agency. She gave Morel the benefit of her knowledge of parliamentary politics and philanthropy in advice less tainted than Green's by uncritical loyalty. Like Katherine Thomasson and CRA London Auxiliary committeewoman Jane Cobden Unwin, Emmott was a leader in the women's suffrage movement. Her concern for the Congo led her to become the President of the CRA Women's Auxiliary.

Both Green and Emmott carved out places of influence for themselves in the male-dominated world of politics, government, and Congo reform. Although insiders in many ways, as women they were also outsiders, trying to influence a power structure that excluded them from most formal roles at this time.

Violet Simpson, another active CRA woman, had spent the 1890s as Andrew Lang's historical research assistant, and then became a writer of historical novels, short stories, and articles about life in bygone days. In 1904–07, she was the Assistant Honorary Secretary of the CRA in London, taking a flat there at her own expense for this purpose. She worked from the *West African Mail*'s London office, where Roger Casement also worked in 1905. When the Harrises came to London in 1906, Simpson joined them at the Association's new offices on Queen Victoria Street.

According to Morel, Casement, and John Harris, Simpson was demanding, difficult, and ineffective, unable to inspire donors or arrange events. Morel avoided addressing these issues in writing, perhaps from misplaced chivalry. While unhappy to be ordered about by "General Simpson," Casement noted that

---

[45] Sandra Holton, "Gender Difference, National Identity and Professing History: The Case of Alice Stopford Green," *History Workshop Journal*, no. 53 (spring 2002): 118.

[46] Cheryl Law, *Women, a Modern Political Dictionary* (London: I.B. Tauris, 2000), 58. http://books.google.com/books?id=iTnXdlutlVsC&pg=PA5.

"she spreads the light like any good firebrand,"[47] suggesting she could advocate for the cause. John Harris had fewer compliments to spare. His letters brim with complaints that, despite her constant letter-writing, she accomplished nothing.[48] Eventually, she quit in exasperation. It is difficult to know the origins of these problems, but Simpson's own attitude and actions contributed. She wrote two novels while at the CRA London office; perhaps the diligent work Casement and Harris observed was unrelated to Congo reform. The effect of gender dynamics is harder to discern. An unmarried woman, just a year younger than Morel and devoted to the Association, Simpson viewed herself as a leading reformer. The men did not share this view; to them she was simultaneously office staff and a well-connected professional oddly unable to leverage her network.

With the possible exception of Simpson, the CRA was fortunate in the competence of the comparatively few women who labored for the cause, including the London office staff, particularly the lead clerk, Edith G. Harrington. Morel came to rely on her judgment and talent. Once he sent her to spy out a shady investment group that later misused his name on promotional material to form a concession company in the French Congo.[49] During Morel's 1910–11 Nigeria trip, Harrington ran the London office. She referred policy questions to Mary Morel and others, but otherwise ensured that ordinary business continued. She wrote to Dilke regarding the second 1910 election, asking him about revising the Questions for Candidates pamphlet and offering to convene the Parliamentary Committee. He addressed his reply to "Dear Sir," reflecting his Victorian assumption that office staff showing initiative and competence would be male unless otherwise identified.[50] When it came time to wind down the CRA, Morel wrote her a recommendation for distribution through his friends, the only such note for a woman in the files and the most widely circulated reference. He praised her shorthand, typing, and charming personality, but did not mention her good judgment or how she handled things in his absence.[51] Perhaps Morel wrote in terms that would appeal to male employers without making her seem threatening, but it is possible that he undervalued her contribution.

He did not undervalue Mary Richardson Morel, his wife. Mary convinced him to start the CRA, despite the disruption this would entail for their family. He sometimes engaged a typist when he tried to manage his workload by working at home Thursday through Sunday, but often Mary supplied this assistance in addition to her ordinary work of supervising the household staff and raising the

---

[47] Casement to Morel, 1 November 1905, F8/20:271.
[48] Harris to Morel, 9 November 1905, F8/75:207.
[49] Morel to Harrington, 14 July 1910, F8/34:25.
[50] Harrington to Dilke, 15 November 1910, and Dilke to "E.G. Harrington, Esq.," 16 November 1910, F8/44:399–400.
[51] Morel to Doyle, 6 September 1912, F8/50:130.

children.[52] When Morel was in Africa, Harrington, Harris, and others referred policy questions to her. Her contributions were almost completely hidden, though not from those close to Morel, such as Casement and Cadbury. After Morel's death, she did not follow Green in creating a career and public identity for herself. Mary Morel was a vital support to a public man and his work but not an independent actor on the public stage.

On the surface, Alice Harris presents a contrast to Mary Morel. Her photographs of the human toll of Leopold's regime made her name known even before she spoke at hundreds of meetings in Britain, America, France, and Switzerland. Determined to continue a shared career with her husband, they became Joint Secretaries of the London Auxiliary in 1906–08, CRA Joint Organising and Traveling Secretaries in 1908–10, and Joint Organising Secretaries of the Anti-Slavery and Aborigines' Protection Society after that. Yet similarities with Mary Morel show how gender operated to maintain men as their partnerships' primary public faces.

Alice Seeley Harris, a silk-works manager's daughter, came from a middle-class family related to imperial historian John Seeley. After time at King's College London, she entered the Civil Service at age 20, working for the Accountant General in the London General Post Office. She volunteered with local missions through F.B. Meyer's Regent's Park Church and Christ Church. Meyer inspired her to become a missionary in Africa, though she hesitated because of her parents' objections.[53] She met John Harris, another Meyer protégé, when she needed a substitute teacher for her Sunday afternoon class. She was 25, he 21 and training to be a missionary with the Guinnesses. Shortly thereafter, she left the Civil Service to learn nursing at the Guinness-run Doric Lodge training center for women. In January 1897, the Congo Council refused her application to go to Africa because there were too many women in the field already.[54] Showing persistence, she applied again in April, and the Council deemed her well suited but needing language skills.[55] In November 1897, they agreed to send her in the spring, pleased by her "stable character" and Meyer's warm recommendation.[56] In January 1898, the Council expressed consternation that she had become engaged to John Harris without permission. Their policy forbade marriages until both parties had lived in the Congo for a year to reduce the risk of losing two missionaries if either found it physically or mentally unsuitable.

---

[52] F10/11:227, 28 May 1904.

[53] Sybil Oldfield, "Harris, Alice," in *Woman Humanitarians: A Biographical Dictionary of British Women Active between 1900–1950* (London: Continuum, 2001), 94–7; Alice Harris's autobiography, Brit. Emp.; Rachel Whitehead, "The Aborigines Protection Society and the Safeguarding of African Interests in Rhodesia," (PhD diss., Oxford University, 1975).

[54] Congo Council, 28 January 1897, Reel 11, Vol. 2, 34.

[55] Congo Council, 29 April 1897, Reel 11, Vol. 2, 56.

[56] Congo Council, 25 November 1897.

Figure 4.1 Alice Seeley Harris
Source: Flyer by The Lecture Agency.

The Council approved their engagement with the proviso that they marry in the Congo.[57] Due to changes in the traveling party, the Council revised its decision on 22 April, and let them marry before sailing, on 6 May; Guinness and Meyer attended.[58] The Council resolved to never again allow such a marriage.[59] If the Harrises' defiance of the policy indicated their determination, their success nonetheless required Meyer's support.

Alice and John's devotion to their work trumped other considerations, including child-rearing. Their first child was born at the Baringa mission. Six weeks after the birth of their second while on furlough, they left both children in the RBMU children's home to return to the Congo. Two more children came, and they left all four in the care of others for long periods.

Like several other RBMU missionaries, Alice Harris had brought a camera to the mission to document the work, the local environment, and how people lived. Her photographs of the regime's effects made her famous; they became a key reform campaign feature in the press, in books, in exhibitions, and most often in magic lantern lectures.

The Harrises were not the first missionaries to criticize the regime, but they would be the most effective. They were not involved in the campaign against the Congo regime before 1904, and had no connection with Casement's report.[60] In 1904, John Harris sent lengthy letters to the Congo and Abir officials about the treatment of the local people. Alice may have penned the letters, which were in French. John met with May French Sheldon on her investigatory journey later that year and tried to draw her attention to atrocities. By testifying before Leopold's Commission of Inquiry in late 1904, John became famous. Alice transcribed his testimony, which Morel printed in the *West African Mail* along with John Weeks's.[61] Leopold never released the Commission's proceedings, so these letters gave the only glimpse into the real conditions described to the Commission and brought the Harrises from obscurity to prominence.

As they prepared for a furlough in 1905, John Harris suggested a British and American speaking tour to Morel, featuring Alice's photographs. He urged Morel to deploy Alice: "Mrs Harris is an intelligent woman, a most thoughtful and able speaker—cannot you use her to plead the cause of the women and children on the Congo—some people that withstand the pleadings of men are powerless before a lady."[62] However, when Casement, Cadbury, Morel, and

---

[57] Congo Council, 28 October 1897 and 27 January 1898, Reel 11, Vol. 2, 80.
[58] *Regions Beyond*, June 1898, 269. Other chronologies in recent literature are not supported by evidence. John Peffer, "Snap of the Whip/Crossroads of Shame," *Visual Anthropology Review*, Vol. 24, Issue 1 (Spring 2008) 60, 64; Grant, *Civilised Savagery*, 31, 40.
[59] Congo Council, June 1898.
[60] Oldfield, "Harris," 94; Ó Síocháin and O'Sullivan, *Eyes of Another Race*, 263–4.
[61] *WAM Congo Supplement*, July 1905.
[62] Harris to Morel, 8 May 1905, F8/75:169.

Meyer discussed the upcoming lectures, they ignored this offer. Her standing changed with the American tour. John Harris wrote of "the remarkable reception given to Mrs Harris's addresses wherever she goes, so much so that we have been asked to separate ... Apparently there is something distinctly pathetic in a woman appealing for defenceless Africans" as he had predicted.[63]

When they returned to Britain in 1906 to run the newly formed London Auxiliary, Alice lectured, giving over 200 talks in the next four years, some with John but most on her own, including in Switzerland and Paris. Women such as Kingsley, Shaw, and French Sheldon had been on the lecture circuit for some time, as had women speaking for women's causes such as suffrage and social purity campaigns, so the presence of a woman was not unusual. By 1912, she had reached the pinnacle of public speaking; her name appeared on Christy's Lecture Service advertisements alongside celebrities such as Winston Churchill, Ernest Shackleton, and Roald Amundsen.[64]

While there is ample testimony to her speaking ability, understanding her capabilities as an officer of a humanitarian organization requires attention to silences. Few letters to or from her survive in the CRA and Anti-Slavery Society archives. The reformers seldom mentioned her except as a speaker. Unlike Violet Simpson or her husband, she was not the subject of complaint. Praise for the London Auxiliary or the Organising Secretaries' work mentions John Harris or "Mr and Mrs Harris" but not Alice alone. With John's more extensive lecturing and given her administrative experience with the GPO, she must have played an important role in the office. She had more education, connections, and general cultural capital than her husband, a plumber's son, illustrated by her correspondence from the Congo with Lord Fitzmaurice, her father's friend.[65]

While the evidence suggests a determined personality of significant ability, the archives' silence implies a modest personal presentation. Though Alice was no stranger to the public, John was their partnership's public face. While he hobnobbed with Holts and Cadburys and developed connections to prominent public men such as Lord Cromer, she stayed in the background. When he committed some real, trivial, or imagined error at the CRA, he alone bore Morel's wrath, though one imagines that his wife participated in, knew about, or possibly opposed his actions. Mary Morel was technically a housewife and Alice Harris always had a paid position, but they both devoted themselves to their husbands' success. Alice may have undertaken their shared career aware of his weaknesses as well as his strengths. She could work at his side and thereby lend him the benefit of her abilities while giving him all the credit. If this was the case, they sailed their partnership safely through assumptions about gender roles and

---

[63] Harris to Buxton via J.G. Alexander, 31 January 1906, Brit. Emp. s.18, C82/77a.
[64] Brit. Emp. s.19 D4/5.
[65] Brit. Emp. s.353.

the proper structure of a marriage. Alice Harris could have more conventionally supported her husband's work without public credit, as Alice Stopford Green and Mary Morel did. Certainly the near-silence in the archives and her husband's far more visible presence in the corridors of power suggest a traditional public subordination. Her challenge to the conventions of the time manifested itself in her appearance as "Joint Secretary" with her husband. More than the shared career, it was the public acknowledgment of it on official letterhead as well as her listing for Christy's speakers' bureau that recognized her as a married woman in a public career.

As noted above, women were an audience valued for their potential as supporters of Congo resolutions, as donors to the cause, and as part of grassroots organizing. The organization perceived itself and its chief actors pursuing a masculine battle for justice and rights. Women played important roles, constrained by their own expectations and by a culture that undervalued their contributions. As Davidoff and Hall have written about a somewhat earlier period, "Some divisions between men and women were enshrined in bricks and mortar, some in custom and practice, and others in association rules and regulations, but none were so set as not to be open to contestation and negotiation."[66] While formal rules held women back less in Edwardian Britain, the force of custom and practice retained much of its old power.

Religious Affiliation

In Edwardian Britain, people with formal religious affiliation were in the minority. The almanacs reported that about eight-and-a-half million people were members or communicants of religious denominations in Great Britain in 1911, less than a third of the adult (16 and over) population. But this did not imply an atheist majority. The nineteenth century's long debate between rationalism and religion left a broad swath of the population not tied to a church but still identifying as Christian. With little connection to specific doctrines or rituals they appeared to take their religion without much theology.[67] There were areas of resurgence. A revival of evangelical enthusiasm found expression in robust support for overseas missions, humanitarianism, and political activism. These were the people Guinness was thinking of when he argued that the CRA's real supporters would be "pronounced Christian men and women."[68]

Guinness was correct; much of the CRA's financial wherewithal came from men and women with a strongly felt religious affiliation. The donor database

---

[66] Davidoff and Hall, *Family Fortunes*, 429.
[67] Helen Merrell Lynd, *England in the Eighteen-Eighties* (London: Oxford University Press, 1945), 340–45.
[68] Guinness to Morel, 2 February 1904, F4/3:87.

includes religious affiliation for over a fifth of the named individual donors with reasonable certainty (465 of 2,034). These people provided two-thirds of all individual donations, or £7,328. The following table compares each religion's proportions in British society in 1911 with the religiously identified donors:

Table 4.4 Religious affiliation

Identified Religion	UK Overall	Great Britain only	CRA donors by population	CRA donors by donation
Presbyterians	13.6%	15.3%	6.7%	8.7%
Methodists	6.7%	9.8%	6.7%	7.6%
Congregationalists	3.8%	5.8%	7.1%	2.1%
Baptists	3.3%	4.9%	14.0%	5.2%
Welsh Calvinist Methodist	1.4%	2.2%	0.0%	0.0%
Unitarians	0.3%	0.3%	2.6%	4.1%
Society of Friends (Quakers)	0.2%	0.2%	27.3%	55.7%
Unspecified Nonconformists	–	–	3.7%	3.6%
All Nonconformists	29.3%	38.4%	68.1%	87.0%
Roman Catholics	43.5%	27.7%	0.9%	0.2%
Anglicans	24.7%	30.4%	29.5%	12.4%
Jews	1.8%	2.7%	1.3%	0.4%
Other	0.7%	0.8%	0.2%	0.0%
	100.0%	100.0%	100.0%	100.0%
N =	12.8 Million	8.5 Million	465	£7,328

Sources: Robert Currie, Alan D Gilbert, and Lee Horsley, *Churches and Churchgoers: Patterns of Church Growth in the British Isles Since 1700* (Oxford: Clarendon Press, 1977); *Whitaker's Almanack* (London, 1912). Unitarian estimates by Alan Ruston and Andrew Hill via email from Rev. Dr David Steers.

Among this population, the Quakers were the largest group by financial contribution (£4,080 or 56 percent), and retained that place even subtracting the 25 largest donors. However, we cannot conclude that Quakers as a group flocked to support the CRA. The 127 Quaker donors were a tiny minority of the 20,000 British Quakers; others focused on the peace movement and social issues.

Baptists and Congregationalists were the next most common donors, giving at a much lower average level. Methodists and Presbyterians occupied middle ranks, with a few Unitarians giving at above-average levels. Altogether,

Nonconformists made up over two-thirds of all donors and nearly seven-eighths of the contributions, with Anglicans accounting for almost all the rest—like the Baptists, giving at a lower average value.

Roman Catholics were almost completely absent. Even without Ireland, Catholics accounted for 27 percent of the religiously affiliated population of Great Britain, but barely any of the CRA's financial supporters. Only five were identifiable: the Irish peer Lord ffrench, Lord Clifford of Chudleigh, Sir Edward Russell (proprietor of the *Liverpool Daily Post*), Alex Johnston (Sir Harry Johnston's brother), and a Miss Agnes Gibbs who wrote to *The Tablet* to encourage Catholics to consider reform. Others who helped without contributing money were the Duke of Norfolk (the leading Catholic peer in Britain), who lent his name rather late in the campaign, and a handful of priests such as Monsignor McKenna, who helped to set up Derby's town's meeting.[69] Their support highlights how seriously the CRA failed to attract Catholics.

Despite the low rate of religious affiliation in Great Britain, most donations were provided by religiously affiliated people. This was also true of the older overseas humanitarian groups. By 1905, Morel had come to understand what Guinness meant. After the March 1905 financial appeal to the Quakers, he increasingly used religious figures such as Meyer and Anglican hierarchs to bolster his requests for money. When John Harris became active in fundraising, he could use his status as a reverend as well as his eyewitness accounts to good effect.

Commercial Interests and Other Occupations

Congo apologists often claimed that Liverpool merchant interests funded and directed the reformers. Morel's hidden subsidies from Holt gave this lie a grain of truth. But was the CRA initially dependent on British merchants with interests in Africa?[70] A historian of John Holt's enterprises calls him the only such merchant to support the CRA.[71] As it turns out, eight British merchants with African interests accounted for £190 of the £880 the CRA collected in its first year, and Holt gave £170 of that, far outstripping Irvine, Swanzy, and the others. Eight African merchants of other countries gave £29 in the first year, led by Ludwig Deuss at £10. Two merchants in the Calcutta trade also contributed. The remainder of the first year's funds came from an assortment of bankers, manufacturers, humanitarians, lawyers, aristocrats, religious figures, and others. Morel's minimal success at collecting donations from British merchants in 1904

---

[69] F10/14:661, 699.
[70] Grant, *Civilised Savagery*, 64.
[71] Cherry Joan Gertzel, "John Holt: A British Merchant in West Africa in the Era of Imperialism" (PhD thesis, Nuffield College, Oxford, 1959), 604.

was a high-water mark. The proportion given by merchants fell year after year. Even including wholesalers and merchants who did not trade with Africa, under £800 of the CRA's funds in 1904–13 came from merchants. This is 10 percent of the donations from identifiable occupational groups as shown Table 4.5.

Table 4.5   Occupational breakdown of donations

Occupation	Donations		Individuals	
Manufacturers	£4,004	52%	64	15%
Merchants	£803	10%	47	10%
Bankers	£636	8%	12	3%
Clergy	£480	6%	200	See text
Philanthropists/Activists	£400	5%	8	2%
Gov't Officials	£284	4%	8	2%
Aristocracy—rentiers	£224	3%	10	2%
Writers	£214	3%	20	5%
Politicians	£206	3%	3	1%
Stockbroker	£125	2%	1	0%
Retail Trade	£100	1%	4	1%
Lawyers & Judges	£95	1%	15	3%
MDs	£65	1%	27	6%
Other	£179	2%	15	3%
All identified occupations	£7,815	100%	434	

The clergy (reverends, bishops, and so on) are almost half of the donors in Table 4.5, but this is because they are so readily identifiable by their honorifics and titles, unlike other occupations. It is more accurate to say that clergymen were 10 percent of all individual donors.

Manufacturers provided by far the largest financial contribution. They tended to have strong religious convictions. A dozen active and retired bankers contributed almost as much as the merchants. The Quakers figured disproportionately among bankers and manufacturers, though not at all among merchants.

The movement's attraction for clergy and philanthropists is not surprising, but the amount contributed by government officials (mostly retired) reminds us that government service employed many wealthy and/or noble employees in the Edwardian age. The aristocracy made up a much smaller proportion than Morel had hoped in the heady early days. Medicine and law were noteworthy for stinginess; they constituted 10 percent of the identifiable donors but gave only 2 percent of the donations.

The issues at stake drew writers. Some contributed non-financially. H. Rider Haggard let his name appear as a "supporter" and Stacpoole wrote *The Pools of Silence*. The adventure novelist Cutcliffe Hyne, who had been to the Congo and written a novel critical of its conditions in his popular Captain Kettle series, *A Master of Fortune*, lectured for the CRA at Bradford and wrote for the *WAM*.[72] The 1906 boys' adventure book *Samba* by Herbert Strang (the pseudonym of George Herbert Ely and Charles James L'Estrange) brought the Congo problems to a younger audience. Mark Twain was more generous; he let the CRA publish his satirical *King Leopold's Soliloquy* and keep the proceeds. Arthur Conan Doyle did all these things: lent his name, wrote *Crime of the Congo* for the movement's benefit, spoke at seven meetings or more, and gave money, too, though only about £10. Violet Simpson donated more than that, and Canadian novelist Sir Gilbert Parker even more, though neither author's books matched the sales of Sherlock Holmes. The most generous author was George Freeland Barbour, whose fortune came not from his religious writings, but from a cotton textile inheritance. The adventure novelist Ralph Durand donated only £4, but he also helped the London Auxiliary and spoke at meetings when the Harrises were not available. Joseph Conrad wished the movement well, but his public help was limited to a single letter for publication, parts of which appeared in Morel's *King Leopold's Rule in Africa*. The two Congo stories he had published in the 1890s, *Heart of Darkness* and "An Outpost of Progress," helped spread the word. Conrad recruited the journalist and author R.B. Cunninghame Graham, who participated in the movement and donated annually from 1909 to 1913. It is difficult to discern common motives among the writers. Most of the writers do not seem to have found inspiration in the religious principles that motivated so many others, but their imaginations may have been more open to the suffering described by the reformers.

In class terms, the aristocracy's support was feeble, with the notable exception of Lords Lonsdale, Monkswell, and Beauchamp—and the latter two appear as having occupations. Working-class support was similarly meager, due to limited income. Working-class donors may have given many of the small donations, but even if all donations below ten shillings belonged to this class, it would total only £222. This is unlikely; average wages for all classes was 26 shillings a week; ten shillings was half or more of a workingman's wages.[73] The professional middle class made up almost all the rest of the occupationally identifiable donations, mostly in small amounts.

---

[72] Myers Literary Guide, "Charles John Cutcliffe Wright Hyne," http://www.sclews.me.uk/m-hyne.html; *WAM*, 25 November 1904, 818.

[73] Craig Lindsay, "A Century of Labour Market Change: 1900 to 2000," *Labour Market Trends* 111, no. 3 (March 2003): 141.

The presence of Africans deserves some attention. At least three West African MDs donated, and one, Moses da Rocha, was later active in the Nigerian independence movement. Several other Africans contributed, primarily traders and government officials. One South Asian donated: E.W. Jayewardene, Ceylon's chief judge and the father of a future Ceylonese president. The colonial donations were small, likely by necessity. They represent the small exceptions to the story of race in the CRA, which was an almost completely white and metropolitan organization that aimed to help colonized Africans who had few effectual ways to help themselves short of armed rebellion. The Congolese could and did use the Congo Free State's court system, but in doing so they risked their lives. If they survived the arduous journeys required to attend regional courts and superior courts in the lower Congo, they often faced murderous reprisals when they returned home. African CRA supporters were most often British subjects. Some, like the doctors, found the story of Leopold's misrule compelling though they had not been to Congo. Da Rocha and others wanted to improve colonial rule all over Africa. Others had worked in the Congo and supported the movement because of what they had seen. The most notable, Hezekiah Andrew Shanu, gave the CRA money and invaluable information before being driven to despair by the boycott that the Congo Free State carried out against his store in Boma. He committed suicide in 1905.

By and large, the CRA hewed to a position on race that owed much to Kingsley, Holt, and Fox Bourne. Africans shared a common humanity with Europeans that entitled them to certain basic rights of liberty and property. Although paternalistic at best and at times condescending, the CRA's official literature and much of its unofficial correspondence reflected this view. These documents generally portrayed educated Africans and those of African descent with dignity, such as Shanu, Edward Blyden, and Booker T. Washington. The large CRA meeting that Casement arranged at the Holborn Town Hall on 7 June 1905 symbolically conveyed respect for Africans by including the Hon. J.J. Thomas, a Sierra Leone councilor, on the platform.[74] Casement, more attuned than many other reformers about the importance of African voices, also urged Guinness to bring Africans with him on his lecture tour in 1904, but this does not seem to have happened.[75]

Ordinary Africans received less consideration, but appeared in printed documents sympathetically, except if they participated in violent excesses. Evidence of racism is not hard to find among even the CRA's most stalwart fighters, usually in the form of condescension. Alfred Emmott routinely referred

---

[74] *Gold Coast Leader,* 29 July 1905, 4.
[75] Casement memorandum, March 1904, F4/5:165–205.

to the Africans as "niggers," but none of the other leading reformers did so. Morel and Holt use the word only when quoting their adversaries.[76]

Reformers sometimes criticized the European men who took African concubines, though they seem worried less about miscegenation than about the violation of religious principles or human rights involved. The sensitive subject of interracial marriage is almost invisible. Though both George Grenfell and Ludwig Deuss had married black women, this topic does not come up in the Congo correspondence. Alice Stopford Green, in a private letter, noted "his white wife!" in a list of Frederick Douglass's faults, suggesting that the silence on interracial marriage may have masked some hostility.[77] A discussion of race would be remiss if it did not include the African-American missionary, Rev. William Sheppard. His part in the reform agitation appears elsewhere in this volume, culminating in the Congo Free State's accusation of libel against him.

Only 25 women appear in the occupational study; most middle-class and upper-class women did not work for pay. Many engaged in volunteer work, but this work did not amount to an occupation because their primary responsibility centered on the home.

The donors had commitments to other causes: temperance (a few dozen), peace (especially among Quakers), ending the opium trade, antivivisection, women's suffrage, anti-slavery, and the APS. A strong thread of social reform appears for wealthy philanthropists and less well-off activists such as Gandhi's friend Muriel Lester and the Social Christian Scott Holland. Mary Kingsley's acolytes, Dennett and Durand, followed Morel into Congo reform.

Though the reform movement claimed universal appeal, the demographics of its leaders and donors convey specific characteristics: the CRA was above party politics but leaned Liberal, nonsectarian but mostly Nonconformist with a disproportionate Quaker influence, and appealed largely to the middle class. The hard-headed secular businessmen that Morel hoped to unite with the religious community largely stayed away, with donations flowing to the CRA primarily from the religiously committed sector of the commercial class involved in good causes in Britain and overseas.

---

[76] Holt to Morel, 27 July 1904 and 30 June 1905, F8/85:366, 386; Morel, *Nigeria* (London: Frank Cass, 1968, first published 1911), xxxv.

[77] Green to Morel, F8/72.

Chapter 5

Alliances

> We are thinking of inviting all organizations interested in the Congo question to join with us in a friendly conference to consider the best means of using further influence, thro' our own Government or other channels, on Congo authorities.[1]—H.R. Fox Bourne, 1904

To put sustained pressure on the British government, the Congo Free State, and Belgium, the Congo reform movement needed to bring multiple interests and groups into a united campaign. This was clear after the failure of Stead's IU Congo Committee. From the start, the CRA's initial Executive Committee was to include people from the worlds of humanitarianism (Fox Bourne), religion (Guinness), commerce (Holt), politics (Emmott and Dilke), and crusading journalism (Morel). The Association's strategic alliances fell within these categories, with the proviso that religion was not so easily categorized. Missionary societies, churches, and para-religious organizations were potential religious allies, and Guinness was not effective as a gateway to any of them.

As independent organizations, these groups were not always willing to subordinate their views and objectives, making for alliances that could be contentious as well as helpful. While difficulties with allies could take the form of personal conflicts, these conflicts often sprang from substantial divergence of interests. Alliances, a method of accomplishing the CRA's work, also shed light on the motivations that underlay the movement and some of the forces that impeded its work, as shown by this consideration of the CRA's connections to the major humanitarian, missionary, church, and commercial organizations

Humanitarian Societies

With its Congo reform activism preceding the CRA by seven years, the Aborigines' Protection Society was a natural ally, but Fox Bourne had initially refused to join the Executive Committee. By late May 1904, his pique had abated, the CRA had shown its staying power, and the benefits of a combined effort began to outweigh his other concerns. Fox Bourne then hoped that each group would take on duties that played to its strengths. The CRA would hold

---

[1] Fox Bourne to Buxton, 5 May 1904, Brit. Emp. s.18, C76/89.

public meetings, collect information, and publicize it, while the APS used "such influence as it possessed" in the Foreign Office and with MPs, while maintaining ties with Belgian reformers.[2] However, the CRA's field of action expanded as Morel developed his own connections and the confidence to use them. By early 1908, Fox Bourne admitted that the CRA had rendered it unnecessary for the APS to do anything more than keep its members informed.[3] The vision of one organization representing everyone interested in Congo reform had finally come to pass.

Fox Bourne's sudden death on 2 February 1909 led to the merger of the Aborigines' Protection Society and the British and Foreign Anti-Slavery Society on 30 June of that year. The resulting British and Foreign Anti-Slavery and Aborigines' Protection Society became the CRA's closest working partner. Before the merger, Morel and the CRA had a complicated relationship with the Anti-Slavery Society. The Society had been only minimally involved in the Congo controversy in the 1890s.[4] Its longtime Secretary, Charles Allen, had helped start the Brussels Anti-Slavery conference and supported Stanley's explorations for Leopold.[5] He and the Society hesitated to take a stand as the stories of forced labor and atrocities trickled out. Not until 1895 did the *Anti-Slavery Reporter* mention the matter by reprinting a *Daily Chronicle* interview with an unnamed missionary describing the "reign of terror" that had depopulated towns under a "system [that] is radically bad" and reprinted information about the practice of taking women hostage to coerce the men to collect rubber. But the *Reporter* was skeptical of this evidence, and expressed hope that the posthumous publication of E.J. Glave's Congo diary would shed light on the matter.[6] Although Glave's diary corroborated the allegations, there followed five years of silence until the *Reporter* reviewed *Pioneering on the Congo*, the reminiscences of the Baptist Missionary Society's Rev. William Holman Bentley, who had been stationed on the Congo for over 20 years. Bentley praised the Congo government and did not mention the allegations of excesses, leaving the *Reporter* flummoxed, despite other testimony that had emerged that year.[7]

Allen's successor as Secretary, Travers Buxton, and the Society's President, Sir Thomas Fowell Buxton, decided that the Society's previous support for Leopold gave it a responsibility to speak out about the problems. Reflecting this new approach, the *Reporter* denounced the methods of the Congo Free State

---

[2] *APS Annual Report for 1905*, 10.
[3] *APS Annual Report for 1907*, 10.
[4] Dennett to Secretary of Anti-Slavery Society, 27 February 1890, Brit. Emp. s.22 G/32.
[5] Annie Coombes, *Reinventing Africa* (New Haven: Yale University Press, 1994), 68, 82.
[6] *ASR*, December 1895, 261–5.
[7] *ASR*, December 1900, 146.

as "horrendous" and "flagrant," and the Society fully supported the APS and the IU Congo Committee.[8] Travers Buxton provided the names of Anti-Slavery subscribers to Stead and gave Guinness letters of introduction to take on his planned speaking tour.[9]

The *Reporter* now commented frequently on the Congo, giving credit to the Aborigines' Protection Society and Stead for raising the issue's profile and to other organizations for making representations to Parliament.[10] But the *Reporter* mentioned only the editor of the *West African Mail*, and did not name Morel until July 1904 or the CRA until October.[11] Travers Buxton wrote only four letters to Morel in the CRA's first two years, all impeccably correct but cool. Fox Bourne and Joseph Alexander were his main contacts in the reform movement.

The reason for Travers Buxton's diffidence is not explicit in his correspondence. His aloofness seems to have resulted from some combination of personal feeling and fundamental differences in approach. Buxton and Morel would have formed opinions of each other while serving on the IU Congo Committee. Temperamentally, Buxton was far more placid and formal than Morel, who was both energetic and much quicker to take offense. On top of this, the CRA's formation undermined Anti-Slavery's strategy of following the lead of the APS. If Buxton saw the CRA as the result of Morel's insolence and disrespect to Fox Bourne, it is entirely possible that this feeling could have outlasted even Fox Bourne's own hostility to the new organization.

Buxton's attitude changed after John Harris asked him to become Treasurer of the CRA's new London Auxiliary in 1906, where they worked closely together. Harris was a fount of ideas for improving the Anti-Slavery Society and positioning it strategically for a wider role, preferably after merging with the APS and/or the CRA. He encouraged it to be more active in the Congo reform movement, for example, by convincing the Society to approach the Kaiser about the Congo question during his state visit to Britain.[12] Harris introduced the Society to leading Congo reformers outside its purview, such as Green and Gilmour. This new closeness manifested itself at the Anti-Slavery Society's 1906 annual meeting, attended by London CRA representatives Harris, Stopford, Durand, and Simpson, usefully countering the presence of Congophile Irish MPs McKean and Nolan.

---

[8] *ASR*, May 1902, 63; Buxton to T.F. Buxton, 7 and 23 May 1903, Brit. Emp. s.19 D1/2:184, 211.

[9] Buxton to Stead, 13 May 1903; Buxton to T.F. Buxton, 18 December 1903, Brit. Emp. s.19 D1/2.

[10] *ASR*, October 1903, 118–20.

[11] *ASR*, February 1904, 14–22; July 1904, 91–8; October 1904, 127.

[12] Buxton to T.F. Buxton, Brit. Emp. s.19 D1/3:652.

By 1906, the Congo appeared in almost every issue of the *Reporter* and on the agenda for almost all the Society's Committee meetings.[13] They passed Congo resolutions, researched legal issues, and wrote to the Foreign Office, sometimes at the CRA's request.[14] After reading Morel's *Red Rubber*, Travers Buxton canceled the Society's conference celebrating the hundredth anniversary of the 1807 abolition of the British slave trade in favor of supporting Congo meetings.[15] This commitment to the Congo did not bring Buxton much closer to Morel, and neither did their relationships with William Cadbury.

Like Morel, the Anti-Slavery Society supported Cadbury during the cocoa scandals. Many Congo reformers including Monkswell and *Spectator* editor St Loe Strachey had joined Fox Bourne and the APS in attacking the chocolate firms for trying to work with the Portuguese. In contrast, Travers Buxton, Morel, and Harris did what they could to undermine this criticism until the fateful moment in March 1909, just after Fox Bourne's death, when Cadbury led the British chocolate makers to boycott cocoa from São Tomé and Príncipe. Notwithstanding Cadbury's fears about its efficacy, the long-delayed boycott was the only action that led to any improvement in the islands' recruitment and management of labor.[16] In a further irony, Morel said the Anti-Slavery Society was insufficiently supportive of Cadbury.[17] Buxton suspected that this attack came because he had "stupidly" (Buxton's word) not invited him to a conference on the subject.[18]

As early as 1907, Buxton described Harris's brain as "seething" with the concept of merging the APS and the Anti-Slavery Society, hoping to create a "vigorous united organization" with or without the CRA. Buxton told the Quaker E.W. Brooks, the only person on the Committees of all three groups, that Harris would be a "splendid organising secretary" of an amalgamated society.[19] The opportunity arose in late 1907 because of an abrupt fall in APS donations to only 75 percent of the income of the previous seven years.[20] However, talks foundered after successful fundraising in 1908, enabling Fox Bourne to oppose any plan that diluted his authority.[21]

---

[13] Brit. Emp. s.20 E/2:12; *ASR*, 25–7.

[14] Buxton to Alexander, 11 July 1906, Brit. Emp. s.19 D1/3:268; Buxton to Grey, 15 October 1907, Brit. Emp. s.18 C166:31.

[15] Buxton to Fox Bourne, 10 January 1907, Brit. Emp. s.19 D1/3:401, 410.

[16] Satre, *Chocolate*, 183.

[17] Buxton to Morel, 9 October 1908, Brit. Emp. s.19 D1/4:316–18.

[18] Buxton to Brooks, 15 October 1908, Brit. Emp. s.19 D1/4:354.

[19] Buxton to Alexander, 19 and 27 December 1907, Brit. Emp. s.19 D1/3:813, 821; Buxton to Brooks, 31 January 1908, Brit. Emp. s.19 D1/3:883–4.

[20] Buxton to T.F. Buxton, 10 December 1907, Brit. Emp. s.19 D1/3.

[21] Buxton to T.F. Buxton, 23 November 1908, Brit. Emp. s.19 D1/4:453.

During 1908 and 1909, Harris's Anti-Slavery activities grew. For example, he went to William Cadbury to discuss how the Society could support him on the cocoa issue. More often his efforts focused on Travers Buxton, advising him on how to organize and publicize a cocoa meeting and on his interactions with Grey, a subject where his advice prevailed over that of Brooks and Monkswell.[22]

After the 1909 merger of the APS and Anti-Slavery, Buxton revived the idea of John Harris as organizing secretary. The Committee made the offer jointly to John and Alice in December 1909. They accepted and left the CRA on 31 March 1910.[23] Fresh from their experience as organizing secretaries of the Congo Reform Association, they reorganized and re-energized the amalgamated British and Foreign Anti-Slavery and Aborigines' Protection Society, infusing it with the energy of the CRA and later influencing policy at multinational organizations such as the League of Nations and the International Labour Organization.[24]

Relations between the CRA and Anti-Slavery warmed considerably thereafter. Travers Buxton, now on the CRA Executive Committee, began writing more cordially to Morel and collaborated with him more often, as when they jointly telegraphed Meyer to ask for a Free Church Council resolution on the Congo.[25] More importantly, Harris ensured that the two groups would present "an absolutely united front" on the Congo.[26] In many ways, the amalgamated Society was a better partner than either the APS or old Anti-Slavery Society had been. The tensions between Morel and Harris, which had so disturbed the CRA, were easier to manage with Harris leading a different organization.

The Congo Reform Association did not embrace other potential humanitarian allies. It was common for humanitarian groups to support each other's causes, but for the most part Morel did not. For example, in 1910 the Subject Races International Committee sponsored a conference that included the Anti-Slavery Society, Positivist Society, and others—but the CRA demurred.[27] Morel cooperated for a while with the League of Honour founded by one Archdeacon Potter, which intended to provide common services to humanitarian groups, but in a speech from the platform at a League meeting in 1911, Morel called the project unnecessary.[28]

---

[22] Buxton to T.F. Buxton, 8 May 1908 and 16 October 1909, Brit. Emp. s.19 D1/4:33, D1/5 384; Buxton to Alexander, 11 June 1908 and 30 October 1908, Brit. Emp. s.19 D1/4:94, 393; Buxton to Harris, 30 June 1908, Brit. Emp. s.19 D1/4:133.

[23] Letters, December 1909, Brit. Emp. s.19 D1/6:26, 31, 65.

[24] Nworah, "Aborigines' Protection Society," 90–91; see also Claude Welch, Jr, *Defining Contemporary Forms of Slavery: Updating a Venerable NGO* (Buffalo: Legal Studies Research Paper Series Paper 2008–002), 3.

[25] F8/108:33.

[26] Harris to Lidgett, 25 April 1910, Brit. Emp. s.19 D3/1:191.

[27] Brit. Emp. s.19 D2/1.

[28] League of Honour pamphlet, Brit. Emp. s.19 D2/3:2.

Missionary Societies

Historian Kevin Grant rediscovered and reprioritized missionaries as key actors in the reform movement, not just supporting cast. They created popular outrage and support for reform through hundreds of atrocity meetings, held mostly at churches from 1905–08. He further argues that the missionaries turned around a failing reform campaign, countering the dominant Morel-centered narrative.[29] Grant's work is an important corrective to the neglect of the 1980s and 1990s, but it swings the pendulum too far in the other direction, as previous chapters have shown. Missionary involvement did help to create a mass movement through the sheer number of meetings and the missionaries' ability to tap into deep wells of religious feeling. However, these meetings and the founding of auxiliaries had an incremental, not revolutionary, impact on the organization's finances and the CRA was not failing before they joined the movement. This section highlights the ways several missionary organizations contributed to or hindered the cause. Readers interested in further details should consult the detailed descriptions of Daniel Lagergren, Ruth Slade, and Robert Burroughs.[30]

Previous chapters have analyzed the Regions Beyond Missionary Union's many contributions to the reform movement: introducing Sjöblom to Fox Bourne in 1896, Guinness's role in the CRA's founding and his many creative ideas, testimony about conditions in the Congo, speakers, and, most of all, loaning the Harrises to the CRA, which boosted the campaign and affected the future of overseas humanitarianism. On the other hand, Guinness was unreliable, controversial, and unable to help the movement build connections into the churches.

Starting in 1909, the RBMU stopped supporting the reform movement, attributable to its efforts to work with the new Belgian administration and severe internal problems. For years, the Guinness missions had raised £20,000–£29,000 annually to run its global missions and its East London Training Institute, whose main operations were Harley House or Harley College (for men), and Doric Lodge (for women). With the death of Guinness's father, Rev. Henry Grattan Guinness, in 1910, revenues fell significantly.[31] In addition, the RBMU confronted dissension in the Congo missions and at Harley House, where an attempt to dismiss the principal alienated students and staff. Guinness compromised at Harley House and went to the Congo in 1910 to conciliate insubordinate missionaries, contracting the illness that was to kill him in 1915.

---

[29] Grant, *A Civilised Savagery*, 60, 65–76.

[30] Lagergren, *Mission and State*; Slade, *English-Speaking Missions*; Slade, "English Missionaries"; Robert Burroughs, *Travel Writing and Atrocities: Eyewitness Accounts of Colonialism in the Congo, Angola, and the Putumayo* (New York: Routledge, 2011).

[31] *Annual Charities Register and Digest* (London: Longman's, Green, 1910); RBMU Directors, 31 December 1903, 26 January 1905, 22 February 1906, 19 November 1909.

His efforts were ineffective; the malcontents, led by Congo reform stalwarts Rev. Somerville Gilchrist and Rev. Harry Whiteside, agitated against Guinness until 1913, supported from London by John Harris.[32] The RBMU directors addressed these problems by diluting Guinness's power and saving money by selling a steamer and closing Doric Lodge and Harley House.[33] In the midst of all this, the British Vice-Consul discovered that Guinness's son-in-law was smuggling rifles into the Congo to trade for ivory.[34] It is no wonder that Morel heard almost nothing from the RBMU after 1909. Not only was the RBMU working with Belgium to obtain new missions, its personal conflicts, institutional controversies, and financial worries distracted its beleaguered leader.

The American Baptist Missionary Union (ABMU) had close ties with the RBMU. The many ABMU missionaries, including Murphy and Sjöblom, had trained at Harley House. In the 1890s, after ABMU missionaries failed to interest local officials in their stories of rubber-related atrocities, Rev. Charles Harvey and Dr Aaron Sims alerted the mission's American headquarters, which sent their report via the US State Department to Van Eetvelde, the head of the Congo government in Brussels, on the commonly held assumption that Leopold's wayward officials were spoiling his benevolent intentions.[35] Van Eetvelde played into this, feigning ignorance of the circumstances. He promised an investigation and punishment for the guilty.[36] He also pointed out that Sims had previously made light of the rubber collection problems and had praised the Congo Free State. This introduces a common problem in the early Congo reform agitation: the ambivalence of missionaries. Knowing a limited territory, dependent on Congo officials, focused on conversion, and often willing to countenance coercion, many missionaries had said favorable things about the Congo Free State. As even Morel admitted, some Congo officials were men of good will toward the local people and thus earned missionary praise on their own merits. For missionaries stationed in areas not subject to rubber collection or coercive requisitioning, the stories told by their brethren or native refugees were just hearsay. The Congo government used these favorable comments to great effect in its fight against the reformers, even when the missionaries had clearly changed their opinions.[37]

---

[32] Harris to Rev. J. Howell, 22 May 1912, Brit. Emp. s.19 D3/5:503; RBMU Directors, 31 January 1913; Harris to Meyer, June-July 1910, Brit. Emp. s.19 D3/1:686; Harris to Meyer, 4 September 1912, Brit. Emp. s.19 D3/6:428.

[33] RBMU Directors, 2 June 1909 memorandum; RBMU Directors, 31 March 1910.

[34] Acting Consul Campbell to Grey 25 August 1910, FO 881/9854:42.

[35] William Roger Louis, "The Stokes Affair and the Origins of the Anti-Congo Campaign, 1895-1896," *Revue Belge de Philologie & d'Histoire* 43, no. 2 (January 1965): 577, 584; Lagergren, *Mission and State*, 143.

[36] Lagergren, *Mission and State*, 139-40.

[37] Lagergren, *Mission and State*, 141.

The ABMU missionaries were the most active in reporting Congo misrule in the mid-1890s, but they muted their criticism from 1898–1903 in the hope of reforms, out of respect for the BMS's advice, and out of concern for the safety of the missions. Leopold had even appointed the ABMU's own Dr Sims to the Commission for the Protection of the Natives.[38] Unlike Grenfell, Sims thought the Commission boded well and that Leopold had heard their criticisms.[39] But the Commission, designed to be powerless, turned out to be useless. After meeting with Rev. William Morrison of the Presbyterians in 1903, the ABMU leadership decided to speak out again even if it jeopardized their missions.[40] Its missionaries appeared at Congo meetings in Britain and America. Thomas Barbour, the ABMU's Foreign Secretary, rallied other American missions, organized the US Congo Reform Association and worked closely with Morel.[41] The ABMU's early involvement helped instigate the Congo campaign in the 1896–97 and intensify it in 1903–04. Its officers and missionaries were mainstays of the American agitation until it ended in 1909.

Already a century old and with long experience on the Congo, the Baptist Missionary Society (BMS) of Great Britain was well placed to aid the reform movement, if it chose to do so. Unlike the ABMU, which operated on the lower Congo up to Stanley Pool, the BMS had stations along the upper Congo between Stanley Pool and Stanleyville at the great bend in the river. While there was no rubber collection in the immediate vicinity of the river, the government demanded military recruits, porters, fuel, and food of the local people. The BMS Congo missions had distinguished personnel who could command public attention if they wished, including the explorer-missionary Rev. George Grenfell and his colleague Rev. William Holman Bentley, author of *Life on the Congo* (1887) and *Pioneering on the Congo* (1900). In London, the redoubtable BMS Secretary, Alfred H. Baynes, exercised firm leadership and considerable diplomatic skills.[42]

For a long time Grenfell and Bentley refused to believe that misgovernment was widespread. Grenfell responded to personal testimony, however, as we saw in his 1896 meeting with Sjöblom. Traveling with Casement in late 1903 shattered his last illusions. He resigned from the Commission for the Protection of the Natives, but without much effect. Not only had the powerless Commission not met in six years, its legal basis had expired in March 1903.[43] Nonetheless,

---

[38] Lagergren, *Mission and State*, 195–6.
[39] *Baptist Missionary Magazine* 77, no. 10 (October 1897): 543, http://books.google.com/books?id=fgjPAAAAMAAJ&pg=PA67.
[40] Lagergren, *Mission and State*, 311.
[41] Lagergren, *Mission and State*, 254, 288, 311, 325.
[42] Lagergren, *Mission and State*, 49.
[43] Lagergren, *Mission and State*, 328; Phipps to Lansdowne, 18 May 1903, FO 403/338 no. 51, Osborne transcription.

his resignation freed him to take a stand against Congo misgovernment in a 1903 letter to *The Times*, in 1904 Commission of Inquiry testimony, and, most dramatically, when he repudiated the rank of Chevalier of the Order of Leopold, causing Harris to exult, "Mr Grenfell has thrown the State completely over!"[44] Grenfell's new attitude did not prevent Congo apologists from citing him as a supporter for years to come.[45]

BMS missionaries who had assisted Casement or testified at Leopold's Commission of Inquiry began to come forward, joining the ABMU and CBM missionaries in publicly denouncing the Congo State.[46] Even then, Baynes refused to change his policy when Morel asked for information, preferring to deal privately with the Congo government. In 1905, Rev. K.H.C. Graham, on the lower Congo, wrote to his fellow BMS missionaries urging them to send information to Morel and "like Weeks and Scrivener ignore instructions from home."[47] In Britain, the Baptist Union's President, Rev. John Clifford, moved against Baynes and secured his retirement in late 1905.[48] Officially, this was for health reasons, but his exit was slow; he worked in tandem with his replacement until 1907, but his influence dwindled.[49] Sir George W. Macalpine, BMS Committee Chairman, initiated cooperation with the CRA in January 1906. He gruffly chided Morel for complaining about the BMS's previous reticence, but Morel and Meyer showed him that these descriptions were accurate.[50] Macalpine threw himself into the cause, personally donating over £86 to the CRA and making BMS missionary Kenred Smith available to address public meetings in March 1906, the first of nine BMS missionary lecturers. Smith

---

[44] *WAM*, 14 April 1905, 63; Harris to Morel, 22 July 1905, F8/75:174; Sir Harry Hamilton Johnston, *George Grenfell and the Congo* (London: Hutchinson & Co., 1908), 377.

[45] *Bulletin officiel de L'État Indépendant du Congo No 8. Etoile de service*, trans. Fédération pour la Défense des Intérêts Belges à L'étranger, 1904, F13/3:1; *Catholic Herald*, 8 December 1904, F9/3:36–8; Scrivener to Morel, 19 February 1905, F9/16; Samuel to Morel, 5 January 1906, F8/125:58.

[46] Weeks and Scrivener letters, *Organ*, July 1904, 64–8; *WAM Congo Supplement*, August 1904, 112–13; Reports on ABIR (Frost, Harris, and Stannard), Katanga (Dugald Campbell), Bangala (Weeks), *WAM*, 7 July 1905, 344–7; Rev. W.B. Frame to Morel, 16 March 1904, F9/6:52–6; Casement to Morel, 9 March 1905, F8/18:137–9. See also Slade, *English-Speaking Missions*, 265 ff.

[47] Harris to Morel, 22 July 1905, F8/75:174.

[48] Harris to Morel, 18, September 1905, F8/75:195.

[49] B.R. Wheeler, *Alfred Henry Baynes, JP* (London: Carey Press, after 1944).

[50] Macalpine to Morel, 15 January, 24 January, and 13 February 1906, F8/105:1, 4, 7; BMS pamphlet, "The Congo Question and the Baptist Missionary Society," July 1909, F13/4:1. Meyer to Morel, 31 October 1906, F8/108:10.

assured Morel, "You will be glad to know that the Baptist Missionary Society is now thoroughly in sympathy with Congo Reform."[51]

With the support of Macalpine and Baynes' successor, Rev. C.E. Wilson, the BMS worked closely with the Congo reform movement. They paid the price of having their applications for new mission stations denied by both the Congo Free State and then Belgium.[52] The Baptist Missionary Society, the last missionary organization to officially join the cause, ironically stayed with it longer than any other.[53]

The American Presbyterian Congo Mission (APCM), active in the Kasai river valley, was important to the movement at several key moments. As previously discussed, Morrison, its local head, had protested about slave-raiding and the imposition of heavy taxes by local officials in 1898. Morrison came to Britain and spoke at one meeting, the only APCM missionary to do so. After the CRA's founding, Morrison, Sheppard, and Rev. L.C. Vass sent Morel stories of misdeeds in the Kasai. Chapter 7 tells how the Kasai Company's libel suit against Morrison and Sheppard backfired, producing reams of positive publicity for the reformers.

After the trial, the APCM dropped out of reform history. The mission forced Sheppard into retirement ostensibly for health reasons, but really because of evidence of repeated adultery.[54] Morrison wrote to Morel just once after this, congratulating him on his 1911 testimonial.[55]

Other missionary societies, such as the Plymouth Brethren, the Foreign Christian Missionary Society, and the Swedish Missionary Society, played minor parts in the reform campaign, usually by providing evidence to Morel or to their home offices. Most notably, on 11 January 1906, they joined the other Protestant Missions in an appeal to the world about Congo misrule. Fifty-two missionaries signed, representing not only the UK and US, but also Canada, Germany, Sweden, Norway, and Denmark.[56] It was a rare show of unity. As the Belgian regime eliminated the worst abuses and worked with the missions, cooperation lapsed, the victim of distance, competition, and internal concerns.

The collaboration of the missionary societies and the CRA was a marriage of convenience. The CRA aimed to enshrine rights and justice in laws and administrative practices, but the missionary societies' primary goal was to bring Christianity with as few impediments as possible. Morel's own feelings about the missionary societies reflected Mary Kingsley's hostility to their interference with

---

[51] Kenred Smith to Morel, 19 March 1906, F8/105:12. Donations from Donor Database.
[52] 31 December 1907, FO 881/9093; FO 881/9590; FO 881/9889:114.
[53] *Organ*, October 1911; Harris to Morel, 27 January 1911, F8/77:416.
[54] Pagan Kennedy, *Black Livingston* (New York: Viking, 2002), 190–91.
[55] Morrison to Morel, 16 January 1911, F8/77:418.
[56] *Organ*, 1906, F4/29.

African culture and his difficulties obtaining their cooperation.[57] The Executive Committee, even with its religious element, was not useful in securing missionary alliances despite the presence of Guinness. The BMS's long hesitation and Guinness's vacillation did nothing to alleviate suspicions. Even in late 1906, during the time of greatest cooperation, Casement fretted that the missionary societies were trying to turn the Congo question to their own interests.[58] This was not a marriage for better or worse. If the viciousness of Leopold's regime had temporarily united the missionaries and the CRA, the reform of that regime quickly exposed their divergent interests. The controversies and frustrations should not blind us to the benefits of their collaboration. Bound together by a common enemy into a difficult relationship, the CRA's alliance with the missionary societies, while it lasted, was enormously productive for the Congo reform movement.

Churches

If the missionaries enabled the reform movement to draw attention to abuses, create a climate of popular indignation, and provide solid evidence of ongoing wrongdoing, religious bodies in Britain gave the movement weight, offered venues for popular mobilization, galvanized fundraising, and boosted the movement's influence among those who might never attend an atrocity meeting. Most major churches endorsed the CRA: the Society of Friends, Baptist Union, Congregational Union, Presbyterian churches, Wesleyan Methodist Synod, and the Anglican Convocations.[59] These groups supported the CRA until its dissolution.

The Baptist Union had committed itself to Congo reform at Clifford's instigation before the founding of the CRA. The elderly but still active leader of the Nonconformist conscience convinced the annual meeting of the Baptist Union in April 1903 to authorize collaboration on the Congo question with other religious, missionary, and philanthropic groups.[60] The Baptists worked with the APS, IU Congo Committee, and CRA. The Baptist Union continued on this path, passing Congo resolutions at almost every annual meeting. Clifford joined the CRA Executive Committee and cooperated with many of Morel's initiatives.[61] Subsequent Baptist Union Presidents George White (1903–04), F.B. Meyer (1906–07), and George Macalpine (1910–11), and other officers such as Herbert Marnham and Rev. John Shakespeare, were heavily involved. Morel spoke to Baptist Union annual meetings in 1906 and 1907 to an overwhelming

[57] Morel to Fox Bourne, 11 October 1906, F10/14:305.
[58] Casement to Morel, 12 November 1906, F8/22:359.
[59] *Organ*, May 1907, 8; E.D. Morel, *Great Britain and the Congo: The Pillage of the Congo Basin* (London: Smith Elder, 1909. Reprint, New York: Howard Fertig, 1969), 16.
[60] Lagergren, *Mission and State*, 307.
[61] Morel to Clifford, 4 June and 7 December 1909, F8/32:12, 23.

142   *British Humanitarianism and the Congo Reform Movement, 1896–1913*

reception.[62] Baptist churches, chapels, and organizations held Congo meetings far more often than did any other religious group, as shown in Table 5.1 below.

Figure 5.1   Rev. John Clifford
Source: Portrait by John Collier [Public domain] via Wikimedia Commons.

---

[62] *Organ*, November 1906, 21–4; Morel to Cadbury 9 October 1906 F8/12:40; Morel to Rev. G. Burden, 2 October 1907, F10/15:931; *Organ*, October 1907, 10–11.

Table 5.1 Recorded Congo meetings by religious affiliation

Church affiliation of meeting location or sponsor	Number of meetings
Baptist	344
Methodist	75
Congregationalist	72
Anglican	40
Presbyterian	26
Friends	14
Union Churches (Nondenominational Protestant)	13
Unitarian	5
Church of Christ	2
Jewish Synagogue	1
Known church affiliation	**590**
Church-related but affiliation not known	45
Subtotal, all religious venues	**635**
Private, club, and municipal locations	382
Total meetings with known locations and/or religious sponsors	**1014**

Notes: Four meetings appear in two categories and are adjusted out of the totals.
Source: Meetings Database.

Baptists played an integral part in convincing the Foreign Office that a broad swath of British public opinion wanted it to press for Congo reform. Its leading figures were prominent exponents of rallying the faithful and lobbying the government in the spirit of the Nonconformist conscience.

With fewer than 23,000 members in the UK, the Society of Friends could never claim to represent broad popular support and carried little weight in the corridors of power. Their wealth and prominence in particular fields did not translate into formal or informal political influence. Tellingly, when Sir Henry Campbell-Bannerman, the leader of the Liberal party, received an invitation from George Cadbury, he had to ask the party Whip to explain who the man was.[63] Major CRA donor Alexander Peckover, who became the first Quaker peer in 1907, never spoke on the Congo or any other topic in his 12 years in the House of Lords.

The Friends had long spoken out against injustice, including the concentration camps and farm-burning tactics of the British in the Boer War, and had passed

---

[63] Campbell-Bannerman to Herbert Gladstone, 17 November 1899, Add. 41215:143.

a Congo resolution on 4 March 1904, shortly before the CRA's founding.[64] The monetary and organizational support of a small number of wealthy Friends made them important players in the reform movement. They took the unusual step of sending J.G. Alexander and E.W. Brooks with John Harris to Berlin in December 1905 to express their concerns directly to the German government.[65] William Cadbury not only secured the publication of the 1905 appeal for funds in *The Friend*, he helped convince the Friends as a body to endorse the reform campaign. As the largest donor to the CRA and as Morel's friend and patron, his opinions helped shape the CRA's policies. The Quakers on the Executive Committee assisted in similar ways.

The CRA's links to the Congregational Union relied on a few leading men, including notable preachers Rev. R.J. Campbell and Rev. Campbell Morgan and three chairmen of the Congregational Union: Dr Robert Horton, Sir Joseph Compton Rickett, MP, and Rev. Silvester Horne, MP. All five donated to the CRA; Campbell and Horne served on its Executive Committee. Despite this backing, institutional and parishioner support for Congo reform never approached that of the Baptists. The annual meetings did pass Congo resolutions in 1906, 1907, and 1909.[66] However, when Horne brought Morel to speak at the 1907 meeting of the Congregational Union of England and Wales, the delegates seemed uninterested, a disappointing contrast to his enthusiastic reception at the Baptist Union.[67] Although larger than the Baptist church, the Congregationalist emphasis on decentralized authority may have made its congregations less susceptible to the influence of its leading figures and less likely to take action in unison.

The Methodists' Congo work was a paler version of the Baptists'. The Wesleyan Methodist Conference of 1907 formally committed the body to Congo reform just after the Presbyterians. That October, the Methodist Committee of Privileges notably instructed its ministers to support the reform effort and to send resolutions to Grey.[68] The 1908–09 President of the Methodist Conference, Rev. J. Scott Lidgett, was on the Executive Committee from 1904, though his influence was slight. Robert Whyte of the Presbyterians joined the Executive Committee in 1909. Members of the Methodist, Presbyterian, and Unitarian churches donated to the CRA, hosted some meetings, and attended Congo events, but the latter two groups had even fewer formal organizational ties with the CRA.

---

[64] Alexander, reply to *Petit Blue, Aborigines' Friend*, June 1904, 111–14.
[65] Buxton to Alexander, Brit. Emp. s.19 D1/2:998.
[66] *Daily Post*, 13 October 1909, 380 HOL I 4/11:6; *Organ*, November 1906, 21–4, F4/30.
[67] Morel to Harris, 11 May 1907, F10/15:573.
[68] *Organ*, November 1907, 56.

National, regional, and local Free Church Councils were vital. The idea of assembling representatives of all the Nonconformist churches in a locality started in the late 1880s; there were over 500 Councils in 1899. As they spread, the possibility of a national council to represent and coordinate the interests of all non-Anglican Protestants electrified the imaginations of leading Nonconformists. The National Council of the Evangelical Free Churches formed in 1895 and became the chief advocate for Nonconformists on political issues such as education and disestablishment, major imperial concerns such as Ireland and South Africa, and moral questions such as ending slavery, liquor, gambling, Sunday labor, and prostitution.[69] The network of Free Church Councils also communicated common positions on non-doctrinal issues from the center outwards through local councils to member churches. In the process, it accustomed the leaders of the denominations to working with each other, as they did on the Congo reform campaign.

Like the Baptists, the Free Church Councils had backed the reform campaign early.[70] In 1905, its former President, Rev. F.B. Meyer, led the National Free Church Council to take a much more active role. A man of energy and charisma, the ubiquitous Meyer has already appeared in connection with the RBMU, the Baptists, and the PSA Brotherhoods, as well as inspiring Alice Harris to become a missionary. In August 1905, his protégé John Harris convinced him to get further involved in freeing "that Devil-cursed tract of Africa."[71]

Meyer made the difference in building a strong alliance. Though Guinness had long argued that the CRA needed to awaken the Nonconformist conscience, most religious leaders had not responded to the overtures of the somewhat skeptical Morel and of Guinness himself, who had many contacts but little influence.[72] Meyer soon had made the National Free Church Council one of the CRA's most reliable allies. His appeal in 1906 may not have pulled in as much money as he hoped, but it generated a tremendous demand for literature and launched a flood of requests for Congo meeting speakers.[73] In March 1907, the Council invited Morel to speak at the annual conference in Leeds. Shortly thereafter, Meyer secured their cooperation in a nationwide effort:

> At the Free Church Committee meeting, I was able to induce the President to draw up a strong letter which is to be published in all the religious press and the

---

[69] Bebbington, *Nonconformist Conscience*, 61–72; *ASR*, February 1895, 41; J. Compton Rickett to Campbell-Bannerman, 3 March 1902, Add. 41237:18–22; Rev. G. Campbell Morgan, D.D., "Church Federation in England," *American Monthly Review of Reviews*, November 1905, 592–5.
[70] *ASR*, July 1903, 90–93.
[71] Meyer to Morel, 30 August 1905, F8/108:2.
[72] Guinness to Morel, 7 October 1905, F8/74:62.
[73] Harris to Morel, 7 September 1906, F8/76:268.

Figure 5.2 Rev. F.B. Meyer
Source: Dr H.G. Guinness, These Thirty Years (London: RBMU, 1903), 9.

daily newspapers next week, signed by himself and all the Vice-Presidents and Officials, and urging the Free Church ministers throughout the country to preach strenuous sermons on the Congo matter ... All the Committee are really more in earnest about this than in any similar matter I remember.[74]

Meyer remained an important conduit to the National Council. Morel and Travers Buxton jointly asked Meyer to convince the Free Church Council to pass a resolution to strengthen the government against recognition in 1910.[75] The annual national meeting passed Congo resolutions in six of the seven years from 1906 to 1912. Meyer also was the first to propose that the CRA bring together Nonconformists and Anglicans to impress the government with the unity of all Protestant Christianity on this issue.[76]

The Committee of the National Free Church Council overlapped significantly with the Congo Reform Association. Of its 43 Committee members, officers, and past Presidents in the 1906–07 term, 18 participated in the CRA.[77] Almost all of them donated money, nine spoke at Congo meetings, and nine served on the CRA's Executive Committee. This led to a community of interest at the highest levels that helped hold the alliance together.

Regional and local Free Church Councils invited Congo reformers to speak at 64 or more of their meetings. They sponsored several Congo Sundays in the peak years of 1907–09.

In Parliament, the National Council had a committee of MPs, led until 1907 by CRA donor Sir Robert W. Perks and thereafter by CRA Executive Committee member Sir George White. In theory these MPs would support the National Council's positions, leading Morel to boast to Lalla Vandervelde in 1906 that the CRA had 225 Nonconformist MPs "absolutely drilled and prepared to strike whenever I give the word."[78] He exaggerated; the Nonconformist MPs never did act as one to push a major Congo reform measure.

In speeches and in print, Morel complimented the "splendid work" of the CRA's two closest religious collaborators, the Free Church Councils and the Baptist Union.[79] The Free Church Councils even set aside their bitter dispute with the Anglicans over the Education Act to appear with them at Congo meetings, sign joint letters to the public and government, and attend deputations to the

---

[74] Meyer to Morel, 5 April 1907, F8/108:14; Wuliger, "Economic imperialism," 163.
[75] Morel and Buxton to Meyer, 6 March 1910 or 1911, F8/108:33.
[76] Meyer to Morel, 23 November 1905, F8/108:6.
[77] *Free Church Year Book* (London: National Council of the Evangelical Free Church Council, 1906), xvi, 97.
[78] Morel to Mme Vandervelde, 8 November 1906, F10/14:549.
[79] *Organ*, January 1907, 34.

Foreign Office.[80] The Free Church Councils were perhaps the most efficacious of the CRA's allies.

Although the Nonconformist conscience was the religious heart of the campaign, the prestige and formal political roles of the Anglican Church's leaders also played an important part in the movement. Morel frequently talked about Anglican support in his speeches and in the *Organ*. By 1909, the Archbishop of Canterbury had put himself in the movement's front ranks. On the other hand, the Anglican Church fell well behind the Nonconformists by every quantitative measure. This in part is due to the relative decline of the church. There were more Nonconformist church members than there were people attending Anglican Easter services in the UK as a whole and in Great Britain (see Table 4.4). Even in England and Wales, where the Church of England was the established church, Bebbington concludes that there were more active Nonconformists than active Anglicans by the early 1900s.[81] However, the Church of England was larger than any single Nonconformist church and had great institutional weight.

The first high-profile Anglican to support the Congo Reform Association was the Bishop of Liverpool, the evangelical Anglican Francis Chavasse, who appeared on the platform at the inaugural meeting of the CRA and joined the Executive Committee. The nationally known Canon of St Paul's Cathedral and founder of the Christian Social Union, Henry Scott Holland, also joined early on, consistent with his habitual activism. Over the next few years, 12 more bishops subscribed, and a few others, plus the two archbishops, signed letters or appeared on platforms. Two bishops stand out. Arthur Winnington Ingram, the Bishop of London, became involved in 1906.[82] In his long tenure, he involved himself in many causes, some puritanical, such as purity (for), condoms (against), corporal punishment (for), and night clubs (against), while as his support for charities and women's suffrage showed compassion and interest in fairness.[83] He preached on the Congo often, at Morel's request notifying the press in advance at least once.[84] He worked with Chavasse to put the Congo problem on the 1906 Anglican conference agenda.[85] With John Harris's help, he convened the first church-sponsored meeting to unite Anglican and Free Church ministers, which called on all London clergy to hold Congo meetings.[86]

[80] *Organ*, February 1907, 32.
[81] Bebbington, *Nonconformist Conscience*, 2.
[82] Wuliger, "Economic imperialism," 142–3.
[83] Paul Ferris, *Sex and the British: A Twentieth-Century History* (London: Michael Joseph, 1993) 8, 38, 88, 93; Charles Herbert, *Twenty-Five Years as Bishop of London* (London: Wells Gardner, Darton & Co. Ltd., 1926), 95; S.C. Carpenter, *Winnington-Ingram* (London: Hodder and Stoughton, 1949), 166–7.
[84] F8/103:10, 11.
[85] Ingram to Morel, 25 September 1906, F8/103:2.
[86] F8/76:334.

Edward S. Talbot was even more supportive than Chavasse and Ingram. He had been the first head of Oxford's Keble College and during the reform years was successively the Bishop of Rochester, Southwark, and Winchester. A High Churchman, like Ingram, he also worked closely with Nonconformists. Meyer had recommended Talbot in late 1905 as the best person to bring together Nonconformist leaders and the Anglican hierarchy for the CRA.[87] Talbot proved to be a good ally, donating money, taking the platform at meetings, corresponding frequently with Morel, and serving on the Executive Committee beginning in 1907.

The most prestigious Anglican convert to the Congo reform movement was the Archbishop of Canterbury. Randall Davidson had risen through the Anglican ranks while cultivating leading political figures. He advised Queen Victoria, Prime Minister Balfour, and two previous archbishops before Balfour had him elevated to the see of Canterbury. National leaders consulted him on political matters and he used his influence to advocate for a few nonreligious causes. Although he had made remarks in the House of Lords on 3 July 1906 critical of the Congo situation, his first contact with Congo Reform Association was to refuse a suggestion from Morel some months later that he associate himself publicly with the cause to increase the pressure on the Foreign Office.[88] He feared that strident criticisms would be counterproductive: "You realise I am sure, how liable we are to do harm when we want to do good."[89] Davidson discouraged Lord Mayo from initiating a debate in the House of Lords in January 1907, advocating patience.[90] When Morel asked about a public letter that spring, he again counseled restraint. "I am somewhat afraid of multiplying letters and 'messages' about the Congo in such degree as to weaken their effectiveness."[91] However, he was coming around to Morel's point of view. The Convocation of Canterbury endorsed Congo reform on 3 May 1907, a few months after the Convocation of York had done the same thanks to Chavasse.[92] This seems to have been the turning point. Davidson would no longer follow the position of his predecessor who had kept silent about the Bulgarian massacres.[93] He expounded his new view to Grey while discussing another humanitarian cause, the troubles in Macedonia:

---

[87] Meyer to Morel, 23 November 1905, F8/108:6; MS Emmott 3, f294.
[88] 159 Parl. Deb. (4th ser.) (1906) 1587.
[89] Davidson to Morel, 5 November 1906, F8/14:7–8; MS Emmott 3 f. 364
[90] Mayo to Morel, 31 January 1907, F8/107:3.
[91] Davidson to Morel, 12 April 1907 F8/14:11.
[92] Morel, *Great Britain and the Congo*, 18; Chavasse to Morel, 22 February 1907, F8/102:13.
[93] Gary Bass, *Freedom's Battle* (New York: Knopf, 2008), 276.

> I do want to press this point, that the greatest evil, in my judgment, of all would be, that we should know the evils that are going on and that we should be content to do nothing. Nothing—absolutely nothing—is more likely to sap the moral sense of our own people than that we should be aware of ghastly deeds taking place, that we should be able in some degree to diminish them, and that for one reason or another we should not be doing so.[94]

On 29 July 1907, in the Lords, he said that the Foreign Office's acquiescence in Leopold's delays was not consistent with public opinion.[95] His signature was the first on the CRA's 1907 "Appeal to the Nation."[96] Davidson later told Grey that the Anglican hierarchy supported whatever actions would convince Belgium to institute major reforms.[97]

Davidson and Morel maintained a brisk correspondence during these years.[98] Morel turned to him whenever the government and the Foreign Office gave the appearance of indifference. It is important to note, as Davidson and Morel did not, that while Davidson lent the movement legitimacy in Westminster and among Anglicans, his personal interventions had little effect on policy in the House of Lords or in the corridors of Whitehall.

When Morel decisively broke with Grey in June 1909, he asked Davidson to lead in getting a manifesto signed by the religious leaders, but Davidson hesitated, not wanting to associate himself with Morel's public attacks on Grey and the Foreign Office.[99] That fall, having taken the pulse of the country, Davidson told Morel that public opinion was not nearly as supportive as he seemed to think:

> There is therefore the more need of meetings carefully conducted, and not open to the accusation of being mere ebullitions of enthusiastic feeling on the part of the few. I believe the more the matter is studied the stronger will be the support we shall obtain in England. I hope during the next week or two to have the opportunity of talking with a good many public men on the subject and of using any influence which I may personally or officially possess.[100]

---

[94] Quoted in G.K.A. Bell, *Randall Davidson, Archbishop of Canterbury*, Vol. 1 (London: Oxford University Press, 1935), 548.

[95] 179 Parl. Deb., (4th ser.) (1907) 412.

[96] *Organ*, November 1907; Davidson to Morel, 25 October 1907, F8/14:13.

[97] Davidson to Grey, FO 881/9530:176.

[98] The files contain 55 letters from Davidson or his secretary and more than two dozen from Morel.

[99] Morel to Davidson, 30 June 1909 F8/14:44.

[100] Davidson to Morel, 23 October 1909, F8/14:79.

Davidson's insight led to a large religious "demonstration" at the Albert Hall in November 1909. The Albert Hall meeting was the work of a "religious committee" organized by John Harris and Talbot. Officially independent, it nonetheless boasted all the usual CRA names. The Archbishop himself presided. Davidson, Ingram, Clifford, Lidgett, Horne, and the Bishop of Oxford spoke, and the platform included numerous clergymen and 90 Congo reform stalwarts, including Monkswell, Mayo, seven Bishops, 30 MPs, Morel, the Harrises, Guinness, Green, Doyle, Gilmour, Fox, and Brabner.[101] Messages of support arrived from another ten Bishops, the Archbishop of York, and German, Swiss, and French religious groups. The meeting succeeded in re-establishing the movement as an expression of public opinion in Britain.

Talbot cautioned Morel that the Anglican Church was more careful than the Nonconformists to distinguish between religion and politics, and less willing to get excited for a cause. The Anglican Church as a whole gave the movement much less tangible support than the Nonconformists. Fewer than half of the 43 English bishops made any contribution to the cause including writing letters of support and under a third donated money.[102] The Bishop of Birmingham spoke for many when he argued against taking a stand on the Congo question at the diocesan conference of 1909.[103] Unlike the Nonconformists, the Anglican Church resisted "Congo Sundays," because "the clergy and their congregations have a great dislike of special Sundays and it is very rarely that we can impose them."[104] Anglicans sponsored 40 of the identified meetings, mostly meetings of the Men's Societies that were the Anglican answer to the PSAs. In terms of donations, the clergy were more active than laypeople. Of the 137 clergymen donors whose religion we can identify, not including bishops, 58 were Anglican, accounting for just over half the value of identifiable clergy donations. However, among the donor base as a whole, only 12 percent of all individual donations came from Anglicans who were almost a third of the donors. The overall picture is of uneven support.

The Anglican Church's connections to the Congo reform movement were top-heavy, enhancing the respectability of the cause among the public and speaking in the Lords and in Whitehall. The Anglican clergy were far less active than the Baptists. The Congo Reform Association had the active support of several leading men, but the agitation in individual parishes left much to be desired in a movement that claimed to represent the broader public.

---

[101] *Organ*, 1910, 417–30, 451–2.
[102] Robert Withycombe, "The Anglican Episcopate in England and Australia in the Early Twentieth Century," *Journal of Religious History* 16, no. 2 (December 1990): 154.
[103] *Organ*, 1910, 456.
[104] Southwark to Morel, 21 March 1907, F8/131:9.

Commerce

The CRA set out to unite the worlds of philanthropy, religion, and commerce. Despite the efforts of Morel and Holt, the third leg was never as strong as the other two.

Within the business world, two groups had direct stakes in the outcome: rubber manufacturers and African merchants. Comparing the rubber companies to the chocolate firms is instructive. After years of investigation, the chocolate firms boycotted cocoa from the islands, but rubber firms stood aloof from the Congo question. George Cadbury made the connection, writing "I have often longed that some great india-rubber manufacturer would take the same course that my nephew, Mr W.A. Cadbury, adopted, and it might have had years ago some influence in bringing public opinion in Belgium to bear on the awful conditions existing in the Congo."[105] There were numerous rubber companies, however, and they did not have the close relationships or moral compass that led the big three chocolate firms to concern themselves with the issue of their suppliers' labor, however slowly.

The rubber industry's evolving attitude appeared in their chief organs of opinion, the biweekly *India-Rubber Journal* of London and the monthly *India Rubber World* of New York. In 1900–03, both papers came to believe the evidence of misrule. The *Journal* took a strongly reformist position that led to some hostile Congophile correspondence, while the *World* took a longer view, worrying that the reckless, forced exploitation was going to exhaust the Congo's rubber.[106] By fall 1904, both publications retreated from their positions. At the end of Morel's US visit, the *World* became agnostic: "Comment upon the purely political aspects of the Congo controversy is beyond the scope of the *India Rubber World*. We do not even know whether there is, or is not, a basis for the charge that commercial rather than humane motives have inspired ... [the reform campaign]."[107] The *Journal* reversed its position completely. It had criticized May French Sheldon when she embarked for the Congo in 1904 as the tool of the Congo Free State, but on her return it approved of her favorable reports about the Congo administration.[108] The paper reproduced a book that argued that forced labor was a philanthropic way to teach Africans how to work. The changes at both journals suggest that Leopold's Press Bureau had paid them for favorable coverage. Although the *Journal* continued to challenge "Mr Morel and his friends" for the next few years, the arrival of a new editor in 1907 caused the

---

[105] Quoted in A.G. Gardiner, *Life of George Cadbury* (London: Cassell, 1923), 249.
[106] *IRW*, 1 July 1903, 328; *IRJ*, 30 March 1903, 335; *IRJ*, 31 August 1903, 223.
[107] "Rubber and the Congo Question," *IRW*, 1 November 1904, 34.
[108] *IRJ*, 21 November 1904, 521; 12 October 1903, 372; 2 January 1905, 18.

paper to embrace neutrality.[109] At about the same time the *World* again began treating the reformers' allegations as fact. However, like Morel, neither journal at any time advocated that the rubber manufacturers do anything different.

The African merchants, except for Holt and Deuss, were lukewarm donors to the CRA. When the Belgian government began opening the country to free trade in 1910, not a single British company made a move to begin trading in the Congo. Far from operating a conspiracy to get their hands on the riches of the Congo, the Liverpool merchants had little interest in this region. Although the sources are silent on the reasons for this, it would appear that the brutality of the regime had damaged the Congo as a land of opportunity for trading. The main British interest in the Congo in these years came from William Lever, a manufacturer. His scheme involved palm-oil plantations, not trading—the plan we have seen Guinness praising in speeches in Chapter 3.[110]

Morel had rested his greatest hopes on the Chambers of Commerce, particularly Liverpool, Manchester, and London. In 1901, he had convinced them to support a resolution against the French Congo for obstructing John Holt's trade.[111] The Congo Free State evil was even more egregious but with the key difference that it had not harmed British companies directly, which dampened interest at the Chambers.

The Liverpool Chamber of Commerce should have been a natural ally. In the 1890s, it had supported humanitarian causes such as ending slavery in Morocco, Uganda, and Zanzibar.[112] John Holt for many years was Vice-Chairman of its African Trade Section and held positions on its governing bodies.[113] Morel had made many contacts that could be useful to the CRA as an honorary member of the Section and served on its Committee starting in 1902, thanks to Alfred Jones, who had not given up trying to woo the younger man and even invested £500 in the *West African Mail* at its founding to this end.[114] However, when it came to rallying the Chamber on the Congo, Holt and Morel had to deal with his active opposition. Now Sir Alfred Jones, he was the African Trade Section's Chairman, the President of the Chamber, and the Congo Free State's Consul in Liverpool.[115] The man who had been Morel's mentor in the 1890s and who

---

[109] *IRJ*, 17 December 1906.
[110] Lever paid Morel, not the CRA, £100 for a report on Nigeria, contrary to Cookey, *Britain*, 278; Lever to Morel, 24 July 1911, F8/100:145.
[111] Liverpool Council meeting, 30 September 1901, 380 COM 1/4:74.
[112] *ASR*, April 1894, 172.
[113] The group's name changed to West African Section only in 1940.
[114] Morel to Gelder, F10/1 39 23; Morel to R. Fox, 31 August 1903, F10/7:411.
[115] African Trade Section, 23 March, 11 May, and 18 May 1903, 380 COM 3/1/1; Morel to Guinness, 17 December 1903, F8/74:16.

had supported him in 1900–1903 to dull his Congo advocacy had become his opponent.[116]

Although the African Trade section's members included several CRA donors, such as James Irvine, Hahnemann Stuart, G.A. Moore, and Joseph Crewdson, Jones was able to quash any discussion of the Congo at the Chamber. Morel refused to run for re-election to the African Trade Section's Committee in 1904, claiming that the leader of the CRA could not serve with the Congo Free State's most effective advocate in Britain.[117] Holt decided against formally challenging Jones on the grounds of conflict of interest because his presidency had otherwise been successful.[118] Caught between Holt and Jones, the Liverpool Chamber could not take a stand on the Congo, a victory for Jones.

After Jones hired May French Sheldon, Lord Mountmorres, and Marcus Dorman as supposedly independent investigators at an expense far exceeding the CRA's annual revenue and distributed literature attacking the reformers, Morel became obsessed with him. When Jones told the Belgian press in 1906 that the CRA was fading away, unsupported by the British public, Morel attacked Jones personally in the press.[119] The next year, Jones put the cocoa scandals on the Section's agenda to focus attention on British complicity in slavery, prompting Holt to publicly question Jones's humanitarian credentials.[120] After some jousting in the press, Morel turned a 4,000-person Congo meeting at Sun Hall, Liverpool, into a forum for denouncing Jones.[121] The Chamber steered a middle ground, voting Jones a message of support and sending a resolution drafted by the African Trade Section to endorse Belgian annexation of the Congo Free State subject to the Berlin Act and Britain's treaty rights, without mentioning the rights of the natives.[122] At long last the Liverpool Chamber of Commerce had, however reluctantly, made a statement in favor of Congo reform. This was their last Congo action, because Grey's policy satisfied them.[123] Holt apologized publicly to Jones, at the same time deploring the Chamber's

---

[116] Morel to Dilke, 1 January 1903, F10/2:86; Morel to Hutton, 3 January 1903, F10/2:88.

[117] Morel to Emmott, 8 June 1904 F10/10:357; African Trade Section, 13 June 1904, 380 COM 3/1/1.

[118] Holt to Morel, 24 December 1904, F8/85:376.

[119] Holt to Morel, 22 October 1906, F8/86:471; 380 HOL I 3/9.

[120] 30 September 1907, 380 HOL I/3/9:90–98; *Organ*, November 1907, 62–4; Joint meeting, General Purposes Committee and African Trade Section, 21 October 1907, 380 HOL I/3/9:90–98; Cadbury to Buxton, 22 October 1907, Brit. Emp. s.18 C79/86; Buxton to Mrs King Lewis and Brooks, 25 October 1907, Brit. Emp. s.19 D1/3:710, 713.

[121] *Organ*, November 1907, 64–6.

[122] Liverpool Chamber of Commerce, Council, 29 October 1907; Section, 11 November 1907, 380 COM 3/1/5; FO 367/70:83.

[123] Guthrie to Morel, 17 February 1910, F9/7:109.

long silence.¹²⁴ Morel's final observation on the matter, "What a miserable body the Liverpool Chamber of Commerce is!" was much the same as Kingsley and Holt's conclusion a decade before.¹²⁵ Jones and Leopold had won most of the rounds. The long struggle to get even a tepid endorsement from the Liverpool Chamber of Commerce highlighted how little support the cause had among the Liverpool commercial community.

The situations in London and Manchester were similar. CRA Executive Committee member Francis Swanzy, a prominent merchant, was Chairman of the West African Trade Section of the London Chamber of Commerce. But just as in Liverpool, a prominent Congophile held a position of great influence: Sir Albert Rollit, MP, Knight Commander of the Order of Leopold and a member of the Supreme Council of the Congo Free State, had been President of the London Chamber from 1893–98 and served as President of the Association of Chambers of Commerce in 1894–98 and 1901–02. He stifled the Congo question in the London Chamber right through 1913. Unlike Jones, Rollitt had no role in the West African Trade Section, so Swanzy could and did convince the Section to act independently several times. In Manchester, the Chamber worried that endorsing reform might jeopardize the Congo market for its manufactures. Arthur Hutton of the African Trade Section occasionally attended Congo events, but only informally.

In November 1907, the Antwerp Chamber of Commerce asked the British Chambers of Commerce to help end the Congo reform campaign.¹²⁶ Morel riposted by asking the Chambers to pass resolutions calling for the restoration of Congo treaty rights in commerce for merchants and natives. He succeeded in ten cities but was stymied by Rollit at the national association.¹²⁷ This spurred the Newcastle and Gateshead Chamber of Commerce to action; for the next two years, Herbert Shaw (Secretary) and Lord Joicey (President) publicized the Congo reform message. In 1909, assisted by John Harris, they led a deputation representing several Chambers to Grey to convey their support for his policy of not recognizing the annexation until Belgium instituted commercial and humanitarian reforms.¹²⁸ In their greatest triumph, Shaw and Joicey obtained the support of 21 chambers for a Congo resolution at the 1910 Associated Chambers meeting over the objections of London, Liverpool and four others.¹²⁹ After this, the alliance with the Chambers withered; Grey and Belgium seemed to be on the right track. They had served the cause of reform, but not as well nor as consistently as Morel had hoped. It is easy to blame the machinations of Jones

---

¹²⁴ *Journal of Commerce*, 12 and 15 November 1907, 380 COM 23/2.
¹²⁵ Guthrie to Morel, 22 February 1910, F9/7:110.
¹²⁶ 21 November 1907, FO 881/9155:178–9.
¹²⁷ Holt to Morel, 30 March 1908, F8/87:529.
¹²⁸ *Organ*, 1909, 142; Morel to Executive Committee, August 1909, F8/145:84.
¹²⁹ Shaw to Morel, 22 February 1910, F8/128:99.

and Rollit. However, Morel's focus on the three most important Chambers where the opposition was strongest blinded him to the possibilities of cultivating the smaller chambers. The 1907 resolutions, 1909 deputation, and 1910 coup at the Associated Chambers meeting showed what was possible with sustained effort from the CRA in partnership with sympathetic men at the Chambers.

Chapter 6

The Internationalist Congo Reform Movement

No pains will be spared in endeavouring to bring about international action for the suppression of abominations against which the Society has been protesting for the past six years or more.[1]—Fox Bourne, 1903

It is possible for men differing in politics, creed, class, and even nationality to combine in common and effective action against systematic wrong-doing.[2]—Morel, 1913

Internationalism

To succeed, the reform movement had to affect events outside the United Kingdom, beginning with international diplomacy. However, the reform agitation had elements better understood as internationalism or what historians call transnationalism. The nineteenth century, when nationalism spread through Europe, also saw the development of internationalism based on national organizations, both governmental and nongovernmental, that reached across borders to build bonds, taking form as international institutions, conferences, and exhibitions. This generated ongoing cross-border connections between individuals from different countries to share knowledge, coordinate practices, and seek solutions to problems.[3] Its prosaic side included practical efforts such as post offices coordinating shipping and trade organizations keeping up with recent developments. Scientists collaborated to advance their fields and activists of every variety internationalized their causes. Internationalism also meant the union of political movements, such as the socialist internationals. At the highest level, internationalism aimed to set up bodies and mechanisms to regulate interstate cooperation and warfare.

Internationalism seemed to offer stability and progress, and this ideological foundation made it, as Daniel Laqua describes it, "a movement, a process, and

---

[1] *Aborigines' Friend*, April 1903, 339–40.
[2] *Organ*, July 1913, 980.
[3] Martin Geyer and Johannes Paulmann, introduction to *The Mechanics of Internationalism*, eds Geyer and Paulmann (Oxford: Oxford University Press, 2001), 1–16.

an outlook."[4] The convening of the first World's Congress of International Associations in May 1910 was its epitome: an institution to determine how international associations could cooperate and to formulate a standard legal framework for their governance.[5]

Among humanitarians, cross-border cooperation had a long history. Amanda Moniz has observed that eighteenth-century philanthropists in American and British voluntary associations saw themselves as an international community of activists.[6] By the late nineteenth century, this form of humanitarian mobilization had spread to other European countries and indeed around the world. Internationalism gave humanitarians additional opportunities. For instance, the Congo reformers considered referring the issue to the International Court of Arbitration and attended the international conferences of other groups.[7]

Whereas internationalism was an idea of the time, transnationalism is a present-day concept that can connote aspects of internationalism or indicate the scholar's construction of a phenomenon transcending national boundaries. Grant, Levine, and Trentmann have pointed out the imperial contribution to transnationalism in developing international law, managing the movement of people and ideas, and generating issues that went beyond the nation-state. Transnational analysis covers phenomena such as diasporas, multiple identities, and cultural hybridization due to dislocation. Most importantly for the present work, transnational communities, connections, and ideas subvert the sovereignty of the nation-state in ways more complex than the application of state-to-state power alone.[8]

From its earliest days, the Congo reform movement had transnational qualities. This study dates the first widespread questions about Leopold's Congo to the advocacy of Williams, an American, and pegs the start of the campaign to the moment when an Englishman, Fox Bourne, publicized the evidence of a Swedish Baptist from an American missionary society. The movement paradoxically succeeded so well as a national movement in Britain in part because it concerned itself with problems external to the British Empire, offering a point of unity after the internal divisions of the Boer War. But notwithstanding occasional fantasies of using unilateral British military pressure to solve the

---

[4] Daniel Laqua, *The Age of Internationalism and Belgium, 1880–1930* (New York: Manchester University Press, 2013), 5.

[5] Brit. Emp. s.18, C85/32.

[6] Amanda Bowie Moniz, "'Labours in the Cause of Humanity in Every Part of the Globe': Transatlantic Philanthropic Collaboration and the Cosmopolitan Ideal, 1760–1815," PhD diss., University of Michigan, 2008), 240–41.

[7] Stead to Morel, 21 May 1903, F4/1.

[8] Kevin Grant, Philippa Levine, and Frank Trentmann, "Introduction," *Beyond Sovereignty: Britain, Empire, and Transnationalism, c. 1880–1950* (Houndmills, Basingstoke, Hampshire: Palgrave Macmillan, 2007), 2–8.

problem, activists and Foreign Secretaries alike generally believed that British action alone would be insufficient to change Leopold's system.

Many of the era's international humanitarian causes had their origins in situations internal to empires that became internationalized when foreigners became interested. In contrast, the Congo Free State's gestation occurred in the burgeoning internationalist trend of the late 1800s. The internationalist spirit was apparent among those interested in Africa. The *Société Géographique de Paris* called an international conference in 1875 to discuss Africa. Savorgnan de Brazza had advocated international cooperation in exploration. A German scientific explorer, Georg Schweinfürth, called for setting up free states ruled by Africans under European protection to end the African slave trade. Drawing on these precedents and ideas, Leopold convened the Geographical Conference of Brussels in 1876 to discuss his proposal to set up African scientific and medical posts in part to end the slave trade. They also endorsed his idea for a permanent central organization, the *Association Internationale Africaine* (AIA), to direct these activities, with national bodies responsible for local publicity, fundraising, and communication with the AIA. Leopold's vision of a strong center and subordinate national bodies went against the dominant model, in which national groups came together to create and direct an international secretariat. Centralization allowed Leopold to play the shell game that ended with his personal vehicle, the *Association International du Congo* (AIC), in control of the Congo, retaining the flag and the aura of the genuinely international AIA. Leopold's new state took concrete form in the world of international relations when, following the examples of the US and Germany, every country attending the Berlin West Africa Conference of 1884–85 recognized the AIC as sovereign. The Conference confirmed these expressions of bilateral legitimacy with a multilateral vote of confidence by allowing the AIC to accede to its culminating treaty. Within months, Leopold renamed the AIC's realm the Congo Free State. Internationalism was a tool Leopold used to achieve his colonial ambitions.

With its origins in the sea foam of internationalism, the Congo Free State initially appeared to be the most attractive international creation of Europe in Africa. Its initial administration, military leadership, and missionaries came from Britain, the US, Italy, Denmark, Sweden, the Netherlands, and elsewhere, as well as Belgium, with workers and soldiers recruited from British colonies. This multinational presence became increasingly Belgian during the existence of the Free State, but never exclusively so.

Agitation for Congo reform took the inverse trajectory, becoming increasingly international. Dennett and Price brought their concerns to Britain in the 1880s and early 1890s. Belgian commercial interests agitated briefly against Leopold's monopolization of trade in the early 1890s without involving other countries. George Washington Williams was the first critic to have a multinational audience. Sjöblom's revelations stirred opinion in Sweden, Belgium, and elsewhere, but sparked a real movement only in Britain. In 1900, Morrison and Sheppard had provided fuel for the British movement and set the stage for a similar one in the United States. Fox Bourne started the movement's transnational nexus through Lorand and Vandervelde.

The first official effort to build bridges between governments occurred in 1903, when Parliament directed the Foreign Secretary, Lord Lansdowne, to confer with the signatories of the Berlin Act. Neither the resulting Note nor the distribution of the Casement Report to the same countries in 1904 led to international cooperation. As described in Chapter 8, this strategy's ineffectiveness was a failure of government internationalism. If the movement was going to express the resolve of the civilized world, then activists would have to create an international consensus of public opinion that governments would follow.

The lessons of the International Union and of Lansdowne's Note were not lost on Morel. Like Fox Bourne, he had tried to stimulate interest in other countries, particularly France and the US. Fully half of his initial plan for the CRA involved building a multinational consensus.[9] Yet this plan, and all subsequent activity, was a country by country process, with different trajectories reflecting each country's character, practices, and interests. The British CRA was essential to the transnational movement in distributing evidence, in spreading the word, and in the advice Morel could provide, but it could not direct events or conjure up functioning affiliates abroad the way it could in Britain.

In today's parlance, Congo reform went viral by 1906, a reflection of the ever-denser network of global connection from faster travel, transport, and communications. The British Empire's Dominions of Canada and Australia, and its future Dominions of New Zealand and South Africa all reverberated with echoes of the British movement. For example, a Congo Balolo Mission representative visiting New Zealand organized meetings and Protestant ministers in Canada prepared a petition.[10] However, no Congo Reform Associations formed in these places, and their governments, lacking authority in foreign affairs, did not act. There were other countries notably absent in the discussions of reform. The government of Sweden-Norway believed that the Congo troubles were the inevitable results of colonial conquest and therefore unremarkable.[11] A few individuals from Russia, the Netherlands, Denmark, Spain, and Portugal made their concerns known to Morel or in their own countries, but there was no sign of anything that could be called a campaign on the part of civil society

---

[9] CRA Plan of Campaign, 31 March 1904, F10/9:764–74.
[10] *Organ*, April 1906, 13.
[11] Liane Ranieri, *Les Relations entre l'État Indépendant du Congo et l'Italie* (Brussels: Académie Royale des Sciences Coloniales, 1959), 151.

or governments in these countries. The Balkan nations were more quiescent still. Much of Europe did not participate in the international movement, and those parts that did were uneven.

European Connections

Austria-Hungary and Italy were most concerned with the Congo Free State's effects on their own nationals. Austrian diplomacy attended to a single case, that of Gustav Maria Rabinek, an Austrian trader who in May 1901 had run afoul of the Katanga Company's rubber monopoly on the Congo's southern borders. After Rabinek appealed his sentence—one so severe that the civil judge at the trial protested in his favor—he died on the long journey to the capital in state custody, with all his goods confiscated by the Katanga Company.[12] This affair linked many countries. The officer who arrested Rabinek, Louis Saroléa, was a first cousin of Belgian Consul Dr Charles Saroléa, a professor in Edinburgh, who debated with Morel in Scotland and America in 1904.[13] Teixiero de Mattos, a Dutch merchant with a Portuguese name trading in British territory and one of Rabinek's creditors, made the affair known by writing to Morel in July 1902. He had issues with the Congo State seizing his goods not long after. Morel's immediate (and initially inaccurate) account of the Rabinek affair came to the attention of German merchant Ludwig Deuss, who had supplied trade goods to Rabinek. Deuss became one of the most passionate and persistent of the reformers, generously supporting the CRA and agitating continuously in Germany for over six years—the only German to do so.[14] While Morel tried to convince the British Foreign Office to take a stand and sparred in the *Morning Post* with Gilzean Reid in February 1903, Rabinek's German connections wrote to *The Times*, Rabinek's heirs sued in Belgian and German courts, Deuss tried in vain to get the German Foreign Office interested, and Austrian diplomacy focused on obtaining a settlement, its only confrontation with the Congo Free State.[15]

Italy's involvement also centered on national concerns. Beginning in 1903, the Italian government agreed to loan Italian army officers to the Congo's multinational military force on half pay. The government approved this initiative, which it had previously refused, in conjunction with a proposal to settle tens of

---

[12] Morel, *King Leopold's Rule*, 285.
[13] *Biographie Coloniale Belge*, Vol. 1, col. 816, and Vol. 7B, col. 336.
[14] Willequet, *Jacques. La Congo Belge et la Weltpolitik* (Brussels: Université Libre de Bruxelles, 1963), 51–2.
[15] *The Times*, 18 June 1904, 4. Rabinek's heir obtained compensation in 1922.

thousands of Italian emigrants in northeast Congo near Lake Kivu.[16] An Italian representative, Captain Baccari, a medical doctor as well as a military officer, arrived in Boma on 1 July 1903 for a yearlong assessment trip to Lake Kivu. When he returned to Italy in the fall of 1904, he disrupted the Foreign Ministry's plans by reporting that Lake Kivu was unsuitable for settlement and that the Congo State deployed Italian officers inappropriately, including requiring them to use violence to collect provisions and rubber. Baccari's sensational accounts of having been poisoned and of the Governor General's attempt to have him declared insane became notorious on his return.[17] The government, determined to offend neither Britain nor Leopold, withheld the report and briefly imprisoned Baccari, spurring some newspapers not suborned by Leopold's cash to undertake their own investigations. Baccari ended up fighting a duel with the Congo's Consul in Genoa on 13 February 1906, which ended with both men lightly wounded.[18] When the government finally released his report, public opinion had become skeptical about Italy's Congo involvement. The emigration scheme died. King Victor Emmanuel halted military recruitment and forbade serving officers from renewing their contracts, and a later act of the Italian Parliament recalled all remaining officers by year end 1906.[19] Leopold's attempt to shield the Free State with Italian involvement had failed; the brouhaha served to keep the issue of Congo misrule before international opinion.

With Italian concerns addressed, the country's interest faded quickly, as the Congo's representative in Italy reported with relief in 1908.[20] The press turned mostly to reprinting Belgian and English Congo articles without taking an editorial stand. In the Italian Parliament, only one delegate continued to bring up the Congo.[21] No organization in Italy pushed Congo reform. The Italian government favored Belgian annexation subject to the terms of the Berlin Act to offend neither Britain nor Belgium. It promptly recognized the annexation.[22]

In Switzerland and France, public interest in the Congo question went much deeper. Dr René Claparède, a public intellectual and journalist in Geneva, began to correspond with Morel as early as 1905 about the Congo. Determined to get Swiss newspapers to enter the controversy and awaken public opinion, he allied with the botanist Dr Hermann Christ-Socin of Basel. They were able

---

[16] Giula Piccolino, "La Civilizzazione A Ritroso: La Questione Congolese E Le Sue Ripercussioni In Italia" (thesis, Universita' Degli Studi Di Firenze, 2004), 134–6.

[17] *New York Times*, 26 December 1904, 4. A court ruled that the poisoning was accidental, and Villa concurred, Ranieri, *Congo et l'Italie*, 185–7.

[18] Piccolino, "Civilizzazione," 201.

[19] *Morning Post*, 13 July 1905, cited in Louis, "E.D. Morel," 163; *The Times*, 19 November 1906, 5; Piccolino, "Civilizzazione," 199.

[20] Van der Burch to de Cuvelier, 11 May 1907, in Ranieri, *Congo et l'Italie*, 222–4.

[21] Adrien van der Burch to de Cuvelier, 11 May 1907, in Ranieri, *Congo et l'Italie*, 226.

[22] FO 881/9093 1907.

propagandists and effective collaborators for the British and the French. He and Christ-Socin wrote books, pamphlets, and letters to the editor. They also held public meetings, including speakers Alice Harris and Morel. On 1 July 1908, Claparède founded the Swiss League for the Defense of the Natives of the Conventional Basin of the Congo (*Ligue Suisse pour la défense des indigènes dans le bassin conventionnel du Congo*) with 136 members. The membership reached 400 a year later, smaller than the CRA's, but larger in proportion to the country's population.[23] Nobody could accuse Switzerland of commercial or colonial designs, and Claparède emphasized its small size and neutrality. This was also a weakness; Leopold and Belgium regarded Swiss opinion as background noise, especially without Swiss government involvement. Swiss activism helped keep the issue alive and neutralized the accusation that it was all about Liverpool merchant interests, but it had no impact on the decisions made about the Congo.

With the French Congo their primary concern, French activists brought passion and energy to the issue. The leaders of the French League for the Defense of the Natives of the Conventional Basin of the Congo (*Ligue Française pour la défense des indigènes dans le bassin conventionnel du Congo*) included the "Kipling of Africa," Pierre Mille, Brazza's former assistant Félicien Challaye, the elderly legal historian Paul Viollet, and the journalist-politician Gustave Rouanet. They had the sympathy of the famous writer Anatole France. However, these men found themselves scarcely able to affect public opinion, which did not distinguish the French Congo from other French colonies, and unable to influence the government. The French government's priority was French Congo. The concession regime there resembled Leopold's, though without the state's direct investment or the same access to military force. The refusal of successive French governments to substantially reform this system prevented them from criticizing Leopold's Congo. The radical editor-politician Georges Clemenceau, who had denounced the Congo Free State in 1896, paid no attention to reformers during his 1906–09 term as prime minister.[24] A personal meeting with Charles Dilke in December 1906 failed to enlist his support. Clemenceau's government recognized the 1908 Belgian annexation without conditions, unlike Britain, Germany, and even Italy.

Coordination among the national movements was difficult. The CRA's British allies had representation on its Executive Committee, but the links to reformers in other countries were personal, usually through Morel. One answer, urged by the Swiss and attempted by the French, was an international organization to coordinate them under an International League for the Defense of the Natives in the Conventional Basin of the Congo (*Ligue Internationale pour la défense des indigènes dans le bassin conventionnel du Congo*), headquartered in Paris, in early

---

[23] René Claparède, "*Ligue Suisse*," *Bulletin Trimestriel*, August 1909, 12.
[24] Lagergren, *Mission and State*, 190, 180–83.

1908.[25] The Norwegian Nobel laureate author and political activist Bjørnstjerne Bjørnson, who had early lent his name to the cause, became its *président d'honneur*, but French men dominated the organization, comprising three-quarters of its initial Committee. It went to work with a will, calling for public support without regard to nationality and issuing pamphlets and a triennial journal, addressing both Congos.[26] The international league lasted about a year. By early 1909, the others had accepted Morel's suggestion to replace it with a consultative committee representing (not overseeing) national organizations, the International Committee for the Defense of the Congo Natives. The French failed to create a truly international Congo reform organization because of the need to operate through national governments. In the end, what mattered to the course of events were the actions of the British, Belgian, American, and German governments.

Germany

The German reform movement took years to organize, beginning in 1903–04, when Alfred Zimmerman, a former colonial official who was chancellor of the German embassy in London, became a committed Congo reformer.[27] He hoped for a European consensus on the rights of Africans under colonial rule. Like Casement, he could not participate in a lobbying organization, but there was no Morel to lead one for him, only Ludwig Deuss. Deuss, like Holt, sympathized with the Africans as people and as customers. He was the only prominent reformer to have married an African woman. Unfortunately, his poor political and organizational sense impeded his well-intentioned efforts.[28] Despite the gradual buildup of support in Bremen, Hamburg, and Berlin, favorable press coverage, and lively debates at the Colonial Society, it took until 1910 to form the German League for the Defence of the Natives of the Congo Basin.

With German allies fragmented, reformers pinned their hopes on the Kaiser. In 1905, the Quakers sent E.W. Brooks and J.G. Alexander to Berlin as a deputation regarding the Congo, possibly with Zimmerman's support. Brooks and Alexander, CRA Executive Committee members, brought along John Harris for eyewitness testimony. They met with German officials but not the Kaiser. The next year, the Kaiser asked his friend Lord Lonsdale for his opinion of the

---

[25] Claparède to Morel, 9 December 1906, F4/14.

[26] *Bulletin Trimestriel*, April, August, December 1908; "*La cession de l'état indépendant a la Belgique*," F13/3/3.

[27] Not to be confused with Arthur Zimmerman, Foreign Minister of Germany during World War I.

[28] Morel to Abel-Musgrave, 2 February 1910, F8/118:26; Willequet, *La Congo Belge et la Weltpolitik*, 51–4, 172–5.

Congo Free State.[29] Morel seized the opportunity, sending a packet of materials via F.W. Fox and Lonsdale, such as the *Speaker* articles of 1900 and a calf-bound copy of *Red Rubber*.[30] When the Kaiser visited England in November 1907, Harris asked the Anti-Slavery Society and the Quakers to sponsor a deputation, but Anti-Slavery deferred to the Friends, who were not able to secure a meeting.[31] Harris then proposed a visit to Berlin, but Sir Thomas Fowell Buxton vetoed the idea, saying that it would be open to misinterpretation.[32] The approaches to the Kaiser were not a productive use of energy. Wilhelm disliked Leopold but did not take up humanitarian causes.[33]

According to the German agent of Leopold's Press Bureau, its subsidies had generated much goodwill for the Congo.[34] The German Congo League formed only after the Press Bureau closed. The alliance between British and German reformers had its benefits. The CRA collected £158 from seven Germans, Deuss, Vohsen, and others kept the controversy alive in the German press, and Morel could showcase their support. However, the reformers had little official impact. Great-power calculations in Berlin, not public pressure, determined the few occasions when the German government supported British pressure on Belgium.

America

The American reform movement was the strongest after Britain's. The American philanthropic tradition was the only one comparable to Britain's in age and depth. Transatlantic cooperation reached back almost as long, and continued to expand through the progressive era.[35] The reformers had the US in their sights from the beginning. Leading British reformers crossed the Atlantic annually for four years to bolster the alliance: Morel in 1904, Guinness in 1905 and 1907, and the Harrises in 1906.

---

[29] F.W. Fox to Morel, 4 November 1906, F9/6:37.

[30] Fox to Morel, 6 November 1906, F9/6:39–40; Morel to Deuss, 12 November 1906, F10/14:598.

[31] Brit. Emp. s.19 D1/3:652; Brit. Emp. s.20 E2/12; Buxton to Morel, 5 October 1907, F9/2:217.

[32] Anti-Slavery Committee, 19 November and 6 December 1907, Brit. Emp. s.20 E2/12; Buxton to Alexander, 10 December 1907, Brit. Emp. s.19 D1/3:821.

[33] Emerson, *Leopold*, 225.

[34] Hochschild, *King Leopold's Ghost*, 240–41.

[35] Moniz, op. cit.; Ann Marie Wilson, "In the Name of God, Civilization, and Humanity: The United States and the Armenian Massacres of the 1890s," *Le Mouvement Social*, April–June 2009: 27–44; Daniel Rodgers, *Atlantic Crossings* (Cambridge: Harvard University Press, 1998).

The ostensible reason for Morel's trip was to bring a memorial to President Roosevelt. Morrison and Guinness believed it would be better to make the trip after the election, but Morel did not know when the election was to take place and was tied to the schedule of his temporary replacement at the *West African Mail*.[36] Roosevelt consented to receive Morel on 30 September 1904 though he considered the request for an audience "a well-meant impertinence."[37] Roosevelt found the 15-minute audience instructive, but the obvious Catholic hostility to the CRA as personified by Cardinal Gibbons of Baltimore worried him with elections coming, and he did nothing.

Morel spent the rest of his three weeks in the US touring the northeast, making speeches and contacting people, armed with introductions from Stead, Parker, Strachey, Harold Spender, Lord Norbury, and others. This led to a meeting with Samuel Clemens (Mark Twain) on 17 October 1904. Twain's assistance for the next 16 months included his satiric booklet, *King Leopold's Soliloquy*, a newspaper interview, speeches, and three trips to Washington to meet with Roosevelt and State Department officials.[38] Leopold's spokesmen, the Belgian ambassador Baron Moncheur and Cardinal Gibbons assisted by Head and Saroléa, could not prevent the formation of the American CRA during Morel's trip, sporting luminaries such as Thomas Barbour, Baptist leader and peace activist, Robert Park, sociologist, Stanley Hall, psychologist and president of Holy Cross, and Booker T. Washington, the prominent African-American. The American CRA organized the Harrises' triumphal tour of 49 cities in 1906. Secretary of State Elihu Root felt that the reformers' arguments were exaggerated and neither he nor Roosevelt believed that the US could intervene because it did not sign the Berlin Act, deliberately to avoid African entanglements.[39]

Policy shifted in December 1906, when the exposure of Leopold's paid lobby in the United States enflamed public opinion, already primed by the Harrises and the American CRA earlier that year.[40] The discovery of Congo payments to a Senate Foreign Relations Committee staff member made this an international incident that transcended worries about the Berlin Treaty. It was this American response, in conjunction with British pressure, that caused the panicked Belgian government to demand and receive a commitment from Leopold to transfer the Congo to Belgium. In a pattern demonstrated in Italy and elsewhere, American hostility to Leopold's rule, the very condition he had spent so much money and

---

[36] Guinness to Morel, 27 April 1904, F8/74:31–2; Morrison to Morel, 16 June 1904, F8/115:14; Morel to Emmott, 2 August 1904, F10/11:477.

[37] Thomas Pakenham, *The Scramble for Africa* (New York: Random House, 1991), 658; Emmott worried that Morel's visit to Roosevelt was inappropriate, F4/5:192.

[38] Hunt Hawkins, "Mark Twain's Involvement with the Congo Reform Movement," *The New England Quarterly* 51, no. 2 (June 1978): 147–75.

[39] *San Francisco Independent*, 11 June 1904.

[40] Hawkins, "Mark Twain's Involvement," 173.

effort to prevent, had come about because of his methods. Reports from the American Consul-General in the Congo at the end of 1907 led to a commitment to joint action with Britain to pressure Belgium for an annexation treaty that would remove the King's authority and improve the condition of the people, an offer Grey took up in 1908. The United States avoided the Berlin question by basing this stance on violations of the 1890 Brussels Anti-Slavery Treaty.[41]

The American CRA had laid the groundwork to make it easy and popular for the government to act. However, government policy shifted again after Taft became President in March 1909. He did not have Roosevelt's personal sympathy for the cause and the united front of the US and Britain dissipated. Also, by mid-1909 the American CRA had fallen apart as its leading men had moved on to other things. The last serving officer, John Daniels, disappeared from view after he married and relocated to Buffalo. Barbour's daughter continued to handle routine correspondence but the movement had faded away after rendering great service.[42]

Belgium

Leopold's Achilles heel was Belgium, the reluctant object of Leopold's plan to make it a colonial power. Leopold's Congo venture depended on a small number of Belgian financiers, military men, and colonial enthusiasts, but even more on Belgium's acquiescence to his activities. In keeping with the country's constitution, the Belgian parliament had formally approved Leopold's acquisition of the Congo crown, but this implied they could disapprove as well. In addition, Leopold was susceptible to Belgian concerns. The dominance of the monarchist Catholic party in Belgium through the Congo Free State period suggested that the government was in the palm of his hand. However, the combination of international pressure and growing criticism in Belgium led the government to act contrary to Leopold's wishes.

Usually mentioned as a corollary to British activism, Belgian anti-Congo efforts deserve their own book to examine their motives and methods. Without Belgian initiative, Leopold's rule might have endured for decades as the concession company regime did in French Congo; Belgian reformers achieved a level of respectability, political influence, and public acceptance that the French reformers never reached.

It did not start out that way. Criticisms from the socialists had little impact; conservatives and liberals were too hostile to the socialists' political program to

---

[41] Paul McStallworth, "The United States and the Congo Question," PhD diss., Ohio State (1955), 313–17.

[42] Morel to Claparède, 23 March 1910, F4/14.

cooperate with them on the Congo. In addition, the Congo was not Belgium's responsibility. In 1895, the Belgian prime minister disavowed any interest in the Congo, even though Belgium had loaned large sums to the Congo Free State.[43] In 1900, parliamentary questions failed on the grounds that Belgium had no responsibilities for the Congo. In 1901, Leopold's former ally, ex-Prime Minister Auguste Beernaert, tried and failed to get Belgium to annex the Congo.

The CRA itself could be an impediment. On occasion, the CRA's actions obstructed progress, particularly when they spurred nationalistic Belgian rejection of British bullying as described by the British envoys to Belgium.[44] Phipps complained that the English reformers' attacks had so alienated Belgians that not even the head of the Belgian Red Cross could concede any justice to their views and his successor Arthur Hardinge wrote that the CRA's denunciations helped "to complicate an already complex situation."[45] Even when the Belgian Parliament prepared to discuss annexation, Hardinge feared that intemperate CRA words would allow apologists to appeal to Belgian patriotism.[46] He wrote along similar lines through 1908: "If Morel and Co. will only stop for a moment their mischievous declamations, which are now one of the best cards in the King's hands, events here appear likely enough to fight for us, without overt action on our part."[47] Hardinge was keenly aware of the importance of letting Belgian reformers take the lead. Even a poorly worded consular report could appear counterproductive, as in early 1910, though the adverse Belgian reaction may have been a negotiating tactic.[48] The complaints of Phipps and Hardinge should not blind us to the fact that Morel, in keeping with the advice of Fox Bourne and Dilke, usually avoided language and actions that would further inflame Belgian public opinion against the reformers.

In fact, the crimes and incompetence of the Congo administration were well known to those Belgians with Congo experience, some of whom had published the information to little avail.[49] The small circle of knowledgeable people who raised questions found themselves further stymied when Belgian public opinion hardened in a nationalist response to British reformers. After this setback, Belgian reform agitation gained strength from the public pronouncements of respected individuals.

---

[43] *Pall Mall Gazette*, 6 November 1895.

[44] Pearson memorandum, 21 February 1906, FO 881/9628:1–2.

[45] Phipps to Lansdowne, 8 September 1903, FO 881/8268:279; Hardinge to Grey, FO 881/9309:80.

[46] Hardinge to Grey, 16 November 1906, FO 881/8923:128.

[47] Hardinge to C. Hardinge, 21 December 1906, FO 881/9823:171 and 20 December 1907, FO 881/9155:181; Hardinge to Grey, 23 January 1908, FO 881/9309:77.

[48] Hardinge to Grey, 10 June 1910, FO 881/9730:153.

[49] Captain Phillip Salusbury, "Defenders of the Congo State," *United Service Magazine*, July 1896, 434–5, 437–8.

The most prominent was Beernaert, a future Nobel Peace Prize winner. He collaborated with the king as prime minister for ten years, but grew insistent that the king should change his policies in the Congo from 1891 on.[50] In 1894, he resigned and split the Catholic Party over proportional representation, taking a small faction with him dedicated to, among other things, prying the Congo from Leopold's control. But he had many interests and doubted that Leopold would give up his colony, "for the sake of the power which this wealth gave him in Belgium, and as a means of accomplishing his costly and magnificent projects."[51] Beernaert became an important arm's-length ally for the reformers in the annexation debates of 1906–08, but he would not dedicate himself to leading them.

Beernaert was not alone in his trajectory from king's man to opponent. The British envoy to Belgium, Constantine Phipps, observed, "Those ... who have suffered shipwreck on the shifting and treacherous sands of the Congo are innumerable," because they had, after years of service, "incurred the disapproval of their despotic master."[52] Alphonse Jean Wauters had been a trusted servant of Leopold's as the editor of the *Mouvement Géographique*, Belgium's leading journal of geography, but became a reformer after falling out with the king. Wauters had found that the Congo Free State's financial statements were false a few years before Morel did, and increasingly cooperated with other reformers.[53]

More important to the cause was the respected professor of colonial law at the Free University of Brussels, Félicien Cattier. His 1898 book on the legal structure of the Congo became the bible for Congo officials, but it also raised criticisms and reminded its readers of the obligations of the Berlin Act and the Congo Free State's constitution.[54] Cattier became increasingly skeptical of Leopold's project, and decided to influence the structure of the Commission of Inquiry as it came into being in 1904. Working with Wauters, Cattier preempted Leopold with a seemingly official announcement of the Commission's powers; Leopold could not announce a lesser mandate without opening himself to severe criticism.[55] Largely because of the Commission's expanded authority, its 1905 report landed the first serious blow against Leopold in Belgium itself. Convinced that Leopold's Congo had to end, Cattier wrote another book in 1906, the same year as Morel's *Red Rubber*. By meticulously outlining the workings of the Congo administration and analyzing the Commission's report, it administered

---

[50] "Auguste Beernaert," *Biographie Coloniale Belge*, Vol. 1 (1948), cols 98–112, http://www.kaowarsom.be/en/notices_Beernaert_Auguste.

[51] Phipps to Lansdowne, 15 May 1904, FO 881/8414:175.

[52] Phipps to Lansdowne, 21 May 1904, FO 881/8414:186.

[53] Marchal, *Morel contre Léopold*, Vol. 1, 19.

[54] Félicien Cattier, *Droit et Administration de l'EIC* (Brussels: Larcier, 1898), especially 136, 331.

[55] Cookey, *Britain*, 124–7.

Figure 6.1   Félicien Cattier
Source: Union Minière du Haut-Katanga, 1906–1956 (Edition L. Cuypers, 1956).

the second serious strike to Leopold's hopes of exploiting the Congo until his death.[56] There is much to be said for the argument that Cattier achieved more in 1905–06 than any other reformer.[57] His colleague at the university, Professor Herbert Speyer, also called for annexation and a new legal framework.

The unexpected entry of another professor broke the monolithic support of Belgian Catholic opinion for Leopold's Congo. Father Arthur-Marie-Théodore Vermeersch, a Jesuit and Professor of Law and Political Science at the Catholic University of Louvain, came out with two books in 1906: *La Question Congolaise* and *Les Destinées du Congo Belge*. For those unmoved by Cattier and Speyer, Vermeersch's coverage of the subject from a perspective both Catholic and respectful of Leopold further damaged the Congo's standing and paved the way for the decision to annex the Congo in December.

Belgium's importance to the reform movement had increased as a consensus formed around annexation. Although it had been discussed for years, the turning point came at a CRA-sponsored meeting in June 1905 at the Holborn Town Hall, arranged by Casement, which endorsed this solution at the insistence of its most prominent speaker, Sir Harry Johnston. Although Morel and others had doubts and might have steered the CRA toward other ideas, Sir Edward Grey's arrival at the Foreign Office locked it in place. Grey wanted a solution that did not increase British responsibilities, that subordinated the Congo government to an elected parliament, and that did not disturb the balance of power in Europe. Annexation met these criteria. It also put the final decision into the hands of the Belgian government and thus the Belgian people and Parliament. Cattier and Vermeersch had called for Belgian annexation. When Vandervelde endorsed Cattier's analysis and solutions, his views became more respectable. The Liberals then joined him to demand an end to the Congo Free State, raising the possibility of parliamentary action.[58] Cattier, Vandervelde, and Lorand worked closely with Morel and Fox Bourne to keep the agitation moving, sharing information and traveling across the North Sea. Cattier even called on the British Foreign Office to encourage them to keep up the pressure.[59] However, Belgian reformers never coalesced into a CRA-like organization. Efforts to unite Speyer, Lorand, Vandervelde, and Vermeersch in a Belgian Association for the Protection of Rights of Congo Natives came to nothing.[60] The individuals who mattered came to the question from such different perspectives that their cooperation was usually *ad hoc*.

---

[56] Cattier, *Étude Sur la Situation de l'État Indépendant du Congo* (Brussels: Larcier, 1906).
[57] Cookey, *Britain*, 155.
[58] Cookey, *Britain*, 156.
[59] Cookey, *Britain*, 157.
[60] Hardinge to Grey, 11 March 1909, FO 881/9530; Claparède to Morel, 20 March 1910, F4/14.

Figure 6.2   Emile Vandervelde
Source: From LSE Library's collections, MOREL/F1/8/1/13.

Even without a mass movement or a CRA-like organization, Belgium made the decisions to expropriate Leopold and institute reforms, thanks to the efforts of a few well-placed experts like Cattier, Vermeersch, and Wauters, to the public revelations of insiders like Charles Lemaire and Stanislaus Lefranc, and to the parliamentary agitation of Vandervelde, Lorand, and others. Because of the confluence of internal factors and external shocks, the Belgian government found itself in an untenable position in late 1906 and again during the 1907–08 annexation debates. After annexation, the same people created the pressure on the Belgian government to introduce reforms, with the assistance of Leopold's heir, Albert, whose 1909 visit to the Congo convinced him that things had to change.

Without international allies, particularly in the US and Belgium, the British were unlikely to have secured annexation or reform short of potentially destabilizing military threats. Less effective allies also assisted, not least by showing that the Congo was not simply a British imperial obsession. The Congo reform agitation was internationalist in that it was a set of interconnected but separate national efforts.

Chapter 7
Contested Representation

> The horror of the Congo Free State must be kept well before the British people, till they insist, in the name of Humanity, that it shall cease.[1]—F.B. Meyer, 1907

Pity the ordinary British citizen who wanted to develop an informed opinion of the Congo question. The literature described two different realities: *The Truth about the Congo* praised the good works of the Congo Free State, but *King Leopold's Rule in Africa* detailed the misrule of a benighted and bloody land. Some pamphlets condemned the intrigues and greed of Leopold, who professed humanitarianism to exploit the Congo, while others said much the same about a shadowy group of British merchants and their humanitarian frontmen, who used compassion as a ruse to seize the country's riches. Missionaries, journalists, explorers, and officials, some on official journeys of investigation, issued supposedly unbiased reports that came to diametrically opposed conclusions, each attacked in turn as tainted by self-interest or hidden subsidies. With the Congo so far away, our perplexed citizen had no way to independently assess these claims and counterclaims. *The Times* complained of "a certain feeling of hopelessness as to the utterly contradictory nature of the evidence given. When versions so entirely discrepant are forthcoming, both from those who claim to have studied the question here and from those who have investigated conditions on the spot, the reader may well-nigh despair of reaching any satisfactory conclusion."[2] Taking a stand meant believing one discourse over another.

The reformers' chief battlefield was representation. The fate of millions depended on whether the reformers' imagined Congo of unchecked exploitation and atrocity would hold more weight with the public, press, and decision-makers than the counter-narrative of a model philanthropic colony with a few swiftly-punished excesses.

A War of Words

The struggle over the Congo was mostly a war of words waged in Europe and America. As Aidan Forth observes, the reformers achieved their aims not

---
[1] Meyer to Morel, 16 April 1907, F4/24.
[2] *The Times*, 25 January 1905, 9.

through social action but by deploying rhetoric.[3] Kevin Dunn calls this process "imagining the Congo," but it involved a discursive shaping of the identities of all parties: Leopold's regime, reformers, and the intended British audience.[4] In her study of cultural power deployed for and against social movements, Ann Swidler outlines how activists confront dominant assumptions by bringing a competing set of images to public notice.[5] The reformers built images that overturned the understanding of the Congo and promoted a British sense of responsibility, publicizing the resulting rhetoric through print, image, and speech to persuade targeted audiences.

Taking their cues from the traditions of overseas humanitarianism and crusading journalism, the leading reformers used information from three broad categories: statistics, administrative practices, and personal testimony.[6] Statistics were available for those who would take the trouble to analyze them, such as Morel, Cattier, and Wauters. Inconsistent and falsified statistics suggested ill intent, and even these numbers exposed the reality of forced labor.

Reformers described the details of the Congo state's administrative practices to portray a system that inevitably produced oppression and atrocities. Even before Morel's 1900 *Speaker* articles indicted Leopold's system, others had deduced that the abuses were the result of the structure and underlying principles of the administration.[7] "The whole system is radically bad," a missionary said in an 1895 *Daily Chronicle* interview and the APS wrote as much to Leopold in 1899.[8] Casement came to this conclusion at about the same time as Morel.[9]

Through adroit publicity of its general principles and its specific regulations, Morel made the Leopoldian system a topic of common knowledge and, more importantly, of official discourse. In 1904, the Foreign Office's Africa department opined that "the whole system of government left much to be desired."[10] Sir Arthur Hardinge, shortly after becoming ambassador to Brussels, used the

---

[3] Aidan Forth, "The Politics of Philanthropy: the Congo Terror Regime and the British Public Sphere, 1884–1914" (MA thesis, Queen's University Kingston, 2006), 72.

[4] Kevin C Dunn, *Imagining the Congo: The International Relations of Identity* (New York: Palgrave Macmillan, 2003).

[5] Ann Swidler, "Cultural Power and Social Movements" in *Social Movements and Culture*, eds Hank Johnston and Bert Klandermans, 3–24, 33, 36 (Minneapolis: University of Minnesota Press 1995).

[6] Joel Best, "Rhetoric in Claims Making," *Social Problems* 34, no. 2 (April 1987): 101–21.

[7] The Congo Free State," *Speaker,* 28 April 1900, 101.

[8] *Anti-Slavery Reporter*, December 1895, 263–4; APS to Leopold, 21 October 1899, in *Aborigines' Friend*, April 1900, 503–5.

[9] Casement to Foreign Office, 30 April 1900, FO 403/304, quoted in Marchal, *Morel contre Léopold*, Vol. 1, 187.

[10] "Current work of the African Dept.," FO 881/8229:44–6.

CRA's language of the "system" with de Cuvelier.[11] Grey and Asquith publicly spoke of the pernicious Congo "system."[12]

To oppose this, apologists praised the system. For example, Mountmorres told the African Trade section of the Liverpool Chamber of Commerce that British colonies should adopt the Congo system of government.[13] But his words carried little weight; his audience knew that Sir Alfred Jones paid his salary. In the critical task of characterizing Leopold's system, the Congo reform movement won the battle.

This was necessary but not sufficient; the reformers needed to marry the understanding of the system with the emotional impact of atrocity stories; neither one alone would do. Murphy's 1895 Reuters article and Sjöblom's 1897 report showed the way with their eyewitness accounts of state-sanctioned looting, burned villages, murder, decapitation, brutal beatings, and hands cut off to prove that cartridges had not been wasted. From the moment he came out as an opponent of the Congo regime, Morel captured readers' attention with stories of cannibalism and mutilation. In his 1903 luridly titled short book *The Congo Slave State*, he sprinkled tales of atrocities throughout to remind readers how the system led to horrific violence.[14] Among atrocity stories, allegations of cannibalism, mutilation of the living or the dead, and grotesque murders such as crucifixion had the most electrifying effect on the public and policymakers. Below in the hierarchy of horror came sadistic torture, rape, extreme flogging, casual murder, punitive murders, abduction of women, village-burning, and fatal imprisonment. The most common atrocities resulted from the officially encouraged practice of taking women and children hostage for rubber production. Apologists defended coercion as necessary to instill habits of labor through discipline and condemned what they said was occasional violence that had no practical benefit; Morel argued that the two were inextricably related.

The Congo Slave State highlights the rhetorical importance of invoking slavery.[15] Morel often called the Congo system worse than slavery, because slave-owners would not countenance the destruction of their own property. Abhorrence of slavery transcended political and sectarian divides, and, Forth argues, brought together otherwise disparate interests and ideologies through an invented tradition that reformers sold to audiences through frequent repetition.[16] In publications such as *The Congo State Is Not a Slave State*, Congo defenders boasted that Leopold had largely ended chattel slavery in the Congo, but the

---

[11] A. Hardinge to Grey, 29 March 1906, Foreign Office Africa no 1 (1906), Cd 3002.
[12] *The Times*, 21 November 1906, quoted in FO 881/8923:133–5; *The Times*, 10 November 1909.
[13] *Congo Supplement to the West African Mail*, May 1905, 309.
[14] Morel, *The Congo Slave State* (Liverpool: Richardson, 1903).
[15] Grant, *Civilised Savagery*, 25.
[16] Forth, "Politics of Philanthropy," 74–5.

apologists lost this battle.[17] The new slaveries of coercion without ownership had become the new moral battleground for activists.

Morel adeptly nurtured sources of information, collected their stories, and publicized them. Dozens of people, mostly missionaries but also travelers, traders, Congo officials, and others, sent him eyewitness accounts of tragedies, stories of recent abuses of power, government documents, and hearsay evidence. The apologists attacked these accounts when possible and ignored them if not, meaning that reliability of sources was the key to success. Fired Congo agents and officers could not be trusted, because, as Dilke put it, "the Congo State employs such desperate adventurers that it is quite impossible to credit their statements after dismissal."[18] Congo agents who quit were only marginally better; they could be playing both sides, like Benedetti, or could be vulnerable to a smear campaign, like Salusbury. This led to a heavy reliance on missionaries, but not all missionaries could be trusted, and even missionaries of integrity could misinterpret what they saw or believe less-than-credible sources.

The reformers' rhetorical strategy invoked abstract concepts such as compassion, justice, and rationality to flatter and inspire. These themes appealed to a British sense of self that had lost some of its force in foreign affairs since the era of Gladstone. In reviving overseas humanitarianism as a concern of the public and government, the reformers fanned the embers of self-confidence in Britain's exceptional identity as the world's most prominent humanitarian power. As Samuel said in the Commons, simplifying a far more complicated past, "It has always been the boast of this country, not only that our own native subjects were governed on principles of justice, but that ever since the days of Wilberforce, England had been the leader in all movements on behalf of the backward races of the earth."[19]

As with every humanitarian cause since anti-slavery, opponents highlighted other ills that needed addressing, or, as Wilberforce had described it, "looked around everywhere for evils, and hugged them all to their bosoms."[20] The Congo's defenders pressed into service Britain's conduct in the Boer War, her punitive expeditions, and her colonial massacres, as well as America's brutal war in the Philippines, Germany's Herrero genocide, and other excesses to question the reformers' single-minded Congo focus. The reformers riposted with the treaties of Berlin and Brussels, the unusual nature of Leopold's regime, and the vast scale of the Congo abuses. When they brought up Britain's own "far from ...

---

[17] Demetrius Boulger, *The Congo State Is Not a Slave State* (London: Low, Marston, 1903).
[18] Dilke to Morel, 30 October 1902, Add. 43897:149.
[19] E.D. Morel, *Red Rubber* (London: Fisher Unwin, 1906), 177.
[20] Brian Harrison, "A Genealogy of Reform in Modern Britain" in *Anti-Slavery, Religion and Reform*, eds Christine Bolt and Seymour Drescher (Hamden, CT: Archon Books, 1980), 123.

stainless" colonial history, they used it to show how much worse Leopold's rule was, thus validating British practices as superior, albeit imperfect, and to defend against the charge of inconsistency.[21]

Reformers repeatedly invoked humanity, signifying the shared human condition, the fellow-feeling that sprang from it, and the benevolence that this connection required. Morel linked humanity to British virtues, writing, "The men of Britain, the men who love fair play and breathe the air of freedom, cannot refuse a helping hand to those down-trodden natives of the Congo, who have appealed to them in the sacred name of humanity."[22] Simultaneously a secular and religious concept, humanity appeared in the appeals of bishops, pastors, activists, and government officials. When the Rev. J.F. Brown talked at a Congo meeting of the "highest ideals of humanity," he indicated benevolence, as did another speaker who said they should follow "the dictates of humanity."[23] Morel's "common cause of humanity" united people across sectarian and racial divides, as did the Methodist F.L. Wiseman's call to aid "humanity Black or White."[24] Similarly, Rev. Elwyn Thomas called for action "in the name of Christ and humanity."[25] Some speakers invoked "the interests of humanity," a more nebulous concept that presumed that the speaker knew what was in mankind's best interest.[26] Grey himself said that the British had the right to protest the situation in Congo irrespective of treaty rights "on ground of humanity."[27] One enthusiastic Baptist could not let go of the term: "humanity has been outraged" and "humanity would condemn" Leopold because his crime "stabs at the heart of humanity" and "stains the name of humanity," and appeals for intervention were "broad-based on common humanity."[28] He quoted James Russell Lowell's anti-slavery poem, "The Present Crisis," invoking a global humanity that felt "the gush of joy or shame" a continent away when a race flourished or suffered. Congo practices thus became "crimes against humanity," a concept developed in the early 1800s but first applied to the Congo by George Washington Williams, and used subsequently by Spender, Morel, and others.[29]

---

[21] Morel, *Red Rubber*, vii; Buxton to Brooks, 13 January 1905, Brit. Emp. s19 D1/2:638; Morel, "Rousing the Country," *Congo Supplement to the WAM*, October 1905, 396.

[22] Editorial, *WAM*, 26 April 1907, 98.

[23] *Organ*, February 1907, 26, 32.

[24] *Organ*, March 1907, 20; *Organ*, June 1907, 14.

[25] *Organ*, April 1907, 22.

[26] J.F. Winnicott, Mayor of Plymouth, Plymouth Town's Meeting, *Organ*, March 1907, 20; Lord Monkswell, York Town's Meeting, *Organ*, February 1907, 22–3.

[27] *Organ*, 1909, 137.

[28] T.E. Ruth to the editor, *Baptist Times*, 22 November 1907, quoted in *Organ*, December 1907, 21.

[29] Thomas Upham, "Suggestions on the Law of Nations," *The Manual of Peace* (New York: Leavitt, Lord, 1836), 351; Harold Spender, *The Living Age*, 4 August 1906, 260–61.

Congo reform rhetoric used the Victorian theme of duty to argue for Britain's legal and moral responsibility.[30] The language of legal obligation sprang from the text of the General Act of the 1885 Berlin Conference and other treaties, especially the provisions committing signatories to free trade and caring for the "moral and material well-being" of Africans. Early on, some claimed that the Berlin Act had created the Congo Free State, an error that Leopold's defenders used to their advantage, but reformers quickly shifted their argument to Britain's legal right and indeed obligation to ensure that other signatories adhered to the treaty.[31] The CRA said Britain's obligation was greater because the Congo Free State owed its existence to British acquiescence.[32] Because moral responsibility was not subject to the same quibbles as legal responsibility, it was a natural line of argument for reformers. Talbot described the nation as "honor-bound" to secure reform, while a fellow bishop called it a "plain duty."[33] Being British (or, as the reformers usually said, English) by itself created this duty, and failing to act would undermine what was exceptional and valuable about being British.

One moral argument with legal overtones described Britain as a trustee of the Berlin Act. Trusteeship had a long history in British political thought, and Congo reform brought it new prominence in the understanding of colonial rule.[34] Andrew Porter describes the trusteeship advocated by the reformers as a hybrid of two intellectual traditions: standards of colonial practice and Burkean restraint.[35] Louis identifies Casement as the champion of trusteeship, illustrated by his warning: "we shall be committing a grave breach of trust" if Britain did not press for reform after Belgian annexation because "we are still trustees under the Berlin Act."[36] Casement equated British inaction with the legal negligence of a trustee failing to act in accordance with the terms of a trust. Others exhorted their audiences to fulfill the trust that Britain had taken on at Berlin. Once the Belgians decided on annexation, Morel urged them to consider the colony as held in trust for its inhabitants, carefully explaining what this meant.[37]

The virtues of the imagined British national character contrasted with the deficiencies of Congo administration. Parliament rang with denunciations of the Congo Free State as an unworthy colonial ruler. "Nobody who had followed

---

[30] Forth, "Politics of Philanthropy," 86–7.
[31] Louis, "The Stokes Affair," 580; Boulger, *Not a Slave State*, 30; Arthur Berriedale Keith, *The Belgian Congo and the Berlin Act* (Oxford, Clarendon Press, 1919), 62–3.
[32] Morel, *Red Rubber*, 196.
[33] *Organ*, January 1910, 456.
[34] Grant, *Civilised Savagery*, 16–21.
[35] Andrew Porter, "Trusteeship," 220.
[36] William Roger Louis, "Sir John Harris and Colonial Trusteeship," *The Bulletin of A.R.S.O.M. (Academie Royale des Sciences d'Outre-Mer) for 1965 and 1966*, Part 6, 840; Casement to Buxton, 2 March 1912, Brit. Emp. D2/3/1.
[37] Morel letter, F8/139:46.

African politics could fail to think that the Congo State, which it was hoped was going to be a great moral agent for the improvement of Central Africa, had very largely failed in the mission for which it was founded," Sydney Buxton said in 1897, a mild statement compared to George Baden-Powell's attack on its "villainy." In the same debate, Dilke observed that "the Congo State did not wish that private individuals should rob the natives, because it preferred to rob them itself" and averred that Arab slavers better represented civilization than their Congo Free State opponents.[38]

When Morel joined the reformers, he used a Belgian legislator's words to describe the Congo rubber regions as a "vast charnel house."[39] The Congo Free State was "an inferno of wickedness, a very abomination of desolation" and its government an "incompetent, blood-stained and corrupt institution."[40] Fox Bourne's *Civilisation in Congoland* called the Congo "a vast field of havoc and spoliation."[41] In his first foray into Congo reform activism in 1903, Stead retraced the thought process that converted skeptics to reformers: "Sir H. Gilzean Reid and Mr Demetrius Boulger would have us believe that King Leopold has converted the Congo Valley into a terrestrial paradise. Mr Morel and Mr Fox Bourne maintain that he has converted it into a Hell; and after making all allowances it is difficult to resist the conviction that they have proved their case."[42] Until 1908, the reformers also inveighed against Leopold personally, using terms such as "political monster" and "international outlaw" in public and allusions to Satan and insanity in private.[43] Morel invoked the worst policies of the Spaniards in the Netherlands and in the New World.[44] He called what was happening in the Congo a "holocaust," a term already in existence to describe human suffering, but here used publicly to mean a mass murder of innocents, perhaps based on Casement's earlier private reference to "a holocaust of human victims."[45]

The polarization of discourse was not to everyone's liking. Some found it troubling to have to choose between a wholly bad and wholly good Congo Free State. Edgar Wallace of the *Daily Mail*, lecturing for the CRA after his own investigatory trip to the Congo, believed that the truth lay somewhere in

---

[38] 48 Parl. Deb. (4th ser.) (1897) 428, 430, 439, 442.

[39] Morel (anon.), "The Congo Scandal V: Red Rubber," *Speaker*, 6 October 1900, 17.

[40] Morel (anon.), "The Congo Scandal VI: Responsibility and Remedy," *Speaker*, 1 December 1900, 228–9.

[41] Fox Bourne, *Civilisation in Congoland*, 303.

[42] "Cannibal Christendom in Africa." *Review of Reviews*, March 1903, quoted in Frederic Whyte, *The Life of W.T. Stead*, Vol. 2. (London: Jonathan Cape Ltd., 1925), 216.

[43] *Red Rubber*, 213; Holt to Morel, 20 January 1904, F8/85:352; Holt to Morel, 18 September 1905, F8/86 392.

[44] Morel, "The Slave State on the Congo," *WAM*, 22 January 1904, 1099–100.

[45] *Organ*, 1911–13, 850; Ward to Morel, 25 August 1903, F8/143:13.

between; there was enough to criticize without making the Congo Free State the embodiment of evil.[46] Those who tried to steer a more nuanced course were mostly unheard or classified on one side or the other. Reformers were never fully comfortable with the equivocating conversion of celebrity colonial administrator Harry Johnston to the reform cause in 1905.[47] Others found themselves denigrated as Congophiles, such as Viscount Mountmorres, who exonerated the state after his Jones-subsidized voyage but endorsed Casement's report as accurately representing the concession companies in the rubber districts.

The relationship of Belgium to the Congo posed ongoing challenges. Belgium had disavowed colonial ambitions, but the Congo's financial backers were Belgians, its government was in Brussels, and Belgians were the largest contingent of its agents. It was with Belgium's permission that Leopold had become the autocrat of the Congo. If they turned against his enterprise, its foundations would crumble. The reformers' best hope was for the Belgian people and legislature to take Congo misrule seriously and induce the government to act. However, as Grey put it, "The Belgian people have been reduced little by little to impotence in regard to the exercise of even a theoretical influence over the management of the Congo territories."[48] They could remedy this by forcing Leopold to give up the Congo.

Some authors have incorrectly seen the CRA as attacking and ostracizing Belgium. Jeff Bass writes that Morel identified Belgian rule as not worthy of a civilized imperial power and Dunn tells us that Morel and the CRA intended to "excise" Belgium from the ranks of civilized countries.[49] Morel's writings do not support this. He did indeed write in 1901 that Belgium's refusal to address the problems in the Congo was unpardonable and in 1902 wrote "The Belgian Curse in Africa."[50] However, the 1901 article attacks Belgium only for not monitoring Leopold, not for any crimes of its own, and the 1902 article does not criticize Belgium or the Belgians after its inflammatory title. After 1903, Morel became careful about rhetorically confusing Belgium with the Congo Free State—a danger Dilke had identified as early as 1897.[51] Bass quotes phrases such as "Belgian occupation" from *King Leopold's Rule in Africa* but these are not Morel's words; he is quoting other, less careful authors. Morel did not tar Belgium with Leopold's crime, though Bass does, by repeatedly writing

---

[46] Wallace to Morel, 23 April 1908, F9/18:10.
[47] Johnston to Dilke, 13 February 1908, Add. 43920:26–8.
[48] Grey to A. Hardinge, 16 March 1908, CAB 37/92/40.
[49] Jeff D. Bass, "Imperial Alterity and Identity Slippage: The Sin of Becoming 'Other' in Edmund D. Morel's *King Leopold's Rule in Africa*," *Rhetoric & Public Affairs* 13, no. 2 (Summer 2010): 284, 291; Dunn, *Imagining the Congo*, 51–4.
[50] *West Africa*, 3 August 1901, quoted in Marchal, *Morel contre Léopold*, Vol. 1, 39.
[51] Morel, "The Belgian Curse in Africa," *Contemporary Review*, March 1902, 358–77; *Aborigines' Friend*, July 1897, 213.

of "Belgian savagery," a term that appears nowhere in Morel's book. On the contrary, Morel warned his readers, "Above all, let us refrain from referring to the Congo as a Belgian Colony, let us avoid writing of a Belgian misrule."[52] Morel wrote privately and publicly that the official position of the CRA was that the Belgian people had no responsibility for the Congo.[53] Grey validated Morel's approach when he told the Belgian ambassador that British anti-Congo sentiment "was not directed against Belgium, and I thought the Association had always been careful to distinguish between the responsibility of the King for the administration of the Congo State, and the responsibility of Belgium, which had hitherto been non-existent."[54]

Apologists, however, often linked Belgium and the Belgians to the Congo, portraying the reform movement as anti-Belgian, both at home, where they called Belgian reformers traitors, and abroad, where they said reform advocates were jealous and eager to hurt Belgium. French Sheldon's five-page letter on the virtues of the Congo Free State referred to "Belgium" and "the Belgians" but never to Leopold.[55]

Belgian annexation in November 1908 complicated the reformers' position. Because the Leopoldian system remained intact for more than a year after annexation, reformers found themselves criticizing the Belgian government while wooing the Belgian people. When apologists accused him of attacking the Belgian people, Morel called it "a perfectly monstrous charge," but it was a difficult distinction to maintain.[56]

Both reformers and apologists attempted to control the discourse, but each side had to refute the other's claims. Morel countered the apologists' accusations of lying, doctoring evidence, and cynical manipulation by interested parties with assertions about the Executive Committee's honor and disinterestedness. When apologists claimed that his indictments reflected conditions from years past, Morel published recent information, often under the rubric "evidence of the month."[57] Some attacked Morel and the CRA with vitriol. Charles Diamond, editor of the *Catholic Herald*, wrote to major newspapers accusing Morel and the CRA of lying about everything: the Congo, the provenance of atrocity photographs, the Association's finances, and its "selfish and sordid motives," while claiming that missionaries of all faiths praised the Congo state—including Grenfell, who was a critic by this time.[58] Diamond went even more fiercely after Guinness, a noted anti-Catholic, saying he would not speak the truth even

---

[52] Morel, *Red Rubber*, 137.
[53] Morel to Davidson, 6 November 1906, F8/14:9; *Organ*, April 1907, 3.
[54] Grey to Hardinge, 16 March 1908, CAB 37/92/40.
[55] French Sheldon to Jones, 10 April 1904, F8/96:130.
[56] Morel to Parker, 7 March 1910, F8/121:65.
[57] *Organ*, June 1908, 19–22.
[58] *Catholic Herald*, 8 December 1904, 36–8, F9/3:36.

under oath.[59] When payments from Leopold ended, some apologists fell silent, recanted, or reversed their positions, but others persisted. During the First World War, Casement's treason and Morel's conviction for violating the Defence of the Realm Act revived some apologists, who claimed that the two men had been German agents since the beginning.[60] With attacks like this, it is no wonder that Morel felt the need to respond, even if it was not always wise to do so.

Photographs as Weapons in the War of Words

The transition from verbal accounts of atrocities to visual representation was not quick. In 1902, Morel had photographs of people with severed hands from two correspondents and reproduced one in *Affairs of West Africa*.[61] But he doubted their worth, noting that the photo did not prove the Congo Free State's culpability.[62] Underestimating the power of atrocity images, neither Morel nor Fox Bourne used photographs in their 1903 publications. As Dilke wrote to Morel at the time, "of course a photograph is no *evidence*."[63]

Grant is likely correct in proposing Roger Casement as a catalyst for more extensive photographic documentation.[64] During Casement's 1903 voyage, the CBM's Rev. Daniel Danielson accompanied him for weeks, photographing the people he interviewed. Danielson used his photographs to illustrate his November 1903 Congo lectures.[65] Although photography was popular among all missionary groups, CBM missionaries were most likely to use their cameras to highlight problems; photos by Danielson, Armstrong, Alice Harris, Rev. Herbert Frost, Rev. Henry Whiteside, and others appeared in Congo reform literature and lantern lectures.

Morel used 26 photographic plates in his next book, *King Leopold's Rule in Africa*, but only six were atrocity photos. A year later, shortly after the Harrises' arrival, Morel published a photo essay called "The Kodak on the Congo" that included photos they brought back, followed by "The Inconvenient Kodak

---

[59] Guinness to Morel, 7 October 1905, F8/74:62.

[60] Comte Louis de Lichtervelde, *Léopold of the Belgians* (London: The Century Co., 1929), 232, 298.

[61] E.D. Morel, *Affairs of West Africa* (1902; repr., London, Frank Cass & Co. Ltd, 1968),, 334, contradicting the belief that no photographs appeared before Casement's 1903 journey. Grant, *Civilised Savagery*, 59.

[62] Morel, *Affairs of West Africa*, 334.

[63] Dilke to Morel 22 May 1902, Add. 43897:14.

[64] Grant, *Civilised Savagery*, 57–8.

[65] Oli Jacobsen, "Daniel J. Danielsen (1871–1916): The Faeroese who Changed History in the Congo," *Brethren Historical Review* 8 (2012), reprint, 5–37.

Again" in 1906.[66] John and Alice put out a pamphlet later that year called "The Camera and the Congo Crime," which included photos by Alice Harris, Whiteside, Armstrong, Frost, and likely Danielson, though his name does not appear.[67] The American and British CRAs used photos and editorial cartoons to good effect to accompany Mark Twain's *King Leopold's Soliloquy*. Photographic evidence of atrocities became a regular feature of the *Organ*.[68]

Morel had set aside his doubts about photographic evidence, but the reasoning behind his hesitation was sound. With the possible exception of a photograph of a flogging in Burrows's suppressed book, the atrocity photographs did not show anyone in the act of beating, torturing, mutilating, or murdering. It was almost impossible to take a photo of an atrocity in progress. When Rev. Dodds set up his camera to photograph men bringing in rubber, state agents removed the whipping post that would have been used to punish inadequate quantity or quality.[69] What appeared was the after-effects of cruel treatment, without anything definitive about how they occurred. Christina Twomey reminds us that the photographs did not exist in a vacuum; for all their emotive power, they required testimony in words for full effect.[70]

The apologists' counter-narrative was that missionaries staged or mislabeled photographs, which was more or less true. Stannard had tied up a man so that Whiteside could photograph him and lied about it when challenged.[71] John Peffer explains that two of Alice Harris's frequently reproduced photos were dramatic re-enactments in which a sentry is about to flog a naked man and guards two women in chains.[72] Photographers posed mutilated, starving, or grieving people for dramatic effect, including the technique, used since 1902, of placing a white cloth behind the subject's arm to highlight the loss of a hand. The famous photo of Nsala contemplating the murder of his daughter was a carefully arranged tableau of onlookers, grieving father, and severed hand and

---

[66] Congo Supplement to the WAM, September 1905, 376–84; *Organ*, February 1906, 1–5.

[67] Harris to Buxton, 17 August 1906, Brit. Emp. s18, C82/78; "The Camera and the Congo Crime," Davidson papers, Lambeth Palace archives; Jacobsen, "Danielsen," 95ff.

[68] For example, *Organ*, December 1906, 14–17; February 1907, 12; May 1907, 38; July 1907, 16–17; September 1907, 1.

[69] *Organ*, September 1907, 1.

[70] Christina Twomey, "Framing Atrocity: Photography and Humanitarianism," *History of Photography* 36:3 (August 2012), 255–64; Twomey, "Severed Hands: Authenticating Atrocity in the Congo, 1903–14" in *Picturing Atrocity: Photography in Crisis*, eds Geoff Batchen, Mick Gidley, Nancy K. Miller, and Jay Prosser (London: Reaktion Books, 2012).

[71] *Organ*, June 1906, 16; Armstrong to Grey, 8 October 1906, FO 881/8923:76.

[72] Peffer, "Snap of the Whip," 67–8; *Regions Beyond*, February 1908, 30; *Organ*, July 1907, 16–17.

foot.[73] An image of a mutilation or flogging moves people more powerfully than a description of a mass murder, especially, as Susan Sontag says, if properly posed to seem authentic.[74]

The necessary response to this visual rhetoric was emotional. Depictions of suffering inflicted on the bodies of strangers engender compassion just as personal exposure to suffering neighbors does. The encounter between compassion and ideas about human agency and responsibility generates what Thomas Laqueur calls a moral imperative.[75] If the cause of the trouble is clear and ameliorative action is possible, then the humanitarian must act. In a recent example, Sierra Leone rebels deliberately escalated violence, especially amputations, to attract international attention: "When we started cutting hands, hardly a day BBC would not talk to us."[76] Visible atrocities arouse the humanitarian conscience. With enough images, they become what some have called "atrocity porn," tapping into a primal psychological force that fixes them in the memory and draws the eye back again and again.[77] Karen Halttunen has argued that British society, having come to condemn the gratuitous infliction of physical pain, found the contemplation of such suffering illicit and thus stimulating emotionally or even sexually. The "traditional social policy of pain" still evident in the Congo became, in the eyes of humanitarian sympathizers, "a modern pornography of pain."[78] Visual studies scholar Sharon Sliwinski draws our attention to the mechanism that turned these images and feelings into support for humanitarian causes: the Congo atrocity images evoked a deeply rooted desire to alleviate the suffering, even though it was beyond remedy because it had already occurred.[79] The reformers channeled that wish into support for future change on the Congo. The deployment of rhetorical strategies through text, spoken as well as written, reinforced the images' credibility and meaning, just as the images reinforced the text. Writers and speakers provided what the readers found most compelling.

---

[73] Morel, *King Leopold's Rule*, 144.

[74] Susan Sontag, *Regarding the Pain of Others* (New York: Farrar, Strauss, and Giroux, 2003).

[75] Thomas W. Laqueur, "Bodies, Details, and the Humanitarian Narrative" in *The New Cultural History*, ed. Lynn Hunt (Berkeley: University of California Press, 1988), 178, 201–2.

[76] Linda Polman, The *Crisis Caravan: What's Wrong with Humanitarian Aid?* (New York: Metropolitan Books, 2010), 167–9.

[77] William Grigg, "War Party's Atrocity Porn," *New American*, 25 January 2005.

[78] Karen Halttunen, "Humanitarianism and the Pornography of Pain in Anglo-American Culture," *American Historical Review* 100, no. 2 (April 1995): 334.

[79] Sharon Sliwinski, "The Childhood of Human Rights: The Kodak on the Congo," *Journal of Visual Culture* 5, no. 3 (January 2006): 356–7.

Lantern Lectures and Other Meetings

Atrocity images had their biggest impact in lantern lectures. Lantern-slide lectures were an established medium; the magic lantern, invented in the seventeenth century, had spread rapidly in the nineteenth century. Lanterns became brighter, more reliable, and less expensive while the price of slides fell rapidly after 1850 as hand-painted slides costing over £20 apiece gave way to easily reproduced photographic slides for 1s (black and white) or 1s 6d (color), before volume discounts.[80]

Lantern lectures were a common form of diversion and education from the 1870s through the early 1900s in Britain. The magic lantern illustrated scientific lectures, entertainment, current events discussion, political campaigns, missionary fundraising, and humanitarian causes. Eleven companies put together lantern lectures for purchase or hire.[81] Some boasted huge collections: E.G. Wood of London claimed the largest inventory with 100,000 slides, while Riley Brothers in Bradford, "The Largest Lantern Outfitters in the World," had a catalog of about 1,500 sets of which over 400 had accompanying lectures.[82] These companies created content by assembling photographs on a theme and preparing a script to be read aloud.[83] The firm would have the narrative "reviewed" or "revised" by an expert in the field. Sometimes, a scientific, religious, or charitable organization would assemble a show or lecture that they made available to members to borrow, hire, or purchase, or to the public through a big lantern lecture firm.

In contrast to the individuals, families, and small groups that rented lectures for one-time use, people seeking to educate, publicize a cause, or raise money would go on extensive speaking tours. In the 1890s, Anti-Slavery employed a commissioned Financial and Travelling Agent and Lecturer who gave 20 lectures at churches, YMCAs, schools, and other public meeting halls in three months

---

[80] W.J. Chadwick, *Magic Lantern Manual* (London: Frederick Warne, 1878), 12, 26; Herman and Ann Hecht, *Pre-Cinema History* (London: Bowker Saur, 1993), 23, 186–7; Sliwinski, "Childhood," 347–8; *The Optical Magic Lantern Journal and Photographic Enlarger* 12 (December 1901): 98–9; James Martin, "Transferred Prints for Magic Lantern," *Photographic News*, 31 December 1869, 626, in Herbert, *Pre-Cinema*, Vol. 2, 297; W.T. Stead, *Annual Index of Periodicals and Photographs* (London: Mowbray House, 1891), 99, http://books.google.com/books?id=hkgUAQAAIAAJ.

[81] Stead, *Annual Index*, 99.

[82] Thomas Cradock Hepworth, *The Book of the Lantern* (London: Hazel, Watson, and Viney, 1894), xiii; David Copeland, "Joseph, William, Herbert, Arnold and Bernard Riley," *Who's Who of Victorian Cinema*, 1996, http://www.victorian-cinema.net/riley.

[83] Richard Abel and Rick Altman, *The Sounds of Early Cinema* (Bloomington: Indiana University Press, 2001), 42–3; Deac Rossell, *Living Pictures: The Origins of the Movies* (Albany: SUNY Press, 1998), 24.

in 1893, of which eight were lantern lectures. He reported, "Of all methods of arousing the sympathies of the British public, these illustrated lectures are most effective, as the hearts of young and old alike are reached and deeply touched by appeals, not only to the ears but to the eyes also, in a manner that will never be forgotten."[84] Lantern lecturers would speak once a day or more. Laura Ormiston Chant addressed over 400 meetings in 12 months during Stead's 1885 Maiden Tribute campaign.[85] In October and November 1900, the Friends' industrial missionaries Mr and Miss Armitage gave 50 lantern lectures.[86] A Peace Society speaker gave 34 talks in nine towns in a single month, including one to 3,000 people.[87] The Harrises' lecturing pace, while admirable, was not unusual.

Missionaries had long used photographs and lantern lectures to promote their missions. T. Jack Thompson's study of missionary photography observes that Guinness was an adept and enthusiastic lantern lecturer beginning in the 1880s, supported by people who prepared the slides, scheduled the talks, and operated the equipment.[88] Lantern lectures on the Congo problem began with Danielson's talks in November–December 1903 and continued in force with Guinness's lectures. However, it was John and Alice Harris who made them into a vital tool for expanding the movement beginning in late 1905. It is likely that most Congo meetings used lantern slides. John Harris continued to use the lantern even after tiring of its complications, observing, "I abominate lantern slides, but I know how an audience loves to see pictures to illustrate the points of lectures."[89] Morel was the exception; as of late 1906, he had not given a single speech illustrated by lantern slides.[90] However, he did not disdain speaking at meetings where others gave lantern presentations, because he knew they were effective. Lantern lectures brought together the immediacy and pathos of the visual, the persuasiveness of human speech, and the longer-lasting messages of accompanying pamphlets.

There were at least three sets of slides used for Congo lecturing: the Guinness set, the Harris set, and a commercial set. There is almost no information about Guinness's. John Harris apparently had three copies of the Harris set made—one for him, one for his wife, and one to loan out.[91] William Riley of Riley Brothers Ltd put together a set of 60 slides in 1906 for his firm and other dealers to sell or rent out for Congo lectures. Riley had Morel's permission to use text from *Red Rubber* and other Congo material to prepare the accompanying lecture. The result was sold as "The Congo Atrocities: A Lecture to Accompany a Series of 60 Photographic

---

[84] *Anti-Slavery Reporter*, ser. 4, Vol. 13, no. 2 (March-April 1893): 102–3.
[85] Bebbington, *Nonconformist Conscience*, 44.
[86] *ASR*, December 1900.
[87] *Herald of Peace*, 2 January 1905, 11–12.
[88] Guinness to Morel, 2 February 1904, F4/3:87–8.
[89] Harris to Meyer, 29 November 1912, Brit. Emp. s.19 D3/7:413.
[90] Morel to Robert Bowran, 12 November 1906, F10/14 589.
[91] Buxton to Joseph Burtt, 14 August 1911, Brit. Emp. S19 D1/9:133.

Slides for the Optical Lantern by W.R. (revised by Mr E.D. Morel and Rev. J.H. Harris) price 6d. May be had from all Optical and Lantern Dealers." There is no evidence of any revisions from either Morel or Harris.[92] As Grant notes, the Riley lecture contained elements of a missionary publicity lecture; it emphasized the role of missionaries, identified the problem as the state undermining the missions' work, and concluded with a demand for more mission stations.[93] This showed that Riley believed his market lay with people focused on religious and missionary issues. It may have been the most widely available lecture, but, contrary to some interpretations, it was neither a CRA standard lecture nor the Harrises' lecture. If someone wanted slides for a meeting, the CRA could lend out the Harris slides or the Riley show.[94] If neither was available, the individual would have to obtain the Riley show from a commercial dealer. The Riley slides' call for a missionary remedy to the Congo's woes did not appear in John Harris's lectures, which, in line with the position of the CRA, demanded a political solution. And, at the end, the Riley lecture included a model resolution based on Morel's standard language; it does not mention missionaries or mission stations.

Lantern lectures had a religious feeling to them and often included singing a conventional hymn or one of several special Congo hymns. The CRA's Liverpool Auxiliary sold a pamphlet of the hymn "Britons awake" for a penny, a stanza of which both Grant and Louis have reproduced.[95] Appropriately for a CRA-sponsored hymn, it encourages the singer to raise his voice for the rights of the natives, not his conversion to Christianity—religious tone used for a secular purpose.[96]

Whether or not the speaker used lantern slides, all meetings intended to appeal both to reason and to emotion. The emphasis differed, however, depending on the venue and the speakers. Larger meetings, town's meetings, and any speech by Morel tended to build outrage through reasoned argument. Smaller meetings, usually at churches, took a more sentimental and more religious tone. The CRA's main themes appeared, including an indictment of the system, but with less erudite exposition. From his first lecture, Harris pitched his talks to this audience, writing Morel, "You appeal to the educated classes and politicians, what I want to do is appeal to the popular mind and while hammering greatly on the system give people an idea of how the thing works out without labouring their minds with a burden of detail."[97]

[92] F13/4/1; Morel to W. Riley, 30 and 31 October 1906, F10/14:446, 469.
[93] Grant, *Civilised Savagery*, 68.
[94] Morel to Rev. S.N. Seaquick, St Mary's Bishopstoke, 13 October 1908, F10/16:860.
[95] "Hymn specially written for Congo meetings" words by Rev. A.T. Brainsby, music by Rev. W. Boyd, Liverpool Auxiliary, F4/41; Grant, *Civilised Savagery*, 68; W.L. Louis "Morel and the Congo Reform Association," in *E.D. Morel's History of the Congo Reform Movement*, eds William Roger Louis and Jean Stengers (Oxford: Clarendon Press, 1968), 210.
[96] See Appendix IV for full text.
[97] Harris to Morel, 19 August 1905, F8/75:179.

The resolution to convey to the Foreign Office and to local MPs marked the high point of each meeting. A prominent local person would propose the resolution, usually with standard CRA language. Several people would give speeches in support, often prepared in advance. Occasionally someone would speak against the resolution or try to. Depending on the size of the crowd, how rowdy the dissenter was, and how well the audience knew the dissenter, he might be heard and answered, heard but not answered, ignored, or ejected from the meeting. Then the resolution would pass with unanimous or near-unanimous support.

Congo reform meetings and thus resolutions were most numerous in 1906–09. The "many" representations Lansdowne received 1903–05 were a mild prelude to the coming flood.[98] In 1906, the Foreign Office received about 300 resolutions; 439 meetings are recorded that year.[99] Some resolutions may have arrived after year-end, and some meetings may not have passed resolutions at all, much to Morel's chagrin. Kenred Smith apologized to Morel in March 1906 for not obtaining resolutions but promised he would in the future.[100] In 1907, however, the Foreign Office received over 1,100 resolutions, far more than the number of recorded meetings. Congo Sundays may account for some of the difference. Congo Sundays endorsed by the Baptists, the Free Church Council, and Liverpool area Protestants from late 1906 through late 1907 would have resulted in many resolutions without formal meetings listed in the *Organ*. Commercial rentals of the Riley Brothers lantern lecture may also have had an impact.

Table 7.1   Congo reform meetings

	Meetings recorded in letters, Organ	Foreign Office records of resolutions received
1904	46	
1905	43	>60
1906	439	300
1907	496	1120
1908	263	283
1909	243	Not given after 1908
1910	37	

Source: Meetings database; 1905 resolutions, Cookey, *Britain*, 149; 1906, FO 881/8850; 1907, FO 881/9093; 1908, FO 881/9414.

---

[98] Lansdowne to A.S. Raikes, 24 August 1903, FO 881/8268, 273.
[99] The challenges of counting meetings are discussed in Chapter 4.
[100] Smith to Morel, 30 March 1906, F4/24.

Over half of the recorded meetings list speakers. The Harrises were the most frequent, with John named at over 400 UK events from 1905–10 and Alice at over 220; because they sometimes appeared jointly, this makes about 530 different events in total, not including their US tour or Alice's French and Swiss meetings. Morel nagged John to apprise him of their meetings, indicating some went undocumented.

Morel was the next most frequent speaker recorded, at 135 meetings, peaking in 1907 with 54 meetings. Following Holt's advice to address only meetings that had a large or important audience, his total fell to 20 in 1908.[101]

Based on Chapter 4's calculations, it appears there were 2,500–3,000 CRA-related meetings in the UK from 1904–13, supplemented by hundreds of meetings that had no connection to the organization. Those who attended typically found them to be moving and memorable experiences.

The Battle in the Press

Much of the rhetorical war took place in the press. The stakes were high because of the British press's pivotal role from the mid-nineteenth century through the early twentieth century, peaking in 1905–10.[102] W.T. Stead may have exaggerated when he wrote that the press had displaced the House of Commons to become "the Chamber of Initiative," but the fourth estate had become a political force to be reckoned with.[103] The press was the conduit bringing the reformers' rhetoric to the reading public, the politically influential, and the politicians and bureaucrats on whom the cause depended. Reformers held two related though apparently contradictory goals; they hoped to shape public opinion and at the same time show decision-makers that public opinion backed their cause. In this age before polling, what appeared in the papers defined public opinion.[104]

This hinged on underlying ideas about the press as a leader or follower of public opinion. Most proprietors and editors believed in their ability to lead public opinion, but the way events unfolded in practice caused recurrent crises of faith. On some issues, the press appeared to sway the public mood while at other times public opinion was impervious to press leadership.[105] This problem was an opportunity, thought Sir Hugh Gilzean Reid, who had been founding

---

[101] Holt to Morel, 16 November 1907, F8/86:521.

[102] Colin Cross, *The Liberals in Power* (London: Barrie and Rockliff, 1963), 80.

[103] W.T. Stead, "Government by Journalism," *The Contemporary Review* 49 (May 1886): 653. http://www.attackingthedevil.co.uk/steadworks/gov.php.

[104] Edward Porritt, "British Public Opinion and the Boers," *Outlook* 64, no. 11 (17 March 1900): 623, http://books.google.com/books?id=vD1YAAAAYAAJ&pg=PA623.

[105] Mark Hampton, *Visions of the Press in Britain, 1850–1950* (Urbana: University of Illinois Press, 2004), 109.

president of the national journalists' association and president of the Society of Newspaper Proprietors and Managers.[106] Gilzean Reid believed the press had come to reflect public opinion rather than lead it, a position not consistent with his efforts to boost the Congo Free State in the press. Reflecting the opinion of the public, not just that of the editor and proprietor, gave newspapers more influence with decision-makers. It is this influence that the reformers sought. Morel had no illusions that rallying editors would by itself be sufficient. He pointed this out to Dilke in early 1904: "You say that Parliament and Press in this country are unanimous. Yes, that is so; nevertheless the country is dead as yet. People don't know about the thing and don't understand it even if they have heard of it ... the British Government will get disheartened and throw up the sponge if we cannot stir up Public Opinion in a more wide-spread form."[107] This mirrored Casement's own argument for the CRA's main objective: "to enlighten, systematically and continuously, public opinion in this country, and abroad, upon the actual condition of the Congo people ... Sporadic meetings and occasional lectures and articles in the press from time to time are not sufficient."[108] A flood of articles, letters, and public meetings were necessary to stimulate interest and convince politicians and bureaucrats that the reformers' position represented public opinion.

Britain teemed with newspapers, with 231 daily papers published in the British Isles and another 2,230 of lesser frequency, most tied to particular political philosophies and parties.[109] When the CRA formed, there were 21 daily newspapers in London alone, which Stead conceptualized in four categories.[110] In the first rank came *The Times* and the *Westminster Gazette* with their limited circulation, reputation for authority, and multi-partisan readership despite their political allegiances.[111] The next group boasted editorial excellence and/or good parliamentary connections and a wider readership, such as the *Daily News, Morning Post, Daily Chronicle*, and *Pall Mall Gazette*. A third group had little influence but the biggest share of advertising, while a fourth group had no influence. Some provincial dailies aspired to the second group, especially the *Manchester Guardian* and the *Liverpool Daily Post and Mercury*. The provincial press included hosts of daily and weekly papers; in Manchester, seven competed

---

[106] "Sir Hugh Gilzean Reid," *Who Was Who*, Vol. 1 (London: A. & C. Black, 1920), 435.
[107] Morel to Dilke, 29 January 1904, F4/3:67–9.
[108] Casement to Morel, 25 January 1904, F8/16:25.
[109] *Newspaper Press Directory*, 1905, cited in *Hazell's*, 1906, 347.
[110] Not including sports papers. Stead, "His Majesty's Public Councilors," *Review of Reviews* 30, no. 180 (December 1904): 604–5; Stephen Koss, *The Rise and Fall of the Political Press in Britain*, Vol. 2 (Chapel Hill: UNC Press, 1984), 1, 28, 30, 68–9; Hampton, *Visions of the Press*, 109, 112.
[111] *Hazell's*, 1906, 347.

with the *Guardian* for readers' attention.[112] In addition, there were weekly, biweekly, and monthly journals of all kinds, such as the *New Age*, *Nineteenth Century and After*, *Athenaeum*, *Economist*, *Spectator*, and *Speaker*. Politicians preferred the press over noisy meetings as an indicator of public opinion.[113]

Morel believed in the power of the press to stir up interest. In 1897, he wrote his *Pall Mall Gazette* article "to urge upon public opinion in this country the need of a little generosity towards the first colonization attempts of a small power," that is, to be less harsh on King Leopold's colonial venture, which, following proper apologist practice, he conflated with Belgium.[114] Within three years, he was writing to educate the public in the opposite perspective. Casement shared his hope that a concerted press campaign would enlighten the public. Casement, though, at times saw failure where Morel saw continued reasons for hope. When the CRA was but nine months old, he was already near despair:

> So with the general public—I find only what I have long been preaching to you, that interest in the Congo question is practically dead. No one cares a d-n about it—and it is quite useless—nay worse than useless to keep on flogging a dead horse. That is my conviction forced upon me. The press paragraphs in favour of our Congo views are only being inserted with ever increasing difficulty by the few friends the movement has: they find growing repugnance to touch the question—or find room for it. I fear you have made some even turn their backs on it ... simply thro' a natural revulsion which many human beings feel to being lectured. That's their view, not mine, but it exists ... You for your part <u>must</u>, my dear Morel, go slower and not bombard them.[115]

Although the "practically dead" sentence has been quoted to show that Casement was ready to give up or that he wanted to intensify the campaign, this letter is a plea to Morel to slow down, because editors' complaints about too many articles and letters worried Casement. However, his fears were groundless. Though they expressed occasional frustrations with Morel's bombardment, as Sir Edward Russell at the *Liverpool Daily Post* did in 1907, the CRA's press penetration only increased for the next four years as a broader public embraced the movement and newspapers both led and followed public opinion.[116]

As an organization that relied on the press to extend its reach to many readers who might never attend an atrocity meeting, the CRA had an extensive and

---

[112] William Haslam Mills, *The Manchester Guardian: A Century of History* (New York: Holt, 1922), 140.

[113] Bebbington, *Nonconformist Conscience*, 154.

[114] Morel (anon.), "A Word for the Congo State," *Pall Mall Gazette*, 19 July 1897; Morel's authorship noted in Marchal, *Morel contre Léopold*, Vol. 1, 20.

[115] Casement to Morel, 14 December 1904, F8/17:96.

[116] Russell to Morel, 31 May 1907, F9/15:42.

varied relationship with the press. Mary Kingsley had expanded Morel's circle of press contacts and shepherded his first anti-Congo article to *Nineteenth Century* and then to *Speaker* despite her worries that it would jeopardize his position at Elder Dempster.[117] Fortunately for Morel, the press had long been skeptical of the Congo. As he noted in 1894, the Congo Free State had been "the butt of very unfriendly criticism" from the English press since its founding, or, as the British ambassador reported in 1897, "M. van Eetvelde [Congo chief minister] complains that that during the past ten years he has never seen anything complimentary said of the Congo in the English press."[118] It is not surprising that the press was generally receptive to Morel and the CRA. The conservative *Morning Post* was a stalwart CRA ally, burnishing the campaign's nonpartisan nature, until the paper's ownership changed in 1908.[119] George Cadbury's *Daily News* was less reliable, despite his support for the CRA, because he exerted less editorial control than most owners.[120] *The Times* was the major holdout among the dailies until Morel won over Valentine Chirol, the foreign editor, in 1906, by providing information, even scoops, in dozens of letters over a six-month period.[121] In consequence, Chirol fired his Brussels correspondent, who for years tilted *The Times* against reform under the influence of Leopold's Press Bureau.[122]

Converting *The Times* meant unanimous support for Congo reform among the London dailies and the leading regional papers except the *Birmingham Daily Post*.[123] This consensus broke down after Morel's 1909 attack on the Foreign Office. *The Times* was the most important casualty, but others also backed the Foreign Office. This may have affected coverage; only one paper published his 1909 press release that the Duke of Norfolk had joined the CRA, a great coup, because he was the leading Catholic peer.[124] The papers continued to support pressure for Congo reform, but many distanced themselves from Morel after this point.

One periodical never deviated: Morel's *West African Mail* and its successor, the *African Mail*, marketed to African merchants and colonial officials. Subsidized by Holt and Cadbury and edited by Morel or, more often, his

---

[117] Kingsley to Morel, 5 [September?] 1899, F8/97A:74.

[118] Morel (anon.), *Pall Mall Gazette*, 22 February 1894, 1–2; Plunkett to Salisbury, 21 May 1897, FO 881/7019:35.

[119] Holt to De Ville, 21 May 1902, F8/84:208.

[120] Morel to Guinness, 30 March 1904 F10/109:735-7; Morel to Gilmour, 24 November 1908, F10/16:957; Cadbury to Morel, 4 November 1907, Cadbury Papers 180/767.

[121] F8/30.

[122] Spender to Morel, 14 June 1907, F8/132:4.

[123] Morel to Meyer, 1 February 1906, F10/13:368; Morel to Cadbury, 28 November 1906, F10/14:751.

[124] Morel to Doyle, 15 October 1909, F8/49:45.

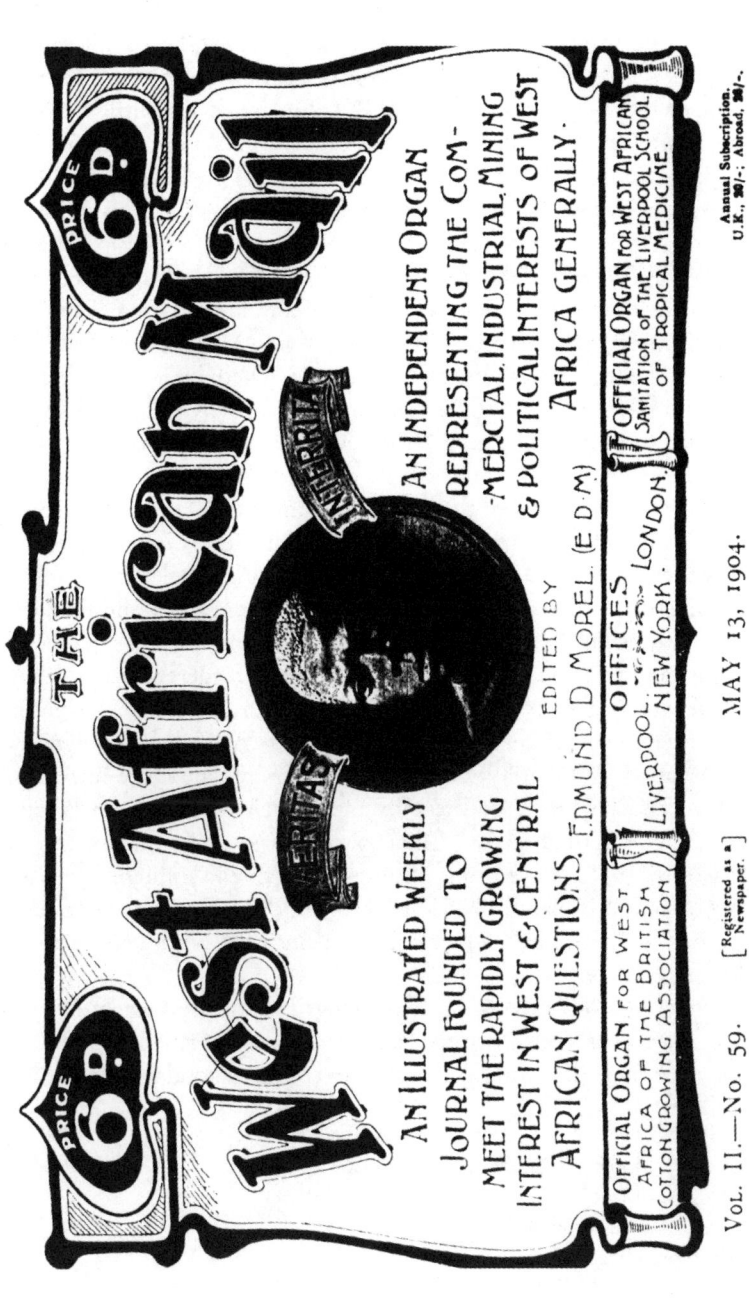

Figure 7.1 *West African Mail* masthead

Source: *West African Mail*, from LSE Library's collections, MOREL/F11/3.

assistant, the weekly paper struggled to increase its small but loyal following of subscribers and advertisers to a level that could bring its finances into the black. Lest anyone forget Morel's underlying motivation, the paper's motto proclaimed *Veritas Interrita* (Truth Undaunted or Fearless Truth). Almost every issue had one or more Congo articles. The *WAM* included a monthly "Congo Supplement" until Cadbury convinced Morel that the CRA's organ should be a standalone publication.[125] Being editor of the *WAM* had the benefit of making Morel a press insider as well as an activist, smoothing his approach to editors at the great national dailies.

The *Aborigines' Friend* and the *Anti-Slavery Reporter* had long reported what other papers said about their activities and causes, and in turn tried to lure the newspapers to amplify their words by reprinting them. Morel intensified these practices, starting with the first issue of the *WAM*, where he included a page of press testimonials for *Affairs of West Africa*.[126] After a CRA deputation met with Sir Edward Grey at the Foreign Office, Morel made sure that the British Press Association sent a full account of the proceedings to all its subscribers. The next month's *Organ* featured the reactions from over 60 periodicals, most of which he gleaned from a clipping service that sent him Congo articles that appeared in other papers.[127] When the CRA put out an "Appeal to the Nation," the *Organ* noted that it had appeared in full or in part in eight London dailies and at least 12 provincial dailies, reprinting editorials from 11 of these papers.[128] This self-regarding coverage showed *WAM* and *Organ* readers that the CRA's positions were widely acknowledged, amplified by Morel's practice of sending hundreds of free copies of the *Organ* to the editors of British, foreign and colonial newspapers, influential politicians and bishops, the more important London clubs, and key allies of the movement such as Green who would distribute them to their contacts.[129] The *Organ* grew steadily, with print runs reaching 2,150 by 1910.[130] Even fundraising had its role in influencing public opinion. Morel sent the March 1905 appeal for funds in *The Friend* to at least 22 other papers.[131] The appeal had weak fundraising results but kept the issue in the public eye.

Congo reform rhetoric did not go unchallenged in the press. Even the most supportive of papers sometimes printed letters from people criticizing the CRA or defending Leopold; the ensuing controversy could be good for circulation.

---

[125] Cadbury to Morel, 17 October 1905, F8/11:65.
[126] *WAM*, 3 April 1903, vii.
[127] *Organ*, December 1906, 9–13.
[128] *Organ*, November 1907, 6–9.
[129] Distribution lists, F4/5:218–49 and F10/9:988–9.
[130] F4/10:289.
[131] Pamphlet, 24 March 1905, F10/12:66–7; Morel to Editor, 5 April 1905, F10/12:116.

A typical example, discussed in Chapter 3, was the exchange in the *New Age* with Catholic MP Hilaire Belloc.

More serious was outright opposition. Leopold's Press Bureau, which paid Belgian, German, and other papers for friendly coverage, found the large British papers less susceptible to its financial inducements, but the Congo had supporters among smaller newspapers and journals, paid or not. Cutcliffe Hyne notified Morel that a "big newspaper editor here in the north" refused to review *King Leopold's Rule in Africa* because the other side paid better.[132] The unnamed paper might have been one of Sir Hugh Gilzean Reid's. The *Liverpool Journal of Commerce* was for the most part Jones's mouthpiece. Jones's reach went much farther, however. Just after the CRA began, he planted an attack on Morel in the *Liverpool Daily Post*, bought 10,000 copies of the paper, put piles of them on African steamships, and sent them to everyone he could think of, including every MP.[133]

The South African-born editor of *African World and Cape-Cairo Express*, Leo Weinthal, was hostile to Congo reform because he opposed the African rights advocated by Morel's *West African Mail*. He was sure from his own experience that Africans were like children who needed to be compelled to work. The initially civil debate between Weinthal and Morel deteriorated as Weinthal began to call the CRA the tool of West African merchants and Morel accused Weinthal of taking (and twisting) *WAM* articles without attribution. Finally, Weinthal wrote that "further correspondence between us—private or otherwise—is out of the question," suggesting that Morel, in a missing letter, had accused him of being on Leopold's payroll.[134]

Charles Diamond's *Catholic Herald* was the most passionately hostile paper, attacking the CRA and Morel as the morally bankrupt tools of sinister interests who would do anything to hurt Catholicism and destroy Leopold's creation. He tried unsuccessfully to persuade or bully other papers into cutting their links to Morel. His chief impact seems to have been to make British Catholics wary of the reform movement.[135] Their suspicion was understandable, because relations with Protestants were not peaceful. Liverpool had anti-Catholic marches, meetings, and even rioting in 1906 and 1909, the latter leaving one person dead

---

[132] Cutcliffe Hyne to Morel, 13 November 1904, F8/199.

[133] Morel to Brabner, 20 June 1904, F10/11:368; Morel to Green, 20 and 21 June 1904, F10/11:365, 379.

[134] Weinthal to Morel, 31 August 1903, F4/24 and 1 September 1904, 17 and 22 April 1908, F9/18:60ff.

[135] Diamond to *Morning Post*, 9 December 1904, F9/3:41; "British Catholics and the Congo Question," *WAM*, 14 April 1905, 50–51. Arthur Conan Doyle and Francis Bourne, Catholic Archbishop of Westminster, *Morning Post*, 5 November 1909, 380 HOL I-4/11:11.

and driving 157 Catholic families (and, in retaliation, 110 Protestant families) from their homes.[136]

The reformers found that their rhetoric, even when exemplary, brought with it certain risks in the marketplace of ideas. When opponents attacked Morel or the CRA in the press, Morel would usually respond with guns blazing, sometimes jumping to conclusions and often overreacting to statements that he might better have left unanswered.[137] In the CRA's early months, Cutcliffe Hyne, who had been to the Congo, lectured for the Association, wrote for the *WAM*, and wrote a Congo novel, complained, "You give too much prominence to missionary evidence. No doubt all the missionaries whose evidence you print are excellent men; but beyond doubt also there are a lot of missionaries on the Congo who are extremely bad eggs and the Powers that be and the public here know it and when they see 'letter from the Rev. Blank of the Particular Baptist Methodist Mission of Botato' they either don't read or don't swallow it."[138] Relying on an alliance of humanitarianism, commerce, and religion meant three points of vulnerability rather than one. Some attacked humanitarians (as Morel had previously done) as ineffectual do-gooders. The involvement of businessmen triggered speculations about a hidden profit motive. The agitation's religious backers could become too fervent. Socialists could find both commercial and religious activism problematic. Ramsay Macdonald noted in 1908, "I find that a great many are under the impression that it is a mere Non-Conformist hubbub," illustrating that the Nonconformist conscience was not necessarily a strength.[139]

The War of Words in the Courtroom

The Congo Free State provided ammunition for the rhetorical arsenal of the reformers, who quoted official bulletins, trade statistics, reports of warfare, and legal actions. Of these, legal actions were the most sensational, including libel trials against critics of the regime and the trials of Congo officials for abuses. In this record, three libel trials against people who had spoken ill of the Congo Free State loom large: Burrows (1903–04), Stannard (1906), and Sheppard (1909). The conviction of Captain Guy Burrows for libel in a British court seemed to damage the reformers, though unfairly, as Morel argued. Burrows was a former Congo officer who had defended it against Salusbury's accusations, but turned

---

[136] Hugh McLeod, "Protestantism and British National Identity," in *Nation and Religion: Perspectives on Europe and Asia*, eds Peter van der Veer and Hartmut Lehmann (Princeton: Princeton University Press, 1999), 55; Ian Henderson, "George Wise" http://www.ulsterbulwark.org/George-Wise-of-Liverpool%28330364%29.htm.

[137] Chirol to Morel, 31 October and 22 November 1907 F8/30:53, 56.

[138] Cutcliffe Hyne to Morel, 23 July 1904, F9/8:197.

[139] Macdonald to Morel, 10 February 1908, F8/106:18.

against it when his request for reappointment was refused. He then published a book, *The Curse of Central Africa* (dismissed by Morel as of no value), that made accusations against another officer that he was unable to substantiate in court when the Congo government sued for libel.[140] The apologists used the Burrows trial for years to cast doubt upon all Congo criticism, even though his book contained a damning section by another former Congo employee, Edgar Canisius, that no one questioned.

The trial of Rev. Edgar Stannard for libel against the Congo State had a mixed outcome. Stannard, under instructions from Guinness, would not call any witnesses. Guinness, defying Morel, intended for Stannard to lose to show that justice was unobtainable in the Congo.[141] Instead of a lawyer, Vice-Consul Armstrong was his chief on-the-spot advisor. Stannard ignored Armstrong's advice to answer questions briefly, instead helping the prosecution with long, evasive replies that "invariably" contradicted what Armstrong told him to say.[142] Stannard lost the case when it became obvious that his accusations against a Congo official were hearsay.[143] However, on appeal, without Stannard present to botch his own defense, the court overturned the sentence, assessing Stannard one franc in damages.

In contrast, the Sheppard trial was a triumph for the reformers. In January 1908, Sheppard wrote an article about atrocities for the mission's local publication, the *Kasai Herald*.[144] The Kasai Company sued Morrison and Sheppard for libel.[145] Emile Vandervelde himself came to the Congo to defend the men. The court dismissed the case against Morrison on a technicality, but Vandervelde secured acquittal for Sheppard while exposing the hypocrisy and venality of the Kasai Company and the entire Congo edifice.

Trials of Congo officials highlighted the weakness of Congo justice. Courts were more likely to convict lower-level employees than more senior officials, who often went out of the reach of the Congo Free State by traveling to Belgium, apparently with official connivance. On appeal, judges reduced or eliminated sentences. No matter what the verdict, every trial was an opportunity for the reformers. If the judge found the defendant guilty, this confirmed the violence inherent in the system. If the judge acquitted the defendant, the Congo Free

---

[140] Morel to Councillor W. Denton of Liverpool, 30 March 1904, F10/9:722.

[141] Armstrong to Nightingale, 27 April 1906 FO 881/ 8786, 158; Morel to Wilkes, 8 February 1907, F10/15:135.

[142] Nightingale to Grey 17 August 1906, FO 881/8923:54–6; Armstrong to Grey, 8 October 1906, FO 881/8923:76.

[143] Nightingale to Morel, 18 August 1906, F8/119:17.

[144] Pagan Kennedy, *Black Livingstone* (New York: Viking, 2002), 162–3; Slade, *English-Speaking Missions*, 368; *Kasai Herald*, January 1908.

[145] FO 881/9530.

State had perverted justice to protect itself. The escape of a defendant to Belgium spoke for itself.

The Congo reform movement was not a spontaneous public outcry, but a widespread agitation fostered by reformers to exert pressure on the government by spurring and embodying public opinion, which needed care and feeding if it was not to wither away. It was not enough to present the facts to the public. The Congo was too far away and its situation too unfamiliar. The reformers needed to make their vision of the Congo and of Britain vivid to the public through words and images.

The reformers tapped into long-established tropes of Britain as compassionate, just, and responsible to remind or convince the British that their virtues would lead them to act on this issue. They invoked multiple meanings of humanity as reasons for action. Their strategy helped their compatriots to reimagine themselves as nobler, more humane, and more just. Like other Europeans before them, they invented a new Congo.[146] To overturn the carefully crafted image of the Congo Free State as a philanthropic enterprise, the reformers conveyed a dissenting image of a sordid and bloody tyranny that enslaved, tortured, and murdered indiscriminately while reducing people to the status of expendable tools for the accumulation of wealth.

By 1906, the reformers had triumphed in the battle of representation; Leopold's apologists had become the dissenters from the new trope. Their continued defense helped Leopold maintain his competing truth claims right through his surrender of the Congo to Belgium. Dunn argues that the reformers succeeded in part by reviving the original picture of the Congo as a place of evil and depravity. It seems, rather, that the locus of evil had shifted from the Congolese, now seen as victims, to Congo Free State officials and concession companies. Belgian annexation made this rhetorical battle more difficult as Morel and others had foreseen. They could not demonize Belgium the way they had demonized Leopold, even when Belgium seemed to be continuing the Leopoldian system in the first year after annexation. Yet Belgium had to act to secure reform.

The rhetorical battle for the hearts and minds of the British people lasted from the first complaints right through the final stage of reforms. Morel, the Harrises, and other leading reformers proved to be indefatigable in the war of words and images, which was necessary if the public were to act on the construction of British virtues. They used venues, technologies, and practices previously deployed by humanitarians, crusading journalists, religious campaigners, and political reformers to make their reimagined Britain and Congo a discursive reality for a large section of the British public. Through the press as well as the written resolutions passed at meetings, they were able to claim to represent public opinion and thus brought weight and legitimacy to the issue in the eyes of the politicians and bureaucrats.

---

[146] Dunn, *Imagining the Congo*, 48.

Chapter 8

Politicians and Bureaucrats: The Art of the Possible

> The state of affairs with which we have to deal is without precedent. It is so scandalous that if neither Belgium nor any other Power will act, we must use all the means at our disposal, short of undertaking the administration of the Congo ourselves, to put an end to it.[1]—Sir Edward Grey to the Cabinet, 1909

The 1890s showed that the Congo regime would make no substantive changes in response to criticism, whether private or public, measured or sensational, friendly or hostile. Reform would come only through the exercise of power: through international coordination, unilateral British military action, or the Belgian political process. All three required the British government to take a strong stand, as Morel recognized, "How can it be stopped? Only ... by publicity and popular pressure upon the Governments ... [to] force it upon the world's diplomacy."[2] The Congo reformers had set themselves a difficult task, but they succeeded in altering British diplomacy to be more consistent with their ends.

Morel's complaints about the Foreign Office and Sir Edward Grey permeate most historical accounts that deign to notice the Foreign Office at all. Three historians, William Roger Louis, S.J.S. Cookey, and John Bremner Osborne, Jr, revised the Morel-generated narrative of Foreign Office vacillation to portray it as an active, autonomous agent, making choices that both helped and hindered reform.[3] The present study builds on their work to create a new understanding of Grey as a protagonist of reform when he took office in 1905 and as the main actor after 1908, applying the decisive pressure to ensure Belgian annexation and implementation of reforms.

---

[1] Cabinet papers, 16 March 1908, CAB 37/92/41.
[2] *Congo Supplement to the WAM*, June 1905, 317.
[3] William Roger Louis, "The Triumph of the Congo Reform Movement, 1905–1908," *Boston University Papers on Africa*, Vol. 2, edited by Jeffrey Butler (Boston: Boston University Press, 1966); Cookey, *Britain*; John Bremner Osborne, Jr, "Sir Edward Grey, the British Consular Staff, and the Congo Reform Campaign," (PhD diss., Rutgers University, 1971); Osborne, "Wilfred G. Thesiger, Sir Edward Grey, and the British Campaign to Reform the Congo, 1905–9," *Journal of Imperial and Commonwealth History* 27, no. 1 (January 1999): 59–80.

The reformers' chief target was the British Foreign Secretary, who in these years operated at the peak of the position's power and autonomy.[4] Lord Salisbury, Prime Minister and Foreign Secretary until 1900, set the pattern, working in secrecy because he believed that the technical expertise required made foreign policy ill-suited to governance by the Cabinet and incompatible with electoral politics.[5] The next Foreign Secretaries were Henry Petty-Fitzmaurice, 5th Marquess of Lansdowne (Unionist) from 1900–05 and Sir Edward Grey (Liberal) from 1905 on. Despite their different affiliations, their policies were similar, focusing on the relative decline of British power in an increasingly unfriendly world. They prioritized good relations with France and Russia to neutralize threats from those countries and to serve as counterweights to an assertive, powerful, and erratic Germany.

Lansdowne and Grey sat at the intersection of institutional identities. They were politicians, active in the Lords and Commons, respectively, though only Grey had to face the voters in parliamentary elections. They were also bureaucrats, running a professionalized government department whose permanent staff worked within set procedures and traditions.

The Foreign Secretary's power was not unlimited. The Prime Minister could remove him, not a serious risk for Lansdowne or Grey. The agreement of the Prime Minister or the Cabinet was advisable though not essential for major policy changes that might lead to political or international complications. The House of Commons had the right to question the Foreign Secretary or his representative, who could answer as he wished, but it was wisest to meet the questioner at least halfway to avoid political difficulties. Because the Commons set the budget, MPs of both major parties routinely proposed cutting the department's funding or the Foreign Secretary's salary by £100. These amendments were a tool to create a debate, not a real financial threat; in 1900–13, all such amendments either were withdrawn after discussion or failed the ensuing vote. The House of Commons could intervene directly in foreign policy by passing a resolution that required the government to act, as with the 20 May 1903 resolution that the government confer with the Berlin Act signatories regarding the Congo.[6] This was a powerful tool not often used; the ruling party was unlikely to challenge its own Foreign Secretary, and the opposition usually could not muster the votes. The 1903 Congo resolution, passed without a division in a "very thin house," prompted Lansdowne to issue two diplomatic Notes to other countries and to instruct Casement to undertake his journey.[7]

---

[4] Zara Steiner, *The Foreign Office and Foreign Policy, 1898–1914* (Cambridge: Cambridge University Press, 1969), 200, 209.

[5] John Darwin, *The Empire Project* (Cambridge: Cambridge University Press, 2009), 78.

[6] 122 Parl. Deb. (4th ser.) (1903) 1289–332.

[7] Fitzmaurice, 122 Parl. Deb. (4th ser.) (1903) 1325.

The ultimate parliamentary weapon was to vote against the government. However, this was available only for the most important issues. The CRA's own nonpartisan strategy militated against this, because such a vote would have split the movement. A parliamentary vote against the government on the Congo issue was not a possibility at any time during the campaign.

Public opinion was a useful but not powerful tool. The Foreign Office's largely upper-class permanent staff believed that foreign policy stood above the tides and fads of public opinion. However, Zara Steiner notes that its officials took account of the views of the most knowledgeable segment of the public, which they collected via the press, through discussions with the representatives of religious, humanitarian, and commercial bodies, from MPs and Parliament, and from informal contacts with prominent people. These views could stimulate discussions among officials, open or close off policy possibilities, and prioritize particular issues.[8]

The reformers tried to influence the Foreign Secretary through Foreign Office personnel, through letters and visits, by applying parliamentary pressure, through the force of public opinion as expressed in the press, public meetings, and resolutions, and by the intervention of influential individuals. By providing information and analyzing its implications, groups like the CRA could affect the policy-making process. The CRA's influence in the Foreign Office peaked when it fulfilled this role and broke down after Morel attacked the Foreign Office.

Lansdowne and Congo Reform

Long before Casement's report, Salisbury had asked the Foreign Office staff to keep a running catalog of reports of Congo brutalities, envisioning a time when they might be useful.[9] Much of this information came from Edward Bannister (Casement's aunt's husband, Vice-Consul 1893–95) and William Pickersgill (Consul 1892–98). Skeptical of Bannister, the Foreign Office asked Pickersgill to review the situation after the April 1897 debate in the House of Commons. Pickersgill substantiated Bannister's reports and expanded their critique through observation and meetings with missionaries. The unpublished version of his report anticipated almost all of Casement's 1903 criticisms.[10]

Although Pickersgill convinced the Foreign Office and Salisbury that the Congo administration was brutal and mendacious, Assistant Undersecretary Sir Francis Bertie vetoed the recommendation of Clement Hill, the African

---

[8] Steiner, *Foreign Office*, 158, 172, 197, 199–200, 212.
[9] Cookey, *Britain*, 22–55.
[10] "Congo Atrocities: Remarks by Mr Pickersgill," 1 June 1897, FO 881/7015.

Department head, that Britain should address the issue.[11] Britain wanted to secure the upper Nile, an aim not well-served by provoking Leopold, especially when evidence from missionaries and traders was seldom firsthand and European courts would not accept testimony from natives.[12] Bertie, backed by Salisbury, felt that only the treatment of British subjects was a fit subject for diplomacy; the press would have to see to the general misrule of the Congo. Lord Salisbury refused the subsequent 1900 APS request to intervene, saying the fate of the Congolese people was not Britain's affair.[13]

However, Salisbury's Foreign Office made a fateful decision in its waning months. Until late 1900, the Consul for Portuguese West Africa, French Tropical Africa, and the Congo Free State resided in Loanda, with a Vice-Consul in the Congo. Since Pickersgill's transfer in 1898, the Loanda Consul had been Roger Casement. As Consul and on a special Boer War assignment, Casement had peppered the Foreign Office with analysis and advice about the Congo cruelties. In October 1900, Salisbury reversed the previous arrangement by moving Casement to the Congo with his Vice-Consul in Loanda. The Foreign Office had deliberately put a known critic of the Congo in a more senior position on the spot, suggesting that Salisbury did not intend Leopold's immunity from criticism to be permanent.

Lansdowne became Foreign Secretary in November 1900, and soon prepared a draft dispatch, approved by King Edward, protesting the awarding of monopoly concessions for extended terms, the "appalling cruelty" of forced rubber collection, and the use of lethal force to compel labor. Fox Bourne had inspired this by arguing that Leopold's lease of British territory made Britain responsible for his Berlin Act compliance there.[14] However, Lansdowne did not send the dispatch, and then refused requests from Fox Bourne and Dilke to take up the Congo. The Congo Free State did not appear in the Africa Department's 1902 annual review.[15]

This hesitation came from several factors. Lansdowne believed that only the assembled Berlin Act signatories could address the Congo, but reconvening them could reopen other African issues.[16] The Foreign Office thought that its evidence was legally insufficient; even Casement relayed hearsay about conditions in the interior.[17] In addition, the Foreign Office fretted that

[11] Cookey, *Britain*, 50, 54–5; Steiner, *Foreign Office*, 38–9.
[12] Osborne, "Grey," 13, 17–18.
[13] *Aborigines' Friend*, August 1900, 551–2.
[14] Lansdowne to Phipps, January 1901, draft, FO 800/117, cited in Osborne, "Grey," 29; Osborne, "Grey," 21–2, 28.
[15] "Current Work of the African Dept.," 1902, FO 881/7764.
[16] Lansdowne to Dilke, 13 March 1902, Add. 43917, cited in Louis, "Casement," 101.
[17] Farnall minute, Addison's memorandum, 11 May 1903, FO 10/803, quoted in Louis, "Casement," 101.

Parliament would complain about the suppression of previous evidence, so it continued suppressing evidence rather than deal with criticism for its inaction during the previous six years.[18] The Foreign Office feared attacks from MPs more than arguments with Leopold. Only public opinion could challenge its refusal to act against the Congo.[19]

Lansdowne's Foreign Office did defend British interests. A French Congo concession company had confiscated property from two British merchant houses, John Holt Co. Ltd. and Hatton & Cookson. Holt and Morel orchestrated a barrage of newspaper articles and chamber of commerce resolutions that led the Foreign Office to protest formally to France. Morel drew the incorrect conclusion that the method of agitation, not the issue, made the difference.[20] He pursued the same tactics regarding the Congo Free State, creating the public opinion that the Foreign Office had feared. To educate Parliament, MPs posed Congo questions to the Foreign Office's Parliamentary Undersecretary, Lord Cranborne, on seven of the 42 days the House of Commons was in session before 20 May 1903, including giving notice on 22 April that they intended to place a bill before the House. On 20 May, Samuel put forward the resolution, supported by Dilke, Emmott, and Conservative Sir John Gorst.

Prime Minister Arthur Balfour intervened to soften the resolution, rather than trying to crush it by forcing a division of the House or by arguing for a narrower interpretation of Britain's responsibilities. He would not have wanted to risk defeat on this peripheral but nonpartisan question, especially when the Foreign Office itself admitted that the evils were real. In taking this middle ground, he and Cranborne encouraged the indictment of the Congo. In consideration of what Cranborne called "public opinion not only in England but throughout Europe," their action required Lansdowne to act on his sentiments.[21]

The Foreign Office hoped to avoid unilateral action by pushing the matter to the court of arbitration in The Hague.[22] However, Lansdowne undermined this by pursuing incompatible goals: to be cautious while expressing British concerns, and to respond to Parliament but not to intervene. His solution was to place responsibility on the Berlin signatories. Lansdowne signaled this via a Note to the British representatives in each capital on 8 August 1903. Although the three-page document shared concerns about the Congo Free State and its adherence to the Berlin Act, it provided no evidence and softened its tone with statements such as "His Majesty's Government do not know precisely to what extent these accusations may be true." After conferring, if they found

---

[18] Farnall minute, 5 June 1903, FO 10/805.
[19] Cookey, *Britain*, 86; Farnall minute, 3 April, on Fox Bourne to Salisbury, 27 March 1902, FO 10/773, quoted in Louis, "Casement," 101.
[20] Osborne, "Grey," 42.
[21] 122 Parl. Deb. (4th ser.) (1903) 1289–332.
[22] Fox Bourne to Morel, 19 June 1903, F8/66:129; FO 881/8229:42–6.

that the Congo Free State had not fulfilled its obligations, they should "make representations." However, he did not disclose the information in the Foreign Office files and did not propose any practical means of conferring. He closed by inviting suggestions, which "might" include resorting to the Hague Tribunal.[23]

Lansdowne's Note was simultaneously a thunderbolt, because no country had so publicly and officially made such broad charges against the Congo Free State, and at the same time a diplomatic trifle, because it recommended nothing and did not require an answer. He hoped that the Berlin signatories would do something without Britain leading the effort.

The Commons resolution forced Lansdowne to turn to Casement. The Congo Consul had proven erratic in his advocacy for the Congolese. He had originally requested and received permission to investigate conditions in the interior in 1902, but canceled the trip so he could improve the consul's residence in Boma before going to Britain for his health.[24] When Casement returned to the Congo in 1903, Lansdowne refused his renewed request because he wanted "materials for an indictment" about the mistreatment of British subjects, a subject fully within British rights of remonstration.[25] However, the 20 May resolution meant that the Foreign Office needed recent, official, firsthand information, so Lansdowne instructed Casement to begin his trip as soon as possible.[26]

Balfour's words and Lansdowne's Note meant that Britain would have to present Casement's report to foreign governments, Parliament, and, inevitably, the public. The report substantiated with direct testimony and evidence the nature of the Congo system that Casement had harped on since 1900. In February 1904, the Foreign Office released the report to Parliament and the signatories, largely intact with one major change. Lord Cranborne had left the Foreign Office on the death of his father, Lord Salisbury, and Earl Percy had succeeded him as Undersecretary. Percy recommended handling the Casement report privately with Leopold and perhaps an international commission.[27] Lansdowne, mindful of Parliament, opted to make it public, but took the advice of the new Lord Salisbury to substitute coded initials for the names of

---

[23] "Despatch to certain of His Majesty's Representatives abroad in regard to alleged Cases of Ill-treatment of Natives and to the Existence of Trade Monopolies in the Independent State of the Congo," FO Africa No. 14 (1903) Cd. 1809.

[24] B.L. Reid, "A Good Man—Has Had Fever: Casement in the Congo," *Sewanee Review* 82, no. 3 (Summer 1974): 460–61.

[25] 8 May 1903, FO 10/804; Louis, "Casement," 102; Lansdowne, 3 May 1903 minute on a letter from Fox Bourne, FO 10/803, quoted in Louis, "Casement," 107.

[26] Casement received 4 June 1903, diary entry, in Ó Síocháin and O'Sullivan, *Eyes of Another Race*, 230.

[27] Cookey, *Britain*, 97–8.

both perpetrators and victims.[28] Percy also proposed that they keep the report temporarily confidential to use in bargaining with Leopold, but Lansdowne wanted the Berlin signatories to take responsibility for next steps, so there was no initiative to suppress or bowdlerize it, apart from the coded initials.

The success or failure of the report hinged on the quality of the evidence. In transmitting Casement's report to the Berlin Act signatories on 12 February 1904, Lansdowne said it related the present state of affairs, but again he did not make concrete suggestions, merely asking when he could expect answers to his 8 August 1903 Note.[29] Osborne takes the contrarian position that Lansdowne thought that Casement failed to provide irrefutable evidence, citing a 19 April 1904 dispatch from Lansdowne to the Congo government.[30] Unfortunately, he relies on a truncated extract of this dispatch from a 1959 biography of Casement, shown below with italics indicating the missing words:[31]

> *With regard to the application, renewed in the Notes, for previous Reports from British Consular officers,* it is necessary to explain that these Reports, though forwarding testimony upon which reliance could apparently be placed, were founded on hearsay, and lacked the authority of personal observation, without which His Majesty's Government were unwilling to come to any definite conclusion unfavourable to the Administration of the Congo State. Moreover, some of the Reports are of old date; *the Congo State had admittedly been very active in pushing forward occupation of the country,* and it would be unjust to bring forward statements regarding a condition of affairs which may have entirely passed away.[32]

The full text is neither a criticism of the Casement report (Osborne) nor evidence of Lansdowne's hostility to Casement (Singleton-Gates and Girodias) because it responded to the Congo Free State's second request for the suppressed consular reports *predating* Casement. It merely shows that the Foreign Office did not want to release the previously suppressed reports. The omissions, which create a false impression of Lansdowne's view of Casement's report, have their explanation in Singleton-Gates's connection to the intelligence services,

---

[28] Salisbury memorandum, 26 January 1904, FO 10/807, cited in Martin Ewans, *European Atrocity, African Catastrophe* (London: Routledge, 2002), 199. Casement had initially urged the protection of witnesses through this kind of anonymity.

[29] Lansdowne to HMG's representatives, 12 February 1904, FO Africa No. 1 (1904), Cd. 1933.

[30] Osborne, "Grey," 49; Osborne, "Thesiger," 61–2.

[31] Maurice Girodias and Peter Singleton-Gates, *The Black Diaries of Roger Casement* (New York: Grove Press, 1959), 196.

[32] Lansdowne to Phipps, 19 April 1904, Africa No. 7 (1904) Cd. 2097, 41. A previous request appears in Phipps to Lansdowne, 15 May 1903, FO 403/338:47.

identified by Angus Mitchell; the omitted text appears to have been part of the campaign to make Casement's already controversial reputation into something wholly unsympathetic to justify his 1916 trial and execution.[33]

Although the atrocity stories in Casement's report garnered the most attention, they were vulnerable because they were sometimes unverifiable and often years old.[34] However, the report contained much more than atrocities. It demonstrated the system's cruelty in statements from state and company officials, firsthand evidence of hostage-taking, and other illustrations of coercive methods.[35] It was also, as Burroughs observes, a traveler's account: observations and conversations presented in chronological order about a journey through a small part of the upper Congo.[36] With the exception of the testimony of Epondo, a mutilated boy who recanted his story that State soldiers had wrecked his hand, the Casement report stood up under the deluge of criticism from the apologists and the State. Casement's descriptions of past atrocities were memorable, while the less sensational, but current, evidence about misrule in the rubber zones was more important.

The impact of Casement's report on public opinion was profound. It gave the British government's imprimatur to the charge of pervasive and systematic Congo misrule and was an essential step in the chain of events that led to reform. It also exposed a weakness in British diplomacy.

Britain's Envoy Extraordinary and Minister Plenipotentiary to Belgium and the Congo Free State was Sir Edmund Constantine Henry Phipps. At his final posting in a diplomatic career that began in 1858, Constantine Phipps was at his best conveying official views between governments, often with sympathy and understanding. When Lansdowne publicly called the Congo government's conduct into question in the August 1903 Note, Phipps began to undermine the new policy without Lansdowne's knowledge, confusing his interlocutors in Belgium and creating the impression that he supported the Congo regime.[37] He told the Italian Minister to Brussels that he did not believe the accusations and that the Note was an insincere attempt to please factions in the Commons.[38] To the Germans, he spoke more plainly; their government need not reply, and the whole affair would soon be "lost in the sands."[39] Phipps urged Germany

---

[33] Angus Mitchell, *Sixteen Lives: Roger Casement* (Dublin: O'Brien Press: 2013), 363.

[34] Osborne, "Thesiger," 61.

[35] Osborne, "Grey," 50–54; original report, FO 881/8564; edited report, FO Africa No. 1 (1904) Cd. 1933, 21–81.

[36] Burroughs, *Travel Writing*, 49–71.

[37] Cookey, *Britain*, 77; Louis, "Morel and the Reform Association," 193.

[38] Gerbaix de Sonnaz to Foreign Minister Tittoni, 24 December 1903, in Ranieri, *Congo et l'Italie*, 149.

[39] Wallwitz to Bülow, 15 July and 28 October 1903, quoted in Willequet, *Congo Belge*, 83.

and France not to "burn their fingers" by cooperating.[40] He told the Belgian Minister to London that profit-seeking Liverpool merchants were behind Congo criticism, an accusation he duly reported to the Foreign Office when Van Eetvelde relayed it back to him a few months later.[41]

Phipps was steering a complicated course. He had supported Casement's proposed journey to settle the "bitter controversy" with unimpeachable "practical details as to the system in force" from "so experienced and careful an observer," and, at the same time, to show Casement the benefits of Leopold's rule.[42] No simple Congophile, Phipps was cynical about Leopold's control of the press and his use of money to make friends and buy silence.[43] He warned Gilzean Reid that information generally known in Belgium undermined his advocacy for Leopold.[44] In his last letter to Grey, Phipps wrote that he had never denied Congo maladministration; he disliked being grouped with apologists like Gilzean Reid.[45]

As Phipps tried to find a balance after the Foreign Office had publicly criticized the Congo, he crossed the line into insubordination, contradicting his government's policy and subverting the will of the House of Commons. He relayed arguments from the Congo administration against Casement's report plus his own critique. Casement's dispatches during his journey, which he had found "valuable" at the time, now struck him as too sweeping.[46] Casement responded with energy and some anger. Lansdowne forwarded their letters to each other, reinforcing a growing acrimony that illuminated aspects of the official British approach in 1904. The cornerstone of Lansdowne's Congo policy was that Britain lacked standing to act alone, and he was "afraid of a snub," as Dilke put it, from the other signatories.[47] Although he backed Casement's report, he allowed Phipps free rein against it. This equivocating strategy suited Lansdowne's sentimental concerns about Congo misrule, his professional belief that there was little Britain could do, and his anxieties about the Congo Free State's *tu quoque* arguments.[48]

---

[40] Willequet, *Congo Belge*, 82–3.

[41] Lalaing to Favereau, 8 July 1903, cited in Ewans, *European Atrocity*, 264; Phipps to Lansdowne, 5 February 1904, FO 403/351, no. 17.

[42] Phipps to Lansdowne, 20 September 1902, FO 403/327 no. 56; Phipps to Lansdowne, 21 March 1903, FO 403/338, no. 130.

[43] Phipps to Lansdowne, 1 May 1903, FO 403/338, no. 40; Phipps to Lansdowne, 18 July 1903, FO 403/338 no. 90.

[44] Phipps to Lansdowne, 11 June 1903, FO 403/338, no. 6.

[45] Phipps to Grey, 19 January 1906, FO 800/42; Phipps to Campbell, 27 September 1902, FO 10/773, no. 71, quoted in Cookey, *Britain*, 78.

[46] Phipps to Lansdowne, 23 October 1903, FO 403/338, no. 159.

[47] Dilke to Morel, 20 June 1903, F8/40:49.

[48] Lansdowne Minute, 11 March 1905, FO 10/815, cited in Louis, "Triumph," 282.

The responses to Lansdowne's note and the Casement report were weak. Sweden said that its citizens did not confirm the reports; Russia abstained from any conclusion as an uninterested power; the Netherlands and Portugal did not want to pursue the issue; and the Austrians did not reply at all.[49] France would do nothing and Germany did not reply. Of the three countries willing to consider the Casement report, Italy declined to proceed, the US was not a Berlin Act signatory, and the Ottoman Empire, under international criticism for its actions in Armenia and Macedonia, was an ally of little value.[50]

The international responses proved to be useless, but the Foreign Secretary moved the cause forward through an unforeseen gambit. The Congo Free State's rebuttal mentioned a new impartial investigation to test Casement's statements.[51] Inspired by a CRA letter critiquing this Leopold-appointed commission, Lansdowne raised the stakes by welcoming the "announcement that a searching and impartial inquiry will be made against the administration of the Free State, and that if real abuses or the necessity for reform should be thereby disclosed, the central Government will act."[52] By publishing this, Lansdowne had boxed in the king. Leopold made the commission a foregone conclusion by demanding an unredacted copy of the Casement report for its use; Lansdowne agreed after extracting a promise to protect witnesses from retaliation.[53] Chapter 6 discussed how Cattier and Wauters with Fox Bourne's help continued Lansdowne's strategy until the Commission of Inquiry met a standard of effectiveness and impartiality unusual among Leopold's creations.

As Percy said, "There has never been a policy of which it might be said as truly as of this one that it was the policy not so much of His Majesty's Government as the policy of the House of Commons."[54] Lansdowne responded to the House of Commons resolution by taking modest actions of critical importance. By sponsoring and distributing Casement's report he gave the allegations of misrule international credibility, and by helping to redefine Leopold's Commission of Inquiry he set in motion the process that would reform the Congo.

Grey's Arrival at the Foreign Office

Sir Edward Grey brought an active commitment to Congo reform, true to his speech in the Commons in June 1904, where he said that the Congo Free State

---

[49] FO 403/351 nos 42–6, 88, Osborne notes.
[50] 135 Parl. Deb. (4th ser.) (1904) 1281.
[51] Phipps to Lansdowne, 13 March 1904 FO Africa No. 7 (1904), Cd. 2097, 23.
[52] Lansdowne to Phipps, 19 April 1904, FO Africa No. 7 (1904), Cd. 2097, 40–41; Campbell to Morel, 1 October 1904, F8/57:25.
[53] Cookey, *Britain*, 116.
[54] 135 Parl. Deb. (4th ser.) (1904) 1272.

had failed as "the mandatory and trustee of the other European Powers" to promote philanthropy and free trade, for which "the European Powers had a responsibility" because "the European good name was in question." In his view, the mistake of 1884–85 was to recognize a "private irresponsible Government"; therefore, the Congo government should be responsible to a representative European parliament. With the other Berlin signatories silent, the situation required the British to interfere alone, however reluctantly, with the country's support, by appointing more consuls and threatening consular jurisdiction to increase the pressure on Leopold, followed by an international conference to revise the Berlin Act. Noting the "gruesome unanimity" of the House of Commons, he cautioned MPs not to tie the government's hands by dictating specific actions. This speech marked him as a reformer and set the broad outlines of his approach when he became Foreign Secretary 18 months later.[55]

With Grey at the Foreign Office, Belgian annexation became Britain's preferred solution. Histories generally credit Sir Harry Johnston for this remedy; in 1904, he floated the idea in *The Times* on 2 June and at the 7 June APS Congo meeting.[56] When Casement organized the Holborn Town Hall meeting of 7 June 1905, Johnston worked with him to get Morel to agree to a resolution advocating annexation. This resolution, by itself, did not make annexation the CRA's official policy because it had not been endorsed by the Executive Committee; indeed, Johnston was still trying to convince Morel it was the best approach in 1908.[57] Nonetheless, after that point, it was the only serious option on the table.

The idea predated Johnston's involvement. Several Belgians had argued for annexation, beginning with Beernaert in 1900, followed by Wauters and Cattier.[58] Morel had argued for Belgian annexation in 1900 and 1902, but against it in 1903 because he feared Leopold's continued influence and Belgian unwillingness or inability to change his system.[59] Given his belief in parliamentary oversight, Grey settled on Belgium as the best country to annex the Congo.[60] What changed British foreign policy was not Holborn Town Hall but Grey's arrival at the Foreign Office.

---

[55] 135 Parl. Deb. (4th ser.) (1904) 1287–90.

[56] Louis, *Ends of British Imperialism* (London: I.B. Tauris, 2006), 165–7; *The Times*, 2 June 1904, 4 and 8 June 1904, 3.

[57] Fox Bourne to Morel, 22 October 1905, F4/6:37; Dilke to Morel, 6 February 1908, Add. 43897:210; Johnston to Dilke, 13 February 1908, Add. 43920:26; Johnston to Morel, 13 June 1908, F8/93:161; Resolution in Morel, *Evidence Laid before the Congo Commission of Inquiry* (Liverpool: Richardson, 1905), 90.

[58] *The Times*, 6 May 1901, 13; Cattier to Morel, 1906, F9/3:54.

[59] "Belgium and the Congo," *Speaker*, 24 March 1900, 668–9; Morel to Guinness, 24. November 1903, F10/1:281–90; Morel to Fox Bourne, 25 June 1903, F10/7.

[60] Grey in Commons, 3 May 1906, FO 881/8786:71.

After Balfour and the Conservatives fell from power in December 1905, six reformers took high office. Emmott, Samuels, and Beauchamp resigned from the CRA Executive Committee to ascend to the Cabinet, joined by John Morley and John Burns, while Lord Aberdeen became Lord Lieutenant of Ireland. But most important was the new Secretary of State for Foreign Affairs. As a Liberal Imperialist, Grey had supported the Boer War and for a time opposed Campbell-Bannerman's leadership of the party. After Campbell-Bannerman's first choice for Foreign Secretary, Lord Cromer, declined, he asked Grey as part of his strategic embrace of the Liberal Imperialists, which helped reunite the party and enabled it to capitalize on concern about free trade and ethical issues to win a sweeping election victory in January 1906.[61]

This pleased most reformers, with Gertie Emmott's comment typical: "I really am hopeful that a Liberal Government may do something more to push things—men like Edward Grey ... are keen I think that there should be reform."[62] Casement, who thought Lansdowne "honest but weak," saw Grey's appointment more pessimistically: "I am sorry Grey has gone to FO—he will be, more or less, a friend of Leopold, I fear. These Imperialists are not to my heart!"[63] Events proved that Emmott's assessment more accurate than Casement's, but Grey's methods were to try the reformers' patience.

Like his idol Gladstone and Morel himself, Grey brought an earnest moral sense to politics, with a similar inability to see facts that might contradict his self-image. Ambitious, with a strong sense of public responsibility, he was also a deeply private man. After his wife died in a freak accident two months into his tenure as Foreign Secretary, he dedicated himself more fully to his government work, while still escaping to the country when he could. Friends and critics alike honored him for honesty, moral rectitude, sincerity, and loyalty. Yet he was not always straightforward, and never less so than when withholding information from Parliament and the Cabinet; Harry Johnston called him "wedded to secrecy."[64] Because he gathered the thoughts of his permanent officials before making a decision, some worried that he deferred to their judgments. These traits determined his approach to his job, his relationships with Morel and the CRA, and his Congo initiatives.

Grey's relationship to reform has seen multiple interpretations. The research conducted for this study supports Osborne's conception of Grey as a willing reformer, bolstered by the CRA but not driven by it. The reformers did not intimidate him, and, contrary to Morel's arguments, his missteps were not the

---

[61] Biagini, *British Democracy*, 3–4.
[62] Gertie Emmott to Morel, December 1905, F8/54:119.
[63] Casement to Morel, 8 September 1905, F8/20:252; Casement to Morel, 14 December 1905, F8/20:289.
[64] Johnston to Morel, 10 April 1913, F8/92:196.

result of fear, weakness, and vacillation, but misjudgments about the main actors in Belgium.

Grey described the Foreign Secretary's work as falling into four areas: preventing threatening political changes, preventing further expansion of the Empire, promoting commerce and peace, and using Britain's influence "to promote humanitarian objects in the world."[65] He admired Gladstone's policies, which inflected political calculation with moral considerations.[66] The Congo was not a sideshow or distraction, but an important concern. Europe remained the Foreign Office's main preoccupation, but he would not forget or set aside the Congo. Grey's negotiations and Cabinet briefings show that his drive for Congo reform was as sincere as Morel's and his position was similar to the CRA's, consistent with his previous statements.

Contemporaries, historians, and Grey himself emphasized how much his policies carried forward Lansdowne's. As Parliamentary Undersecretary, Grey chose Lansdowne's brother Lord Fitzmaurice, like Grey a known reformer. Seven months later, Fitzmaurice could say, "I am glad ... we are able to look back with complete agreement upon the policy of our predecessors."[67] Yet Grey's policies were different in emphasis and execution.[68] Grey quickly went well beyond his predecessor's weak Congo policy.

The reformers' unhappiness with Phipps had increased; Dilke excoriated him for saying that the deficiencies in the Commission for the Protection of the Natives were not the Congo government's fault.[69] In September 1905, Sir Arthur Rollitt, MP, referenced in Chapter 5 as an apologist with influence in the Chambers of Commerce, made a speech at Liège that reassured his Belgian hosts that the British public considered reports of Congo misrule to be "a calumny," a remark he later repudiated but which seems to have earned him promotion to Grand Officer of the Order of Leopold.[70] Reuters reported that Phipps led the applause after Rollitt spoke, which he fruitlessly denied.[71] The Liège incident irredeemably tarnished him as an apologist.[72] Grey would not find reassurance in the Foreign Office files, where his dispatches called for greater understanding of the Congo Free State's problems. As of 21 January 1906, Grey replaced him

---

[65] Speech upon receiving the freedom of the city of Newcastle, *ASR&AF*, October 1913, 146.
[66] Edward Grey, *Twenty-Five Years: 1892–1916* (New York: Frederick A. Stokes, 1925), xxvii.
[67] FO 881/8923:3.
[68] Keith Robbins, *Sir Edward Grey: A Biography of Lord Grey of Fallodon* (London: Cassell, 1971), 135, 144; Steiner, *Foreign Office*, 87–8.
[69] 135 Parl. Deb. (4th ser.) (1904), 1237.
[70] "Virtue Rewarded," *WAM*, 27 October 1905.
[71] "King Leopold's New Recruit," *WAM*, 8 September 1905, 569.
[72] "Liège Pantomime," *WAM*, 29 September 1905.

with a more astute diplomat: Sir Arthur Hardinge, cousin of Charles Hardinge, Grey's Permanent Undersecretary at the Foreign Office.

Humanitarians mistrusted Arthur Hardinge because he had countenanced the continuation of slavery as Britain's representative in Zanzibar. He reciprocated, thinking the humanitarians unrealistic and extreme in their demands. He also felt that the new Liberal Cabinet was prone to sentimentalism concerning slavery and other local customs of Africans that offended European sensibilities.[73] However, Grey found him an able partner. He was superior to Phipps in perceptiveness, creativity, and subtlety. He had earned first-class honors at Oxford, spoke at least eight languages and learned Flemish while in Brussels—unlike Leopold.[74] He took a hand in policy development through carefully argued suggestions to Grey.[75] Once Grey made a decision, Hardinge would carry it out.[76] When Cuvelier asked him why the Congo Free State received so much more scrutiny than the French Congo or other colonies, Hardinge answered as Grey would have: systematic abuses in the Congo Free State provoked much more complaint than the merely local abuses elsewhere, and without a legislature through which public opinion could act, the administration was "absolute and irresponsible."[77]

The Foreign Office staff generally agreed on the Congo's problems, but had many opinions regarding policy choices. Grey's secrecy, caution, and independence led many reformers to fret that the staff influenced him with their hostility. Stead published such an analysis in 1907, entitled "The Eclipse of Sir Edward Grey," illustrated with a cosmology that showed Permanent Undersecretary Charles Hardinge obscuring his chief's face, "throwing the firmament into darkness."[78] Foreign Office documents show a different picture. Though interested in his staff's opinions, Grey chose alternatives that fit his overall policy and priorities most closely. On the Congo question, the Foreign Office papers show senior staff increasingly making proposals intended to further Grey's policy goals.

During the Lansdowne years, a few Foreign Office staffers had unofficially talked with the reformers. From 1906–08, those contacts grew as similarity of purpose brought greater cooperation. Foreign Office officials, including

---

[73] Osborne, "Grey," 99; Arthur Hardinge, *A Diplomatist in Europe* (London: Jonathan Cape, 1927), 194.

[74] Henry Lane Wilson, *Diplomatic Episodes in Mexico, Belgium, and Chile* (New York: Doubleday, 1927), 126; Emerson, *Leopold*, 7.

[75] Hardinge to Grey, 7 June 1906, FO 403/373, 100.

[76] Louis, "The Philosophical Diplomatist: Sir Arthur Hardinge and King Leopold's Congo, 1906–1911," *Bulletin of A.R.S.O.M. (Academie Royale des Sciences d'Outre-Mer) for 1968*, 1402–30.

[77] Hardinge to Grey, 29 March 1906, FO Africa No. 1 (1906). Cd 3002.

[78] "The Tchinovnik of the Foreign Office," *Review of Reviews* 36, no. 216 (December 1907): 566–75. http://books.google.com/books?id=gHIAAAAAYAAJ&pg=RA1-PA566.

Fitzmaurice, passed confidential information on to Morel.[79] The Foreign Office acted on Morel-supplied information and often posed questions the CRA suggested to the Congo government. Morel helped shape Foreign Office thinking on many questions.

The Congo government suspected undue influence. When Phipps relayed Grey's criticisms to Cuvelier, the Congo Foreign Minister understandably wondered if Morel had written it, especially as its substance had already appeared in the *Organ*.[80] When Grey asked Cuvelier for the Commission's proceedings, Cuvelier refused, imagining some sinister CRA design.[81] Like Phipps, Hardinge brought Cuvelier problems that Morel had publicized.[82]

Grey viewed the Belgian solution more optimistically than the CRA; Belgian annexation would help the Congolese with minimal repercussions to international relations.[83] The CRA worried that Belgium lacked colonial experience, its legislature and public seemed uninterested, Leopold's political influence and his subsidies seemed limitless, and Belgium had no broad-based movement for reform.[84] Leopold had taught the Belgians that colonies should contribute to the public purse, contrary to the usual colonial practice. Cromer and Nightingale agreed with many Belgian Socialists that Europe should internationalize the Congo, while others urged assigning the Congo to France, Germany, and/or, more controversially, Britain.[85] The Africa Department's E.A.W. Clarke agreed with Morel's concerns but endorsed Grey's position that "the control of the Powers will be much stronger after the annexation."[86] Morel believed Belgium would be more difficult to pressure than Leopold, due to the potential for international complications and prickly Belgian nationalism. He and Grey were both correct. Belgium wanted reform more than Leopold did, but getting satisfactory reforms would require a heavier hand than Grey imagined.

Grey's Foreign Office and Congo Reform

The CRA believed Foreign Secretaries would act only when pushed. In March 1906, the CRA Parliamentary Committee increased the pressure by posing

---

[79] Fitzmaurice to Morel, 19 May 1906, F8/59:96.
[80] Phipps to Grey, 11 January 1906, FO 881/8715:7.
[81] Hardinge to Grey, 29 March 1906, FO 881/8786:1–2.
[82] Hardinge to Grey, 6 April 1906, FO 881/8786:10.
[83] Grey in Commons, 3 May 1906, FO 881/8786:71; Law to Morel, 20 June 1907, F8/98 13; Grey, *Twenty-five Years*, 190–93.
[84] For example, Morel to Emmott, 15/16 April 1907, F10/15:456.
[85] Cromer/Harris interview, 25 January 1908, F8/35:5; Nightingale to Morel, 6 January 1907, F8/119:26; FO 881/9854:184–5.
[86] Clarke memorandum, 22 January 1907, FO 881/8996.

five questions in the Commons over four days and sending a delegation led by Ramsay MacDonald to Grey on 19 March.[87] They mistook Grey's less urgent timetable for inaction.[88] Grey's belief that Belgium would eventually do the right thing repeatedly led him to give them more time. Morel dissented strongly: "The enlightened Belgian Government theory is all my–eye ... [it] is a rotten concern as at present managed."[89] Grey also worried that Belgium might respond to pressure with a German alliance.[90]

Critically, the reformers did not know what Grey communicated to Brussels until long afterwards. As a result, many doubted his intentions. But for the time being, most leading reformers, even Casement, were willing to grant Grey's goodwill, though they believed he needed prodding to overcome his natural caution and the Foreign Office staff's braking efforts.[91]

Leopold's June 1906 announcement of reforms met with public criticism from Cattier and confidential derision from Foreign Office staffer G.S.H. Pearson, who analyzed them for Grey.[92] Based on Pearson's analysis, Grey spoke disparagingly in Parliament on 5 July, prompting a bizarre letter from Leopold listing 37 grievances with Grey's speech. Grey, with dignity, replied that it was not usual or desirable for the British Foreign Secretary to have a direct correspondence with the Sovereign of the Congo State.[93]

The 1906 reforms were the first iteration of a pattern of missed deadlines. In July, Grey told Parliament he would wait until autumn before committing to specific actions. To the CRA's chagrin, Grey's patience was elastic; autumn passed and Grey continued to wait in the hopes that Belgium "unembarrassed" by British pressure would act to take over the Congo.[94]

One sign that Grey's patience was not a mask for inaction came at the annual Guildhall banquet inaugurating the new Lord Mayor of London, a traditional venue for presenting Government policies. Lord Ripon, speaking for Prime Minister Campbell-Bannerman at the Guildhall on 8 November 1906, said that if Belgium did not do its duty to reform the Congo, Britain would act, reflecting Grey's policy.[95]

Unconvinced, the CRA prodded Grey with parliamentary questions, press campaigns, a proliferation of meetings and resolutions, agitation in his home

---

[87] Trevelyan, MacDonald, and Wason questions, March 15, 20, 22, and 27, 1906, FO 881/8715:79, 86, 89, 95.
[88] Macdonald to Morel, 20 March 1906, F8/106:6.
[89] Morel to Harris, 8 November 1906, F10/14:551.
[90] Harris to Buxton, 17 August 1906, Brit. Emp. s.18 C82/78.
[91] Casement to Morel, 21 August 1906, F8/22:345.
[92] Pearson "Memorandum," 15 June 1906, FO 881/8786:128–39.
[93] FO 881/8850; FO 403/374:28.
[94] 160 Parl. Deb. (4th ser.) (1906) 323–4; *Organ*, December 1906, 1–6.
[95] *Washington Post*, 10 November 1906, 1.

constituency, pressure from influential people at home and abroad, and a torrent of memorandums.[96] Morel's 20 November 1906 *tour de force* was a deputation of commercial, religious, press, and philanthropic men, bringing memorials from nine cities, to meet with Grey, Fitzmaurice, Barrington, and Vice-Consul Armstrong, home on leave. Grey concurred with their diagnosis, discussed the parameters of British policy, and concluded, "If the Constitutional Government of Belgium, responsible to a free Parliament as it is, will take the matter in hand ... they will in our judgment provide the best remedy because what they will do will be to produce not a list of reforms for the Congo, but an entire change of the system of government."[97] He advised the deputation not to offend the Belgian government or people so they could feel free to choose without embarrassment or constraint. If Belgium would not act, then Britain would again approach the signatories before undertaking unilateral action. Thanks to Morel, favorable reports of the deputation appeared in over 50 papers, giving the reformers the publicity they wanted in Britain and abroad.[98]

This was the backdrop for the 13 December 1906 memo by Foreign Office staffer A.W. Clarke regarding Grey's options under treaty, on the understanding that his superiors had decided that "the time for remonstrance is at an end, and that the moment is approaching for decisive action." He considered and rejected Morel's proposals in *Red Rubber*: cease to recognize the Congo and bring British subjects under consular jurisdiction, refuse to admit ships flying the Congo flag to British ports, and withdraw the exequaturs issued to consuls of the Congo Free State. These actions would annoy Leopold but, "he must by this time be quite aware of what we think of him and the proceeding would otherwise have absolutely no effect." Clarke considered prohibiting Congo rubber imports but decided this would be too disruptive. He saw four options based on treaty rights: consular jurisdiction, an International Commission for Congo navigation that could close the Congo River, a conference, and arbitration. Of these, only a conference held much hope of creating real change. To convince the signatories to agree to meet, he suggested approaching them privately. If this failed, arbitration would be the last resort. Clarke's peaceful solutions informed Foreign Office discussions for two years.[99]

Not for the last time, just as Grey was on the verge of taking stronger action, the situation changed and the clock started over again. The Belgian Prime Minister announced on 14 December 1906 (the day after Clarke's memorandum) that

---

[96] Morel to Cadbury, 1 October 1906 (dated added later), F8/12:33.
[97] *Organ*, December 1906, 5.
[98] *Organ*, December 1910.
[99] A.W. Clark, "Memorandum as to Possible Modes of Dealing with the Congo Free State," 13 December 1906, FO 881/8486.

the Belgian cabinet would move quickly to annex the Congo, relieving Grey of the need to proceed with Clarke's recommendations.[100]

Expectations of a quick annexation came to naught as Belgian politicians embarked on protracted negotiations with each other and a very stubborn Leopold. Grey spent 1907 examining policy options, trying not to interfere. He said in the Commons on 15 May that Belgian annexation had to completely change the system of government to be satisfactory, qualifying this on 2 August by observing that the Belgian legislature's efforts should proceed, "not complicated by introducing in them the idea that Belgium had to act under the menaces or threats from other parties."[101] Similarly, Campbell-Bannerman's 1907 Guildhall address rebuked the Congo government but then backtracked, saying, "The British Government had no intention whatever of interfering with the rights of any power."[102] J.A. Spender, *Westminster Gazette* editor and confidant of leading Liberals, interpreted this as "a carefully worded warning to the Belgian people."[103] The Belgian press did not agree, contrasting Campbell-Bannerman's courteous tone with the CRA's menacing "Appeal to the Nation" appearing at the same time.[104]

Then, quite dramatically, the Congo appeared in the King's Speech opening Parliament on 29 January 1908, when the Government laid out its program for the coming year:

> My Government are fully aware of the great anxiety felt with regard to the treatment of the native population in the Congo State. Their sole desire is to see the government of that State humanely administered in accordance with the spirit of the Berlin Act, and I trust that the negotiations now proceeding between the Sovereign of the Congo State and the Belgian Government will secure this object.[105]

Edward VII was in sympathy with this position, reflecting his own feelings expressed to Leopold in 1903: "The King cannot, therefore, feel attracted towards a Sovereign, whether he is a relative or not, who, he considers, has

---

[100] Hardinge to Grey, 15 December 1906, FO 881/8923:159.

[101] FO 881/9093, no. 2.

[102] *The Times*, 11 November 1907; *Speeches by the Rt. Hon. Sir Henry Campbell-Bannerman* (London: The Times, 1909); Campbell-Bannerman correspondence, British Library.

[103] J.A. Spender, *The Life of the Right Hon. Sir Henry Campbell-Bannerman* (London: Hodder and Stoughton, 1924), 372n.

[104] Hardinge to Grey, 16 November 1907, FO 881/9155:129.

[105] *Organ*, February 1908, 4.

neglected his duty towards humanity."[106] Responsibility is hard to pin down, but Campbell-Bannerman, recovering from a heart attack, may have approved the insertion on Grey's recommendation, which itself likely came from a meeting Morel had at the Foreign Office.[107] The King's Speech reflected the Government's commitment to Congo reform.[108] It was a far cry from Lansdowne's tepid request for suggestions in 1903–04.

The November 1906 deputation had inaugurated a personal connection between Morel and Grey from 1906–08, including private meetings, private exchanges of letters, and lengthy memoranda by Morel, interrupted from October 1907 to June 1908 after Morel pushed too hard.[109] Throughout these years, Grey circulated Morel's letters and reports to Hardinge and other Foreign Office officials. They expressed gratitude for Morel's analyses and, on Grey's instructions, continued to share confidential information with him.[110] In October 1908, Grey endorsed the CRA's decision to continue agitating for reform even after the annexation.[111]

By this time, the Foreign Office and the CRA shared a common vocabulary and set of concepts. Their understanding now perfectly aligned, their chief difference was how quickly Britain should adopt more confrontational strategies. Monkswell observed, "It is curious to note how Grey and Fitzmaurice when out of office were all for action and Lansdowne and Percy when in office for delay, and now their opinions are reversed with their positions."[112] The responsibility of office swamped good intentions with international complexities and potentially damaging side-effects. For Grey, options such as consular jurisdiction became weapons to hold in reserve, pending a worsening situation. As Walter Langley had written, "we are as anxious as [Morel] can be to remedy the lot of the native, although we differ from him as to the advisability of moving at the present time."[113]

Patience in Europe did not mean idleness in the Congo. In May 1905, Lansdowne had appointed two Vice-Consuls for the upper Congo, Jack Proby

---

[106] Edward to Leopold, 4 November 1903, Royal Archives, Add. MSS. A.4/31, quoted in Philip Magnus, *King Edward the Seventh* (NY: Dutton, 1964), 321.

[107] "Campbell-Bannerman," *Dictionary of National Biography*, Second Suppl. 1 (London: Macmillan, 1912), 310–11, http://books.google.com/books?id=bMkcAQAAI AAJ&pg=PA310&lpg=PA310; Clarke and Wellesley, FO 991/9155:82.

[108] Mayo to Morel, 31 January 1907, F8/107:3.

[109] Morel to Grey, 25 September and 18 October 1907, F8/60; FO to Morel, 25 October 1907, F8/60:159; CRA to Grey, 1 July 1908, FO 403/400:1–2.

[110] Langley to Morel, 29 January 1909, F8/62:221. Grey to Langley, 16 March 1909, F8/62:254–6.

[111] Grey to Morel, 28 September 1908, F8/60:196; Morel to White, 9 November 1908, F10/16:897, 899.

[112] Monkswell to Morel, 7 January 1907, F8/111:2.

[113] Langley minute, Clarke memorandum, 18 October 1906, FO 403/388:82.

Armstrong in Leopoldville and George Babington Michell in Stanleyville, with instructions to visit surrounding regions and report on conditions.[114] Grey extended their reach, budget, and authority. Within a day of issuing his first diplomatic salvo to Cuvelier, he telegraphed Consul Arthur Nightingale to authorize the Vice-Consuls to embark on tours to gather current information.[115]

In April 1907, Grey replaced Nightingale with Captain Charles Francis Cromie, and added a third Vice-Consul, George Bailey Beak, in Katanga. Both had extensive experience; Cromie had been Consul-General for French West Africa and Beak was a former colonial official and published author. Beak, like other vice-consuls, arrived thinking that Morel and the missionaries exaggerated, but found their stories true "in all particulars."[116]

Cromie reported that the 1906 reform decrees had been largely ineffective, as predicted. After he died in October 1907, his successor, Sir Wilfred G. Thesiger, became Grey's star Congo consul. Using the Thesiger family's private papers and Foreign Office documents, Osborne has established Thesiger's importance to the reform effort.[117] The Foreign Office chose Thesiger because of his success handling difficult assignments in Belgrade and St Petersburg. During 18 months in the Congo and subsequent time in Britain, he was a key player in Grey's reforming efforts. He undertook his own journeys—far longer than Casement's—as well as coordinating the journeys and reports of his Vice-Consuls, whose number rose to four on his recommendation. He developed his own opinion of the ineptitude and weakness of the Congo Free State, its officials baffled by the contradictory decrees of the King-Sovereign and, with only 3,913 Europeans resident in January 1908, far too understaffed to administer such a vast country. His reports acknowledged instances of competent administration but confirmed the general misrule.

Grey routinely sent Thesiger's memos to Hardinge and Hardinge's to Thesiger for comment as he forged his tactics. The caliber of the men involved led to a productive interchange as they analyzed each other's ideas in the context of Grey's overall strategy.

Thesiger was unusual in his distance from the CRA, refusing to correspond with Morel because he considered it inappropriate for an official to deal directly with a lobbyist.[118] (Nightingale, Casement, and some Vice-Consuls corresponded with Morel; Armstrong and Beak donated to the CRA.) Thesiger did, however, analyze several of Morel's papers for Grey.[119]

---

[114] Villiers to Michell and Armstrong, 18 May and 24 July 1905, FO 403/364.
[115] Grey to Nightingale, 28 March 1906, FO 403/372:97.
[116] Beak memorandum, FO/881/9123.
[117] Osborne, "Thesiger," 69–78.
[118] Thesiger to Morel, 1 May 1909, F8/115:133.
[119] Thesiger memorandum, 10 September 1908, FO 881/9476:89–92.

During Thesiger's tenure, Belgium annexed the Congo without announcing any reforms; indeed, Belgian Colonial Minister Jules Renkin claimed nothing was wrong with Leopold's system. The British government refused to recognize the annexation, a policy that Hardinge had first floated in May 1907.[120] Thesiger concluded that Belgium would need British pressure to move forward because the powerful forces of throne, church, and capital wanted to keep things as they were.

The Cabinet

When he worried about international complications, Grey consulted with the Cabinet. In preparation for a February 1908 Commons debate, he told the Cabinet that British and American consuls reported that Congo conditions had worsened while annexation was under discussion. He would soon announce that Britain would find Belgian annexation satisfactory only if the government and legislature had power and responsibility.[121] The Cabinet concurred and the House of Commons passed a resolution supporting the government's Congo policy without a division.[122]

On 28 May 1908, Grey informed the Cabinet that Belgium had responded to his diplomatic initiative with a commitment to reform. He also brought a 31-page memo based primarily on Thesiger's work on taxation and currency, the first major memorandum that did not rely on CRA information. Grey was reducing his dependence on reform advocates in favor of growing Foreign Office expertise. He recommended, and the Cabinet adopted, the policy of "reserving our definite recognition of the annexation until it is seen how it is proposed by the Belgian Government to put their reassurances into practice."[123] The Cabinet reaffirmed its position when it approved Grey's firm communication with the Belgian government that October.[124]

When annexation occurred without a reform program, Grey called publicly on Belgium to thoroughly reform Leopold's system and announced that Britain and the US had jointly refused to recognize the annexation. On 25 February 1909, Grey told the House of Commons that Britain would recognize the annexation only when Parliament had the chance to discuss a Belgian reform plan, publicly stating what he had privately committed to White and Morel the

---

[120] Osborne, "Grey," 156–7; Hardinge to Grey, 10 May 1907, FO 403/387, no. 59; Hardinge to Grey, 20 December 1907, FO 881/9155:181–5; Grey minute, ibid., 186–7.
[121] CAB 41/31/45, 24 February 1908.
[122] 184 Parl. Deb. (4th ser.) (1908) 1833.
[123] 28 May 1908, CAB 41/31/58.
[124] 28 October 1908, CAB 41/31/69.

preceding year.[125] For the next four years, Grey applied judicious pressure while waiting to bring the issue before the Commons until he was sure of support. Some reformers believed Grey would recognize the annexation when it suited him without telling anyone beforehand. But Grey kept his word. It may have been the only major foreign policy question he voluntarily brought before the House of Commons for approval, partly because the undivided Commons had set government policy in 1903 and endorsed it in 1908, and partly because he recognized the breadth and depth of public feeling on the issue.[126]

On 14 March 1909, he informed the Cabinet that the system of administration and forced labor remained, but "the systematic cruelty and wholesale atrocities, that created such indignation in the time of King Leopold, have come to an end."[127] It seemed that the long-awaited reform plan was imminent. However, the next day's Belgian reply repeated the same vague assurances to adhere to the Berlin and Brussels treaties.[128] To make matters worse, the United States, which had been an effective partner for Grey for two years, became increasingly distant after President Taft's inauguration.[129]

Grey's optimism turned to frustration. He decided to pursue arbitration of commercial questions, where the US still had an interest. In May he told the Cabinet that the CRA believed that Belgium acted in bad faith, suggesting he had some sympathy with this idea.[130] He feared that progress would be slower than anyone would find satisfactory, perhaps requiring strong measures to speed things up. After Morel's input, Grey notified the Cabinet on 9 June that he had decided against arbitration. He told the Belgian Foreign Minister on 11 June, the same day a CRA-sponsored religious delegation led by the Archbishop of Canterbury came to argue against arbitration.[131] For Morel, "Grey with another of his volte faces has, as a result of pressure (mark that!) thrown arbitration over board," showing "the indefiniteness and looseness which characterises our diplomacy in the matter."[132] This was unfair; Morel's 21 May arguments had led Grey to drop arbitration, not the religious deputation. Confronted

---

[125] 1 Parl. Deb., H.C. (5th ser.) (1909) 960–61; White–Grey interview, 30 June 1908, F8/145:31.

[126] 184 Parl. Deb. (4th ser.) (1908) 1871.

[127] 14 March 1909, CAB 37/115/18.

[128] Lalaing to Grey, 15 March 1909, *Accounts and Papers*, 1909, Cd. 4396, ix, 565, cited in Cookey, *Britain*, 240.

[129] Cookey, *Britain*, 241–2.

[130] 19 May 1909, CAB 37/100/89; Cabinet meeting notes, 19 May 1909, CAB 41/32/17.

[131] Cookey, *Britain*, 244; Cabinet papers, 9 June 1909, CAB 41/32/20; Morel to Davidson, 30 June 1909, F8/14 44.

[132] Morel to Lidgett, June 1909, F8/101:8; Morel to Davidson, 30 June 1909, F8/14:44.

with Belgian intransigence, Grey kept the pressure on and contemplated more forceful measures.

The religious leaders had considered telling Grey they would back a war for reform, but calmer heads prevailed.[133] Advocacy of war was not new. Guinness had suggested seizing Boma in 1906.[134] In 1907, Holt wrote, "If we had the spirit of our ancestors we should long ago have finished this iniquity by the mouth of the Cannon and the rifle."[135] Even Brooks, a Quaker, endorsed using gunboats to stop rubber shipments, consoling his pacifist conscience by believing this would not lead to war.[136]

The Break with the Foreign Office

The loose alliance between the Foreign Office and the CRA ended in mid-1909. Morel's impatience with Grey had grown. In private correspondence, Grey assured Morel that he had always "put the moral and human consideration in front" when dealing with the Congo question.[137] However, several CRA members openly deprecated Grey, particularly Monkswell, who wrote, "It must sooner or later come to a fight with the FO" as early as 1907.[138] He reminded the House of Lords that "Ministers are the servants and not the masters of the people. The people of England are day by day issuing their instructions to Sir Edward Grey with more emphasis."[139] Casement thought that Grey was insincere.[140] Holt let his righteous indignation direct itself at Grey: "Nightingale told you rubbish when he told you Grey wanted to act … What crass timidity or weakness stops him?"[141] The eminent lawyer and scholar Sir Francis Channing, MP, was "utterly disheartened and disgusted" by Grey's "coldness and slackness," and accused him of staining British honor by waiting for humanitarian issues to sort themselves out.[142] It is no wonder Morel wrote Grey: "Though it may appear strange to you, I am a moderating influence in the councils of the Congo Reform Association."[143] He told Channing that opposing Grey, and thus the government, would be "a fatal tactical mistake." Grey had "always displayed exceptional courtesy and

---

[133] Talbot to Morel, 12 June 1909, F8/131:39.
[134] Harris to Morel, 21 September 1906, F8/76:275.
[135] Holt to Morel, 25 October 1907, F8/86:517.
[136] Brooks to Morel, 3 February 1908, F9/2:202.
[137] Grey to Morel, 6 January 1907, F8/60:128.
[138] Monkswell to Morel, 9 January 1907, F8/111:3.
[139] *Organ*, July 1907, 18, and August 1907, 5.
[140] Casement to Morel, 13 December 1907, F8/22:389.
[141] Holt to Morel, 27 May 1907, F8/86:506.
[142] Channing to Morel, 12 September 1907, F8/28:3.
[143] Morel to Grey, 28 December 1906, F10/14 885ff.

kindness in my few dealings with him," and was "anxious to do the right thing, and a man of scrupulous honour."[144] As he summarized in October 1908, "If I had adopted the views of some of my friends two years ago, the influence which the Association enjoys with the Foreign Office would have disappeared, and we should have been driven into opposition to Sir Edward Grey—a course absolutely fatal to the ends we have in view."[145] Morel was only half right: attacking the Foreign Office would end the CRA's influence, but would not be fatal for the cause.

Grey had admirers, friends, and even confidants among the reformers. Cromer, Chirol, Chavasse, Gilmour, St Loe Strachey, and Harold Spender contested the criticism with generally accurate information about Grey's intentions and actions.[146] Dilke too believed that Grey had moved closer to the CRA's positions.[147] Harris maintained faith in Grey while Morel's hostility grew.[148] Parker and Mayo were bellwethers who supported Grey in 1908 but turned on him in 1909.

Morel's impatience was souring into mistrust; Grey was lukewarm, Morel believed, because Foreign Office officials opposed reform, including both Hardinges.[149] Langley tried to explain: "Sir E. Grey represents and alone represents H.M.G. [His Majesty's Government] and the Foreign Office and it does not matter an atom what other people say or think on the subject. This is not a constitutional fiction: it is a simple fact and I hope that you will dismiss from your mind any theories which do not square with it."[150] In late 1908, trying to stay positive, Morel orchestrated a "National Manifesto" supporting Grey's non-recognition policy, though he thought it weak.[151]

By April 1909, Morel was writing in increasingly furious tones about Grey's slothful Congo policy, which he linked to fear of Germany.[152] He repeated his vow not to attack Grey, but his resolve was ebbing. At the Foreign Office on 21 May, he condemned arbitration, proposed immediate consular jurisdiction, and advocated ending all trade in Congo goods. He said Belgium would quickly come

---

[144] Morel to Channing, 31 January 1907, F10/15:76.

[145] Morel to Brooks, 13 October 1908, Cadbury 180/324.

[146] Memo of Spender-Cromer interview, 18 January 1908, F8/35:1; Cromer to Morel, 6, 9, and 19 March 1908, F8/35:42, 43, 46; Cromer to Morel, 15 August 1908, F8/35:50; Chavasse to Morel, 28 January 1908, F8/102:15; Spender to Morel, 26 May 1909, F98/132:14.

[147] Dilke to Morel, 5 May 1908, F8/42:154.

[148] Buxton to T.F. Buxton, 11 September 1907, Brit. Emp. s.19 D1/3:638.

[149] Morel to Cromer, 14 February 1908, F8/35:32; Morel to Parker, 15 May 1908, F8/121:36.

[150] Langley to Morel, 15 July 1908, F8/ 61:185.

[151] *The Times*, 23 December 1908; *Organ*, 1909, 26–8.

[152] Morel to White, 14 April 1909, F8/145:49.

to terms because the appearance of British or American warships would set the whole Congo ablaze with a rebellion that would leave not a single Belgian official alive.[153] Morel also threatened to deal with government inaction by leading a storm of unprecedented protest. Charles Hardinge observed that Morel's ideas showed him an "honest fanatic" with a "swollen head," a reasonable conclusion from Morel's fantasies about the slaughter of Belgians and unprecedented protests. The Foreign Office took Morel's advice on arbitration and agreed with him on the potential next steps, just not the timing. As Gilmour reported, Grey was not ready to use force—yet.[154] When Grey noted that Morel "was prepared for universal war," he ordered, "This record of what he proposes must be kept."[155] Grey was also preparing for war, but at a further remove and as a last resort.

Morel convened the Executive Committee the same day he visited the Foreign Office. No minutes exist, but Harold Spender later apologized to Morel for being unpleasant over the risk of war with Germany, so Morel must have brought it up. It had galled Morel when Grey asked if the CRA was ready for war over the Congo a month before.[156] Then, on 27 May, in the House of Commons, Grey said, "If this question were rashly managed it might make a European question, compared with which those with which we had to deal in the last few months might be child's play," and pointed out the absurdity of advocating a "peaceful blockade" when a blockade was an act of war that could have far-reaching consequences, including raising "a European question ... of the gravest kind."[157]

Morel saw Grey's speech as the last straw and launched an opening salvo entitled "Is England Turning Craven?" in the *Morning Post* of 3 June. That Conservative-leaning daily must have gladly printed this attack on the Liberal government. Gilmour visited the Foreign Office on 6 June, where staff expressed concern about Morel's willingness to risk war, believing that "the public would shrink, as Morel did not, from the logical consequences" of a bellicose policy toward Belgium.[158]

Grey's 27 May remarks did not say that Britain would never use forceful measures, but, as he later explained, was meant to convey that the government would have to prepare any such measures carefully and use them only if necessary. But Morel reacted as if Grey had said that he would never consider stronger measures. In his fury, he ignored the possibility that a precipitate attack on the Congo would have been a declaration of war against Belgium, an officially neutral country that could call on its other guarantors, France and Germany, to

---

[153] G.R. Clerk, memorandum, 21 May 1909, FO 367/165.
[154] Gilmour to Morel, 5 June 1909, F8/69:7.
[155] Grey minute, quoted in Cookey, *Britain*, 245; Osborne, "Grey," 219–21.
[156] Hudson (for Dilke) to Morel, 19 April 1909, F8/43:230.
[157] 5 Parl. Deb., H.C. (5th ser.) (1909) 1395–6.
[158] Memorandum, 6 June 1909, F5/1.

come to its aid, just as it would call on Britain and France in 1914. Morel, the amateur diplomatist, could not imagine either country risking war with Britain over this issue. Most historians notice the June 1909 break with the Foreign Office, when they notice it at all, as Morel's first major attack on the foreign policy apparatus. It should also be considered a watershed for CRA-Foreign Office relations.

Before launching his attack, Morel sounded out his closest allies. Col. Stopford thought Grey had surrendered to German opinion and suggested sending him a white feather.[159] Parker called Grey "lamentably weak."[160] Holt agreed, though he did not yet understand how momentous this was for Morel.[161] Others advised restraint. Talbot urged Morel not to "make a definite break between Grey and yourself."[162] The Edinburgh Auxiliary expressed sympathy with Grey's speech and Bournemouth trusted that Grey knew his business.[163] Spender reported that Grey's position had not changed since the CRA Executive Committee voted him its support in November.[164] Harris, temporizing between Morel and Grey, offered to see the Foreign Secretary to "reinforce our position."[165]

Morel, as usual, favored the responses that backed his anger and ignored the others. Before convening the Executive Committee meeting to endorse his stand, he "cross[ed] the Rubicon" with a diatribe in the *Review of Reviews* condemning Grey, the Foreign Office, British fear of Germany, and the Anglo-French entente, followed by a similar article in the *Organ*, where he claimed that Grey's speech gave "a moral shock to the whole country," confusing himself with the reading public of Britain.[166] These interlocking concerns outlived the Congo question to form the basis of Morel's wartime agitation.

Alfred and Gertie Emmott were aghast: "Why have you made a general attack on Foreign policy with which our Association has nothing whatever to do?"[167] Lord Cromer stepped back from the movement to dissociate himself from this new "fire-eating" policy.[168] The attack on Grey had made the German Colonial

---

[159] Stopford to Morel, 8 June 1909, F8/134:14.
[160] 1 June 1909, Parker correspondence, F8/121:43.
[161] Holt to Morel, 1 June 1909, F8/87:591.
[162] Talbot to Morel, 26 May 1909, F8/131:35.
[163] John Baird to Morel, 6 June 1909, F9/2:1; J.A.V. Smythe to Morel, 4 June 1909, F9/16:156.
[164] Spender to Morel, 9 June 1909, F8/132:22.
[165] Harris to Morel, 9 June 1909, F8/132:19.
[166] Cline, *Morel*, 72; *Organ*, June 1909, 193–6.
[167] Gertie Emmott to Morel, 23 June 1909, F8/55:250.
[168] Cromer to Talbot, 9 June 1909, FO 633/18, cited in Louis, "Morel and the Congo Reform Association," 204.

Minister "a little shy of us."[169] Gilmour deplored this "grievous business."[170] Talbot argued that such a broad attack was unwise.[171] Paget, the Bishop of Oxford and President of that auxiliary, fretted, but, like others, reaffirmed his support for the Congo cause.[172] St Loe Strachey, editor of the *Spectator*, who supported the use of force, found the article "unfair and wrong-headed," and its arguments "childish," "hopelessly amateurish and unwise." Strachey worried "that it will do terrible mischief to the cause which you have at heart." As for his attack on Grey, "I can only say that Grey's opinion must be held to be worth a hundred times more than yours." He wondered if he could remain a CRA member "when ideas so wild are propagated in its name" and asked if Morel had the authorization of the Executive Committee (of which he was a member).[173] Morel wrote an equally lengthy rebuttal, complaining, "No man could have done more to back Sir Edward Grey than I have," and accusing Grey of betraying the CRA.[174] He also claimed that "no article I have ever written was written with more deliberation, and with less impulsiveness," true in the sense that this had been brewing for a long time, but false in that it was a hasty overreaction to Grey's comments, which most reformers, such as Holt, and most historians have not seen in the same apocalyptic light.[175]

Though thinking Morel had not "done the Congo cause any favors by ... censuring their general control of foreign affairs," Casement nonetheless wrote, "I don't like being that abject thing to say 'I told you so!' but I have never trusted Grey" and "I feel sure Grey has been a traitor all along. He gulled [the] CRA."[176] Green joined in, finding Grey to be the "priest of humbug or we may say of hypocrisy" after years of saying he was trustworthy; she, Morel, and Casement had come together on this point as on others.[177] Their reassurances gave Morel strength to carry on his campaign against the Foreign Office.

There is no documentation of the "best-attended" Executive Committee meeting on 7 July 1909. Morel likely received its backing, though it passed no public resolutions, perhaps because Morel's attack made that temporarily unwise. Morel continued his offensive, publishing *Great Britain and the Congo Question* in September. Here he called the Foreign Office's Congo policy

---

[169] Talbot to Morel, 9 and 15 June 1909, F8/131:38, 40.
[170] Gilmour to Morel, 21 June 1909 on reading the advance proofs, F8/69:2.
[171] Talbot to Motel, 1 July 1909, F8/131:41.
[172] Bishop of Oxford to Morel, 23 June 1909, F8/120:6.
[173] Strachey to Morel, 1 June 1909 and 22 June 1909, F8/135:19, 21; Morel, "Humanitarianism and Sea Power," *Spectator*, 5 June 1909, 890.
[174] Morel to Strachey, 23 June 1909, F8/135:1.
[175] Holt to Morel, 28 June 1909, F8/87:592.
[176] Casement to Morel, 23 June, 29 June, and 12 July 1909, F8/23:415, 424, 426.
[177] Green to Morel, 20 June 1909, F8/72:218.

"inconsistent and feeble."[178] He published letters between himself and Lord Lonsdale, friend of King Edward and Kaiser Wilhelm, to show that Germany would not back Belgium against British pressure.[179] He continued attacking Grey, though Gilmour scolded him for "bad practice," writing "Do you think, even holding the views you do, that it is really good tactics to hold up the F.O. to public obloquy and scorn as incompetent or ill-informed on the international situation?" [180] Morel thundered that Grey had forced him into this position, but Gilmour considered Morel the instigator. Morel was fighting a one-sided battle by this time, because Grey had qualified his May statements in a 22 July Commons debate, making them a minor point, not a statement of policy.[181] The damage was done. Many press outlets treated Morel's letters and articles more cautiously, and he had affected some of his relationships. The Emmotts do not appear to have corresponded with him for the next two years, but Strachey did stay on the CRA Executive Committee. More seriously, Morel had jeopardized the CRA's ability to affect events and gained nothing for the Congo in return.

The break led to a fateful incident. On 9 June, Harris had proposed that he meet with Grey to bridge the gap. He later informed Morel that he and Spender were to see Grey on 20 July. Morel "forbore" to cancel the meeting though he thought its timing poor. Harris's failure to brief him for three days after the meeting (at Spender's misguided suggestion) led Morel to once again spectacularly lose his temper, calling Harris insubordinate and disloyal.[182] At Holt's urging, Morel superficially reconciled with Harris and Spender the next week, but the affair convinced the Harrises that they had to leave the CRA. It also transferred the Foreign Office link that had once been Morel's to Harris, which he carried to the Anti-Slavery Society in April 1910.[183]

Grey did not immediately treat the break as permanent, instructing Langley to continue sharing information verbally with Morel.[184] Morel sent letters to Grey with missionary evidence, recommendations, and resolutions. However, the Foreign Office no longer needed Morel because it could rely on its consuls and its in-house expertise. The CRA's name largely disappeared from the Foreign Office's Congo reports. Its remaining use to the Foreign Office was to communicate the mood of the country and to convince Belgium that

---

[178] Morel, *Great Britain*, 117ff.

[179] Morel to Lonsdale, 27 and 28 September, F9/11; Lonsdale to Morel, 4 October 1909, F9/11.

[180] *The Times*, 5 October 1909; Gilmour to Morel, 5 October 1909, F1/1/10.

[181] 8 Parl. Deb., H.C. (5th ser.) (1909) 652.

[182] Morel to Harris, 23 July 1909, F4/10:49.

[183] Harris to Hodgkin, 25 July and 22 September 1910, Brit. Emp. s.19 D3/1:881 and 2:459.

[184] Grey to Langley, 12 July 1909 F8/62:260.

cooperation with the diplomatically worded demands of the Foreign Office was better than the rough justice the CRA espoused.

Unbeknownst to the CRA, Grey's patience was ending. When Thesiger returned home in mid-1909, Grey had him outline Britain's options if Belgium did not cooperate. Thesiger advocated that Britain propose a six-part reform scheme: rights of private traders, freedom to establish factories on the upper Congo, native rights to sell forest products, abolition of taxes in produce and labor, a general and moderate currency tax, abolition of the rubber and ivory monopolies, and equal treatment for Catholic and Protestant missions.[185] He recommended coercive steps if Belgium did not respond: consular jurisdiction, occupying Boma and Matadi, and seizing customs. Thesiger's report quickly became the basis for official British policy.[186]

Thanks to Grey, and not the CRA, Britain came to the brink of an international crisis over the Congo in October/November 1909. Despite Hardinge's assurance on 5 October that a comprehensive reform announcement was likely, Grey prepared for the worst.[187] Cookey says that the CRA's renewed campaign changed Grey's policy, but the Cabinet and Foreign Office records show consistency of tone and purpose, while CRA activity was diminishing.[188]

On October 19, Grey informed the Cabinet, "We are approaching the time when the Cabinet must take a serious decision on the question of the Congo. For the last year this question has been in an irregular and anomalous state, which cannot be prolonged indefinitely, and which circumstances might at any moment make impossible." Grey presented Thesiger's memorandum and proposed a year-end deadline, after which he would invoke consular jurisdiction and end even unofficial recognition. If Belgium still refused to cooperate or to call a conference, Britain should prepare to resort to force, because "We cannot sit still and go on watching a system which we have denounced, not only as contrary to humanity, but also as being contrary to our treaty rights. Much less could we countersign the continuance of this system by recognising the annexation."[189]

The Cabinet discussed the question on 27 October, just after Grey's speech in Sheffield, his only public Congo speech.[190] The Cabinet adopted his recommendation in full.[191] Ironically, the next day, Renkin announced Belgium's

---

[185] Thesiger memorandum, 22 August 1909, FO 881/9691, 104–8.
[186] CAB 37/100/118, 19 October 1909; Osborne, "Thesiger," 75–8.
[187] Hardinge to Grey, 5 October 1909, FO 881/9691:156.
[188] Cookey, *Britain*, 251.
[189] Grey memo to Cabinet, 19 October 1909, CAB 37/101/142.
[190] *Organ*, October 1909, 353–4.
[191] Cabinet minutes, 21 & 27 October 1909, CAB 41/32/38:39.

comprehensive Congo reforms. Britain's firm stand was obsolete. Morel never knew how close Britain had come to going to war over the Congo.[192]

Coming less than two weeks after the Cabinet meeting and Renkin's announcement, Asquith's Guildhall speech of 9 November 1909 reflected the new reality. Asquith had hitherto shown no interest in the Congo, as shown by his correspondence with Grey and his remarks in Parliament.[193] However, his five-minute Congo speech at the Guildhall Banquet of 9 November 1909 was the most extensive made by any Prime Minister. After describing ongoing Congo misgovernment, Asquith abruptly changed tone to welcome Belgium's reform program.[194] He likely prepared a warlike speech to rally the public behind a tougher approach to Belgium, should one be necessary, then altered it after Renkin's reform announcement. His welcome was conditional; Britain would need to see reforms in action.

The CRA found the Belgian reforms inadequate in content, because they did not address the concession companies and did not return most of the land to local ownership, and in timing, because reforms phased in geographically through 1912. They guessed, as did the consuls, that Renkin intended to maximize revenue before ending the rubber tax. They also found Renkin's continued defense of Leopold's system even while ending it infuriating and a possible mark of insincerity. Because Morel did not trust Grey to address these points, the CRA embarked on a new phase of the campaign, beginning with a resolution from the Executive Committee on 10 November demanding that Belgium enact the whole reform program at once.[195] Large meetings in nine cities climaxed in the Royal Albert Hall "Protest of Christian England" (really Protestant England) on 19 November, the Archbishop of Canterbury presiding. It was not officially a Congo Reform Association meeting, though CRA mainstays Harris and Talbot had arranged it. The speakers called on the British government to demand improvements to the reform program.

Morel continued to complain about Grey's "lamentably bad" performance, telling his correspondents, "He has only done something when kicked."[196] Yet we have seen that Grey no longer allowed the CRA to affect his path. Morel misinterpreted the relationship between CRA activity and Grey's actions, mistaking coincidence for causality. The Foreign Office papers show that Grey's course through 1909 was largely unaffected by Morel.

---

[192] Cabinet minutes, 3 November 1909, CAB 41/32/40.
[193] Asquith Papers.
[194] Guildhall speech, *The Times*, 10 November 1909.
[195] *Organ*, 1910, 450.
[196] Morel to Guthrie, 23 February 1910, F9/7:111.

In April 1910, Morel authored a Parliamentary Memorial signed by 162 MPs asking Asquith for consular jurisdiction by August 1911 if Belgium did not accelerate and improve its program. Asquith demurred, referring them to Grey's speeches.[197] To Morel's chagrin, the Parliamentary Committee accepted the government's strategy of monitoring the pace and effectiveness of reforms. Before the 14 July 1910 Executive Committee meeting, he told Holt, "All I can tell my Committee is that we must hang on, watching events, taking every opportunity we have of pushing forward a pawn on the chess-board."[198]

He did not know that Hardinge had condemned the use of threats at this juncture as counterproductive and instead recommended "sustained and steady diplomatic pressure. I do not hold with Mr Morel that our refusal to recognise annexation is a *brutum fulmen* [an inert thunder] at which Belgium scoffs. It is, on the contrary, a real grievance."[199] Grey concurred and adopted a policy of "benevolent expectancy," a phrase Morel misinterpreted, announcing that the CRA was "resisting the undisguised attempt of the Foreign Office and those whom it inspires to drop the whole question ... Victory would have been complete but for the sorry performances of the Foreign Office."[200]

Grey kept his promise to bring papers to Parliament, primarily consular reports. The long-serving Armstrong, Acting Consul in February 1910, had doubted that the imminent reforms would mean much.[201] Grey declined to appoint him Consul and told the Cabinet in March 1910 that the situation was still uncertain.[202] Consul Mackie and his Vice-Consuls reported in 1910–11 how the Belgian reform plan unfolded. Having served as Acting Consul in 1905, Mackie could contrast the new regime with the old. The next Consul, W.J. Lamont, continued to report progress. By early 1913, the consuls deemed the reforms to be largely effective (see Chapter 9). The Cabinet concurred with Grey's recommendation to recognize the annexation.[203] He brought the question before the House of Commons on 29 May 1913 and notified the Belgian ambassador on 27 June that Britain had recognized the transfer of the Congo to Belgium.[204]

---

[197] Asquith to White, 12 July 1910, F4/10:121.
[198] Morel to Holt, 1 July 1910, F8/88:688.
[199] Hardinge to Grey, 10 June 1910, FO 881/9730:153.
[200] Grey in Commons, *Organ*, 1910, 552–60; "The Outlook," 28 May 1910, *Organ*, 1910, 489–91.
[201] Armstrong, Memorandum, 1 February 1910, FO 881/9730:14–16.
[202] Cabinet minutes, 9 March 1910, CAB 41/32/53.
[203] Grey's memo to Cabinet, 14 March 1913, CAB 37/115/18; Cabinet minutes, 20 March 1913, CAB 41/34/10.
[204] 53 Parl. Deb., H.C. (5th ser.) (1913) 345–459.

Grey the Reformer

To succeed, the reformers required the commitment of the Foreign Secretary, representing the British government, to pressure the Congo Free State and Belgian governments. Lansdowne's Foreign Office made progress by commissioning the Casement report and prodding Leopold on the Commission of Inquiry's powers. Grey came into office committed to ending Congo misrule, and with little involvement by Prime Ministers, Britain's Congo policy lay in his hands. He believed that Belgian annexation was the best antidote; therefore pressure must be judicious so as not to jeopardize this alternative, giving the Belgian legislature, government, and public time to take each step. Grey preferred moral persuasion and diplomatic pressure, but his patience had limits. In the October 1909 crisis, he was preparing for consular jurisdiction, closing the Nile, or military force if other tactics failed. Renkin's reform announcement rendered this plan unnecessary, and Grey returned to diplomatic pressure. Grey's patience and behind-the-scenes methods led Morel and others to feel betrayed. Unable or unwilling to understand, they sought other explanations in his character, the permanent staff's hostility, and, for Morel, the structure of British foreign policy. When Morel reoriented the CRA's stance to treat Grey as an enemy instead of a slow-moving ally, he sharply reduced its influence. Whereas the CRA in 1906–08 had collaborated with the Foreign Office, after the 1909 crisis, its chief role was to give Grey the excuse of public opinion for continuing pressure along the lines he had already set. The initiative had passed fully to the Foreign Office. Sir Edward Grey delivered the triumph of the Congo reform movement.

Chapter 9

Effectiveness

That this Association, founded in March 1904 with the object of restoring to the natives of the Congo the rights guaranteed them under the Berlin and Brussels Acts, of which they had been deprived by their European rulers, and of putting an end to the barbarities inflicted upon them ... records the belief that its main purposes have now been secured and that its labours may be honourably brought to a conclusion.[1]—resolution passed unanimously at the Congo Reform Association's final meeting, 16 June 1913

The chief gauge of the movement's effectiveness should be on its own terms: the degree to which it achieved its goals in improving the lives of millions of Congolese people. However, the understanding of effectiveness has become confused. Questions that appeared settled in 1913 are now open, in many cases not as new areas of inquiry, but instead as assertions about the movement's success or failure.

Wuliger observes that the world was "more intent upon the appearance of poetic justice" than in real reform and argues that CRA's goals were as unmet in 1953 as they were in 1911.[2] Citing "reports of misgovernment," Grant describes a movement that dissolved before its work was done because public interest had dissipated and the Foreign Office was about to recognize the annexation for unspecified reasons.[3] These interpretations imply that the reformers' resolutions, speeches, letters, and telegrams at the June 1913 meeting were uniformly products of hypocrisy, unleavened by honest acknowledgement of unfinished work.[4] For Hochschild, the CRA failed "to save millions of lives," possibly because it took years to accomplish its work or possibly because the reforms were incomplete; there is no explanation for this estimate. After assessing the post-reform years, Hochschild concludes that the reform effort missed its mark because forced labor never disappeared and subsequently expanded.[5] Sliwinski, drawing on Grant and Hochschild, says that the movement ended, "not with a bang, but with a whimper."[6] Ewans paints a more nuanced picture of the post-reform years

---
[1] *Organ*, July 1913, 1008.
[2] Wuliger, "Economic imperialism," 287, 319.
[3] Grant, *Civilised Savagery*, 77.
[4] *Organ*, July 1913, 1008–20.
[5] Hochschild, *King Leopold's Ghost*, 277–9.
[6] Sliwinski, "Childhood," 353.

and eschews judgments on effectiveness.[7] Didier Gondola's survey of Congolese history stresses the continuity of the Congo Free State and the Belgian Congo, without acknowledging that any reforms occurred at all from 1909–12.[8] In his view, reformers succeeded only in accelerating the takeover of the Congo by a rapacious Belgium he characterizes inexplicably as "poor." (Belgium, routinely described as rich by Belgians and foreigners alike, had Europe's 3rd highest per capita GDP in 1913, after the UK and Switzerland, and ahead of France, Italy, and the Netherlands.[9]) Of course, even a prosperous Belgium could find the riches of the Congo intriguing; this was not the least of King Leopold's legacies.

In sharp contrast to these assessments, Louis, Osborne, Cookey, and Echenberg consider the movement a success, without making much of a study of the post-reform Congo.[10] Stengers, a specialist in the Belgian Congo, writes that the reforms of the first years of Belgian rule genuinely improved the conditions of life.[11] Renton, Seddon, and Zelig grant that after 1913 things changed significantly even if the change was not completely liberating.[12] Using the observations of contemporaries and scholars of Congo history, this chapter will evaluate the movement's impact by comparing its goals to the post-reform situation and identifying what actions and methods led to this outcome.

The Impact of Reforms

In 1912, Morel wrote to René Claparède, "There is no doubt that the condition of affairs in the Congo is infinitely better; and we ought to rejoice that it is so."[13] The CRA's leadership believed the movement had succeeded, with three major caveats. First, the Belgian government had not granted Africans land rights according to customary collective ownership. Although Parker felt this goal was not only unimportant but misguided, others saw land rights as the reformed Congo's chief flaw.[14] Second, the Colonial Minister could revoke

---

[7] Ewans, *European Atrocity*, 236.

[8] Ch. Didier Gondola, *History of Congo* (Westport, CT: Greenwood Press, 2002), 78.

[9] Angus Maddison, *HS-8: The World Economy, 1–2001 AD* (Paris: OECD Publishing, 2003), 262, Table 8c.

[10] Louis, "Triumph," 302–3; Osborne, "Thesiger," 59; Cookey, *Britain*, 313; Echenberg, *Morel*, 205.

[11] Jean Stengers, "The Congo Free State and the Belgian Congo," in *Colonialism in Africa*, eds Lewis H. Gann and Peter Duignan (Cambridge: Cambridge University Press, 1969), 270–71.

[12] David Renton, David Seddon, and Leo Zelig, *The Congo: Plunder and Resistance* (New York: Zed Books, 2007), 50.

[13] Morel to Claparède, 14 October 1912, F4/14.

[14] Parker to Morel, 1 June 1912, F8/121:126.

the reforms as easily as he had promulgated them; the reformers would have preferred parliamentary action to make the changes more permanent. Finally, Belgian intentions to encourage plantations, if implemented, would require large numbers of wage laborers who could be obtained only by compulsion.[15] Subsequent events validated these concerns.

Apart from these issues, Morel and the other reformers repeatedly said they had largely achieved what they set out to do, and the Foreign Office agreed. The reports from the Congo tracked overall improvement. Within a year of annexation, atrocities diminished, suggesting improved accountability and control under Belgian rule. The reform program announced in late 1909 began to go into effect in July 1910. Just a few months later, Acting Consul Gerald Campbell, hitherto a severe critic of Belgian rule, reported a rapid improvement in conditions:

> With a few exceptions missionaries and traders alike report that the treatment which the natives in the interior are receiving at the hands of the State officials has perceptibly improved. These reports have been received since the reform decrees came into force on the 1st July last ... enquiries are, moreover, being held into such occurrences as have come to the knowledge of the Government. There are signs that the former régime ... is undergoing a radical change, and that it is the wish of the Government that the new decrees which aim at the betterment of the condition of the natives shall be sincerely interpreted.[16]

By May 1911, Consul Mackie observed that the reforms had gone better than the consuls expected, noting, "there is substantial ground for the belief that crime and oppression are now the exception and not the rule" and the government showed determination in investigating and punishing those responsible for the now unusual cases of oppression.[17] The following month, he said local officials had become much more hesitant to use lethal force because of the administration's constant admonitions and King Albert's well-known interest in the welfare of the Congolese people.[18] A year after the Kasai Company lost its monopoly, Morrison penned his most positive assessment to date: "I believe the new Government is making an honest effort to improve conditions. Things are far from what they ought to be, but we hope that more time will see further

---

[15] John Harris, "Section II," *Present Conditions on the Congo* (London: Denison House, 1911), 1–10.
[16] Memorandum, Campbell to Grey, 25 October 1910, FO 881/9854:93.
[17] Mackie to Grey, 30 May 1911, FO 881/9889:119–57.
[18] Mackie to Grey, 2 June 1911, FO 881/10047:1.

improvement."[19] The new *Commission pour la Protection des Indigènes* reported in 1911 that the reforms had made an enormous difference.[20]

In 1912, after visiting the Congo, John Harris told the CRA Executive Committee, "To be able to say to-day that that we could find nowhere in the Congo any atrocities committed upon the natives with the toleration of the Government, is, I think, an extremely satisfactory situation." He also gave voice to the caveats noted above and observed that the people of the Congo were still the most impoverished and oppressed in Africa.[21] Later that year, Morel expressed the same general sentiments to Vandervelde.[22] Vandervelde was of like mind, writing that the Belgian reformers' chief task now was to ensure that the reforms became permanent.[23]

Six months after the last wave of reforms, the Foreign Office observed "immense improvement in the condition of the country, which has resulted from the application of the reform decrees. Complaints were seldom heard, and those responsible for isolated cases of ill-treatment of the natives received proper punishment."[24] Morel's final letter to the Foreign Office listed the three caveats but concluded, "The Association fully and gladly recognises that the contents of [the last two white books] show the state of affairs in the Congo has undergone an immense change for the better." Though noting "much that is regrettable," the CRA concluded that the post-reform Congo was nothing like Leopold's Congo Free State.[25]

To understand this change in affairs and measure the CRA's effectiveness, specific reforms matter—not only their content but also how well they curtailed practices that the reformers saw as crimes against humanity. Grey, like the CRA, understood that misrule was inherent in the system. His first dispatches as Foreign Secretary called for the Congo Free State to end the abuses that "are constantly being brought to my attention," and condemned the combining of administrative and commercial functions, whereby the state acted like a private company and concession companies had state powers.[26] His goals in 1906 fell under the general rubric of achieving the Berlin Act's provisions for free trade and amelioration of the moral and material conditions of the indigenous population. The means was to be Belgian annexation, which had been mooted by Morel in 1900, alluded to by Grey in 1904, recommended by Johnston in

---

[19] Morrison to US Consul-General at Boma, 29 June 1911, FO 881/10047:20.
[20] Anstey, *King Leopold's Legacy*, 48.
[21] *Organ*, August 1912, 788, 803–6.
[22] Morel to Vandervelde, 30 September 1912, F8/139:105.
[23] Vandervelde to Morel, 28 April 1913, F8/139:106.
[24] H.S. Seymour, Memorandum, FO 881/10211:1.
[25] Morel to Foreign Office, 16 April 1913, FO 881/10316:105–20.
[26] Grey to Phipps, 9 January 1906, Africa No. 1 (1906) Cd. 3002; Grey to Hardinge, 16 April 1906, FO 403/373:19.

the same year, and advocated by the CRA's Holborn Town Hall meeting in June 1905. It became the official Foreign Office objective when Grey came into office in December 1905. Morel and others were skeptical of Belgium's willingness and ability to put things right, but Grey's vision trumped all others, and the CRA accommodated itself to Belgian annexation.

For over a year after Belgium announced the impending annexation in late 1906, Grey refrained from specifying reforms in the belief that the Belgian Parliament would accompany annexation with acceptable reforms. However, when it became clear in March 1908 that Belgium had no reform plan, Grey laid out requirements for a "radical alteration of the existing system," based on his 1906 ideas, with additions suggested by Morel and the consuls. As approved by the Cabinet in April 1908, enunciated in Parliament on 27 July, and echoed by the US, Grey put forward six objectives, which remained constant thereafter:[27]

1. Relief from excessive taxation
2. Introduction of currency
3. Ending forced labor for commercial purposes
4. Granting the Congolese sufficient land to let them freely trade the products of the soil
5. Free trade for Europeans
6. Ending the monopoly concessions and disentangling commerce and administration.

Grey's 1908 objectives were identical to the 1904 Programme of the Congo Reform Association, plus the demand, also added by the CRA, for the introduction of currency. Both the Foreign Office and the CRA supplemented these core conditions with ancillary changes, such as judicial independence and putting Protestant and Catholic missions on equal footing. The CRA and Foreign Office never adopted the broader hopes of some reformers for a new standard for African rule. The CRA and the government worked to ensure that the Congo became more like other colonies, not superior to them.

In gauging the movement's success by reviewing each requirement, there are two considerations to keep in mind. First, the Congo's size was a barrier to uniform results; a reform effective in some districts might be ineffective in others, interpreted as a success or a failure according to one's perspective. Second, the resurgence of some practices complicated the story in subsequent years.

Relief from excessive taxation came as the reforms reached each region. The new rules replaced all labor and in-kind taxes (including rubber, wood, and food)

---

[27] Grey to Hardinge, 27 March 1908, circulated 7 April 1908, CAB 37/92/44; Wilson to Van der Elst, 7 April 1908, FO 403/399; Memorandum to Cabinet, 23 June 1908, CAB 37/94/88; 193 Parl. Deb. (4th ser.) (1908) 974–5; Grey to Lalaing, CAB 37/95/124.

with a head tax that the administration intended to increase as currency became more common.[28] In the Lower Congo and Stanley Pool areas, where annual head taxes already existed at the level of 12 francs and 9 francs, respectively, the government reduced the taxes. Taxes in newly reformed areas began at 5 or 6 francs per adult male, plus 1–2 francs for every wife beyond the first, with the intent to increase these to 12 francs.[29] Mackie observed that the new tax policy quickly had beneficial effects:

> The dispirited people, released from the burden of excessive taxation in kind, are growing more reassured and contented, many natives who migrated to French territory are returning to their former homes, the birthrate is already on the increase, sleeping sickness shows signs of abatement, and the tax in currency in many of the wealthier districts cheerfully and willingly paid.[30]

Vice-Consul Campbell reported similar benefits. Before the reforms, when Campbell went into a village, nearly all the men would come forward to complain about the injustice of the taxes. On his 1911 tour of the lands reformed in 1910, this did not happen at all:

> Natives who, little more than a year ago, were spending from ten to twenty days monthly in an exhausted forest searching for rubber, and inhabitants of riverine towns, compelled to labour five and six days weekly in supplying State posts with fish, are now left in peace to gain in their own way the money for the payment of the tax which is levied by the government.[31]

The initial post-reform taxation levels had uneven impacts. In some copal-producing areas, a person could earn his year's taxes with a single day's work.[32] At the other extreme, it was almost impossible for local people to earn enough to pay taxes in the newly opened Kivu region, which was not yet a part of the colonial economy.[33] According to Acting US Consul-General John W. Dye, a tax payment of 12 francs in poorer districts would require about three to five days each month. While this compared favorably to the pre-reform taxation levels that forced people to work 10–22 days per month, this exceeded what was reasonable and customary elsewhere, and little of what was collected paid for activities that directly benefited the inhabitants. He also heard reports in

---

[28] Granville to Grey, 29 October 1909, FO 403/410:169.
[29] Hardinge to Grey, 8 December 1909, FO 403/410:269–70.
[30] Mackie to Grey, 30 May 1911, FO 403/405:119.
[31] Campbell to Mackie: 27 May 1911, FO 403/425:156.
[32] Mackie to Grey, 30 May 1911, FO 403/405:119.
[33] David Northrup, *Beyond the Bend in the River: African Labor in Eastern Zaire, 1865–1940* (Athens, OH: Ohio University Center for International Studies, 1988), 89.

1911 of tax collectors exceeding their authority by flogging men and women without cause and extorting food and animals.[34] This problem occurred even in the Lower Congo, where money taxation was longstanding: "The collection of taxes has ever been attended with abuses, such as pillage, extortion, and cruelty, usually perpetrated by black subordinates but winked at by white officials. In this there has been little change for many years."[35] The administration responded to taxation concerns on an *ad hoc* basis, in some places negotiating collective payments by village, and in others granting temporary reductions in taxation levels, while trying to root out abusive tax collectors. In July 1914, the colonial government addressed concerns with inequity by authorizing local officials to assess taxes at their discretion between 2 and 24 francs annually, depending on local resources.[36]

By 1912, the tax regime represented a substantial improvement over previous practices. Though still higher than in many other African colonies, taxes no longer destroyed the fabric of most people's lives. Because it took years to expand taxation to cover even half the eligible taxpayers, most people did not pay the head tax for much of the decade after the reforms took effect.[37]

The pressures of war altered taxation. During the First World War, the government, now completely dependent on the Congo for revenue, doubled taxes.[38] In addition, new laws promulgated in 1917 increased penalties for nonpayment, authorizing forced labor to compensate for nonpayment of taxes.

Congo taxation policy met the goals of Grey and the CRA by ending the previous regime that had required the Congolese to spend one-third to two-thirds of their existence working to fulfill tax obligations. Even when taxation levels doubled during the war, they did not reach this level. Regarding taxes, the reformers could boast that they had successfully transformed the Leopoldian system to something far less oppressive.

Currency introduction, which took longer than expected, was otherwise a success. The government injected currency into the economy by paying for food and labor in coin.[39] Within a few years, there was enough coin circulating in most areas to make paying taxes in currency possible.

The verdict on forced labor cannot be so clear. Grey and the CRA had called for an end to forced labor for commercial purposes. Many reformers hoped for an end to all forced labor, but this did not square with the objective of a Congo colony run on the same basis as other African colonies. Many African

---

[34] Dye report, 11 July 1911, FO 403/426:34.
[35] Dye to Mackie, 22 August 1911, FO 881/10047:24.
[36] Anstey, *King Leopold's Legacy*, 48.
[37] Northrup, *Beyond*, 86.
[38] Samuel H. Nelson, *Colonialism in the Congo Basin 1880–1940* (Athens, OH: Ohio University Center for International Studies, 1994), 124.
[39] Granville to Grey, 29 October 1909, FO 403/410:169.

colonies, including most British colonies, used forced labor for purposes defined by authorities as being of public utility, such as road-building, though not all Africans would have agreed that they benefited from these projects.

Renkin's reform program ended forced labor for commercial purposes, at least on paper, and reduced government forced labor contracts to three years.[40] In 1910, Renkin declared that the government would no longer use forced labor even for works of public utility, such as the new railroad line being constructed in the Great Lakes territory, where 5,000 laborers found themselves free to go or stay.[41] Renkin was at his least sincere on this issue. Later that year, Vandervelde complained that forced labor continued.[42] Furthermore, some government rubber and cocoa plantations were using forced labor, as Morel and Harris had feared.[43] When the new British Minister to Belgium, Francis Villiers, asked Renkin about the use of forced labor in 1911, the Colonial Minister replied that forced labor did not exist on plantations or elsewhere.[44] This appears to have been a lie. In 1912, Morel highlighted the discrepancy between the repudiation of forced labor and its continuation in three areas: government activities such as the military, government-controlled commercial work such as state-run plantations, and private company work with broader benefits such as railroad labor.[45] In the same year, the American Consul praised the ending of commercial forced labor almost everywhere but similarly noted continued forced labor at government mines and plantations.[46]

Analyzing the persistence of forced labor for state-run commercial purposes, David Northrup identifies the cause: the government's rejection of field officers' proposals to make wage levels competitive with private firms, thus undermining the free labor market. Because workers opted for better-paying commercial employment, government mines and plantations could not find workers at substandard wages, and the state turned to compulsion rather than increasing wages.[47] This had ripple effects. Wage-earners short of money could not support the food markets essential to a proletariat, so the state began coercing local people to bring products to the markets near state-run enterprises.[48]

---

[40] Ibid.
[41] Hardinge to Grey, 8 December 1909, FO 403/410:268; Hardinge to Grey, 22 January 1910, FO 881/9730:9.
[42] Hardinge to Grey 4 February 1910, FO 881/9730:17.
[43] Report from Consul Dye, 11 July 1911, FO 403/426:34; Dye to Mackie, 22 August 1911, FO 881/10047:24; Lamont to Grey, 17 January 1912, FO 881/10142:14.
[44] Villiers to Grey, 16 May 1912, FO 881/10142:69–70.
[45] *Organ*, August 1912, 745–8.
[46] Vice-Consul-General Ross Hazeltine, report, 16 December 1912, US State Department, Africa #547, General Correspondence (1912), 53.
[47] Northrup, *Beyond*, 88.
[48] Northrup, *Beyond*, 89.

The limited geographic scope of these enterprises does not refute the charge that the government, in these places, continued to force people to work.

Privately owned companies raised wages to attract workers, and sometimes could not attract all the workers they needed. The Forminière mines moved from forced labor in 1912 to methods that included both free labor and coerced labor in 1913.[49] When forced labor had legally ended, many mines and plantations turned to private labor recruiters, obliged by the terms of their government licenses to attract men with practices consistent with a free labor market. In practice the authorities did little to constrain the recruiters' zeal. Also, even after the 1910–12 reforms, government officials required that chiefs provide men to work on mines and plantations.

The First World War brought about a notable setback in the implementation of a free labor ideology. With Belgium erased from the map of Europe, its exiled government could wage total war only by demanding sacrifices from its African colony. Authorities regarded mining, particularly gold mining, as sufficiently vital that they set aside the 1910–12 reforms when they deemed it necessary. The same was true for forced labor for porterage, which returned on a huge scale during the war, as it did in Britain's East African colonies. Restraints on labor recruiters vanished; during and immediately after the war, the authorities tolerated hostage-taking and manhunts. Complaints from state inspectors and the laborers themselves eventually led to a burst of government action in the mid-1920s to curb the worst abuses.[50] Belgian inspectors, able to get their voices heard after the war, made headway in reducing, but not eliminating, forced labor practices that had revived during the war.[51] It was not until the late 1920s that wages for Africans finally began to rise sufficiently to keep pace with inflation, thanks to three government actions: government monitoring of labor recruiters, ending the requirement that chiefs provide labor, and construction of sufficient roads (ironically conducted with forced labor) to make porterage largely unnecessary.[52]

For all his prevarication (in both senses of the word), Renkin significantly reduced the scope of forced labor, apparently believing that it was an undesirable practice with a certain utility that made its complete elimination impractical.[53] In agriculture, he attempted to reap its benefits while avoiding the abuses of the Leopoldian forced labor regime by reinventing the practice as compulsory cultivation. In 1917, he replaced village obligations to the government with a program in which the villagers would grow cash crops under the stern eye of

---

[49] Northrup, *Beyond*, 95, 97.
[50] Anstey, *King Leopold's Legacy*, 59–60.
[51] Northrup, *Beyond*, 101, 102, 117.
[52] Anstey, *King Leopold's Legacy*, 87–8, 111; Northrup, *Beyond*, 160.
[53] Robert Edgerton, *The Troubled Heart of Africa: A History of the Congo* (New York: St Martin's Press, 2002), 160.

colonial officials.[54] The villagers would then sell the resulting cotton, coffee, foodstuffs, and so on, at prices fixed by the state.[55] After the war's end, his successors expanded this program.

Once again merging taxation and forced labor after a 20-year respite, new rules in 1933 formalized the practice of requiring all male villagers without paying jobs elsewhere to work 60 days a year, or five days a month, on work of importance to the local community. During the Second World War, this labor tax doubled to 120 days, and expanded to once again include porterage and wild rubber collection, reviving for the war's duration two activities that the Congolese people loathed. Though rubber collection ended in 1945, some other requirements lingered for years.[56]

Under the guise of paternalism, the Belgians developed new forms of compulsion. For example, officials might force the inhabitants of an area afflicted by cold weather to make blankets, or compel people short of food to expand their area of cultivation. Historian Roger Anstey calls this "paternalist coercion" because officials saw it for the inhabitants' own good. Belgian administrators resorted to compulsion more often than officials in other colonies, with the effect on local people depending heavily on whether the officials were what Anstey called "good paternalists."[57] Whether or not there was a net physical benefit, compulsion robbed people of agency and led to threats, imprisonment, beatings, and other forms of punishment for failure to obey orders.

The reforms failed to eliminate commercial forced labor. After a significant decline, it had expanded, albeit less lethally and less extensively than in the Congo Free State. Renton, Seddon, and Zelig describe the post-1913 exploitative relationships in the Congo as changing from largely master/slave to largely boss/worker, a significant improvement though still oppressive.[58] The reformers achieved a salutary change that failed to meet their goal.

The fourth objective, granting the Congolese sufficient land to let them freely trade the products of the soil, contained two closely linked changes to solve a single problem. Under Leopold's system, all the products of the soil beyond village garden plots belonged to the government, which collected them through taxes in kind or in labor. The old regime treated any trade in these products as theft of state property. The reformers' twofold remedy was to restore traditional land rights and to legalize trading, but Renkin focused on the latter. With the reform program, the government surrendered its claim to the products of the

---

[54] Jean-Philippe Peemans, "Capital Accumulation in the Congo," in *Colonialism in Africa, 1870–1960, Vol. 4, The Economics of Colonialism*, eds Gann and Duignan (Cambridge: Cambridge University Press, 1975), 176–7.
[55] Edgerton, *Troubled Heart*, 168–9; Nelson, *Colonialism*, 125.
[56] Anstey, *King Leopold's Legacy*, 145–7, 159.
[57] Anstey, *King Leopold's Legacy*, 77–8.
[58] Renton, Seddon, and Zelig, *Congo*, 50.

soil, allowing the local people to gather them freely and sell them to private traders.[59] This single change broke the back of Leopold's system. However, Renkin refused to re-establish Congolese collective land rights, reserving for the colonial government the right to grant any European or African the legal title to what he persisted in calling "vacant lands" (in reality land traditionally under the control of nearby villages). Although Morel had earlier ranked land ownership as less vital than land access, it was an important goal.[60] Hardinge, like Morel, found this to be the least satisfactory part of Renkin's reforms. The US Vice-Consul-General urged without success that the state should at least compensate the local people when it took so-called vacant land for its own purposes or to sell to companies.[61] The reformers were uneasy with good reason. In the decades that followed, the colonial government granted vacant lands and even inhabited areas to plantations owned by the state and private firms. For its palm-oil concession, Lever Brothers obtained rights to parcels collectively one-fourth the size of Belgium.[62] This practice affected a much smaller fraction of the Congo than Leopold's concessions, but could pose real hardship for any Congolese directly affected.

The right of the Congo people to freely buy and sell generated benefits quite quickly. As the number of private traders grew from 2 in 1910 to over 1,000 in 1917, competition forced prices up for forest products, food, and fish.[63] Some traders were rogues, but the colonial government dealt with these cases as they came to its attention.[64] Even with wartime constraints, the free-trade regime was largely beneficial to those Congolese able to take advantage of it by virtue of location, accessible products, and personal initiative. Renkin's commitment to free trade was sincere; he rebuffed requests from large companies to limit the activity of small traders and to cap prices.[65]

However, after Renkin's departure in 1918, large firms found a more sympathetic ear. Renkin's successor replaced free trade with a managed-trade regime that benefited the large companies at the expense of the Congo people and the small traders. The Congolese confronted prices fixed by the firms or the state and no longer subject to supply and demand. Private traders found themselves hampered by new regulations. By the end of the First World War, five companies controlled 70 percent of the business of the Congo.[66] They took on some civic functions, such as provision of housing, medical care, and education,

---

[59] Granville to Grey, 29 October 1909, FO 403/410:168.
[60] Morel to Johnston, 21 October 1908, F8/92:178.
[61] US Vice-Consul-General, 16 December 1912, 54.
[62] 1,875,000 acres = 2929 sq. mi.
[63] Nelson, *Colonialism*, 121.
[64] Anstey, *King Leopold's Legacy*, 59.
[65] Nelson, *Colonialism*, 123.
[66] Edgerton, *Troubled Heart*, 169.

though not tax-collecting. The reformers had largely achieved what they wanted in the period 1912–18, but the state impeded the market's operation after 1917 and eroded its beneficial effects.

Renkin made free trade available to Europeans on the same 1910–12 schedule as his other reforms. He replaced the prohibitive 5,000-franc fee for opening a trading station with moderate taxes on rubber, while limiting land purchases by individual Europeans.[67] He also put in severe restrictions on ivory sales to protect government revenue and preserve the elephants.[68] Europeans paid an upfront ivory fee, but they could keep all the ivory if it was properly documented; indigenous people had no fee but they had to give the government half of the ivory they collected.[69]

The free-trade regime of the 1910–18 period, accompanied by a partially free labor market, brought significant material benefits to many Congolese, as the reformers had predicted. This regime began to erode under the pressure of war and then more quickly after Renkin's departure as the larger firms gained privileges, limited competition, and reduced wages and producer prices. Real wages fell by two-thirds by 1920, not regaining the levels that they had achieved in the free-trade period until the 1940s. Although this trend was not unique to the Congo, the reformers' almost-complete success in this regard gradually became a partial success.[70]

Leopold's 1906 reforms had made only a small dent in the entanglement of commerce and administration, but Renkin went much further. He replaced the old monopoly concessions with much smaller freeholds of more limited powers for fixed terms that he could revoke if they failed to meet certain standards. New concessions, such as Lever's palm-oil concession, had to pay a minimum wage of at least .25 francs per day, maintain schools and medical facilities, and meet food, housing, and sanitation requirements.[71] Dispatches from headquarters in the old Abir territory "were always enjoining moderation in all dealings with the natives and so constantly dwelling on the serious responsibility the officials would incur by recourse to any measure of severity."[72] This did not guarantee improvement. In late 1912 the US Consul advised that the reform of the concessions was not complete; some companies retained some municipal duties, and with them, the right to use forced labor.[73] However, maintaining a concession now required minimally acceptable treatment of the local people. The reconfigured Lomami concession treated the Congolese so badly even after the reforms that

---

[67] Granville to Grey, 29 October 1909, FO 403/410:169.
[68] Campbell to Grey, 25 October 1910, FO 881/9854:103–4.
[69] Hardinge to Grey, 22 January 1910, FO 881/9730:9.
[70] Peemans, "Capital Accumulation," 187–8.
[71] Northrup, *Beyond*, 93.
[72] Mackie to Grey, 2 July [June], 1911, FO 403/426:1.
[73] US Vice-Consul-General, 16 December 1912, 53.

the state shut it down in 1915.[74] Also, under free labor, employees could show their discontent by leaving. In one of Lever's concession areas, Elizabetha, when laborers left over poor conditions, employment fell from 4,000 in 1915 to 1,500 in 1918, leading to better treatment as well as tighter control over movement.[75]

Renkin undertook ancillary reforms as well. The hiring of Belgian colonial inspectors helped ferret out problems, though metropolitan authorities often disregarded their advice about policy. Despite inspectors' warnings, metropolitan misunderstandings about African authority patterns, land use conventions, and religious beliefs led colonial authorities to unnecessarily disrupt local society.[76] Renkin increased the pay of the colonial civil service, reducing their incentive to enrich themselves by other means. Appointed chiefs, called medal chiefs, frequently abused their authority, leading to waves of reforms of mixed efficacy.[77] However, these considerations are only tangentially relevant to unwinding what Hardinge called "a great fabric of oppression" in the six areas discussed above.[78]

The reformers were neither liars nor hypocrites when they proclaimed that the reform movement had largely succeeded in 1913. The excessive taxation of the past was gone, never to return. Belgium had introduced currency to facilitate markets and money taxes. Forced labor for commercial purposes had ended in theory and diminished significantly in practice until its resurgence during and after the war. Although they did not have title to their traditional lands, the Congolese enjoyed the benefits of access to land and free trade that eroded but did not disappear after 1918. Free trade for non-African individuals and companies similarly flourished in full force for a few years; even the more restrictive practices of the 1920s provided far more commercial liberty than Leopold's regime had. The old concession companies lost most of their lands and powers; many fizzled out. Concessions henceforth operated at a higher standard of responsibility. The reformers could claim that their programs appeared largely successful in 1913. By the 1920s, the picture was muddier, but, whether we call it a flawed triumph or a partial success, conditions were superior to those of the red rubber regime.

In general, the reforms softened the colonial rule over the Congo by ending the most violent and oppressive features of the Congo Free State, but many underlying attitudes and even structures had remained, facilitating the return of forced labor, the introduction of paternalist coercion, and the weakening of the free-trade regime.[79] Renkin's priorities, state-promoted economic development

---

[74] Lamont to Grey, FO 403/443:25; Northrup, *Beyond*, 94.
[75] Northrup, *Beyond*, 94.
[76] Anstey, *King Leopold's Legacy*, 49–57.
[77] 1911 report, *Commission pour la Protection des Indigènes*, cited in Anstey, *King Leopold's Legacy*, 48.
[78] Hardinge to Grey, 8 December 1909, FO 403/410:271.
[79] Nelson, *Colonialism*, 114–16.

and untrammeled free markets, were in conflict. It was free markets, and thus the people's prosperity, which later colonial secretaries sacrificed to speed development. In terms of taxation and forced labor, the effect of the reforms was to replace the brutal oppression of a large portion of the population with less vicious forms of oppression. Northrup suggests that the total burden may have been the same, just spread out to a larger number of people.[80] His calculus of comparative suffering fails to account for differential impact. Although precise calculations are impossible, it is clear that the gap between a flogging and a public humiliation is wide, and the gap between murder and flogging is wider still. Sadistic punishments that end in death may be worse than simple murder, while forced labor, compulsory agriculture, or other forms of oppression, for all their deplorable effects, have far lower costs. By ending the old system, with its extreme violence and societal disruption leading to starvation, epidemics, and population decline, the reforms and thus the reformers reduced the toll on the people of the Congo.[81] The economic burden may have been similar, but the toll of human suffering had become less.

Analyzing Causality: What Led to Congo Reform?

Causality is a fraught category of analysis; if one event preceded another in time, it did not necessarily cause the succeeding event to occur. In Geoffrey Elton's formulation, the historian can avoid this pitfall through "argument backwards."[82] In this view, causality is best understood not by looking forward from some occurrence, but in looking backward from the outcome and tracing how it came to occur.

In examining the question of how the movement caused change, there are several potential pitfalls to avoid. The first mistakes temporal sequence for cause and effect. For instance, the movement's internal dynamics and growing popularity, altered decisively by the Harrises in 1905–06, had nothing to do with Grey's becoming Foreign Secretary. Yet it was the accession of a committed reformer that changed British foreign policy in 1906, not the Harrises' activities. A more complicated example concerns the ebbing of the movement in 1910, a time when the Harrises left the CRA, the number of lantern lectures fell, and Morel added other interests to his Congo activism. The Harrises' departure did not cripple the movement; their move to Anti-Slavery enabled better cooperation with Morel. As the present work has shown, the falloff in CRA

---

[80] Northrup, *Beyond*, 117.
[81] Mackie to Grey, 30 May 1911, FO 881/9889:119–57.
[82] Geoffrey R. Elton, *Return to Essentials* (New York: Cambridge University Press, 1991), 7.

meetings and donations followed two key events: the 1909 Belgian reform program and the Parliamentary Committee's mid-1910 decision to adhere to Grey's policy of watching and waiting. Had the Belgian reforms failed, the MPs, the CRA, and Anti-Slavery could have revived the campaign.

The second pitfall is to overlook the transnational component of the movement, particularly American involvement and, even more importantly, the Belgian reformers who played critical roles at several junctures, both privately, as when Wauters and Cattier influenced the powers of Leopold's Commission of Inquiry, and politically, where Vandervelde, Lorand, Beernaert, and others altered the annexation process to limit Leopold's influence, making reforms possible. Speyer, Cattier, Vandervelde, and Lorand advocated the same reforms that Grey and the CRA did.[83] This section will seek to avoid both the misreading of causality and a narrow focus on Britain in delineating the chain of causality from 1913 backwards.

The main sequence of events that led to the improved conditions of 1913 includes the following milestones:

> 1903 May: The Samuel Resolution passed by the British House of Commons
> 1904 February: Casement Report published
> 1904 July: Commission of Inquiry launched
> 1905 October: Commission of Inquiry report published
> 1906 December: Belgian consensus to annex the Congo
> 1908 November: Belgian annexation of the Congo
> 1909 October: Reform plan announced
> 1910–12: Belgian reforms put into effect
> 1913 June: British recognition of annexation and dissolution of the CRA.

In 1913, atrocities had largely ended, and the reform program was in place. The participants had different understandings of how this occurred. Belgian Colonial Secretary Jules Renkin adamantly maintained that the reforms were largely his own idea, implemented because the colony needed new rules to reflect current conditions, needs, and goals. The CRA, on the other hand, trumpeted how the conscience of the British public had overcome opposition from Leopold, Belgium, and the British Foreign Office to obtain needed remedies. These competing narratives helped everyone—promulgators and audiences alike—understand what had occurred in the context of their own goals and beliefs. Renkin, defending Belgian sovereignty and hoping to become Prime Minister one day, could not give any credit to the British reform movement or

---

[83] Granville to Grey, 1 November 1909, FO 403/410:199–200.

government.[84] Similarly, most reformers, having worked so hard for so long, had difficulty acknowledging that the initiative had passed to the Foreign Office and Belgium years before.

The following section reads the chain of causality backwards to identify the most influential factors in creating the outcome. The Belgian reform program had addressed most of the reformers' demands and created change for the better. The symbolic representations of this consensus included the formal British recognition of the Belgian annexation on 27 June 1913, the vote to dissolve the CRA on 16 June 1913 at London's Westminster Palace Hotel, the Parliamentary debate of 29 May 1913 where MPs endorsed recognition, and, the step that paved the way for all the others, the CRA Executive Committee vote to support recognition on 25 April 1913. Grey had given the House of Commons the consular reports, fulfilling his promise that Parliament would have the chance to review the situation before Britain ended its pressure for reforms. These actions resulted from the favorable reports of the British consuls.

While the reforms were not perfect, the colonial government worked to ensure that the new rules took effect through instructions, administrative changes, and inspections. The Colonial Council included men such as Cattier, Speyer, and Vandervelde who reminded Renkin of the need for real improvement. Until 1913, British consuls were the watchdogs, reporting progress and problems through Grey to the Belgian government; implementation of the reforms was more thorough because of their voluminous reports. Grey also applied judicious pressure to encourage completion of the reform program by making suggestions, such as recommending that Belgium replace the top officials of the colony, by posing questions, such as his inquiries about the fate of the concessionary companies, and by delaying recognition until he had favorable reports in hand for all reformed areas, despite Belgian hints about earlier recognition.[85] Leopold's inhibiting effect on the process ended with his death in December 1909.[86]

Between the November 1909 and June 1913, the CRA undertook initiatives such as the massive 19 November 1909 Albert Hall demonstration, the April 1910 Parliamentary Memorial, and at least 25 reports, resolutions, memorials, and other letters Morel sent to Grey. However, in terms of causality, these initiatives had no impact on the structure, pace, or effectiveness of the Belgian reforms. During these years, the CRA played a secondary role without direct impact on how the reforms unfolded.

---

[84] Harding to Grey, 8 December 1909, FO 881/9854 268–70.

[85] Grey to Hardinge, 15 April 1910, FO 881/9730:109; Grey to Granville, 13 July 1910, FO 881/9854:7; Hardinge to Grey, 15 July 1910, FO 881/9854:14–16; Grey to Villiers, 17 July 1912, FO 881/10245:7.

[86] Hardinge to Grey, 4 February and 13 March 1910, FO 881/9730:17, 84.

As previously described, the reform program was effective in successive Congo regions in July 1910, July 1911, and July 1912. The minor changes in regulation and bigger changes in tone that occurred between annexation and July 1910 had the salutary but limited effect of a reduction in atrocities, according to the British consuls.

Because Renkin's reform program announced on 29 October 1909 essentially went into effect without modification from 1910–12, it is important to understand what led to it. The Belgian annexation was the necessary, but not sufficient, precondition. Before annexation, in a communiqué of 12 July 1908, the Belgian government had committed to several major reforms as soon as the Belgian Parliament voted for annexation and the Colonial Law: eliminating the labor tax, ending abuses, expanding village land rights, and allowing the Congolese people to trade freely.[87] The CRA was right to be skeptical; contrary to this commitment, no reform program appeared when the Chamber of Deputies approved annexation on 20 August 1908 or when annexation occurred three months later, on 15 November.

The Belgian government was not prepared to follow up on the promise of reform made in the 12 July 1908. Leopold still influenced the government and particularly Renkin, though Cattier and Speyer had confidence that Renkin and Belgium would do the right thing in the end.[88] Although Hardinge later described Renkin as determined to implement reforms, if only out of self-interest, he seemed more focused on the political present.[89] On taking office, he denied systematic or widespread misrule in the Congo Free State, but acknowledged reforms were needed, reforms that no outside power could dictate, thus precluding recommendations from Grey and the CRA. He knew he had to act. Prince Albert, soon to be the next King, "had frankly admitted that the King's system of administration had given rise to grave abuses, which would have, for the sake of Belgium's good name as a civilised and progressive State, to be removed."[90] After Albert spent three months in the Congo in 1909, his interest in reform became common knowledge.[91] Renkin also examined Congo conditions in person; he was absent from Brussels for six months (22 April to mid-October 1909) on his own voyage of inquiry to the Congo, leaving the Belgian foreign minister to deal with the increasingly impatient Grey.

The year-long delay may have suited Renkin's purposes as a middle course between inaction, favoring Leopold and his cronies, and aggressive change as advocated by Albert and the reformers. However, by delaying, he gambled with

---

[87] Enclosure, Davignon to Lalaing, 12 July 1908, Africa No. 4 (1908), Cd. 4178.

[88] Cattier to Morel, no date, F9/3:54–5; Hardinge to Grey, 3 February 1909, FO 881/9530:49.

[89] Hardinge to Grey, 8 December 1909, FO 881/9691:268–70.

[90] Hardinge to Grey, 17 May 1909, FO 881/9530:195–6.

[91] *Liverpool Daily Post*, 18 December 1909, 11.

possible diplomatic or even military hostilities between Belgium and Britain. Unbeknownst to Renkin or to Morel, Grey had won the British Cabinet's support for stronger measures just before Renkin presented his reforms.

Though Renkin never admitted as much, the reform program appeared to owe much of its substance to the proposals from Grey, the CRA, and Cattier. At key moments, Cattier came to Britain to ask the Foreign Office and the CRA to keep up the pressure.[92] While Cattier's prominence in Belgium lent weight to his ideas, the pressure applied by Grey ensured that they would be included. The British could play the heavies while Cattier and Speyer could be more supportive. In direct communiqués and less formal messages sent through Hardinge and Lalaing (the Belgian ambassador to Britain), Grey conveyed what Britain expected in a reform program and emphasized that the country's patience was not inexhaustible.[93] In this light, Grey's unusual promise on 25 February 1909 that he would consult with Parliament before recognizing the annexation was part of a strategy to pressure Belgium, preventing him from recognizing the annexation for anything less than a fully effective program.

Belgian annexation had made this possible; the Congo Free State had to end for reforms to occur. However, annexation occurred two years after 13 December 1906, when the Belgian government announced the pending *reprise*. At issue were the terms on which Belgium would annex the Congo. Leopold demanded the continuation of his system, a role in colonial governance, personal control over Congo Crown Domain lands, respect for existing concession contracts, and large financial commitments to himself, his family, and his building programs. The king's position weakened as negotiations continued through a parliamentary election and three prime ministers, each less sympathetic than the last. The final terms included none of Leopold's initial demands except scaled-back financial commitments.

In the two years from the Belgian commitment to annexation in December 1906 to the actual annexation of November 1908, the most important changes occurred in Belgium with British and American support.[94] Britain's involvement was at first somewhat muted; Grey's error, never forgiven by Morel, was to agree with the Belgians that detailed reform plans could wait until annexation. However, this missed opportunity did not preclude other forms of British involvement. The Belgian opposition went so far as to invite British and American pressure on the government during the annexation debates.[95] King Edward's

---

[92] Cookey, *Britain*, 157.
[93] Grey to Hardinge, 27 March 1908, Africa No. 2 (1908), Cd. 4079, 2; Grey to Davignon, 4 November 1908, Africa No. 5 (1908), Cd. 4396, 1; Grey to Davignon, 11 June 1909, Africa No. 2 (1909), Cd. 4701, doc. 2; Hardinge to Grey, 1 October 1909, FO 881/9691:155.
[94] FO 881/9309.
[95] Hardinge to Grey, 24 April 1908, FO 881/9309:193.

1908 speech seems to have reminded the Belgian government of the urgency in the international arena.[96] As Grey became more impatient, his messages became more specific; by May 1908, he had given the Belgian government an outline of the desired reform program.[97] Interestingly, the timing of Belgium's August 1908 vote to annex was Hardinge's doing; the Belgian government had taken his suggestion to call a special summer legislative session to deal with the Congo question.[98]

The British reform movement contributed to the erosion of Leopold's position in these years. During the Belgian debates of December 1906 to October 1908, the CRA published and rallied and thundered with all the gusto of an organization at the peak of its popularity and prowess. Although it had played little part in educating Belgian public opinion, the British campaign ensured that the Belgian Parliament and people stayed aware of their country's embarrassment. Other than this, it had little effect on the course of events in Belgium in these two years. This should not be surprising; the CRA's prime target was the British government. More than 1,300 resolutions inundated the Foreign Office and the desks of MPs in 1907–08, supporting Grey's calls for annexation, urging him to convene an international conference, and demanding stronger action to convince the Congo Free State to start reforms even before annexation. The last demand failed, but the CRA's analysis and information helped the Foreign Office and its publicity conveyed how strongly British public opinion wanted improvement.

The Belgian consensus on annexation in late 1906 was a pivotal event in the story of Congo reform, completely reversing the positions that had prevailed through 1905. Until this moment, the Belgian cabinet had supported Leopold's plan to keep the Congo for life and insisted that Congo affairs were not Belgium's concern. No parliamentary party except Beernaert's Young Right endorsed annexation, and the matter barely registered in public opinion.

The dramatic Belgian change resulted from the confluence of domestic and international events from October 1905 to December 1906 that removed the scales from their eyes regarding the king and his Congo Free State and made annexation inevitable. The avalanche began with the long-delayed release of the report of Leopold's Commission of Inquiry on 30 October 1905. Despite Leopold's best efforts to occlude the report's content and spin what could not be hidden, it condemned the Congo system of rule, even while praising its accomplishments. In the ensuing 12 months, the campaign's most influential books appeared. The CRA issued at least a dozen publications, including the damning (and popular) "Evidence Laid before the Congo Commission of

---

[96] Hardinge to Grey, 4 and 8 February 1908, FO 881/9309:89ff.
[97] Hardinge to Grey, 9 May 1908, FO 881/9309:201–11.
[98] Hardinge to Grey, 13 May 1908, FO 881/9309:216.

Inquiry" in French and English. Morel wrote his most famous book, *Red Rubber*, at this time. However, it was not Morel's work that awakened Belgian opinion; they had ignored his denunciations for years. Belgian authors woke sentiment in Belgium and turned the ripple caused by the Commission's report into an irresistible force.

The first volley came from Wauters in the *Mouvement Géographique* of 19 November 1905, condemning the Congo Free State based on the Commission's report and the missionary evidence published by Morel. By January, the Catholic religious press had begun to turn against Leopold, stung by accusations that Catholic missions had ignored Congo misrule and to some degree had been complicit in it.[99]

In February, Cattier's *Etude de la Situation de l'Etat Indépendant du Congo* analyzed the Commission's report, linking it to his previous book and contradicting its conciliatory tone. Unlike the Commission, Cattier highlighted Leopold's rule as the heart of the problem. He advocated Belgian annexation and revealed that the Congo Free State had borrowed far more money from Belgium than it needed to cover its early deficits, leading to suspicions of financial shenanigans.

Cattier's book caused a sensation in Belgium and helped convince Vandervelde to support annexation.[100] When the Socialist party, not surprisingly, would not accept this remedy, Vandervelde asked for and received permission to advocate for annexation separately from the party. On 20 February, quoting from Cattier's book and revealing specifics of the Press Bureau's corruption of a Belgian paper, Vandervelde launched what became the five days' debate beginning 27 February in the Chamber of Deputies.[101] Also influenced by Cattier, the Belgian Liberals decided to demand annexation, forming a united opposition that spanned the political spectrum from Vandervelde through the Liberals to Beernaert's Young Right party. They voted to examine previous Belgian legislation that had set the legal framework for a Belgian takeover.

Shortly thereafter, Father Vermeersch's *La Question Congolaise* appeared. Although he was more careful than Cattier to praise Leopold, his status as a Jesuit and his access to reports from Belgian Catholic missionaries gave his book additional weight among the Catholic population of Belgium and the conservative Catholic Party.[102] Later that year, Speyer reissued his 63-page

---

[99] "Belgian Catholic Censure," *WAM*, 19 January 1906, 1024.

[100] Wilson to Secretary of State, 5 March 1906, *Papers Related to the Foreign Relations of the United States, Part 1* (1909), 89, http://books.google.com/books?id=dhNHAQA AIAAJ&pg=PA89.

[101] "Verbatim Report of the Five Days' Congo Debate," 16 December 1906, 59th Congress, Senate 2nd session, no. 138, http://books.google.com/books?id=zBJHAQAAI AAJ&pg=PA209.

[102] Morel, *Great Britain*, 89; Vermeersch, *La Question Congolaise*, 179, 267ff.

booklet, *Comment Nous Gouvernerons le Congo*, and Vermeersch wrote *Les Destinées du Congo Belge*. The three professors stirred Belgian public opinion against Leopold and the Congo situation far more effectively than British reformers could.

Slow to understand the gravity of the situation, Leopold further inflamed political opinion in a June 1906 royal manifesto that dismissed annexation and claimed that his rights over the Congo were the fruits of his own expenditure and labors, contrasting with Cattier's narrative that he had used Belgian money to build a colonial empire using the forced labor of Africans.[103] Leopold also announced onerous conditions for annexation, when and if he consented. He managed to alienate many members of the monarchist Catholic party, who joined the opposition by November 1906 in demanding annexation. Fox Bourne sent a well-timed letter to Belgian deputies endorsing Belgian annexation, a tactic that, combined with Grey's similar statements, finally laid to rest most Belgian fears of British intentions.[104]

Though Leopold still had the support of the prime minister and Cabinet, trouble brewed in the international arena. Clemenceau's French government announced some tepid reforms to its concessionary regime in French Congo in conjunction with its settlement of its dispute with Britain.[105] On 6 December, the Belgian prime minister and leading members of the Cabinet, deeply concerned about the international situation, asked the king to agree to annexation to forestall what the foreign minister believed was the imminent danger of a conference and partition, though Leopold met their demand with an ambiguous reply.[106]

The impetus to the king's capitulation in the days after 6 December came from the United States.[107] The American Congo Reform Association had prepared the ground for two years since Morel's 1904 visit with meetings, with literature, and by publishing Twain's sarcastic *King Leopold's Soliloquy* at Morel's urging.[108] The Harrises had stirred up the public as they lectured in the US in late January and February 1906, generating thousands of telegrams, petitions, and letters to the Senate. Roosevelt, who had been sympathetic, if inactive, since Morel's visit, indicated in November that he was considering joint diplomacy with Britain.[109]

---

[103] Emerson, *Leopold*, 255.
[104] Cookey, *Britain*, 166–8.
[105] Cookey, *Britain*, 180.
[106] Stengers, *"Vers la reprise du Congo par la Belgique: La décision," Congo, Mythes et réalités* (Paris: Duculot, 1989), 171–2.
[107] Emerson, *Leopold*, 256–7.
[108] Morel to Park, 9 May and 20 June 1905, F10/12:217, 307.
[109] Cookey, *Britain*, 170.

What tipped the scales in the US was the exposure of the American Congo lobby in early December 1906 by disgruntled apologist Henry Kowalsky, including the revelation that the lobby had bribed a Senate Foreign Relations Committee staff member. Events moved quickly after the revelations appeared in print on 9 December. Senator Lodge put forward a motion on 10 December to support the President in any action he might take, and the US officially offered to cooperate with the British on 11 December. On 13 December, Leopold publicly assented to annexation, the quicker the better. The next day, with the blessing of the king and the prime minister, the Belgian Chamber voted to annex, with 128 votes in favor, 2 against, and 29 abstentions. Any temptation Leopold had to reverse or fight this decision was smothered by his visit to Paris on 16 December 1906, where the new prime minister, Clemenceau, seems to have conveyed that Leopold could expect no help from France.[110]

Absent a threat to bring down the government, the majority Catholic party and especially Leopold's ally, Prime Minister Smet de Nayer, would not have brought annexation to the Chamber unless the king agreed. Stengers demonstrates that foreign pressure made the difference.[111] The king's reversal on annexation was a triumph for the British reformers. The CRA had succeeded in its efforts to create a clamor in Britain and beyond, particularly through the US, which gave added weight to Grey's insistent diplomacy.

The Belgian reformers played a crucial role that has been underappreciated in most historical writing. They changed the mood in Belgium and, together with the CRA and Grey, had made possible the decision to annex in December 1906. Without such a decision at this time, when Belgian interest and international fears peaked, other outcomes would have become possible due to flagging Belgian public interest, British impatience, and royal intransigence. The international consensus that Leopold and the Belgian foreign minister feared might have come to pass.[112] Contrast their panic with the British Foreign Office's perspective of its own limited power and options. Britain was acting alone, except during US cooperation from December 1906 to March 1909. Foreign Office information indicated that other countries were at best neutral on the Congo question, despite occasional criticism of Leopold.

The Commission of Inquiry's report appeared nearly a year after it had completed its journey. The CRA's 96-page "Evidence Laid before the Congo Commission of Inquiry" pamphlet, made possible by Cadbury's £600 gift, contained missionary testimony not otherwise available.[113] This prompted the Congo authorities to issue the long-delayed Commission report on 30 October

---

[110] Stengers, *"Vers la reprise,"* 173–4; Cookey, *Britain*, 177.
[111] Stengers, *"Vers la reprise,"* 173.
[112] Stengers, *"Vers la reprise,"* 173–4.
[113] Morel to Beauchamp, 10 July 1905, F10/12:375.

1905; without directly quoted testimony and laden with compliments to the Congo government, it must have seemed less dangerous than the CRA's popular booklet. Thus the report's publication resulted from the CRA's activities.

The creation of the Commission in 1904 was a direct result of outside pressure. Lansdowne, Cattier, Wauters, and Fox Bourne capitalized on Leopold's misstep of mentioning an inquiry to turn what everyone thought of as a whitewash into a thorough re-examination of the areas Casement had covered.

The Casement journey and report resulted from the Congo debate and Samuel resolution of 1903. Although the resolution's supporters hoped for an international conference, the debate and resolution of 1903 set the process in motion. These vital first steps were entirely the result of the overlapping and collaborating campaigns of Fox Bourne, Stead, and, most importantly, Morel.[114] There is irony in the realization that the reformers' greatest success, achieved contrary to the wishes of the Foreign Office and without the help of Belgian reformers, occurred before the formation of the CRA.

The CRA's first two years, when it was at its weakest in terms of members, public meetings, and finances, were also the years of its greatest importance to the cause. With Lansdowne in the Foreign Office, the impetus for reform and the spread of the message came primarily from the Congo Reform Association. When Grey became Foreign Secretary, its importance changed because of his commitment to reform; its prodding was less important, but it educated him and influenced his positions from 1906–09. Its effect on events decreased as time went on, until, by late 1909, its ability to alter the outcome had almost vanished. This is not to say that its activities after 1909 had no value. It kept public opinion alive to the Congo question, maintained an active agitation in the press, gave Grey the cover of public dissatisfaction to pursue his policies, and alarmed the defenders of the old regime. The Association spurred international interest and supported Belgian reformers. Nonetheless, this section has shown that its direct role in bringing about the critical events of Congo reform diminished over time.

The Human Element: Interpersonal Relationships and Emotional Responses

Ever since Wuliger unearthed the Morel papers in the early 1950s, interpersonal tensions have loomed large. As Wuliger put it:

> Fox Bourne hated Guinness; Guinness and Stead detested Dilke; Mrs Green abominated both Guinness and Fox Bourne; EDM [Morel] loathed John Harris; Harris was jealous of EDM. The missionary societies had a gray reputation. The Chambers of Commerce were contemptuous of the Aborigines' Protection

---

[114] Emmott to Morel, 31 December 1903, F8/53:34.

Society. The APS was horrified by the commercial taint. The *Morning Post* people were irritated at finding themselves in the same boat with what they called "professional humanitarians."[115]

Others have taken this issue farther; Grant asserts that dissension "split the ranks of the Congo reformers" in 1908.[116] It is legitimate to ask how these animosities affected the movement. For instance, hostility to Dilke kept Stead at arm's length from the CRA. Relations with Guinness went through periodic crises until he embraced the Belgian government, yet he rendered great service to the movement in 1904–06. Fox Bourne overcame his hostility to the creation of the CRA and joined its Executive Committee. Green's animosities usually coincided with Morel's and made him feel justified in his dislikes, but in the end Morel did what he could to work with anyone interested in reform.

The relations between Harris and Morel require further examination because of their centrality. Their relationship was far more complex than Morel's occasional temper tantrums might suggest. John Harris could justifiably cite grievances with Morel, but not his oft-repeated complaint that Morel would not share the credit. Morel publicly and privately praised the contributions of John and Alice Harris from 1905 to 1913.[117] He raised money for the Harrises when their personal expenses exceeded their salary.[118] Upon their departure, and in their presence, he told the Executive Committee,

> It is impossible to speak too highly of the energy and devotion they have shewn, and of the immense amount of labour they have put into the movement. I should not like to hazard a guess at the number of meetings they have addressed throughout this country in the last few years—certainly they have run into many hundreds ... Mr Harris' capabilities as an organiser have been invaluable to the Association, and were well exemplified in the Albert Hall gathering, for whose organisation he was entirely responsible ... During the last year, Mr Harris has been responsible for the financial side of the Association's work, and he has carried out that work with efficiency and success.[119]

---

[115] Wuliger, "Economic Imperialism," 72.

[116] Grant, *Civilised Savagery*, 76.

[117] For example, "Rousing the Country," *WAM Congo Supplement*, October 1905, 395–8; "He has done magnificent work," Morel to Cadbury, 31 July 1906, F4/7:23; "the great services rendered by Lord Monkswell and Mr and Mrs Harris," Executive Committee, 21 January 1908, F4/9:21.

[118] Ralph Durand to Buxton, 17 January, 26 January and 2 February 1907, Brit Emp. s18, C80/102–4; Morel to Cadbury, 24 January 1907, F8/12:53.

[119] Executive Committee, 15 March 1910, *Organ*, May 1910, 532.

At the CRA's final meeting, where the Harrises' exclusion from the platform prompted John Harris's complaint about sharing credit, Morel announced,

> I must testify to-day, and it gives me great pleasure to do so, to the very great services rendered to the cause by Rev. John Harris and Mrs Harris, whose activities the Congo Balolo Mission generously placed at the disposal of the Association ... who afterward and for some time acted with indefatigable energy and success as Organising Secretaries of the Association, addressing hundreds of meetings all over the country and contributing powerfully to the enlightenment of public opinion.[120]

Both because of his periodic difficulties with Morel and because he feared being unemployed after the CRA's work was done, Harris began thinking about leaving the CRA as early as 1908, but he and Alice stayed on until 31 March 1910, after almost five years' service. Morel's personal opinion of Harris deteriorated, reinforced by the CRA Treasurer, Harold Brabner, who never lost an opportunity to attack the "perfect little snake" in extreme terms on often trivial matters, by Green, and by Casement, who claimed Harris was "not very straight" with him.[121] Yet, except during the occasional eruption, Morel suppressed his animosity. His interpretation of Harris's careless inaccurate remarks as lies led him to believe that Harris told people in 1911 that Morel had diverted money from the CRA. In 1912, he wrote Holt (who continued to have good relations with Harris),

> He and I keep perfectly friendly. But between you and I and the gate-post I cannot like the man. However, he is a force to reckon with ... and long as he uses his influence in the right way that is the main point. He grows, however, personally, more and more distasteful to me as time goes on.[122]

Harris, on the other hand, notwithstanding his own jealously and grievances, considered Morel one of his closest friends. When he and Alice went on their year-long trip to Africa in 1911–12, he asked Morel to be one of three men who would advise his executors about arrangements for their four children and raise money in the event John and Alice did not survive the trip. Also, for this journey, worried that the Congo authorities might tamper with his mail, Harris set up a secret code with Morel, not any of his other trusted humanitarian friends such

---

[120] *Organ*, July 1913, 1019–20. Of course, though he was always willing to praise Harris for his work, Morel had a far higher opinion of his own importance to it, which other reformers—including John Harris—constantly reinforced.
[121] Brabner to Morel, 20 January 1911, F8/34:71 and 26 June 1911, F4/10:182; Casement to Morel, 16 December 1909, F8/13:27.
[122] Morel to Holt, 7 October 1912, F8/89:899.

as Travers Buxton or Harold Spender. Morel suppressed his growing dislike for Harris in the interest of the cause they supported and Harris treated Morel like a trusted friend and ally, especially after he left the CRA. As Harris put it in a 1911 letter to Morel: "When the fight is over, if we live to see that day, we must try and have a happy evening together, when we will dismiss everything but that which has been bright and happy."[123]

The key to understanding how the movement functioned despite personal animosities was Morel's longstanding principle that the reformers had to subordinate their personal feelings, as when he tried to cajole Stead into working with Dilke. Because of this attitude, Morel's drama with Harris did not significantly impede the reform movement. When it came to the battle with Leopold, the movement stayed united despite personal issues.

The reformers did sometimes hurt their cause by misinterpreting the actions of others. The CRA saw every positive step by the Foreign Office or Belgium as a vindication of its most recent actions. Morel's break with the Foreign Office was perhaps the most egregious setback masquerading as a tactical victory. Morel believed that the campaign against the Foreign Office convinced Grey to prepare for stronger action against Belgium, though Grey's preparations for sterner measures sprang from his own judgment and Thesiger's reports.

The Reform Movement's Effectiveness

If the reformers did not argue for self-determination for the colonized or for an end to colonial rule, we cannot then deem their cause to have failed because colonial rule continued. Most Congo reformers found colonialism acceptable and even desirable as long as it was administered well. It was not obvious to Holt and Morel that colonial rule *necessitated* coercion and violence; they imagined that the right kind of colonialism could respect and leave intact local cultures while peacefully suppressing their most repugnant practices. The old liberal proposition that full legal equality and self-determination was only for those who were ready for it had faded in Europe, but it continued in colonial theory. Morel's language of rights distinguished between civilized nations, where the full panoply of rights should apply, and subject races, who should be entitled to a much smaller set of rights. Nonetheless, though many of the movement's adherents wanted nothing more than to end the murders, rapes, and mutilations of Leopold's regime, the CRA's leadership had a radical agenda. Its radicalism lay not in its program, which aspired to make the Congo like other colonies, but in applying the principle formalized a century later by the UN General Assembly as the Responsibility to Protect: if a state fails in its responsibilities

---

[123] Harris to Morel, 9 March 1911, F8/77:427.

by committing crimes against humanity, other countries have an obligation "to use appropriate diplomatic, humanitarian and other peaceful means ... to help protect populations from genocide, war crimes, ethnic cleansing, and crimes against humanity," with military action as a last resort.[124] This wording resonates with the sentiments of the CRA and Grey. Like the UN today, neither Grey nor Morel contemplated ending all violence, exploitation, or oppression, but sought to overturn the administrative and economic basis of the system Leopold created. Had the reforms completely succeeded, the resulting colony would nonetheless have shared the racist traits of all African colonial regimes, using implicit and explicit violence to maintain imperial rule.

Those who deem that the reformers failed are arguing that they should have pursued different goals, such as the end of colonial rule or transforming the Congo into a model colonial state. This is an inappropriate standard. Condemning the Congo reform movement because it was not anticolonial or because the Belgian colony was not a paragon has little to do with the question of whether the CRA was effective in achieving its ends. The Belgian Congo of 1913 justified British recognition and the end of the CRA; the less-than-satisfactory aspects, such as the land question, were not amenable to further pressure as they had been partially satisfied. Overall, the result appeared to be better than passing marks for the reformers.

In 1913, the reformers could fear but not predict that conditions would erode in the future. If the reforms in 1913 looked like an incomplete success, the later years emphasized the incompleteness. After 1915 and especially 1918, Belgium adulterated or even reversed reforms because of pressure for development, perceived needs of total war, and oppressive paternalism. New problems arose. The Belgian Congo from the 1920s was one of the more oppressive colonies in Africa. This was nonetheless an improvement. The situation in 1922 and 1944 was worse than in 1913, but these three points in time were all far better than anything between 1890–1909. The governance of the Belgian Congo did not lapse back into the systemic, widespread horrors of the Congo Free State. The success of Grey and the Congo Reform Association had ended the years of hell, but it had not made a paradise.

The reformers had made this possible. The years of their biggest impact were 1900–05, when the Belgian reformers were powerless and the British Foreign Office would not take up the question on its own. It is in these years, particularly 1903, when the activists rallied educated public opinion and deployed parliamentary allies to tap the powers inherent in the House of Commons to force the British government to act against its inclination in exposing the Congo question to international scrutiny and take actions toward securing reform.

---

[124] United Nations, "2005 World Summit Outcome," 31, http://www.who.int/hiv/universalaccess2010/worldsummit.pdf.

Under Grey the Foreign Office became an advocate of Congo reform. The CRA supported and educated him for the next few years until Morel's break with the Foreign Office damaged those connections. Thereafter the CRA reminded the Foreign Office and the world of Britain's ongoing popular interest in the question, but it no longer determined or decisively influenced events.

Conclusion

> I think when the history of the Congo Reform Association is read in retrospect and cold blood, it will not be lacking in lessons which have a bearing on many other controversies past and, no doubt, future too.[1]—Edward Talbot, Bishop of Winchester, at the final CRA meeting, 16 June 1913

At the Westminster Palace Hotel on 16 June 1913, the Congo Reform Association celebrated the successful completion of its efforts. The movement had drawn on a rich British tradition of overseas humanitarianism, reforming journalism, and public mobilization. After the isolated voices raised from time to time since 1886 and the Aborigines' Protection Society's ineffective efforts in the late 1890s, the movement gathered steam in the early 1900s when Morel, Stead, and Guinness began their own campaigns in parallel with the APS, culminating in the Commons resolution of May 1903, which led a reluctant Conservative government to take its first steps on the path to ending the reign of terror on the Congo. The resolution set in motion Casement's report, which in turn led to the formation of the Commission of Inquiry and the CRA in 1904. The chain of events that followed in the British Foreign Office, Belgium, and elsewhere changed the conditions of life for many Congolese. If the reformers who gathered in 1913 had known that Belgium would dilute some reforms and reverse others in both wartime and peacetime during the next three decades, it would have dampened their mood but not crushed it; their chief satisfaction was in ending the Leopoldian system and the widespread atrocities it had spawned.

Despite its special characteristics, the Congo reform movement was less unique in motives or methods than its leaders and its historians have claimed. Its participants believed in the virtues of free trade, abhorred cruel treatment of colonized people, and thought of their activism as way to regenerate Britain as well as the Congo. The movement tapped into the Nonconformist conscience, then at its peak influence in British politics, as well as the more secular ideas of the Aborigines' Protection Society and Mary Kingsley's Liverpool Sect. The union of commercial, religious, and humanitarian players strengthened the movement, both by linking different constituencies and by attracting people who represented all three areas: deeply religious business owners who had supported humanitarian organizations for years before they joined the CRA.

---

[1] *Organ*, July 1913, 1014.

Most of the CRA's structures and practices fit into the tradition of British overseas humanitarianism: in its Committee and aristocratic President, its hard-working Honorary Secretary, its auxiliaries, its lantern lectures, its newsletter and pamphlets, its methods of gathering information, its lobbying of Whitehall and Parliament, and its international contacts. The CRA came to conform to common practice such as audited accounts, published donor lists and financial statements, meeting minutes, and using the Committee to vet (most) major policy changes. Morel could, with the Executive Committee's support, impose discipline on the movement to ensure that Britain and the world heard consistent messages regarding the problems, their origins, and solutions. Morel exemplified this discipline, particularly in his belief that all adherents should set aside personal acrimony to work together to further the cause. Morel himself, while giving this advice to Stead and others, lived by it as well in the way he dealt with John Harris, who periodically enraged him and whom he came to dislike.

The CRA perpetuated the gendered leadership structure of its constituencies and the political structure it sought to influence. In its relationship to the relatively small number of women who had important formal or informal roles, the movement did not anticipate the rapid expansion of women's public roles in the twentieth century, but remained firmly planted in a late-Victorian world of informal, behind-the-scenes, and subordinate roles for women. Alice Harris most nearly made an exception to this pattern, with her official titles, photography, public speaking, and organizing, but even she conceded the limelight to her husband.

The Executive Committee was primarily Liberal in its political affiliations, more religious than the population of Britain as a whole, younger than its peers, and largely London-based. Most of the business of pleading for money fell to Morel and Harris. Individual donors provided seven-eighths of the CRA's income, while branches accounted for a twentieth of the funding (excluding London) and meeting proceeds another twentieth. Most money came from donors who tended to be religious and connected to manufacturing. The donors who made up the heart of the movement numbered fewer than 2,100 people— a good showing, but hardly a mass following. The movement's claim to popular support rested on its press activity and its many meetings. In both venues, the CRA fought the war of words essential to the cause of reform, transmuting Leopold's Congo Free State from philanthropic venture to untrammeled evil. They invoked justice, compassion, and rationality in the service of humanity in all its meanings: the shared human condition, the fellow-feeling that sprang from it, and the benevolence that this connection required. The meetings qualified Congo reform as a mass movement and generated a flood of resolutions as well as press attention. Large town's meetings called by local mayors and bigger demonstrations at the largest meeting venues in London, Liverpool, and elsewhere were most significant because they brought local political structures into supporting reform, helped the formation of auxiliaries, and brought together a more diverse audience than a small church meeting might. The Riley Brothers lantern slides indicate, however, that the discussion had to a degree escaped the discipline and control of the CRA.

The story of Congo reform was a single strand in the complex web of Edwardian Britain. The CRA allied with religious, missionary, humanitarian, commercial, and international groups to achieve its goals. While these groups necessarily had different priorities, viewed collectively, they contributed significantly to the cause. The Foreign Office, however, was the irreplaceable vehicle available to exert formal power in service of reform. Reformers informed, advised, badgered, and collaborated with the Foreign Office, but came to view diplomats as obstacles to reform. Having used Parliament to compel Lansdowne's hesitant cooperation, the reformers welcomed Grey into the Foreign Office in 1905. As this study has shown, they were right, in that Grey pursued reform for over seven years, and wrong, in that he was not subject to the CRA's discipline. Over time, Grey freed himself from dependence on the CRA, relying increasingly on his consuls, his representatives, and his staff for information and policy recommendations. Morel may have complained, "Victory would have been complete but for the sorry performances of the Foreign Office," but the triumph of 1913 was largely Grey's.[2] The CRA had become far less relevant to the conduct of policy since Morel went on the attack against Grey and the Foreign Office in June 1909.

Stripping away the fog of events and controversies, a chain of causality comes into focus leading to the 1913 declaration of victory. The activities of Fox Bourne, Stead, Guinness, and Morel, rallying public opinion to their side as manifested via the press, brought about the Samuel resolution of May 1903. To satisfy that resolution, Lansdowne ordered Casement to produce a report of conditions in the interior. This report had three notable consequences: it made the condemnation of Congo conditions the British government's official view, it sparked the CRA's formation, and it led Leopold to counterattack with his own Commission of Inquiry. Lansdowne, Wauters, and Cattier ensured that the Commission would be far more independent and impartial than Leopold intended. Its report was more momentous than Casement's, because its findings, as amplified and interpreted by Cattier, seriously embarrassed Belgium. This embarrassment, exacerbated into a serious domestic and international situation for Belgium by Leopold's arrogant assertion of prerogatives and the revelations of his unscrupulous methods, brought about the Belgian consensus in December 1906 that the country should annex the Congo, the very policy Grey had argued for since coming to office a year before. This decision led to the November 1908 annexation after lengthy delays to determine how much say Leopold would have

---

[2] "The Outlook," *Organ*, May 1910, 489–91, 496.

over the annexation terms and over the future Belgian Congo. The outcome was a financial settlement for Leopold, his projects, and his family, but complete government control over the Belgian Congo. The annexation's failure to come with reforms disappointed Grey and infuriated the CRA. Grey increased the pressure on Belgium through diplomatic means, both through diplomatic communications and the very public policy of not recognizing the annexation, and moved closer to taking forceful measures. Morel broke with Grey, ending the substantive influence of the CRA at the Foreign Office. Just after Grey obtained the Cabinet's concurrence to Thesiger's plan to go beyond diplomatic methods, Renkin announced a full reform plan on 29 October 1909, which went into effect from 1910 to 1912. The CRA's Parliamentary Committee endorsed Grey's policy of benevolent expectancy in 1910, which further reduced the CRA's role. By 1913, consular reports indicated that the reforms had been put into place in the entire country and that they had been largely, though not completely, effective.

This proposed chain of causality is in itself a story of the flow of power through formal and informal institutions. At the end of the chain lay a seemingly immovable object: a colonialist's hold on the Congo as a vehicle for generating money regardless of the human cost. None of the reformers had any direct way to dislodge the resulting system from the Congo. There were only two alternatives. Belgium could move against Leopold, but pressure from foreigners tended to entrench Belgians in defense of the king and his project. Alternatively, they needed the Foreign Office to prod the Berlin signatories to use their latent power or to wield Britain's formidable power alone, but Salisbury's and Lansdowne's Foreign Office refused to do so. The only power that could move a reluctant Foreign Office was Parliament, so the reformers undertook the publicity and lobbying campaign that led to the Samuel resolution. Public opinion, as expressed in the press and through energetic lobbying of individual MPs, became a powerful force in its own right at that moment. As they had hoped, the parliamentary resolution not only moved the Foreign Office to send Casement out, but triggered the whole chain of events described above. From 1905 on, the Foreign Office under Grey advocated Congo reform, making the Congo Reform Association's efforts to exercise power in the UK increasingly redundant and ultimately irrelevant. The chain of events, however, did what no British reformer could do; it brought about a consensus in Belgium that led to annexation. Artful pressure from the Foreign Office ensured that the reform program that followed would overturn Leopold's system and its consular monitoring helped ensure that Belgium would fully implement its own program.

As a history of the reform movement, this study has cast its leading figures in a different light. Grey, Fox Bourne, Guinness, Vandervelde, and Cattier share center stage with Morel and Casement. John and Alice Harris, recently proposed as the keys to a truly popular agitation that succeeded where Morel failed, appear as important contributors to a movement that did not, as it turned out, depend for its influence solely on its popular manifestations in meetings.

Decentering Morel does not mean belittling his importance, calling his strategies failures, or writing the story without him. He had by 1902 placed himself in the line of fire and remained there for the duration. His early insights into the nature of Leopold's regime became the center of the critique. The 1903 Samuel resolution owed more to Morel than to any other single activist. As the Congo Reform Association's leader, his unrelenting and effective dedication to the cause and mastery of relevant facts made that movement more notable than many of its contemporaries. More than any other single person, he molded the CRA's principles and practices. It was also Morel who condemned the organization to reduced influence and relevance in the corridors of power with his 1909 attack on the Foreign Office. The speakers at the Morel testimonial dinner in 1911 paid tribute to him in unmeasured terms, such as, "Mr Morel has represented and saved the reputation of Europe, the honour of England, and the soul of the Church," but we do not need to follow their lead in exaggerating his important role.[3] He was essential in the movement's early years, but if he had died or left the Congo Reform Association in 1906 or 1909, it would have continued, if in a different manner; that was the benefit of having an organization.

In developing a revised narrative of the Congo reform movement, this study has refuted some interpretations and demonstrated the importance of overlooked events. If the movement sits firmly in the humanitarian tradition, then it cannot be immune to the recent critiques of humanitarianism. In the past two decades, works by economists, political scientists, anthropologists, and historians have enhanced our understanding of the benefits and pitfalls of the interventions of third parties in humanitarian crises.[4] Government policy in one's own country can lead to unintended consequences, but when policy takes as its object peoples and circumstances an ocean away, the damage can be far greater, and the local people have fewer means of influencing its course. No matter how well-intentioned, overseas humanitarian action rests on assumptions about conditions, causes, and remedies based on the presumed superior knowledge, resources, and power of the humanitarians, leading to the

---

[3] Sylvester Horne, 29 May 1911, "The Public Presentation to Mr E.D. Morel," 10, http://www.archive.org/stream/publicpresentati00cromiala/publicpresentati00cromiala_djvu.txt.

[4] Among others: Alex de Waal, *Famine Crimes: Politics & the Disaster Relief Industry in Africa* (London: African Rights & the International African Institute, 1997); William Easterly, *The White Man's Burden* (New York: Penguin Press HC, 2006); Linda Polman, *The Crisis Caravan: What's Wrong with Humanitarian Aid?* (New York: Metropolitan Books, 2010); David Rieff, *A Bed for the Night,* (New York: Simon and Schuster, 2002); Fiona Terry, *Condemned to Repeat? The Paradox of Humanitarian Action* (Ithaca: Cornell University Press, 2002).

use of masked or naked deployments of power in service of a high-minded cause. Indeed, some humanitarian campaigns may have caused damage greater than the help they provided.[5]

This study has already discussed the core contradiction in the Congo reform movement: its espousal of rights for Africans in a colonial context. Reformers and imperialists came at this question from different directions. Morel, the advocate of native rights, and Flora Shaw Lugard, the advocate of ongoing imperial conquest and antagonist of Mary Kingsley, agreed on one important justification for European rule: only state control could prevent swaths of Africa from falling under the control of rogue Europeans who would use the vast disparity in military power to become warlords and exploit Africans ruthlessly—much as Leopold did.[6] Once they had convinced themselves of the necessity of European rule, they then showed how it could prove its worth. Morel argued that the duty of rule could justify itself only by increasing the well-being and happiness of the ruled. Lady Lugard, on the other hand, sought the justification for rule in the development of these countries by teaching the local people to work for the benefit of their European overlords, an argument reminiscent of Leopold's. Both Morel and Lugard believed they were arguing for civilizing or "regenerating" the colonized people under an inevitably imperial system. Opolot Okia has taken the activists to task for being against forced labor primarily because they could see how the arguments of Leopold and even Lady Lugard ultimately discredited colonialism.[7] The contrast between Morel and Lady Lugard makes it clear that this argument is, in a fundamental sense, correct. By judging colonial rule necessary, the reformers prioritized improving the lot of Africans living under it while more conventional imperialists primarily hoped to benefit the ruling Europeans. Both stances were paternalistic in the sense that they believed Europeans knew better than Africans what was good for them and should impose this vision by force if necessary.

The reformers in many ways were naive to think that European colonial regimes could rule beneficently without being subject to the inevitable abuses of power that could be as subtle as a fixed-price cocoa marketing board in the Gold Coast or as overt as the reintroduction of forced labor for commercial purposes in the Congo. Many critics, like Okia, echo Ivan Illich's 1971 critique of humanitarians as part of the system causing the damage.[8] It may be safer to say that because so few challenged colonialism at all, humanitarians and reformers

---

[5] Reiff, "Did Live Aid do More Harm than Good?" *Guardian*, 24 June 2005.

[6] Morel, "The Treatment of Native Races: The Heritage and Duty of the British People," *African Mail*, 2 May 1913, 307–10; Flora Lugard, "The Tropics of the Empire."

[7] Opolot Okia, "Forced Labor and Humanitarian Ideology in Kenya, 1911–1925" (PhD diss., West Virginia University, 2002), 282.

[8] De Waal, *Famine Crimes*, 5.

focused on improving its operation. For Africans the result was imperial rule no matter which side prevailed.

Alex de Waal, building on arguments by Amartya Sen, has argued that humanitarian aid (specifically for famines) is least likely to fail or betray its recipients when local people have political and civil rights and when the humanitarians reinforce local authority structures.[9] Local people had almost no participation in the Congo reform movement. Some fought their oppressors, of course, allowing Morel and the others to use frequent rebellions to highlight the regime's brutality. The people of the Congo gave their grievances, both real and exaggerated, to missionaries and investigators on the spot, and to judges and state officials. However, no European consulted them about remedies or let them debate the relative merits of the Belgian solution versus an international condominium. Belgian annexation, while better than Leopold's rule, developed its own forms of coercion and exploitation that surely would not have had the support of the people had their new overlords consulted them. This highlights the shortcomings in the CRA's vision, accepting as it did the necessity of colonial rule.

At least one group saw further than the CRA to a full set of civil rights for people under imperial rule. Casement, Fox Bourne, and Buxton all participated in the forward-looking Subject Races International Committee of 1907–18, which urged rights for people under imperial rule and proposed that subject peoples have access to the International Tribunal in The Hague so that they could seek justice.[10] The Subject Races Committee represented the united efforts of several organizations, including the Aborigines' Protection Society, Anti-Slavery Society, Egyptian Committee, Friends of Russian Freedom, Georgian Relief Committee, International Arbitration and Peace Association, National Council of Ireland, and Positivists, but its ideas seem to have made little impact on the discourse on colonialism.[11] Two of its main figures, Florence and Henry Dryhurst, had strong ties to Russian anarchists and to the Socialist International, which may have undermined the group's ability to speak to power. Socialists were the main exception to the general acceptance of colonialism. Their calls for the end of all colonial rule did not amount to much; they were seldom near the levers of power in these years.

The Congo reformers' answer to the contradictions simmering below the surface of their arguments was to keep their focus relentlessly on the specific case of Leopold's system of rule which had produced so many outrageous

---

[9] De Waal, *Famine Crimes*, 2–3, 7, 49.

[10] *The Survey* 27, no. 1 (7 October 1911): 1008–9, http://books.google.com/books?id=_HoXAAAAYAAJ&pg=PA1008; "Official Report of the Seventeenth Universal Congress of Peace," 1908 (London: National Council of Peace Societies, 1909), 249–52, http://www.archive.org/stream/officialreportof00univ/officialreportof00univ_djvu.txt.

[11] Sandi E. Cooper, *Patriotic Pacifism* (New York: Oxford University Press, 1991), 179.

consequences. As we have seen, it took 17 years from the start of the movement until the reformers could be reasonably sure that the ultimate colonial evil had ended. For the people of the Congo and the reformers themselves, the fight was worth it. In the words of one analyst:

> For all its failings and limitations, [humanitarianism] represents what is decent in an indecent world. Its core assumptions—solidarity, a fundamental sympathy for victims, and an antipathy for oppressors and exploiters—represent those rare moments of grace when we are at our best.[12]—David Rieff

---

[12] Rieff, "Humanitarianism in Crisis," *Foreign Affairs* 81, no. 6 (November–December 2002): 121.

Appendix I—About the Donor Database

The donor database combines the following Congo Reform Association donor lists published in the *Organ*, excising duplicated donations. Morel listed donations in the order received, and correspondence provides precise dates, permitting analysis over time.

25 Jan. 1904—22 Mar. 1904	Typewritten list, F4:274–6
23 Mar. 1904—31 Oct. 1904	*Organ*, June 1909, 283–90
23 Mar. 1904—17 Sep. 1908[1]	*Organ*, June 1909, 283–90
17 Sep. 1907—17 Sep. 1908[2]	*Organ*, September 1908, 4–6
1 Apr. 1907—31 Mar. 1908: London Auxiliary[3]	*Rising Tide*, April 1908, 25–8
18 Sep. 1908—25 Mar 1909[4]	
18 Sep.—29 Oct. 1908	*Organ*, April 1909, 181
1 April—29 Oct. 1908[5]	*Organ*, April 1909, 181–2
30 Oct. 1908—25 Mar. 1909	*Organ*, April 1909, 183–8
25 Mar. 1909—15 Jun. 1909	*Organ*, June 1909, 291–2
15 June 1909—13 Dec. 1909	*Organ*, January 1910, 483–7
13 Dec. 1909—31 Mar. 1910	*Organ*, April 1910, 605–8
1 Apr. 1910—30 Sep. 1910	*Organ*, October 1910, 657–9
1 Oct. 1910—31 Mar. 1911	*Organ*, May 1911, 701–4
1 Apr. 1911—30 Sep. 1911	*Organ*, October 1911, 743–4
1 Oct. 1911—31 July 1912	*Organ*, August 1912, 856–9
1 Aug 1912—20 Mar. 1913	*Organ*, April 1913, 974–5
21 Mar. 1913—23 Jun. 1913	*Organ*, July 1913, 1044

---

[1] Duplicates removed to create 1 Nov. 1904–17 Sep. 1907.

[2] The total given in the *Organ* is £1,564 but the total of all donations is £1,552.

[3] The London Auxiliary operated in three modes. In the 1906–07 fiscal year, the Auxiliary reported its donors only by their initials and used their donations to fund itself. As with all other auxiliaries, these donations are not tracked here. From 1 April 1907 to 31 March 1908, London donors were recorded in full and all surplus ended up in the coffers of the central CRA; those donations are included here. After 31 March 1908, on Morel's instructions, all London donations were forwarded on to the central treasurer, Harold Brabner, and tracked there.

[4] Starting date printed incorrectly in the *Organ* as 1907; the information did not include 1907.

[5] London.

The donor list has been transcribed and verified to the best of my ability, but this does not eliminate all chance of keying error. The second step was to accumulate each person's donations where possible. In many cases this was obvious, but for questionable cases, donations were united under donors only if there was a good argument for doing so; otherwise they were left separate. Admittedly, this was a judgment call, as one can see from looking at the three listings for Mrs Linscott, two of which probably should have been combined (see also Mrs Little). Thus, the actual number of donors may be somewhat smaller than the numbers reported here.

The linking of donors to religions, occupations, and so on, was done based on various research tools at my disposal, many of which appear at the end of this appendix. Gender and clergy status were almost always apparent from the lists. However, assigning further demographic information was impossible for common names, or names that did not appear in any of my sources. Thus, of 30 donors with the last name Smith, I dared assign information only to two: Reverend Kenred Smith, a unique name active in the CRA, and Samuel Smith, MP. However, for some less common names I assigned demographic information on the assumption that there could be only one person by that name likely to donate to the CRA. This was a judgment call and errors may have occurred.

Shillings and pence have been converted to decimal pounds to facilitate sorting and analysis, counting 20 shillings to the pound and 12 pence to the shilling.

Where available, dates reflect when donation was received by Morel. Donations that went straight to Brabner were receipted by him; I have not found that receipt book. However, all the reports presented donations in the order received (except the initial 1904 list and the London list of 1907–08), so the chronology can be deduced using the dates we do have from Morel's records.

The median donation was £1, but £2 for the religiously identifiable; people who were identifiable by religion were more likely to be more prominent in one way or another than people whose religion was not identifiable using the sources at my disposal.

The donor database and associated files are too large and cumbersome to include here but are available for inspection electronically at www.ashgate.com/isbn/9781472436474.

Partial list of research tools for demographic and biographical information:

Oxford Dictionary of National Biography (multiple editions)
Who's Who (multiple editions)
Who Was Who (multiple editions)
Hazell's Annual (London: Hazell, Watson & Viney Ltd., 1903, 1910, 1911)

American Friends Peace Conference http://books.google.com/books?id=MVUNAAAAYAAJ

Extracts from the Minutes and Proceedings of the yearly meeting of Friends (1905), http://books.google.com/books?id=uGAoAAAAYAAJ

The British Friend 6, http://books.google.com/books?id=oEgrAAAAYAAJ

The descendants of John Backhouse, yeoman, of Moss Side (London: Chiswick Press, 1894), http://books.google.com/books?id=8vQ7AAAAMAAJ

Low's handbook to the charities of London (London: Sampson Low, Marston & Company, Ltd., 1904) http://books.google.com/books?id=n7NbAAAAQAAJ

Victor Plarr, *Men and Women of the Time: A Dictionary of Contemporaries*, (London: George Routledge and Sons, 1899), http://books.google.com/books?id=GigaAAAAYAAJ

Edward Walford, editor, *The Windsor Peerage for 1893*, (London: Chatto & Windus, 1893) http://books.google.com/books?id=ick-AAAAYAAJ

The Popular Guide to the House of Commons, Pall Mall Gazette Extra, February 1906. (London: The Pall Mall Press, 1906), http://books.google.com/books?id=xYIMAAAAYAAJ

The Peerage website, http://thepeerage.com

Appendix II—Congo Reform Association Auxiliaries[1]

Dates given are dates of founding.

1. Liverpool—January 1906
2. London—12 April 1906 ** (merged into central organization November 1908)
3. Stroud—August 1906 or later
4. Northumberland and North Durham (Newcastle)—2 October 1906
5. South Devon (Plymouth)—February 1907 [2]
6. North Devon (Exeter)—May 1907
7. Bristol—3 May 1907
8. Hull—20 June 1907
9. Bournemouth—9 July 1907
10. Manchester and Salford—2 July 1907
11. Brondesbury—after October 1907
12. Hampstead—November 1907
13. Portsmouth—after October 1907 * (not on October 1909 or 1910 list)
14. West Hartlepool—13 December 1907 * (not on 1910 list)
15. Newport and West Monmouthshire—February 1907 **
16. Edinburgh—February 1908
17. Lymington—after October 1907 * (not on October 1909 or 1910 list)
18. Leeds—15 June 1909
19. Bolton—July 1909
20. Redditch—July 1909
21. Oxford—Feb 1910
22. Women's Auxiliary—January 1909 **

* Lasted less than one year.
** Not mentioned in the final list of CRA Auxiliaries in 1913 though there is evidence (donations, representation) that they still existed.

---

[1] Grant, 75, updated to reflect documentation in the Morel files regarding finances, representation on Executive Committee, and reports in *Official Organ*.

[2] There was also listed a Devon County Auxiliary, but this seems to have been a vehicle for Lord Clifford of Chudleigh. The North and South Devon auxiliaries seem to have done the work.

Select Bibliography

Archives

Aborigines' Protection Society papers. Rhodes House, Oxford.
Asquith papers. Bodleian Library, Oxford.
Balfour papers, British Library, London.
Baptist Union and Baptist Missionary Society, Angus Library, Regents Park College, Oxford.
Baring, Evelyn (Lord Cromer). Papers. British Library, London.
British and Foreign Anti-Slavery Society, Rhodes House, Oxford.
Buxton, Sidney. Papers. British Library, London.
Buxton, Travers. Papers. Rhodes House, Oxford.
Cadbury, William. Papers. University of Birmingham.
Campbell-Bannerman papers. British Library, London.
Collier, Robert (2nd Baron Monkswell). Bodleian Library, Oxford.
Davidson papers. Lambeth Palace Library, London.
Dilke papers. British Library, London.
Emmott papers. Nuffield College Library, Oxford.
Gladstone, Herbert. Papers. British Library, London.
Harris, John Hobbis. Papers. Rhodes House, Oxford.
Holt papers. City Library, Liverpool.
Holt papers. Maritime Museum Archives, Liverpool.
Liverpool Chamber of Commerce Papers. City Library, Liverpool.
Morel papers. British Library of Political and Economic Science, London School of Economics. Regions Beyond Missionary Union, film, Harvard University, Cambridge.
Ripon papers. British Library, London.
Samuel papers. Parliamentary Archives, London.
Strachey papers. Parliamentary Archives, London.
Unwin, Jane Cobden. Papers. British Library, London.
British National Archives, Kew.
CAB 37/91–115
CAB 41/23–38
FO367
FO371
FO881
FO10

Empire Online, Adam Matthew Digital Archive, http://www.empire.amdigital.co.uk/Documents/Details/Congo%20Balolo%20Mission%20Record%2019041907.

Newspapers and Periodicals

Aborigines' Friend and Aborigines' Protection Society annual reports.
African Mail
African World
Anti-Slavery Reporter
Anti-Slavery Reporter and Aborigines Friend
Congo Balolo Mission Record
Congo News Letter
Hazell's Annual
India-Rubber Journal
India Rubber World
Journal of the Manchester Geographical Society
Liverpool Daily Post and Mercury
Liverpool Journal of Commerce
Manchester Guardian
New York Times
Official Organ of the Congo Reform Association
Regions Beyond
Review of Reviews
Revue de l'Université de Bruxelles
The New Age
The Speaker
The Spectator
The Tablet
The Times
United Service Magazine
West African Mail
Whitaker's Almanack

Government Publications

British Documents on Foreign Affairs: Reports and Papers from the Foreign Office Confidential Print, Part I: From the Mid-Nineteenth Century to the First World War: Series F: Europe, 1848–1914. Vol. 5, *The Low Countries II:*

Belgium, 1893–1914, edited by David Stevenson. Bethesda, MD: University Publications of America, 1987.

Parliamentary Debates, fourth and fifth series.

Report of the Parliamentary Select Committee on Aboriginal Tribes (British Settlements), Reprinted, with Comments, by the Aborigines' Protection Society. London: William Ball and Hatchard & Son, 1837.

US Department of State, *Papers Related to the Foreign Relations of the United States, Part 1, 1909.* http://books.google.com/books?id=dhNHAQAAIAAJ&pg=PA89.

Foreign Office. Africa No. 8 (1896) C. 8276.

———. Misc. (Africa) No. 459 (June 1898). C. 8649.

———. Africa No. 10 (1903) Cd. 1754.

———. Africa No. 14 (1903) Cd. 1809.

———. Africa No. 1 (1904) Cd. 1933.

———. Africa No. 7 (1904) Cd. 2097.

———. Africa No. 1 (1905) Cd. 2333.

———. Africa No. 1 (1906) Cd. 3002.

———. Africa No. 1 (1907) Cd. 3450.

———. Africa No. 1 (1908) Cd. 3880.

———. Africa No. 2 (1908) Cd. 4079.

———. Africa No. 3 (1908) Cd. 4135.

———. Africa No. 4 (1908) Cd. 4178.

———. Africa No. 5 (1908) Cd. 4396.

———. Africa No. 1 (1909) Cd. 4466.

———. Africa No. 2 (1909) Cd. 4701.

———. Congo No. 1 (1911) Cd. 5559.

———. Africa No. 2 (1911) Cd. 5860.

———. Africa No. 1 (1913) Cd. 6606.

———. Africa No. 3 (1913) Cd. 6802.

Contemporary Published Sources: Books, Pamphlets, and Articles

Anonymous. *An Answer to Mark Twain*, 1907.

Anonymous. "The Congo Free State." A Manuscript from the American Philosophical Society, translated by Melody R. Herr. No date.

Belloc, Hilaire. "Thoughts about Modern Thought." *New Age*, 7 December 1907, 108–10.

———. "The Recess and the Congo." *The New Age*, 8 August 1908, 283.

Boulger, Demetrius. *The Congo State is not a Slave State* London: S. Low, Marston, 1903.

Bourne, Henry Richard Fox. *The Aborigines Protection Society: Chapters in its History*. London: P.S. King, 1899.

———. *The Aborigines Protection Society: Its Aims and Methods*. London: P.S. King, 1900.

———. "The Congo Free State." *The Imperial and Asiatic Quarterly Review and Oriental and Colonial Record*, ser. 3, no. 11 (July 1901): 86–100.

———. *Civilisation in Congoland: A Story of International Wrong-doing*. London: P.S. King, 1903.

Burrows, Guy and Edgar Canisius. *The Curse of Central Africa*. London: R.A. Everett & Co., 1903. http://books.google.com/books?id=JuUqAAAAYAAJ.

Castelein, A. *The Congo State: Its Origins, Rights and Duties: The Charges of its Accusers*. 1907. Reprint, New York: Negro University Press, 1969.

Cattier, Félicien. *Droit et Administration de l'EIC*. Brussels: Larcier, 1898.

———. *Étude Sur la Situation de l'État Indépendant du Congo*. Brussels: Larcier, 1906.

Chadwick, W.J. *Magic Lantern Manual*. London: Frederick Warne & Co., 1878.

Congo Free State, The. *Congo: A Report of the Commission of Enquiry Appointed by the Congo Free State Government*. New York: G.P. Putnam's Sons, 1906.

Congo Reform Association. *Memorial on the Present Phase of the Congo Question*. 1912.

Cromer, Edward Winton, Arthur Conan Doyle, George White, C. Silvester Horne, and Alice Stopford Green. *The Public Presentation to Mr. E.D. Morel*. 1911. http://www.archive.org/details/publicpresentati00cromiala.

Daniels, John et al., *Evidence in the Congo case: Statement in Reply to Professor Starr's Articles in the Chicago tribune*. Boston: Congo Reform Association, 1907.

Dorman, Marcus R.P. *A Journal of a Tour in the Congo Free State*. Echo Library, 2007. Reprint, London: Kegan Paul, Trench, Trübner & Co., Ltd, 1905.

Doyle, Arthur Conan. *Crime of the Congo*. 1909. Reprint, Honolulu: University Press of the Pacific, 2004.

Fédération pour la Défense des Intérêts Belges à L'Étranger. "Mr. Morel's Errors." Brussels: Travaux Publics, 1904.

Gilder, Richard Watson. "Glave's Last Letter and His Death." *Century Magazine*, September 1897, 796–8.

Glave, Edward James. "Cruelty in the Congo Free State." *Century Magazine*, September 1897, 699–714.

Goldman, Charles Sydney. "Introduction." In *The Empire and the Century: A Series of Essays on Imperial Problems and Possibilities*, edited by Charles S. Goldman, xi–xxiii. London: J. Murray, 1905. http://books.google.com/books?id=-hELAAAAYAAJ.

Grey, Sir Edward. *Twenty-Five Years, 1892–1916*. New York: Frederick Stokes Company, 1925.

———. *Speeches on Foreign Affairs*, edited by Paul Knaplund. London: Allen and Unwin, 1931.
Guinness, Dr. H. Grattan, M.D. "Belgian Inhumanity in the Congo." *Missionary Review* XXVI (July 1903), 530–2.
———. *These Thirty Years*. London: Regions Beyond Missionary Union, 1903.
———. "The Congo Problem" "The Condition of the Congo Free State." *Regions Beyond*, February 1904, 39–40.
———. "The Red Flower of Congo Civilisation." *Regions Beyond*, January 1904, 8–9.
———. *"Not Unto Us:" A Record of Twenty-one Years' Missionary Service*. London: RBMU, 1908. http://books.google.com/books?id=N74NAAAAQAAJ.
———. *The Congo Crisis: 1908*. London: RBMU Publications Department, 1908.
Guinness, Dr H. Grattan, M.D. and Bokwala (A Congo Resident). *Bokwala, The Story of A Congo Victim*. London: The Religious Tract Society, 1910. http://ia301533.us.archive.org/2/items/BokwalaTheStoryOfACongoVictim/Bokwala2_text.pdf.
Harris, John H. *Cocoa Production in West Africa*. 1911.
———. *Present Conditions in the Congo*. 1911.
———. *Dawn in Darkest Africa*. London: Smith, Elder, 1912.
Harrison, Frederic. "Empire and Humanity." *National and Social Problems*. New York: The Macmillan Company, 1908.
Herbert Fry's Royal Guide to the London Charities, edited by John Lane. London: Chatto & Windus, 1917. http://www.victorianlondon.org/charities/charities.htm.
Hobson, J.A. "Free Trade and Foreign Policy." *Contemporary Review*, no. 74 (August 1898), 167–80.
———. *Imperialism: A Study*. London: J. Nisbet & Co., 1902.
Johnston, Sir Harry Hamilton, Lawson Forfeitt, and Emil Torday, *George Grenfell and the Congo*. Vol. 2. London: Hutchinson & Co., 1908.
Keltie, Sir John Scott. *The Partition of Africa*, 2nd ed. London: E. Stanford, 1895.
Kingsley, Mary. *West African Studies*. London: Macmillan, 1901.
Lugard, Lady Flora. "The Tropics of the Empire." In *The Empire and the Century*, edited by Charles Sydney Goldman, 817–26. London: J. Murray, 1905. http://books.google.com/books?id=-hELAAAAYAAJ.
Lugard, Lord Frederick D. "West African Possessions and Administrations." In *The Empire and the Century,* edited by Charles Sydney Goldman, 835–60. London: J. Murray, 1905. http://books.google.com/books?id=-hELAAAAYAAJ.
MacDonnell, John de Courcy. *King Leopold II: His Rule in Belgium and the Congo*. London: Cassell, 1905.
Mackintosh, Catherine W. *The Life Story of Henry Grattan Guinness, M.D., F.R.G.S.* London: Regions Beyond Missionary Union, 1916.

Masoin, L.F. *Histoire de l'État Indépendant du Congo*. Namur, 1912.
Milner, Viscount. *Constructive Imperialism*. London: National Review, 1908.
Morel, E.D. *Affairs of West Africa*. 1902. Reprint, London, Frank Cass & Co. Ltd, 1968.
———. "The Belgian Curse in Africa." *Contemporary Review*, March 1902: 358–77.
———. *The Black Man's Burden: The White Man in Africa from the Fifteenth Century to World War I*. 1902. Reprint, New York: Monthly Review Press, 1969.
———. *The Congo Slave State*. Liverpool: John Richardson & Sons, 1903.
———. "The "Commercial" Aspect of the Congo Question." *Journal of the Royal African Society* 3, no. 12 (July 1904): 430–48.
———. *The Treatment of Women and Children in the Congo State 1895–1904. An Appeal to the Women of the United States of America*. 1904.
———. *King Leopold's Rule in Africa*. London: William Heinemann, 1904.
———. *Red Rubber: The Story of the Rubber Slave Trade Flourishing on the Congo in the Year of Grace 1906*. 1906. Reprint, New York: Haskell House, 1970.
———. "The Congo Reform Association and Mr. Belloc." *The New Age*, 21 December 1907, 149–50.
———. *The Congo Tragedy: An Appeal to Parliament*. 1907.
———. "How Long Are We to Wait?" 1907.
———. "More Official Evidence from the Congo." 1907.
———. "Recent Evidence from the Congo." 1907.
———. *The Stannard Case*. 1907.
———. *Great Britain and the Congo: The Pillage of the Congo Basin*. London: Smith Elder, 1909. Reprint, New York: Howard Fertig, 1969.
———. "The Congo Crime." reprinted from *Sunday School Chronicle*.
Morel, E.D., anonymously. "The Belgians in Africa." *Pall Mall Gazette*, 22 February 1894.
———. "A Word for the Congo State." *Pall Mall Gazette*, 19 July, 1897.
———. "Belgium and the Congo State." *Speaker* 1, no. 25 (24 March 1900): 668–9.
———. "Letter to the Editor: Belgium and the Congo State." *Speaker* 2, no. 27 (7 April 1900): 13–14.
———. "Letter to the Editor: The Congo Free State." *Speaker* 2, no. 30 (28 April 1900): 101–2.
———. "The Congo Scandal—I. The *Domaine Prive* and How It Was Created." *Speaker* 2, no. 43 (28 July 1900): 463–4.
———. "The Congo Scandal—II. The Congo Scandal—The Rubber Taxes—How They Are Applied." *Speaker* 2, no. 44 (4 August 1900): 487–8.
———. "The Congo Scandal—III. The Rubber 'Companies' on the Domaine Privé." *Speaker* 2, no. 47 (25 August 1900): 571–2.
———. "The Congo Scandal—IV. The Alleged 'Development' and 'Prosperity' of the State." *Speaker* 2, no. 48 (1 Sept. 1900): 595–7.

———. "The Congo Scandal—V. Red Rubber." *Speaker* 3, no. 53 (6 October 1900): 15–17. http://books.google.com/books?id=B_wnAAAAYAAJ&pg=PA15.

———. "The Congo Scandal—VI. Responsibility and Remedy." *Speaker* 3, no. 61 (1 December 1900): 228–9. http://books.google.com/books?id=B_wnAAAAYAAJ&pg=RA1-PA228.

Mountmorres, William Geoffrey Bouchard de Montmorency. *The Congo Independent State: A Report on a Voyage of Enquiry*. London: Williams and Norgate, 1906.

Oldham, Joseph Houldsworth. *Christianity and the Race Problem*. New York: George H. Doran, 1924.

Olivier, Sidney. *White Capital and Coloured Labour*. London: Independent Labour Party, 1906.

Norman, C.H., "Drifting on the Congo." *The New Age*, 7 March 1908, 365–6.

———. "The Congo Situation." *The New Age*, 27 June 1908, 166.

———. "More Congo Papers" *The New Age*, 29 August 1908, 344.

Phillimore, G.G., The Congo State: A Review of the International Position." *Law Magazine and Review*, 5th series, 29, no. 385 (August 1904): 385–405.

Phillips, Henry Jr, "An Account of the Congo Independent State." *Proceedings of the American Philosophical Society* 26, no. 130 (July–December 1889): 459–76.

"Report of the proceedings of the conference of African merchants on the Congo free state and import duties." Manchester: Manchester Press Company, 1890.

Russell, Robert Howard. "Glave's Career." *Century Magazine*, October 1895, 864–8.

Scrivener, Rev. A., "The Condition of the Congo Free State." *Regions Beyond*, February 1904: 41–5.

Sheppard, William H. *Presbyterian Pioneers in Congo*. Richmond, VA: Presbyterian Committee of Publication, 1917.

Spencer, Herbert. "Imperialism and Slavery." In *Facts and Comments*, 157–71. New York: D. Appleton and Company, 1902.

Spender, Harold. "The Great Congo Iniquity." *Contemporary Review* 90, no. 487 (July 1906): 43–55.

———. "The Congo Scandal." 1907.

Speyer, Herbert. *Comment nous gouvernerons le Congo; Étude critique du projet de loi coloniale organique suivie du texte proposé par le gouvernement*. Bruxelles, Lamberty, 1907. http://www.archive.org/details/commentnousgouv00speygoog.

Stacpoole, H. de Vere. *The Pools of Silence*. New York: Duffield & Co., 1910.

Starr, Frederick. *The Truth about the Congo*. Chicago: Forbes & Co., 1907.

Stead, W.T. *Annual Index of Periodicals and Photographs*. London: Mowbray House, 1891.

———. Review of *Affairs of West Africa and Civilisation in Congoland*. *Review of Reviews* 27, no. 158 (14 February 1903): 183–7. http://books.google.com/books?vid=HARVARD32044092820927&printsec=titlepage#v=onepage&q=&f=false.

———. "Leopold, Emperor of the Congo." *The American Review of Reviews*, July 1903. http://www.attackingthedevil.co.uk/reviews/congo.php.

———. "A Year on the Congo: Mrs. French Sheldon." *Review of Reviews* 30, no. 181 (January 1905): 22–3. http://books.google.com/books?vid=HARVARD32044092820968&printsec=titlepage#v=onepage&q=&f=false.

———. "Ought King Leopold To Be Hanged: The Rev. John H. Harris." *Review of Reviews* 32, no. 189 (September 1905): 246–8.

———. "The Saviour of the Congo: The Quarterly's Tribute to E. D. Morel." *Review of Reviews* 33, no.194 (February 1906): 166.

———. "Belgium and the Congo." *Review of Reviews* 36, no. 216 (December 1907): 588.

———. "The Tchinovnik of the Foreign Office." *Review of Reviews* 36, no. 216 (December 1907): 567–75. http://books.google.com/books?id=gHIAAAAAYAAJ&pg=RA1-PA566.

———. "If Belgium Annexes the Congo: What Then?" *Review of Reviews* 37, no. 217 (January 1908): 55.

———. Congo discussion, *Review of Reviews* 37, no. 219 (March 1908): 228.

———. "After Twenty-one Years." *Review of Reviews* 43, no. 253 (January 1911): 6.

Thesiger, Wilfred G. "How it Strikes an Outsider." *Kasai Herald*, 1 January 1909, 5–6.

Twain, Mark. *King Leopold's Soliloquy*. Boston: P.R. Warren Co., 1905.

Vermeersch, Father Arthur. *La Question Congolaise*, 1906. http://books.google.com/books?id=iXnvUweKbi0C.

———. *Les Destinées du Congo Belge*, 1906. http://books.google.com/books?id=BSgUAAAAIAAJ.

Wack, Henry Wellington. *The Story of the Congo Free State*. New York: Putnam, 1905.

Weeks, Rev. John H. *Among Congo Cannibals*. Philadelphia: Lippincott, 1913.

Williams, George Washington. *An Open Letter to His Serene Majesty Leopold II, King of the Belgians and Sovereign of the Independent State of Congo*. 1890.

Unpublished Secondary Sources: Dissertations, Theses, and Conference Papers

Burroughs, Robert. "Britain's Travelling Eyewitnesses: Narratives of the New Slaveries, 1884–1916." PhD diss., Nottingham Trent University, 2006.

Echenberg, Myron. "The British Attitude toward the Congo Question, with particular reference to the work of E.D. Morel and the CRA, 1903–1913." MA thesis, McGill University, 1964.

Forth, Aidan. "The Politics of Philanthropy: the Congo Terror Regime and the British Public Sphere, 1884–1914." MA thesis, Queen's University (Kingston), 2006.

Gertzel, Cherry Joan. "John Holt: A British Merchant in West Africa in the Era of Imperialism." PhD thesis, Nuffield College, Oxford, 1959.

Hunt, Nancy Rose. "A Nervous Colony: Post-Terror Biopolitics and Belgian Policing of Religious Movements in Congo's Equateur." Paper presented at the University of Michigan Anthropology and History Workshop, Ann Arbor, Michigan, 1 April 2008.

Martens, Daisy S. "A history of European penetration and African reaction in the Kasai region of Zaire, 1880–1908." PhD thesis, Simon Fraser University, 1980.

McStallworth, Paul. "The United States and the Congo Question, 1884–1914." PhD diss., Ohio State, 1955.

Middleton, Ben. "Geographies of Conscience: Britain and the Movement for Congo Reform." Undergraduate thesis, Plymouth University, 2011.

Nworah, Kingsley Kenneth Dike. "Humanitarian Pressure-Groups and British Attitudes to West Africa, 1895–1915." PhD thesis, University of London, 1966.

Osborne, Jr, John Bremner. "Sir Edward Grey, the British Consular Staff, and the Congo Reform Campaign." PhD Thesis, Rutgers University, 1971.

Piccolino, Giula. "La Civilizzazione A Ritroso: La Questione Congolese E Le Sue Ripercussioni In Italia." Thesis, Universita' Degli Studi Di Firenze, 2004.

Renwald, Mary Casilda. "Humanitarianism and British Colonial Policy." Unpublished Doctoral thesis, St. Louis, 1934.

Richardson, Kip. "Profits of Religion: Anticlericalism and the Labor Movement." Paper presented at the American Historical Association conference, Boston, 7 January 2011.

Swaisland, Henry Charles. "The Aborigines Protection Society and British Southern and West Africa." Oxford D.Phil. Thesis, 1968.

Willmington, Susan M.K. "The Activities of the Aborigines Protection Society as a Pressure Group on the Formulation of Colonial Policy 1868–1880." PhD thesis, University of Wales, 1973.

Wilson, Ann Marie. "Taking Liberties Abroad: Americans and International Humanitarian Advocacy, 1821–1914." PhD diss., Harvard University, 2010.

Wuliger, Robert. "The Idea of Economic Imperialism with Special Reference to the Life and Work of E.D. Morel." PhD thesis, Univ. of London, 1953.

Published Secondary Sources

Anstey, Roger T. *King Leopold's Legacy*. New York: Oxford University Press, 1966.

———. "The Congo Rubber Atrocities—A Case Study." *African Historical Studies* 4, no. 1 (1971): 59–76.

———. "The Pattern of British Abolitionism." In *Anti-Slavery, Religion and Reform*, edited by Christine Bolt and Seymour Drescher, 1–37. Hamden CT: Archon Books, 1980.

Ascherson, Neal. *The King Incorporated: Leopold the Second and the Congo*. 1963. Reprint, London: Granta Books, 1999.

Auld, John W. "The Liberal Pro-Boers," *Journal of British Studies* 14, no. 2 (May 1975): 78–101.

Bain, William. *Between Anarchy and Society: Trusteeship and the Obligations of Power*. Oxford: Oxford University Press, 2003.

Bass, Jeff D. "Imperial Alterity and Identity Slippage: The Sin of Becoming 'Other' in Edmund D. Morel's King Leopold's Rule in Africa." *Rhetoric & Public Affairs* 13, no. 2 (Summer 2010): 281–308.

Bauer, Ludwig. *Leopold, the Unloved: King of the Belgians and of Wealth*. Translated by Eden and Cedar Paul. Boston: Little, Brown, and Co., 1935.

Bebbington, D.W. *The Nonconformist Conscience: Chapel and Politics 1870–1914*. London: George Allen and Unwin, 1982.

———. *Evangelicalism in Britain: A History from the 1730s to the 1980s*. Grand Rapids, MI: Baker House Books, 1989.

———. "Atonement, Sin, and Empire, 1880–1914." In *The Imperial Horizons of British Protestant Missions, 1880–1914*, edited by Andrew Porter, 14–31. Grand Rapids, MI: Eerdmans, 2003.

Benedetto, Robert. *Presbyterian Reformers in Central Africa*. New York: E.J. Brill, 1996.

Birkett, Dea. *Mary Kingsley: Imperial Adventuress*. London: Macmillan, 1992.

Black, Jeremy. "The Press: Jeremy Black Charts its Growth in Victorian Britain." *History Review* (March 1998): 31–3.

Blom, Philipp. *The Vertigo Years: Europe 1900–1914*. New York: Basic Books, 2008.

Boisseau, Tracey Jean. *White Queen: May French-Sheldon and the Imperial Origins of American Feminist Identity*. Bloomington, IN: Indiana University Press, 2004.

Brooks, David. *The Age of Upheaval: Edwardian Politics, 1899–1914*. New York: St Martin's Press, 1995.

Brown, Christopher Leslie. *Moral Capital: Foundations of British Abolitionism*. Durham: University of North Carolina Press, 2006.

Burroughs, Robert. "In Conrad's Footsteps: Critical Approaches to Africanist Travel Writing." *Literature Compass* 3, no. 4 (2006): 924–39.

———. "The Travelling Apologist: May French-Sheldon in the Congo Free State (1903–4)." *Studies in Travel Writing* 14, no. 2 (June 2010): 135–57.

———. *Travel Writing and Atrocities: Eyewitness Accounts of Colonialism in the Congo, Angola, and the Putumayo*. New York: Routledge, 2011.

Castryck, Geert. "Whose History is History: Singularities and Dualities of the Public Debate on Belgian Colonialism." In *Europe and the World in European Historiography*, edited by Csaba Levai, 71–88. Pisa: Edizioni Plus—Pisa University Press, 2006. http://www.cliohres.net/books/6/castryck.pdf.

Claeys, Gregory. *Imperial Sceptics: British Critics of Empire, 1850–1920*. Cambridge: Cambridge University Press, 2010.

Cline, Catherine A. "The Church and the Movement for Congo Reform." *Church History* 32, no. 1 (March 1963): 46–56.

———. "E.D. Morel and the Crusade against the Foreign Office." *The Journal of Modern History* 39, no. 2 (June 1967): 126–37.

———. *E.D. Morel 1873–1924*. Belfast: Blackstaff Press, 1980.

Conley, Joseph F. *Drumbeats that Changed the World: A History of the Regions Beyond Missionary Union and the West Indies Mission, 1873–1999*. Pasadena, CA: William Carey Library, 2000.

Cookey, Sylvanus John Sodienye, *Britain and the Congo Question, 1885–1913*. London: Longmans, Green and Co. Ltd, 1968.

Cooper, Frederick, "Conditions Analogous to Slavery." In *Beyond Slavery*, edited by Frederick Cooper, Thomas Holt, and Rebecca Scott, 107–50. Chapel Hill, NC: University of North Carolina Press, 2000.

Curtin, Philip D. *The Image of Africa*. Madison, WI: University of Wisconsin Press, 1964.

Davidoff, Leonore and Catherine Hall. *Family Fortunes: Men and Women of the English Middle Class, 1780–1850*. Chicago: University of Chicago Press, 1987.

Davies, Peter N. *Trading in West Africa*. London: Croom Helm, 1976.

———. *Sir Alfred Jones*. London: Europa Publications, 1978.

Davis, David Brion. "Reflections on Abolitionism and Ideological Hegemony." *The American Historical Review* 92, no. 4 (October 1987): 797–812.

de St Moulin, Léon. "What is known of the demographic history of Zaire since 1885?" In *Demography from Scanty Evidence: Central Africa in the Colonial Era*, edited by Bruce Fetter, 299–325. Boulder, CO: L. Rienner Publishers, 1990.

Dixon, Thomas. *The Invention of Altruism: Making Moral Meanings in Victorian Britain*. Oxford: Oxford University Press, 2008.

Dumoulin, Michel. *Léopold II, Un Roi Génocidaire?* Brussels: Academie Royale de Belgique, 2005.

Dunn, Kevin C. *Imagining the Congo: The International Relations of Identity.* New York: Palgrave Macmillan, 2003.

Eckley, Grace. *Maiden Tribute, A Life of W. T. Stead.* Philadelphia, PA: Xlibris, 2007.

Edgerton, Robert. *The Troubled Heart of Africa: A History of the Congo.* New York: St Martin's Press, 2002.

Emerson, Barbara. *Leopold II of the Belgians: King of Colonialism.* New York: St Martin's Press, 1979.

Ewans, Martin. *European Atrocity, African Catastrophe.* London: Routledge, 2002.

———. "Belgium and the Colonial Experience." *Journal of Contemporary European Studies* 11, no. 2 (November 2003): 168–80.

Fiedler, Klaus. *The Story of Faith Missions.* Oxford: Regnum Books International, 1994.

Fitzmaurice, Andrew. "The Justification of Leopold II's Congo Enterprise." *Law and Politics in British Colonial Thought*, edited by Shaunnagh Dorsett and Ian Hunter. Basingstoke: Palgrave Macmillan, 2010.

———. "Liberalism and Empire in Nineteenth-Century Law." *American Historical Review*, 117 (1), February 2012.

Flint, John E. "Mary Kingsley—A Reassessment." *The Journal of African History* 4, no. 1 (1963): 95–104.

———. "Morel and Morality in West African History." *Canadian Journal of African Studies* 3, no. 3 (Autumn 1969): 637–43.

Frank, Katherine. *A Voyager Out: The Life of Mary Kingsley.* Boston, MA: Houghton Mifflin Co., 1986.

Franklin, John Hope. *George Washington Williams.* Raleigh: Duke University Press, 1985.

Gann, L.H. and Peter Duignan, eds. *Colonialism in Africa 1870–1960.* Cambridge: Cambridge University Press, 1969.

———. *The Rulers of Belgian Africa 1884–1914.* Princeton, NJ: Princeton University Press, 1979.

Gewald, Jan-Bart. "More than Red Rubber and Figures Alone: A Critical Appraisal of the Memory of the Congo Exhibition at the Royal Museum for Central Africa, Tervuren, Belgium." *International Journal of African Historical Studies* 39, no. 3 (2006): 471–86.

Geyer, Martin and Johannes Paulmann. Introduction to *The Mechanics of Internationalism*, edited by Martin Geyer and Johannes Paulmann, 1–16. Oxford: Oxford University Press, 2001.

Gibbons, Herbert Adams. *The New Map of Africa (1900–1916): A History of European Expansion and Colonial Diplomacy.* New York, The Century Company, 1916.

Glaser, John F. "English Nonconformity and the Decline of Liberalism." *The American Historical Review* 63, no. 2 (January 1958): 352–63.

Gondola, Ch. Didier. *History of Congo*. Westport, CT: Greenwood Press, 2002.
Grant, Kevin. "Christian Critics of Empire: Missionaries, Lantern Lectures, and the Congo Reform Campaign in Britain." *Journal of Imperial & Commonwealth History* 29, no. 2 (2001): 27–58.
———. *A Civilised Savagery*. New York: Routledge, 2005.
———. "Human Rights and Sovereign Abolition of Slavery, c. 1885–1956." In *Beyond Sovereignty: Britain, Empire, and Transnationalism, c. 1880–1950*, edited by Kevin Grant, Philippa Levine, and Frank Trentmann, 80–102. Houndmills, Basingstoke, Hampshire: Palgrave Macmillan, 2007.
Grant, Kevin, Philippa Levine, and Frank Trentmann. Introduction to *Beyond Sovereignty: Britain, Empire, and Transnationalism, c. 1880–1950*, edited by Kevin Grant, Philippa Levine, and Frank Trentmann, 1–16. Houndmills, Basingstoke, Hampshire: Palgrave Macmillan, 2007.
Gray, Benjamin Kirkman. *A History of English Philanthropy: From the Dissolution of the Monasteries to the Taking of the First Census*. London: P.S. King, 1906.
Grey, Edward. *Twenty-five Years 1892–1916*. New York: Frederick A. Stokes, 1925.
Gwynn, Stephen. *The Life of Mary Kingsley*. London: Macmillan, 1932.
Halladay, E., "The Debate on the Congo, 1900–1908." *Parliamentary Affairs* 21 (March 1968): 277–84.
Halstead, John P. *The Second British Empire: Trade, Philanthropy and Good Government*. Westport, CT: Greenwood Press, 1983.
Halttunen, Karen. "Humanitarianism and the Pornography of Pain in Anglo-American Culture." *American Historical Review* 100, no. 2 (April 1995): 303–34.
Harlow, Barbara. "Introduction: The Congo: Abominations and Denunciations." In *Archives of Empire v 2: The Scramble for Africa*, edited by Barbara Harlow and Mia Carter. Durham: Duke University Press, 2003.
Harms, Robert. "The End of Red Rubber: A Reassessment." *The Journal of African History* 16, no. 1 (1975): 73–88.
———. "The World ABIR Made: The Margina Lopori Basin, 1885–1903." *African Economic History*, no. 12 (1983): Business Empires in Equatorial Africa: 125–39.
Harrison, Brian Howard. "Philanthropy and the Victorians." *Victorian Studies* 9, no. 4 (June 1966): 353–74.
———. "A Genealogy of Reform in Modern Britain." In *Anti-Slavery, Religion and Reform*, edited by Christine Bolt and Seymour Drescher, 119–48. Hamden, CT: Archon Books, 1980.
———. "Philanthropy and the Victorians." *Peaceable Kingdom*. Oxford: Clarendon Press, 1982.

Haskell, Thomas. "Capitalism and the Origins of the Humanitarian Sensibility" Parts 1 and 2. *The American Historical Review* 90, no. 2 (April 1985): 339–61; no. 3 (June 1985): 547–66.

———. "Convention and Hegemonic Interest in the Debate over Antislavery: A Reply to Davis and Ashworth." *American Historical Review* 92, no. 4 (October 1987): 829–78.

Hawkins, Hunt. "Mark Twain's Involvement with the Congo Reform Movement: 'A Fury of Generous Indignation,'" *The New England Quarterly* 51, no. 2 (June 1978): 147–75.

———. "Joseph Conrad, Roger Casement, and the Congo Reform Movement." *Journal of Modern Literature* 9, no. 1 (1981–82): 65–80.

Hinsley, F.H. editor. *British Foreign Policy under Sir Edward Grey*. Cambridge: Cambridge University Press, 1977.

Hochschild, Adam. *King Leopold's Ghost*. New York: Houghton Mifflin, 1998.

Holton, Sandra. "Gender Difference, National Identity and Professing History: The Case of Alice Stopford Green." *History Workshop Journal*, no. 53 (Spring 2002): 118–27.

Hunt, Nancy Rose. "An acoustic register, tenacious images, and Congolese scenes of rape and repetition." *Cultural Anthropology* 23, no. 2 (May 2008): 220–253.

International Labour Organisation Forced Labour Convention of 1930. http://www.itcilo.it/actrav/english/common/C029.html.

Jacobsen, Óli. "Daniel J. Danielsen (1871–1916): The Faeroese who Changed History in the Congo." *Brethren Historical Review* 8 (2012), 5–37.

———. *Daniel J. Danielsen and the Congo: Missionary Campaigns and Atrocity Photographs*. Brethren Archivists and Historians Network, 2014, available at www.olijacobsen.com.

Keith, Arthur Berriedale. *The Belgian Congo and the Berlin Act*. Oxford: Clarendon Press, 1919. http://books.google.com/books?id=eQ5zAAAAMAAJ.

Kennedy, Pagan. *Black Livingstone*. New York: Viking, 2002.

Kennedy, Thomas C. *British Quakerism, 1860–1920: The Transformation of a Religious Community*. Oxford: Oxford University Press, 2001.

Lagergren, David. *Mission and State in the Congo: A Study of the Relations between Protestant Missions and the Congo Independent State Authorities with Special Reference to the Equator District, 1885–1903*. Uppsala: Almqvist and Wikshells, 1970.

Lambert, David and Alan Lester. "Geographies of Colonial Philanthropy." *Progress in Human Geography* 28, no. 3 (2004): 320–334.

Laqua, Daniel. "The Tensions of Internationalism: Transnational Anti-Slavery in the 1880s and 1890s." *The International History Review* 33, no. 4 (December 2011): 705–26.

———. *The Age of Internationalism and Belgium, 1880–1930.* New York: Manchester University Press, 2013.

Laqueur, Thomas W. "Bodies, Details, and the Humanitarian Narrative," in *The New Cultural History*, edited by Lynn Hunt, 176–204. Berkeley, CA: University of California Press, 1988.

Lichtervelde, Comte Louis de. *Léopold of the Belgians.* Translated by Thomas H. Reed and H. Russell Reed. New York: The Century Co., 1929.

Lindqvist, Sven. *Exterminate All the Brutes.* Translated by Joan Tate. New York: The New Press, 1996.

Lorimer, Douglas A. *Colour, Class, and the Victorians.* New York: Leicester University Press, 1978.

Louis, William Roger. "Roger Casement and the Congo." *The Journal of African History* 5, no. 1 (1964): 99–120.

———. "The Stokes Affair and the Origins of the Anti-Congo Campaign, 1895–1896." *Revue Belge de Philologie & d'Histoire* 43, no. 2 (January 1965): 572–84.

———. "The Triumph of the Congo Reform Movement, 1905–1908." *Boston University Papers on Africa: Transition in Politics.* Vol. 2, edited by Jeffrey Butler. Boston, MA: Boston University Press, 1966. Reprinted in William Roger Louis, *Ends of British Imperialism.* London: I.B. Tauris, 2006.

———. "Sir John Harris and 'Colonial Trusteeship,'" *The Bulletin of A.R.S.O.M. (Academie Royale des Sciences d'Outre-Mer) for 1965 and 1966*, Part 6, 832–56.

———. "The Philosophical Diplomatist: Sir Arthur Hardinge and King Leopold's Congo, 1906–1911." In *The Bulletin of A.R.S.O.M. (Academie Royale des Sciences d'Outre-Mer) for 1968*, 1402–30.

Louis, William Roger and Jean Stengers. *E.D. Morel's History of the Congo Reform Movement.* Oxford: Clarendon Press, 1968.

Marchal, Jules. *E.D. Morel contre Léopold II: L'Historie du Congo 1900–1910.* Vols 1–2. Paris: L'Harmattan, 1996.

———. *L'État libre du Congo: Paradis Perdu: L'Histoire du Congo 1876–1900.* Borgloon: Bellings, 1996.

Matikkala, Mira. *Empire and Imperial Ambition: Liberty, Englishness and Anti-Imperialism in Late-Victorian Britain.* New York: I.B. Tauris, 2011.

McDowell, Robert Brendan. *Alice Stopford Green: A Passionate Historian.* Dublin: Figgis, 1967.

McLeod, Hugh. *Religion and Society in England 1850–1914.* New York: St Martin's Press, 1996.

———. "Protestantism and British National Identity." In *Nation and Religion: Perspectives on Europe and Asia*, edited by Peter van der Veer and Hartmut Lehmann, 44–70. Princeton, NJ: Princeton University Press, 1999.

Mirzoreff, Nicholas. "Photography at the Heart of Darkness." In *Colonialism and the Object: Empire, Material Culture, and the Museum*, edited by T.J. Barringer, and Tom Flynn, 167–87. New York: Routledge, 1998.

Mitchell, Angus. "New Light on the Heart of Darkness." *History Today* 49, no. 12 (December 1999): 20–27.

———. *Casement*. London: Haus Publishing, 2003.

———. "Alice Stopford Green and the origins of the African Society." *History Ireland* 14, no. 4 (July/August 2006). http://www.historyireland.com/volumes/volume14/issue4/features/?id=327.

Mitchell, Donald. *The Politics of Dissent: A Biography of E.D. Morel*. Bristol: Silverwood Books, 2014.

Morris, R.J. "Clubs, Societies and Associations." In *Cambridge Social History of Britain 1750–1950*. Vol. 3, *Social Agencies and Institutions*, edited by F.M.L. Thompson, 395–443. Cambridge: Cambridge University Press, 1990.

Mudimbe, V.Y., *The Invention of Africa: Gnosis, Philosophy, and the Order of Knowledge*. Bloomington, IN: Indiana University Press, 1988.

Mullen, Patrick. "Roger Casement's Global English: From Human Rights to the Homoerotic." *Public Culture* 15, no. 3, (2003): 559–78.

Nelson, Samuel H. *Colonialism in the Congo Basin 1880–1940*. Athens, OH: Ohio University Center for International Studies, 1994.

Northrup, David. *Beyond the Bend in the River: African Labor in Eastern Zaire, 1865–1940*, Athens, OH: Ohio University Center for International Studies, 1988.

———. "Slavery and Forced Labour in the Eastern Congo." In *Slavery in the Great Lakes Region of East Africa*, edited by Henri Médard and Shane Doyle. Athens, OH: Ohio University Press, 2007.

Nworah, Kingsley Kenneth Dike. "New Introduction" in E.D. Morel, *Affairs of West Africa*, vii–xviii. 1902. Reprint, London, Frank Cass & Co. Ltd., 1968.

———. "The Liverpool "Sect" and British West African Policy 1895–1915." *African Affairs* 70, no. 281 (1971): 349–64.

Nzolongo-Ntalajia, Georges. *The Congo from Leopold to Kabila: A People's History*. New York: Zed Book Room 400, 2002.

O'Callaghan, Margaret. "Through the Eyes of Another Race, of a People Once Hunted Themselves." In *Ireland in Transition*, edited by Kieran A. Kennedy. Cork: Mercier Press, 1986.

Oldfield, Sybil. "Harris, Alice." In *Woman Humanitarians: A Biographical Dictionary of British Women Active Between 1900–1950*, edited by Sybil Oldfield, 94–7. London: Continuum, 2001.

———. "Compiling the First Dictionary of British Women Humani-tarians." *Women's Studies International Forum* 24, no. 6 (December 2002): 737–43.

———. "Harris, Sir John Hobbis (1874–1940)." *Oxford Dictionary of National Biography*. Oxford, Oxford University Press, 2004.

Osborne, John Bremner. "Wilfred G. Thesiger, Sir Edward Grey, and the British Campaign to Reform the Congo, 1905-9." *The Journal of Imperial and Commonwealth History* 27, no. 1 (January 1999): 59-80.

Owen, David Edward. *English Philanthropy, 1660-1960*. Cambridge: Belknap Press, 1964.

Owen, Nicholas. "Critics of Empire." In *The Oxford History of the British Empire*, Vol. IV, *The Twentieth Century*, edited by Judith Brown and William Roger Louis. New York: Oxford University Press, 1999.

Pavlakis, Dean. "The Development of British Overseas Humanitarianism and the Congo Reform Campaign." *Journal of Colonialism and Colonial History* 11, no. 1 (Spring 2010).

Peemans, Jean-Philippe. "Capital Accumulation in the Congo." In *Colonialism in Africa, 1870-1960*. Vol. 4, *The Economics of Colonialism*, edited by L.H. Gann and Peter Duignan, 165-212. Cambridge: Cambridge University Press, 1975.

Peffer, John. "Snap of the Whip/Crossroads of Shame: Flogging, Photography, and the Representation of Atrocity in the Congo Reform Campaign." *Visual Anthropology Review* 24, no. 1, (Spring 2008): 55-77.

Phillips, Anne. *The Enigma of Colonialism: British Policy in West Africa*. Bloomington, IN: Indiana University Press, 1989.

Phipps, William E. *William Sheppard: Congo's African American Livingstone*. Louisville, KY: Geneva Press, 2002.

Polasky, Janet. *The Democratic Socialism of Emile Vandervelde*. Washington, DC: Berg, 1995.

Porter, Andrew. "Trusteeship, Anti-Slavery and Humanitarianism" and "Religion, Missionary Enthusiasm and Empire." In *The Oxford History of the British Empire*. Vol. 3, *The Nineteenth Century*, edited by Andrew Porter, 198-221, 222-46. Oxford: Oxford University Press, 1999.

———. "Sir Roger Casement and the International Humanitarian Movement." *Journal of Imperial and Commonwealth History* 29, no. 2 (May 2001): 59-73.

———. *Religion Versus Empire? British Protestant Missionaries and Overseas Expansion*. New York: Manchester University Press, 2004.

Porter, Bernard. *Critics of Empire: British Radical Attitudes towards Colonialism in Africa*. 2nd ed. New York: I.B. Tauris, 2008.

Rahier, Jean Muteba. "The Ghost of Leopold II: The Belgian Royal Museum of Central Africa and Its Dusty Colonial Exhibition." *Research in African Literatures* 34, no. 1, (Spring 2003): 58-84.

Ranieri, Liane. *Les relations entre l'Etat indépendant du Congo et l'Italie*. Brussels: Académie Royale des Sciences Coloniales, 1959.

Rattray, R.S. Review of *The Life of Mary Kingsley* by Stephen Gwynn, *Journal of the Royal African Society* 31, no. 125 (October 1932): 354-65.

Reardon, Ruth Slade "Catholics and Protestants in the Congo." In C.G .Baëta, *Christianity in Tropical Africa*. Oxford, Oxford University Press, 1968.

Reid, B. L. "A Good Man—Has Had Fever: Casement in the Congo." *The Sewanee Review* 82, no. 3 (Summer 1974): 460–80.

Renton, David, David Seddon, and Leo Zelig, *The Congo: Plunder and Resistance*. New York: Zed Books, 2007.

Riding, Alan. "Belgium Confronts its Heart of Darkness." 21 September 2002. http://www.racematters.org/belgiandarkness.htm.

Robbins, Keith. *Sir Edward Grey: A Biography of Lord Grey of Fallodon*. London: Cassell, 1971.

Robins, Jonathan E. "Slave Cocoa and Red Rubber: E.D. Morel and the Problem of Ethical Consumption." *Comparative Studies in Society and History* 54, no. 3 (July 2102), 592–611.

Russell, Bertrand. "Imperialism: The Congo." *Freedom and Organization, 1814–1914*, 450–456. London: Allen and Unwin, 1934.

Samarin, William J. *The Black Man's Burden: African Colonial Labor on the Congo and Ubangi Rivers 1880–1900*. Boulder, CO: Westview Press, 1989.

Satre, Lowell J. *Chocolate on Trial: Slavery, Politics, and the Ethics of Business*. Athens, OH: Ohio University Press, 2005.

Ó Síocháin, Séamas and Michael O'Sullivan. *The Eyes of Another Race: Roger Casement's Congo Report and 1903 Diary*. Dublin: University College Dublin Press, 2003.

Shaloff, Stanley. *Reform in King Leopold's Congo*. Richmond, VA: John Knox Press, 1970.

Slade, Ruth. "English Missionaries and the Beginning of the Anti-Congolese Campaign in England." *Revue Belge de Philologie d'Histoire* 33, no. 1 (1955): 37–73.

———. "King Leopold II and the Attitude of English and American Catholics towards the Anti-Congolese Campaign." *Zaire*, XI, (June 1957): 600–604.

———. *English-Speaking Missions in the Congo Independent State*. Brussels: Academie Royale des Sciences Coloniales, 1959.

———. *King Leopold's Congo*. New York: Oxford University Press, 1962.

Sliwinski, Sharon. "The Childhood of Human Rights: the Kodak on the Congo." *Journal of Visual Culture* 5, no. 3 (January 2006): 333–63.

Stanley, Brian. "Grenfell, George, 1849 to 1906." *International Bulletin of Missionary Research* 21, no. 3 (July 97): 120–24. Dictionary of African Christian Biography website, http://www.dacb.org/stories/cameroon/legacy_grenfell.html.

Stengers, Jean. "The Congo Free State and the Belgian Congo." In *Colonialism in Africa*, edited by Lewis H. Gann and Peter Duignan, 261–92. Cambridge: Cambridge University Press, 1969.

———. *Congo: Mythes et Réalités*. Paris: Duculot, 1989.

———. "Sur la Critiques des Données Demographiques en Afrique" in *Mélanges Pierre Salmon*. Brussels: Université libre de Bruxelles Institu de Sociology, 1993.

———. "Pre-War Belgian Attitudes to Britain: Anglophilia and Anglophobia." In *Europe in Exile*, edited by Martin Conway and José Gotovitch. New York: Berghahn Books, 2001, 35ff.

Stengers, Jean and Jan Vansina. "King Leopold's Congo, 1886–1908." In *The Cambridge History of Africa*, Vol. 6, *From 1870 to 1905*, edited by Roland Oliver and G.N. Sanderson, 315–58. Cambridge: Cambridge University Press, 1985.

Swaisland, Charles. "The Aborigines' Protection Society, 1837–1909." In *After Slavery: Emancipation and Its Discontents*, edited by Howard Temperley, 265–80. London: Frank Cass, 2000.

Swidler, Ann, "Cultural Power and Social Movements" in *Social Movements and Culture*, edited by Hank Johnston and Bert Klandermans, 25–40. Minneapolis, MN: University of Minnesota Press, 1995.

Temperley, Howard. "Anti-Slavery as a Form of Cultural Imperialism." In *Anti-Slavery, Religion and Reform*, edited by Christine Bolt and Seymour Drescher, 335–50. Hamden, CT: Archon Books, 1980.

Thompson, T. Jack. "Light on the Dark Continent: The Photography of Alice Seeley Harris and the Congo Atrocities of the Early Twentieth Century." *International Bulletin of Missionary Research*, October 2002: 146–50.

———. *Light on Darkness? Missionary Photography of Africa in the Nineteenth and Early Twentieth Centuries*. Grand Rapids, MI: Eerdmans, 2003.

Trevelyan, G.M. *Grey of Fallodon*. New York: Longmans, Green, 1937.

Twomey, Christina. "Framing Atrocity: Photography and Humanitarianism." *History of Photography* 36:3 (August 2012): 255–64.

———. "Severed Hands: Authenticating Atrocity in the Congo, 1903–14." In *Picturing Atrocity: Photography in Crisis*, edited by Geoff Batchen, Mick Gidley, Nancy K. Miller, and Jay Prosser. London: Reaktion Books, 2012.

Vangroenweghe, Daniel. "Introduction." In *Le Rapport Casement (Enquêtes et Documents D'Histoire Africaine)*, edited by Daniel Vangroenweghe and Jean-Luc Vellut, 1–26. Louvain: Université Catholique de Louvain, 1985.

———. *Du Sang sur les Lianes*. Bruxelles: Les Editions Aden, 2010. Revision of original Didier Hatier edition, 1986.

Vanthemsche, Guy. "The Historiography of Belgian Colonialism in the Congo" in *Europe and the World in European Historiography*, edited by Csaba Levai, 89–119. Pisa: Pisa University Press, 2006. http://www.cliohres.net/books/6/Vanthemsche.pdf.

———. *Belgium and the Congo, 1885–1960*. Translated by Alice Cameron and Stephen Windross. Cambridge: Cambridge University Press, 2012.

Varouxakis, Georgios. "'Patriotism,' 'Cosmopolitanism,' and 'Humanity' in Victorian Political Thought." *European Journal of Political Theory* 5, no. 1 (January 2006): 100–118.

Vellut, Jean-Luc, editor, "Preface." In *Le Rapport Casement (Enquêtes et Documents D'Histoire Africaine)*, edited by Daniel Vangroenweghe and Jean-Luc Vellut, i–xxi. Louvain: Université Catholique de Louvain, 1985.

———. *La Memoire du Congo: Le Temps Colonial*. Tervuren: Grand Editions Snoeck, 2005.

Walzer, Michael, *Arguing About War*. New Haven, CT: Yale University Press, 2004.

Weisbord, Robert G. "The King, the Cardinal and the Pope: Leopold II's genocide in the Congo and the Vatican," *Journal of Genocide Research* 5, no. 1 (2003): 35–45.

Wheeler, B.R. *Alfred Henry Baynes, JP*. London: Carey Press, after 1944.

Willequet, Jacques. *La Congo Belge et la Weltpolitik*. Brussels: Université Libre de Bruxelles, 1963.

Wolf, Howard and Ralph Wolf. *Rubber: A Story of Glory and Greed*. New York: Covici Friede, 1936.

Index

Aborigines' Protection Society (APS) 22–6, 58, 73–4, 129, 256, 267
    Anti-Slavery merger 98, 133–5
    Committee members 30, 106, 112
    Congo agitation after 1904 211
    Congo agitation before 1904 6–7, 34–9, 55, 141, 176, 204, 261
    Morel differences 41, 45–6
    Stanley criticism 31
    CRA relationship 63–5, 71, 131–5
    finances 87, 89, 91, 95, 112
    promotion of native rights 44
    structure 33, 69, 86
African Mail 75, 85, 194; *see also West African Mail*
Albert I, King of the Belgians (1875–1934) 173, 235, 249
Albright, William A. (1853–1942) 23, 107, 110, 112
Alexander, Joseph Grundy (1848–1918) 23, 69, 107, 133, 144, 164
American Baptist Missionary Union (ABMU) 32–4, 53, 56, 137–9
American Congo Reform Association 7, 166–7, 253–4
American Presbyterian Congo Mission (APCM) 45, 57, 140
Anglicans 1, 50, 106–8, 124–5, 141, 143, 147–51
    evangelical 19, 21
annexation; *see also* annexation headings under Foreign Office; Hardinge; Morel
    annexation in 1908 76, 83, 247, 249
    annexation without reform 183, 200, 219, 221, 249, 264

Belgian annexation as policy
    Congo Reform Association 76, 211, 236–7
    Foreign Office 201, 211, 215, 221–2, 232, 237, 250
    Liverpool Chamber of Commerce 154
    Morel's support for 57
Belgians calling for 168, 211, 250–53, 263–4
British recognition 7, 231, 233, 247–8, 259, 264
British refusal to recognize 101, 155, 221–2, 229, 231, 248, 250
international recognition 162–3
steps toward annexation 76, 95, 168–9, 173, 218, 247, 250–54
treaty negotiations 7, 76, 167, 218, 264
as trusteeship 180
Anti-Slavery and Aborigines Protection Society 78, 113–14, 132, 135, 267
    Harrises as Joint Organising Secretaries 99, 119, 122, 135, 228, 246
Anti-Slavery Society (until June 1909) 22–4, 58, 69, 74, 132–5, 187
    branches 86
    Buxton, *see* Buxton, Travers; Buxton, Sir Thomas Fowell
    CRA relationship 132–3
    Committee 106, 112
    finances 23, 74, 87, 89
    Harris ideas for 96, 98, 133–5, 165
Armstrong, Jack Proby 199, 217, 220, 231
Asquith, Herbert Henry (1852–1928) 101, 177, 230–31
Austria-Hungary 161, 210

Baccari, Captain Eduardo (MD) 162
Balfour, Arthur James (1848–1930) 149, 205–6, 212
Bannister, Edward 32, 37, 59, 203
Baptist church, *see* Baptists
Baptist Union, *see* Baptists
Baptists 1, 143, 179; *see also* American Baptist Missionary Union; Baptist Missionary Society
   Baptist Union 141–5, 147
   churches and chapels 51, 104, 142–3, 190
   CRA donors 110, 124
   leaders 50, 81, 91, 107–8, 139, 141, 145
   in America 166
   Swedish 34, 158
Baptist Missionary Society 32–3, 36, 55–6, 78, 105, 138–41
Barbour, Thomas S. (1853–1915) 166–7
Barclay, Sir Thomas 73, 82
Baring, Sir Evelyn, *see* Cromer, Earl of
Baynes, Alfred Henry 36, 55, 138–40
Beak, George Bailey 220
Beauchamp, 7th Earl (William Lygon) (1872–1938) 72, 77, 108, 111, 127, 212
Beernaert, Auguste (1829–1912) 168–9, 211, 247, 251–2
Belgian Congo 2, 9, 12, 83–4, 234–46, 259, 264
   Baptist Missionary Society relationship 140
   Harris job thoughts 96
   RBMU relationship 95, 137
   reforms 101, 153, 155, 200, 229–31, 240–45, 259
Belgium 173, 193, 201, 234, 247–54, 258–9, 263–4
   Antwerp Chamber of Commerce 155
   apologists 166, 183, 193
   Belgians working in Congo Free State 159, 199–200
   British ambassador 208–11, 240
   British pressure 99, 101, 131, 150, 167, 217–18, 221–2, 232

Congo annexation, *see* annexation
Congo Reform Association's view of 76, 95, 131, 182–4, 224–5, 230, 249
   demonizing? 182–3, 200
   government 75, 153, 221, 234, 237, 248–51, 256; *see also* Belgian Congo
   loans to Leopold 8
   Grey's misjudgments 213, 216–18
   lack of colonial experience 215
   parliament, including Chamber of Deputies 31, 75–6, 95, 167–8, 237, 249–52
   press 31, 34
   public attitude 29, 152, 160, 264
   reaction to Leopold's monopolization 31
   reformers 4, 7, 18, 39, 132, 167–73, 236, 247; *see also* Beernaert; Cattier; Lorand; Speyer; Vermeersch; Wauters
   relation to Congo before 1906 182
   relations with other European countries 162–3, 165–7
   slowness to reform 222, 229
Belloc, Hilaire (1870–1953) 74, 197
Benedetti, Antonio 90–91, 178
Bentley, Rev. William Holman (1855–1905) 33, 132, 138
Berlin Act of 1885 65, 78, 233, 236
   Belgian annexation to conform with 154, 162, 218, 222
   Britain as trustee 36, 204
   Congo violations of 20, 33
   International Association of the Congo accession 6, 159
   reformers' invocation of 78, 169, 178, 180
   revisions to allow import duties 8, 31
   signatories, appeals to 30, 36, 204–7, 211
   signatories, British consultation with 46, 67, 160, 202, 264
   US not a signatory 166–7, 210
Berlin Treaty, *see* Berlin Act
Berlin West Africa Conference (1884–1885) 5–6, 36, 159; *see also* Berlin Act of 1885
Bertie, Sir Francis 203–4

Index

Birmingham 86, 112, 151, 194
Brazza, Pierre Savorgnan de (1852–1905) 159, 163
British honor 18, 20, 223
British parliamentary resolution of 20 May 1903, *see* resolutions: parliamentary, of 20 May 1903
British Cabinet 201–2, 212–14, 221–2, 237, 253, 264
    annexation, refusal to recognize 76, 101
    military force authorized 229–30, 250
    recognition 231; *see also under* annexation
British empire 3, 13–14, 18, 51, 158, 160, 213
British Foreign Office, *see* Foreign Office
Boer War 1, 17–18, 143, 158, 204, 212
Boma 59, 128, 162, 206, 223, 229
Bourke, Dermot Robert Wyndham, *see* Mayo, 7th Earl of
Bourne, Henry Richard Fox (1837–1909) 35, 49, 91, 106–7, 263–4; *see also* Aborigines' Protection Society
    annexation 57, 253
    APS Secretary 69, 74
    APS/Anti-Slavery merger 132, 134
    international connections 39, 45, 157, 160, 168, 171
    cocoa scandal agitation 26, 111, 134
    Colonial Office ties 25
    Commission of Inquiry 255
    Congo agitation 1896–1908 6, 36–7, 39, 46, 67, 131, 255
    leased British territory 204
    CRA founding 60, 63–4, 71, 131–3, 256
    decay of British humanitarian spirit 22–3
    Guinness, concerns about 53, 57–8, 80, 255
    IU Congo Committee 50, 57–8
    Morel relationship 43, 45, 64
    rhetoric 19, 46, 181
    rights focus 34, 44, 128, 267
Brabner, Harold (1863–1951) 71–4, 89, 98, 107, 151, 257, 269–70

Burrows, Captain Guy 79, 185, 198–9
Buxton, Sir Thomas Fowell (1837–1915) 71, 110, 132, 165
Buxton, Travers (1864–1945) 72, 74, 107, 132–5, 147, 267
    Anti-Slavery Secretary 69, 71
    Harris relationship 82, 94, 96, 133–5, 258
    IU Congo Committee 50, 58

Cadbury, George (1839–1922) 110–11, 143, 152, 194
Cadbury, William Adlington (1867–1957) 92, 152, 194, 254
    advice 72–3, 98, 196
    cocoa scandals 77, 111–12, 134–5
    CRA role 77, 86, 91, 93, 109–12, 144, 254
    Morel relationship 75, 112, 116
Campbell, Gerald 137, 235, 238, 244
Campbell-Bannerman, Sir Henry (1836–1908) 17, 20, 143, 212, 216, 218–19
Casement, Roger David (1864–1916) 7, 38, 203–4, 255, 257, 267
    cocoa scandals 26
    CRA founding 29, 57, 60–65, 67, 110–11, 113
    purpose 78, 192–3
    CRA work 1905 115–18, 128, 171
    imperial ideas 13, 180
    investigation 56, 59–60, 184, 202, 206, 264
    pessimism 91, 193
    report 69, 182, 206–10, 232, 247, 261, 263
    ties to Morel and Harris 75, 93
    treason 184
    view of Grey 216, 223, 227
Cattier, Prof. Félicien (1869–1946) 169–71, 173, 176
    as a reformer 210–11, 216, 247–50, 255, 263–4
causality 27, 230, 246–8, 264
Challaye, Félicien (1875–1967) 163

chambers of commerce 7, 27, 42, 46, 153–6, 205, 213, 255; *see also* London Chamber of Commerce; Liverpool: Chamber of Commerce
Church of England, *see* Anglicans
Claparède, René (1863–1928) 162–4, 234
Clemens, Samuel (1835–1910) 26, 127, 166, 185, 253
Clifford, Rev. Dr. John (1836–1923) 50, 81, 107, 139, 141–2, 151
cocoa scandals 8, 26, 77–9, 111, 134–5, 152–4
Collier, John, *see* Monkswell
Commission of Inquiry 7, 91, 247, 251–2, 254–5, 263
   formation 169, 210, 232, 247, 255, 261
   testimony 121, 139, 215, 254
Commission for the Protection of the Natives 33, 138, 213, 236, 245
Congo Balolo Mission (CBM) 82–4, 104, 119, 184; *see also* Regions Beyond Missionary Union
   Congo reticence 31, 34, 51, 53, 83–4
   Congo publicity 55–8, 81
   Harrises 83, 119, 121, 257
   missionary lectures 56, 82–3, 93, 105, 160
Congo Council of the CBM, *see* Congo Balolo Mission
Congo Reform Association (CRA)
   alliances; *see also* Aborigines' Protection Society
      British organizations 81–4, 91, 131–56, 210
      international 18, 161–73; *see also* American Congo Reform Association
   anniversary celebration in 1907 74
   auxiliaries 86–8, 105–6, 114, 136, 262–3, 273; *see also* Congo Reform Association: Liverpool Auxiliary *and* London Auxiliary
   church participation 86, 141–51; *see also* Free Church Councils *and* individual denominations
   disbanding 1–2, 5, 233, 247–8, 261
   discipline 4, 29, 41, 60, 78–85, 96, 262–3
   donors and subscribers 20–24, 26–7, 88–91, 109–14, 123–9, 220, 262
      database 269–70
      demographics 114–15, 123–6, 151
      disclosure 74
      Harris and London Auxiliary 94–6
      individual donors 91, 110–13, 143–4, 147, 154
      value of donations 85–6
   evaluating effectiveness 2, 233–55, 261, 264
   Executive Committee 24, 69–78, 103, 106–9, 183, 262
      auxiliary representatives 87, 102
      APS and Anti-Slavery representation 64, 131, 135, 256
      individual members 107–8, 112, 155, 164, 212, 227–8
      Morel's salary and move 95–6
      policy-making 101, 211, 225–7, 230, 248
      religious leaders on 81–4, 141, 144, 147–9
   finances 67, 71–5, 81–2, 85–91, 123, 255
      customary practices 23–4, 69, 262
      deficits at CRA, APS, and Anti-Slavery 38–9, 87–9
      Finance Committee 72–3, 88, 95–6, 101
      financial reporting 72–4, 88, 94–5
      fundraising 62, 88–91, 96, 109, 141, 256
      individual donations 5, 62, 93, 110–11, 125–7; *see also* Congo Reform Association: donors and subscribers
      money raised at meetings 26, 61, 87–8
      suspicions 74, 183
   Foreign Office relations, *see* Foreign Office
   formation 7, 50, 61–5, 71, 136, 261

goals and objectives 2–4, 69, 74, 78, 99, 233, 237–46
press, *see* press
headquarters move to London 88, 93–9, 102, 116
honorary secretary, *see* Morel, Edmund Dene
impact 67, 234–46, 255, 258–60
limitations 4, 67, 228, 248
Liverpool Auxiliary 72, 75, 82, 87, 104, 189
London Auxiliary 86–9, 94–6, 102, 117–19, 127, 273
    appeal to women 113–14
    Committee 23
    financial management of 73, 86–9, 95, 109, 269
    Harrises loaned to run 81
Manchester Auxiliary 88, 273
methods 69, 71–4, 78, 94–5, 261–2
    humanitarian 23–6, 64
Parliamentary Committee 99–102, 118, 215, 231, 247, 264
president 23, 69, 72, 77–8, 94, 113, 262
press relationships, *see* press
structure 67, 71, 98, 101–3, 113, 262
support for 103–5; *see also* Congo Reform Association: donors and subscribers
women, role of 113–23, 262
Congregationalists 1, 81, 91, 112, 124, 141–2
Conservative Party 99, 106, 212
consular jurisdiction 76, 211, 217, 219, 224, 229, 231–2
consuls, British 7, 12, 38, 220; *see also* Armstrong; Bannister; Beak; Campbell; Casement; Mackie; Michell; Nightingale; Pickersgill; Thesiger
    adding consuls 76, 211, 220
    Foreign Office reliance 228, 237, 263
    reporting on reforms 231, 235, 248–9
Cookey, S.J.S. 91, 201, 234
copal 8, 238
Cranborne, Lord, *see* Gascoyne-Cecil, James

Cromer, Earl of (Sir Evelyn Baring) (1841–1917) 75, 96, 122, 212, 215, 224, 226

Danielson, Rev. Daniel Jacob (1871–1916) 54, 56–7, 184–5, 188
Davidson, Randall, Archbishop of Canterbury (1848–1930) 1, 74, 96, 148–51, 222, 230
Dennett, Richard E. (1857–1921) 29–30, 129, 159
Deuss, Ludwig 110, 113, 125, 129, 153, 161, 164–5
Dilke, Sir Charles Wentworth (1843–1911) 37, 41, 45–7, 62–4, 131, 181–2
    detested by Stead and Guinness 50–51, 53, 55, 63, 255–6, 258
    House of Commons speeches 33, 36–7, 67, 85, 181, 205, 213
    Morel correspondence and advice 168, 178, 182, 184, 209
    other reform roles 78, 93
    Parliamentary Committee 99–101, 118
Doyle, Sir Arthur Conan (1859–1930) 75, 79, 84, 127, 151, 197
Durand, Ralph (1876–1945) 43, 127, 129, 133

Edward VII, King of the United Kingdom (1841–1910) 18, 216, 218–19, 240
Eetvelde, Baron Edmond Van (1852–1925) 36, 54, 137, 194, 209
Elder Dempster shipping firm 8, 39, 41–2, 44, 58, 194
Emmott, Alfred (1858–1926) 71–3, 77–80, 107, 115, 128, 228
    Morel testimonial 75
    Morel's visit to Roosevelt 166
    Parliamentary Committee 99–100
    resignation 212
    role in forming the CRA 7, 50, 58, 62, 64, 131
Emmott, Mary Gertrude "Gertie" (1866–1954) 114, 116–17, 212, 226, 228

evangelicals and evangelicalism 19–22, 34, 93, 123, 148
Executive Committee of the CRA, *see* Congo Reform Association

Fitzmaurice, Baron (Edmond George Petty-Fitzmaurice) (1846–1935) 122, 202, 213, 215, 217, 231
Foreign Office 4, 25, 201–21, 263–5; *see also* Grey; Lansdowne
   attitude to Congo scandals 255, 263
   1901 and earlier 31–2, 35, 37–8, 203–4
   CRA criticism 150, 201, 216–17, 228, 231, 247
   growing expertise 221, 228
   under Lansdowne 56, 69, 176, 204–10, 232, 255
   under Grey 171, 201, 210–21, 232, 235–7, 248, 260
   Casement investigation and report, *see under* Casement
   Cattier and 171, 250
   cocoa scandals 112
   concern about European complications 76, 225–6
   CRA, APS, and Anti-Slavery attempts to influence 26, 69, 99, 132, 134, 149, 196, 203
   French Congo, *see* French Congo
   Harris and 116, 228
   Morel as collaborator 4, 102, 203, 214–20, 251
   Morel's attack on 4, 76, 194, 223–32, 258, 264–5
   Rabinek affair and, *see* Rabinek
   recognition of Belgian annexation, *see* annexationt
   religious lobbying of 143, 148
   resolutions sent to 80, 103, 190, 251
Fox, Frederick William (1841–1918) 30, 34, 36, 64, 107, 165
Fox Bourne, *see* Bourne, Henry Richard Fox
France 7, 17, 20, 39, 84, 215, 234
   Belgian relationship 38, 225–6, 254

   British relationship 38, 76, 202, 205, 209–10, 226
   Congo reform cause in 85, 119, 151, 160, 162–4, 203
   Sjöblom's report 34
   Williams's *Open Letter* 24
Free Church Councils 81, 111, 135, 145, 147–8
free trade 65, 153, 237, 261
   Belgian Congo 243–5
   British attitude toward 20, 212
   Congo commitments to 6, 29, 76, 180, 211, 236
   Morel's and Holt's emphasis on 41–2, 45
French Congo 14, 46, 118, 163, 167, 214, 253
   Holt's dispute 43, 153, 205
Friends, Society of, *see* Quakers

Gascoyne-Cecil, Robert, *see* Salisbury, 3rd Marquess
Gascoyne-Cecil, James, *see* Salisbury, 4th Marquess, a.k.a Lord Cranborne
gender 115, 117–18, 122, 262; *see also* Congo Reform Association: women, role of
Germany 37, 84, 140, 144, 197, 215
   British fear of 76, 202, 216, 224–6
   colonies 2, 178
   Congo reform cause in 7, 85, 151, 161, 163–5, 227–8
   Congo Free State recognition 159
   cooperation with 24, 32, 59
   Phipps dissuaded 208, 210
Gilchrist, Rev. G. Somerville 54, 81, 137
Gilmour, Thomas Lennox (1859–1936) 74, 98, 107, 133, 151, 224–5, 227–8
Gilzean Reid, *see* Reid
Gladstone, William (1809–1898) 13, 91, 178, 212–13
Glave, E.J. (1862–1895) 37–8, 132
Grant, Kevin xi, 63, 87, 93n131, 233, 256
   Harris and Guinness 82–3
   photography and lantern slides 184, 189
   rights orientation 44

Index

role of missionaries 51, 113, 136
transnationalism 158
Green, Alice Stopford (1847–1929) 74–5, 115–17, 151, 196, 227, 255–7
  anti-imperialism 16–17
  brother 71
  Harris and 116, 133, 257
  Mary Kingsley and 43, 115
  political hostess 95
  presidential search 77
  racism 129
  West African Mail investor 90
Grenfell, George (1859–1906) 33–4, 36, 129, 138–9, 183
Grey, Sir Edward (1862–1933) 209–32, 236–7, 247–51, 253–5, 258–60, 263–4; *see also* Foreign Office
  assessments of character 116, 212, 216, 223–4, 226–28, 230
  Belgian annexation 171, 211, 218, 221–3, 236–7, 254
  Belgian responsibility for Congo Free State 182–3
  Cabinet and 221–3
  Harris and 99, 135, 224, 226, 228
  Morel's attack on 150, 223
  pressure from the CRA 87, 100–101, 216–17, 228
  pressure from others 106, 144, 149–50, 154–5
  public statements 101, 103
  reform commitment 7, 177, 179, 201, 212–13, 215, 232, 236–9
  role and practices as Foreign Secretary 202, 213–14, 220
  US cooperation 167
Guinness, Dr. Harry Grattan (MD) (1861–1915) 50–62, 79–84, 106–7, 255–6, 263–4; *see also* Regions Beyond Missionary Union; Congo Balolo Mission
  Albert Hall meeting 151
  anti-Catholic 183–4
  character 7, 56, 58, 60–62, 76, 79–80, 82–4, 136

Congo debates 1904 79
CRA founding 57–62, 131, 136
difficulty securing missionary and church allies 141, 145
equivocation 1890–1903 31, 33–4, 36, 50, 53–7
Harris wedding 121
influence in CRA 80–81, 86, 91, 103, 123, 125
lectures 57–8, 62, 80, 93, 105, 133, 188
lending and releasing Harrises to CRA 95, 136
military option 223
RBMU dissention against 137
Stannard trial 199
US trip 166
Guinness, Rev. Henry Grattan (DD) (1835–1910) 51, 136

Hardinge, Sir Charles (1858–1944) 214, 225
Hardinge, Sir Arthur Henry (1859–1933) 168, 176–7, 214–15, 219–21, 231, 243, 250
  Belgian vote to annex 251
  Morel's view of 224
  reaction to Belgian reforms 243, 245, 249
Harris, Alice Seeley (1870–1970) 67, 119–23, 145, 256, 262, 264
  employment changes 71, 81, 84, 95–6, 98, 147, 257
  lecturing 93, 105, 113, 122, 163, 188, 191
  London Auxiliary 87, 94–5, 99, 102, 114
  photography 121, 184–5, 262
  Women's Auxiliary 114
  women's involvement 113–14
Harris, Rev. John Hobbis (1874–1940) 54, 93–9, 106–7, 119, 145
  Alice Seeley Harris and 119, 121–3
  Anti-Slavery Society and 133–5, 165, 246
  Berlin visit 144, 164–5
  Congo assessment 1912 240

CRA contribution 26, 67, 82, 155, 200
  religious leaders 81, 145, 148, 151, 230
CRA Finance Committee 72–3, 96, 109, 125
employment changes and pay 71, 81–2, 95–6, 98–9, 109, 135–6, 147, 257
Grey relationship 99, 135, 224, 226, 228
Guinness relationship 82–3, 136
lantern slides 188–9
lecturing 81, 93, 105, 113, 122, 163, 188–91, 246
London Auxiliary 87–9, 94, 99, 102, 109, 113–14, 117–18
Morel relationship, *see* Morel: Harris relationship
Putumayo rubber scandals 26
US tour 166, 253
Harrison, Frederic (1831–1923) 16–17, 21
Head, George Herbert 79–80, 166
Hochschild, Adam xi, 5, 233
Hodgkin, Thomas (1831–1913) 34, 73, 76, 94, 108, 110, 112
Holborn Town Hall 128, 171, 211, 237
Holland, Canon Henry Scott (1847–1918) 23, 50, 81, 108, 129, 148
Holt, John (1841–1915) 7, 49, 108, 110, 205, 223, 228
  concern for African rights and well-being 43–5, 65, 79, 85, 112, 128, 258
  correspondence 50, 58, 60–62, 129, 226, 231
  donations and subsidies 61, 90, 110, 112, 125, 194
  Executive Committee and finances 62, 64, 71–3, 77
  Harris and 73, 116, 122, 228, 257
  Kingsley and 42, 115
  merchants and commerce 43, 131, 152–5
  Morel mentor 42–3, 73, 75, 191, 226–8
  Stead's IU Congo Committee 50, 58
Horne, Rev. Charles Silvester (1865–1914) 91, 108, 144, 151

human rights 45, 65, 112, 123, 129, 267
  APS advocacy 22, 25, 34, 36
  limited rights for colonized peoples 44–6, 234, 243, 258, 266–7; *see also* land rights
  African World opposed 197
  CRA program 65, 78, 85, 114, 128, 189, 233
  Foreign Office advocated 229
  guaranteed by Berlin Act 33
  Liverpool Chamber overlooked 154
humanitarianism 77, 81, 106, 131, 136, 186–7
  British 3–4, 17, 20–30, 200, 213, 223, 261–8
  Congo Free State's claims 175
  CRA ideology 12, 87, 109, 176, 198
  Holt's 45, 154
  inspired by Congo scandals 8, 113, 178
  other groups, e.g., APS 34, 102, 106, 135, 158–9, 203
  religious 80–81, 123
  Stead's 49, 65
humanity 16, 19, 31, 128, 179, 200, 219, 229, 262
  crimes against 31, 179, 236, 259

imperialism 14, 17–18, 41
Ingram, Arthur Foley Winnington, Bishop of London (1858–1946) 148–9, 151
International League for the Defense of the Natives in the Conventional Basin of the Congo 163
International Union 49–51, 57–8, 131, 133, 141, 160
Ireland 5, 16, 116–17, 125, 145, 212, 267
Irish Parliamentary Party 116, 133
Irvine, James (1835–1926) 54–5, 83, 125, 154
ivory 6, 8, 137, 229, 244

Johnston, Sir Harry H. (1858–1927) 50, 125, 139, 171, 182, 211–12, 236
Jones, Sir Alfred Lewis (1845–1909) 39, 50, 56, 73, 82, 177, 182

Morel as protégé and enemy 41–3, 153–5, 197

Kingsley, Mary Henrietta (1862–1900) 41–3, 59, 117, 122, 155, 194, 266
  influence after her death 45, 65, 85, 115, 128–9, 140, 261

land rights, Congo 2, 6, 65, 78, 230, 237
  impact of reforms 234, 242–5, 249–50, 259
Lansdowne, 5th Marquess (Henry Petty-Fitzmaurice) (1845–1927) 160, 202–14, 219, 232
  Leopold's Commission of Inquiry 210, 255, 263
  ordering Casement investigation 59, 67, 206, 263
  reluctance to interfere 6, 264
lantern lectures, *see* public meetings: lantern lectures
Liberal Party 17, 20, 114, 117, 143, 171, 218
  CRA adherents 99–100, 106–8, 129
  Liberal government 72, 77, 99, 106, 212, 214, 225, 262
Lidgett, Rev. John Scott (1854–1953) 81, 91, 108, 144, 151
Liverpool 24, 60, 86, 106, 154–5, 190, 197
  Auxiliary, *see* Congo Reform Association: Liverpool Auxiliary
  bishop of 81, 91, 148
  Chamber of Commerce 41–2, 153–5, 177
  commercial interests 8, 42, 125, 153
    accused of plotting to seize the Congo 98, 153, 163, 209
    Elder Dempster shipping firm 8, 39, 41–2, 44, 58, 194
  consulate of the Congo Free State 39, 153
  CRA headquarters 1904–08 71, 94–5, 98
  Daily Post and Mercury 90, 125, 192–3, 197
  meeting to launch CRA 57, 61, 64

Liverpool Sect 42–3, 261
  London Auxiliary, *see* Congo Reform Association: London Auxiliary
London Chamber of Commerce 42, 46, 155
Lorand, Georges (1860–1918) 34, 45, 160, 171, 173, 235, 247
Louis, William Roger 46, 91, 180, 189, 201, 234
Lugard, Lady Flora Shaw (1852–1929) 13–14, 41, 266
Lygon, William, *see* Beauchamp, 7th Earl

Mackie, Horatio George Arthur 231, 235, 238
Manchester 24, 49, 86, 94, 192
  Auxiliary, *see* Congo Reform Association: Manchester Auxiliary
  Chamber of Commerce 42, 153, 155
  Geographical Society 29–30
Matadi 59, 229
Mayo, 7th Earl of (Dermot Bourke) (1851–1927) 107, 149, 151, 224
merchants 36, 106, 125–6, 152–6, 175, 194, 197; *see also* Liverpool: commercial interests
Methodists 1, 108, 110–12, 124, 141, 143–4, 179, 198; *see also* Lidgett
methods, humanitarian 25, 64, 72, 167, 188, 234, 261–2
Meyer, Rev. Frederick Brotherton (1847–1929) 81–3, 108–9, 135, 139, 145–7, 149, 175
  donations 90–91, 125
  Harrises and 119, 121–2
  PSA President 105
Michell, George Babington 220
Mille, Pierre (1864–1941) 163
missionaries 136–41
Monkswell, Baron (John Collier) (1845–1909) 72, 77, 98, 107, 151, 179, 256
  aggressive Congo policy 76, 78, 85
  cocoa scandals 134–5
  donor 110, 113, 127

Foreign Office 219, 223
Montmorency, William Geoffrey Bouchard de, Viscount Mountmorres (1872–1936)
moral superiority of Britain linked to Congo agitation 3–4, 14, 18, 20
Morel, Edmund Dene (1873–1924) 40, 106, 108
　accepting reformed Congo in 1913 1–2, 236–7, 240
　activities after the Congo 246
　Affairs of West Africa 46
　Anti-Slavery relationship, *see* Anti-Slavery, and Buxton, Travers
　atrocities and slavery rhetoric 177
　attacks on 183–4
　background 39, 41
　Barclay affair (offer from Leopold) 73
　Belgian annexation 57, 171, 180, 182–3, 200, 211, 216, 236–7, 250
　Benedetti affair 90–91
　Cadbury relationship, see Cadbury, William
　Casement relationship 59–60
　Chambers of Commerce 153–6
　churches and Free Church Councils 141, 144–5, 147–50
　collecting evidence 178, 183–5
　Congo Reform Association founding 7, 61–5, 67, 84, 261
　Congo Reform Association organizing 68–76, 86–7, 102
　Congo Reform Association president, *see* Congo Reform Association: president
　correspondence 53, 129
　defending Leopold's Congo 41, 193
　disciplining the CRA 67, 76, 78–80, 84–5, 104, 262
　financial difficulties of CRA and *WAM* 89–90
　financial reporting 72–4, 88, 94–5
　finding evidence of Congo system of misrule 6–7, 46, 176
　Foreign Office relationship 4
　collaboration 215–18, 219–22
　break 4, 76, 150, 194, 201, 203, 223–32, 258, 260, 264–5
　Fox Bourne relationship 45–6, 63–4
　fundraising 1904–05 89–91, 109, 126, 262, 269
　Green relationship 116–17
　Guinness relationship, *see* Guinness, Dr. Harry Grattan
　Harris relationship 27, 102, 116, 191, 255–8, 262
　　after 1909 135
　　difficulties 1906–09 73, 85, 88–9, 94–6, 98–9, 102
　　mutual admiration 82–3, 96
　　origins 1905 121–2
　heroic portrayal and self-image 1, 27, 265
　Holt relationship 43, 45
　ideology
　　free trade 15, 46
　　imperialism 17, 258–9, 266
　　responsibility to the unprivileged 19, 44, 179
　　rights 44–5, 240, 258
　importance to movement 3–5, 46, 67, 101, 132, 136, 200, 255, 262–5
　international connections 160–66, 168, 171
　IU Congo Committee crisis 57–62
　journalist 39, 41
　King Leopold's Rule in Africa 127
　Kingsley relationship and inspiration 41–3, 115, 129, 194
　limitations 113, 252
　meetings, speaker at 105, 141, 144–5, 188–9
　merchants and 43–4, 46, 89, 125
　missionary societies 54–6, 81, 84–5, 136–40
　move to London 88, 93–9, 102, 116
　parliamentary influence 67, 99–102, 147, 248
　personal financial needs and subsidies 75, 95, 111–13, 125
　press strategies 192–4, 196–8, 205

recruiting a leader for reform movement, 1901–02 49
Red Rubber and its financing 112, 252
Speaker articles in 1900 45, 176
Stead's hostility to Dilke 50–51, 63
trials 198–200
uniqueness of Congo Free State 26, 41, 181
uniqueness of Congo Reform Association 69
US voyage 72, 89, 152, 253
view of Congo Reform Association 87, 109, 129, 152
West Africa 44, 55
women in CRA 114–15, 117–23
Morel, Mary Florence Yonge Richardson (1874–1951) 118, 122
Morley, John 36, 77, 212
Morrison, Rev. William McCutcheon (1867–1918) 45, 138, 140, 166, 199, 235
motives 27, 127, 152, 261
Mountmorres, *see* Montmorency
Murphy, Rev. John B. (1863–1926) 32, 53–4, 137, 177

Nightingale, Arthur (1859–1926) 215, 220, 223
Nworah, Kenneth Dike Kingsley 43

Osborne, John Bremner 207, 212, 220
Ottoman Empire 18, 49, 210

pamphlets 103, 109, 114, 175, 188–9, 254, 262
 "Camera and the Congo Crime" 185
 international 163–4
 pre-CRA 24, 55, 57–8,
Parker, Sir Gilbert (1862–1932) 1, 100–101, 106–8, 127, 166, 224, 226, 246
Percy, Henry Algernon George, Earl Percy (1871–1909) 77, 206–7, 210, 219
Petty-Fitzmaurice, Edmond George, *see* Fitzmaurice, Baron

Petty-Fitzmaurice, Henry, *see* Lansdowne, 5th Marquess
Phillips, Richard Cobden (1846–1912) 31
Phipps, Sir Edmund Constantine Henry (1840–1911) 168–9, 208–15
Pickersgill, William (1846–1901) 32, 37–8, 203
Pleasant Sunday Afternoon (PSA) Society 105, 145, 151
Positivists 16, 19, 21, 45, 135, 267
press 191–3, 203–4
 apologists' use 27, 31, 41, 91, 154, 183, 209, 218
 CRA plans for publicity 69, 78, 175, 193
 editors and proprietors 1, 71, 103, 106, 115, 191–7
  Congophile 33, 183
  crusading 23, 134
  of *New Age* 74
  of other papers 49, 86, 133–4, 152, 197, 218, 227
  Morel as editor 44, 55, 133
  Russell 90, 108, 125, 193
  Wauters 169
 European 162–5, 169
 humanitarian use 24, 26
 lack of reform coverage 34, 62
 Morel's attack on the Foreign Office 228
 publishing denunciations 31–4, 36–7, 41, 103, 148, 166
 reformers' use 121, 191–98, 200, 216–17, 255, 262–4
  auxiliaries 87
  before CRA 67
  Free Church appeal 147
 religious 109, 145, 183, 252
Press Bureau of the Congo Free State 194, 197, 209, 252
pro-Boers 18, 26
public meetings
 Aborigines' Protection Society 31, 36, 53, 58, 64, 211
 Anti-Slavery 134–5, 187
 attendance estimate 103–5
 auxiliary development 87, 263

CRA method, generally 62, 69, 78–9, 103–5, 132, 263, 265
CRA presidents' attendance, compared 77–8
financial contribution 86–9, 109, 262
Foreign Office pressure via 192, 216
Guinness's
  before the CRA 57–8, 61–2
  CRA meetings 80–81, 83–4, 93, 105
  RBMU-sponsored 57–8, 79, 160
Harrises' 93, 163, 188, 191, 256–7
  CRA payments to RBMU 82
  frequency 93, 105, 119, 191
  organizing religious meetings 148, 151
Holborn Town Hall, 1905 128, 171, 211, 237
humanitarian method 24–5, 62, 74, 81, 187–8
inaugural CRA meeting in Liverpool 61, 64, 148
lantern lectures 24, 29, 80, 121, 184, 187–90, 246, 262–3
missionary atrocity meetings 136, 138, 140
reformers' use 27, 150, 154, 189, 262
religious meetings 105, 141–5, 147–8, 151, 230
resolutions at 80, 103, 144, 147, 190, 200, 203
speakers other than Harrises 105, 127, 139, 147, 149, 179, 191
town's meetings 104–5, 125, 189, 262
women 113–14
public opinion
  Belgian 152, 168, 251, 253
  British 191–3
    Boer War 17
    Casement report impact 208
    of Congo 103, 150–51, 191–3, 255, 257, 259, 263
    CRA plans to rouse 29, 64, 191–2, 200
    Foreign Office impact 143, 203, 205, 232, 251

humanitarian uses, generally 21
  role in reformed Congo 214
  role of fundraising 196
  Stanley's warning to Leopold 33
international 7, 33, 152, 160, 162–3, 166, 253

Quakers 19, 23, 51, 143, 188
  CRA donors 91, 111, 113, 124, 126, 129
  reform movement participation 106, 109, 141, 143–4, 164–5

Rabinek, Gustav Maria (1863–1901) 161
race 13–14, 21, 34, 44, 128–9, 178–9, 258
racism 140–41
Regions Beyond Missionary Union 12, 51–8, 61–2, 73–4, 79–83, 93–6, 136–7; *see also* Congo Balolo Mission
  Harrises and 81–2, 93, 96, 120–21, 137
  Meyer and 82–3, 145
Reid, Sir Hugh Gilzean (1836–1911) 33, 37, 49–50, 54, 73, 161, 181
  newspaper proprietor and editor 33, 191–2
Renkin, Jules (1862–1934) 221, 229–30, 232, 240–45, 247–50, 264
Responsibility to Protect 258–9
resolutions 24–5
  absence of 56
  at CRA meetings 79–80, 103–4, 147, 189–90, 211, 233, 262
  at CRA Executive Committee 230, 277
  other organizations 31 APS, 105, 134–5, BU 141, churches 144, FCC 147, Chamber of Commerce 153–6, 205
  parliamentary, of 20 May 1903 46, 67, 202, 205–6, 247, 263–5
    impact 59, 202, 206, 210, 255, 261
  parliamentary, other 7, 99, 202, 221
  to Foreign Office 190, 200, 203, 216, 228, 248, 251
  women's value in 123
Rollitt, Sir Albert Kaye (1842–1922) 155, 213

Roman Catholics 124–5, 127, 194, 197
  absence of in CRA 106, 109, 125
  anti-Catholic riots 197–8
  Belgian 33, 167, 169, 171, 252–4
  Catholic hostility to CRA 166, 183, 197
  CRA and Guinness seen as anti-Catholic 116, 183, 197
Roosevelt, Theodore 80, 166–7, 253
rubber
  coercive production methods 15, 30, 33–4, 38, 162, 240
    hostage-taking 132, 177, 208, 241
    practices revived in wartime 242
  eradication of vines 12, 152
  impact on Congo 37
  Leopold's reliance on 6, 8, 12
  market statistics 8–12
  monopoly 161
  Putumayo 26, 79
  red rubber agitation 7–8, 26, 137, 181–2, 185, 204
    proposed boycotts or military force 217, 223
    reforms 12, 229–30, 237–8, 244–5
  rubber merchants and manufacturers 90, 152–3
Russell, Sir Edward (1834–1920) 90, 125, 193

Salisbury, 3rd Marquess (Robert Gascoyne-Cecil) (1830–1903) 6, 32, 38, 202–4, 206, 264
Salisbury, 4th Marquess, Lord Cranborne until 1903 (James Gascoyne-Cecil) (1861–1947) 205–6
Salusbury, Captain Phillip 32–3, 36, 54, 79, 178, 198
Samuel, Herbert (1870–1963) 50, 90, 93, 106, 108, 178, 212; *see also* resolutions: parliamentary of 20 May 1903
Sarolea, Dr. Charles 79, 161, 166
Scott Holland, *see* Holland
Shakespeare, Rev. John (1857–1928) 108, 141

Shanu, Hezekiah 128
Shaw, Flora, *see* Lugard
Sheldon, May French (1847–1936) 50, 121–2, 154, 183
Sheppard, William Henry (1865–1927) 45, 129, 140, 160, 198–9
Simpson, Violet 73, 87, 94, 117–18, 122, 127, 133
Sims, Rev. Aaron (MD) 33, 137–8
Sjöblom, Rev. Edvard Viktor (1864–1903) 33–4, 36–7, 53, 136–8, 160, 177
Smith, Rev. Kenred (1866–1949) 78, 139, 190, 270
Society of Friends, *see* Quakers
Spender, Edward Harold (1864–1926) 39, 96, 166, 179, 224–6, 228, 258
  on Executive Committee 89, 108, 225
  on search for president 77
Speyer, Prof. Herbert (1870–1942) 171, 247–50, 252
Stanley, Henry Morton (1841–1904) 5, 30–33, 37, 50, 132
Stannard, Rev. Edgar W. 185, 198–9
Stead, William Thomas (1849–1912)
  crusading journalist 7, 26, 29, 48–9, 188, 191–2, 214, 261
  IU Congo Committee 46, 49–51, 57–8, 131, 133, 255
  CRA formation and after 60–61, 63–5, 166, 181, 255–6, 258, 262–3
Stopford, Col. John George Bernford (1838–1916) 71, 104, 108, 133, 226
Stopford Green, *see* Green, Alice Stopford
Strachey, John St. Loe (1860–1927) 23, 108, 134, 166, 224, 227–8
Swanzy, Francis A. (1854–1920) 46, 50, 108, 125, 155
Switzerland 7, 34, 119, 122, 151, 162–3, 191
  GDP per person 234

Taft, William Howard 167, 222
Talbot, Eduard Stuart, Bishop of Southwark, then Bishop of Winchester (1844–1934) 13, 93, 120, 161, 163, 192, 273